THE DREAM PREVAILS

THE DREAM PREVAILS

A STORY OF INDIA

DIVER, MAUD

GYAN

Published by

Gyan Publishing House
5, Ansari Road
Daryaganj, New Delhi-110002
Phone: 011-47034999, 9811692060
E-mail: books@gyanbooks.com

Distribution Network
gyanbooks.com
India, USA, Canada, UK, Australia

ISBN: 978-93-7447-052-7 (PB)

First Published, 1938

2nd Impression 2026

Printed at: Gyan Press, Delhi.

THE DREAM PREVAILS
Author: DIVER, MAUD

The
DREAM PREVAILS
A Story of India

BOOKS BY MAUD DIVER

THE DREAM PREVAILS

SHIPS OF YOUTH

A WILD BIRD

UNCONQUERED

COOMBE ST. MARY'S

SIEGE PERILOUS

LONELY FURROW

THE STRONG HOURS

FAR TO SEEK

DESMOND'S DAUGHTERS

HONORIA LAWRENCE: A FRAGMENT OF INDIAN HISTORY

BY MAUD DIVER

The DREAM PREVAILS
A Story of India

Fools act and babble; but the dream, in the end, prevails.
HUMBERT WOLFE

HOUGHTON MIFFLIN COMPANY · BOSTON
The Riverside Press Cambridge
1938

TO

LUCY FRANKLIN

UNFAILING CRITIC AND FRIEND

IN GRATITUDE

Who hears me, who understands me, is mine; a possession for all time. . . . So that a friend may well be reckoned the masterpiece of Nature.

EMERSON

Author's Note

THIS book stands complete in itself, but its interest will be enhanced for those who have read *The Singer Passes.*

Like the earlier book, it is a forward-looking study of India's present problems, as well as a story of many contrasting characters, English and Indian. The chief of these, Sir Roy Sinclair, symbolises in himself the clash and ultimate balance between East and West, and embodies the belief that each has something essential, which the other lacks. Can they arrive at working together in harmony?

M. D.

Guide to pronouncing Indian words and names

ā = *ar*	in = *een*
a = *u*, as in bud	ai = *i* as in vine
i = *ee*	ō = as in note
ir = *eer*	u = oo
e = *ai*	

Pathan = *Putār*

Contents

BOOK ONE

THE QUEST

Chief Characters Appearing in This Book

IT HAS been suggested that a list of the chief characters in this book, and their relation to each other, will be useful to readers who are not familiar with my world of North-West India, the Desmond family having now reached a third generation.

SIR VINCENT LEIGH, G.C.S.I., K.C.S.I., Governor of North-West Frontier.
THEA LEIGH, wife of Sir Vincent, daughter of Sir Theo Desmond, V.C.
CAPTAIN THEO LEIGH, D.S.O., eldest son of Sir Vincent.
VERNON LEIGH, R.A.F., youngest son of Sir Vincent.
SIR ROY SINCLAIR, Baronet of Branleigh Beeches, Surrey.
TARA, wife of Sir Roy.
LILĀMANI, daughter of Sir Roy.
ARUNA, first cousin of Sir Roy.
SIR LAKSHMAN SINGH, K.C.S.I., Rajput grandfather of Sir Roy.
SURĀJ MUL, a relative of Sir Roy.
RAJINI, wife of Surāj Mul.
LEWIS BUCHANAN EDOM, American millionaire turned Brahma Samāj.
JOHN LYNCH, Deputy Inspector General of Police.
GRACE LYNCH, wife of John Lynch.
DIXON VERNEY, Police officer under Lynch.
JASPER INGLIS, Commissioner of Peshawar.
CLAIRE INGLIS, wife of Jasper.
CHRYSTAL ADAIR, niece of Claire Inglis.
CAPTAIN LANCE DESMOND, M.C., nephew of Lady Leigh, grandson of Sir Theo Desmond, Assistant Commissioner of Peshawar.
EVE DESMOND, wife of Captain Desmond, daughter of Colonel Ian Challoner.
LIEUTENANTS SHER AFZUL KHAN, ABDUL JĀN, GOPĀL SINGH, SRI NATH, Indian commissioned Army officers.

All of the above characters are purely imaginary.

M. DIVER

Chapter I

What hour shall Fate in all the future find?

LAURENCE BINYON

'I'VE told them — coffee and liqueurs in the side verandah to encourage the moon!'

Grace Lynch looked across the dinner table at her senior guest Mrs. Inglis, the Commissioner's wife. There was a general pushing back of chairs. Everyone stood up — eight of them.

'As if the blatant, overworshipped moon needs encouragement from a mere handful of Feringhis,' remarked her husband, a square, sunburnt man, with curiously pale eyes under rough eyebrows, like a thumb stroke.

'She isn't blatant, and she isn't overworshipped,' young Eve Desmond flatly contradicted him. And Mrs. Inglis asked in her deep, measured voice, 'Which is worse — would you say — to overdo the superfluous, or to underdo the essential?'

'I must have notice of that question! Too abstruse for an after-dinner brain.'

'At the moment,' said his wife in her quick way, 'I vote for overdoing the superfluous, if the young things will stay for coffee, before running off to the dance?'

Her smile and question were for Eve Desmond, a notable young married woman, tall and thin like herself, with a face full of character and a glint of humour in her grey-green eyes.

'Young things — look at her,' she appealed to her fellow-guests — 'putting on middle-aged airs. I ask you — can anyone detect a squiggle of grey in her crinkly hair?'

The large hand of John Lynch closed on her upper arm and gave it a gentle shake.

'You always were addicted to impertinence. And Lance hasn't got a square enough thumb.'

'Just as well — for Lance,' she murmured darkly; and Grace flung an arm round her.

'Let her be. She's privileged. Come on, all of you.'

Out into the moon-splashed side verandah they trailed; Grace and Eve followed by Captain Lance Desmond with Chrystal Adair, the attractive niece whom Claire Inglis had lately brought out from Home. Eve, listening to them, knew that Lance was enjoying himself and was probably being cursed by Flight-Lieutenant Peter Grant for 'obstructing the traffic.' Lance frankly admired Chrystal. He had the Desmond eye for feminine charm: and Eve, after suffering torments of futile jealousy, had arrived at accepting the whole man as he was — a creature of swift susceptibilities and unshakably constant heart.

If he did happen to like them beautiful, he had chosen to love and marry her, though she was no beauty: and he was welcome, if it amused him, to cultivate Chrystal Adair, whose withdrawn manner — quite unrelated to shyness — suggested hidden reserves and stabilities that might make her worth winning as a friend. Eve chose her friends fastidiously, with an instinct for character and a balanced judgment ahead of her years. At three-and-twenty she had passed through deep waters, in spite of an early marriage that came as near perfection as human imperfection could achieve. She had lost her first child in tragic circumstances; had paid the price, in nerve strain, of being artist and woman: but her resilient spirit had triumphed, as it always would, over the worst that Fate could do to her. Life and people had a way of yielding up their secrets to her valiant and very human curiosity. Speculating on that Chrystal girl, with her cool, poised air, she guessed at a point of hidden flame deep down. The crystal might become a fire opal when she fell in love — not with red-headed Peter Grant, if Eve knew anything of her.

As a mere picture, she was enviably good to look at: the eggshell tint of her skin, the honey-coloured hair softly curling in her neck; the wing-like eyebrows above eyes clear as aquamarines, the iris darkly rimmed. In every way she had a finished air that made Eve at times feel rough-cut and ordinary, with her kinked eyebrows and decided Challoner nose, even if she was recognised, by now, as a composer of distinction — a *rara avis* in Anglo-India. One could not expect to have everything; though, being Eve, she wanted everything that life could give.

Lance had been making Chrystal laugh at dinner; and he was talking nonsense to her now; while the defrauded and freckled R.A.F. man listened with a bored air of respect to the platitudes of Jasper Inglis — one of those charming men who give their smiling best to the world and, metaphorically, slouch in slippers at home. Eve had seen both sides of him, so she knew. Grace knew also; and shared in the 'Jasper hate,' as Eve irreverently called it. For the man was nearly double her age, and Commissioner of Peshawar to boot. It was rough luck on Lance being his Assistant Commissioner, which constrained her to 'behave'; and neither Eve nor Grace betrayed a hint of their 'hate' to Claire, whose loyalty to a patently unsatisfactory husband was of the clear-eyed order.

Tonight Claire had been enjoying her talk with Lynch, the kind of man she could sincerely admire; and Lynch in his own blunt way returned the compliment. Normally he avoided women; but this one had brains and character written all over her broad face, with its decided features and fine eyes, her only beauty. One could talk to her 'as man to man'; and he loitered with her now in the drawing-room to discuss a curious coin he had picked up in the city. Coins, maps, and ethnology were his main diversions from the police work that devoured his days. Happily he had married a wife who knew the meaning of work. As Doctor Grace Yolande, she had run a Border mission hospital for ten years, had been a skilled surgeon; and she still ceaselessly devoted herself to the welfare of India's women and children.

Very much intrigued over his coin, he invited Claire to examine the new 'find' with a magnifier, heedless of the fact that her coffee was cooling itself in the verandah.

A discreet cough interrupted him; and the voice of his *chāprassi* announced: 'Khan Sahib Sher Afzul Khan.'

'*Salaam dō*,' said Lynch, and slipped his treasure into a waistcoat pocket as he turned to greet the 'Khan Sahib,' a tall man of powerful build wearing Punjab Cavalry Mess uniform; in appearance a British subaltern, noticeably tanned; in fact, a Yusufzai Pathan, son of his own wild hills, stepson of Harrow and Sandhurst — a commissioned Indian officer. Dress, manner, and the clipped moustache were patently English. The strongly modelled nose and jaw, the tawny hazel eyes were as patently Pathan.

'Come along in, Afzul,' Lynch genially greeted him. Better than most of his kind, he recognised that these young Indian officers — commonly called Brindians — needed just that extra touch of friendliness too seldom proffered by the white Brahmins and Kshattryas [1] of British India.

Afzul Khan came forward and bowed to Claire, who knew him well. 'Sorry if I interrupt, sir, but I have to see Captain Desmond about tomorrow's gymkhana programme. I was told I should find him here.'

'You'll neatly catch him before he hops off to the Club dance. Come on, Claire, to your nice cold cup of coffee!'

As the three entered the verandah, Claire noticed how the Pathan's eyes sought Chrystal, where she stood with Grant in a patch of moonlight: her casque of fair hair and her yellow dress bathed in its unearthly glamour. The child was magnetic to men; the more so for her air of cool detachment. Her mind being unclouded by race prejudice, she was friendlier with these Brindian officers — with Sher Afzul in particular — than most girls were apt to be out here; frankly interested in 'a new specimen,' if nothing more. Claire, though she liked Sher Afzul, sincerely hoped it *was* nothing more.

A remark from Lance drew the girl into his brief talk with

[1] Warrior caste.

the Pathan. They were very good friends; and when programme details had been settled, Desmond invited Afzul to 'Come and join the dance.'

The Pathan smiled and shrugged his shoulders.

'No party — no partners.'

'Join our party,' Lance encouraged him. 'And I vouch for two.'

Still obviously hesitating, he said in a low tone: 'Thanks — I would like to come. But I don't wish to dance with anyone — who would rather not.'

Lance twitched an eyelid.

'I know all about that. Trust me — and come along.'

As the five of them departed, Lynch emptied his coffee cup and half stifled a yawn.

'*Naryān!*' he said, putting up his hand; and Grace laughed.

'*You* invoking the gods!'

'As how?' asked Inglis, mildly amused.

'It means "Great God,"' Grace enlightened him, 'a prayer for protection; because a gaping mouth invites a demon to hop down your throat and torment your inside. Or a part of your soul might escape with fatal effect! That's the real origin of the gesture — not for courtesy but for protection.'

Jasper Inglis considered her with his sceptical smile.

'Learned woman you are.'

'It's not learning,' she retorted, suspecting sarcasm. 'It's living in close touch with these people for fifteen years.'

She was checked by the whirr of the telephone bell and the voice of a *chāprassi*. The Burra Sahib was speaking from Government House.

Lynch sprang up. In Peshawar men were prepared for any emergency at any time of the day or night.

'Sir Vincent — at this hour? Excuse me, Inglis.'

And he vanished, leaving Grace with the other two.

Inglis, deep in a cane chair, yawned without ceremony, and winked at Grace.

'A bit of my soul escaped that time! Sorry. But I had a rotten night, and my tiresome heart's a bit groggy.'

'You shouldn't have played that last set of tennis,' said Claire in a practical voice.

'Didn't mean to. The woman tempted me! And this climate dissolves good resolutions.' He pulled out his cigar-case, with a guilty grin at his wife. 'May I damn the Doctor Sahib, and send another one up in smoke?'

The query was for Grace, who answered lightly, 'As far as I'm concerned, you're welcome to make a burnt sacrifice of them all.'

'Happy thought! A man in my case must live dangerously — and take his chance of going up in smoke himself.'

The familiar tag and gesture of courage fell flat, but there remained the hollow satisfaction of a forbidden cigar. Having lit it, he leaned back, not troubling to make talk, neither knowing nor caring how he was hampering theirs by his silent presence.

Very soon Lynch reappeared.

'Sir Vincent wants me round there,' he announced. 'They've got the wind up over the vanished Sinclair. His Holiness, the Guru Maharāj, who spirited him away, seems to have mislaid him somewhere in the hills around Kashmir ——'

'John, *don't* talk like that,' Grace checked him with a touch of asperity. 'What *has* happened, really?'

'That's what I'm to hear about. And, by the way' — he looked hard at the abstracted Commissioner 'All this in the Secret Department. Got that, Inglis?'

'Got it. You likely to be back soon?'

'Can't say.'

'Well, I think I'll be rolling home. I had a rotten night' — out it came again, as he rose to his feet; but the tragic statement fell on stony ground.

'I can't let Claire run away so soon,' was all that Grace had to say about it; and Jasper glanced at his wife.

'How do you propose to get back, *ma chère*? Can't send the car for you. Nussar Ali has a Trades Union mentality.'

Lynch turned in the doorway.

'Hand him over to me. I'll cure him. Claire needn't hurry. My man will roll her home.'

'Very good of you.' Inglis thanked him without enthusiasm; but Lynch had vanished. The big, deliberate man could move like a lightning streak at need. 'Efficiency without noise' was his rule of life and the motto of his service. While others discussed what should be done, he would leave them discussing — and do it. Inglis — efficient also in his own line — lived and worked in an I.C.S.[1] groove. Seeing Lynch as a mere policeman with an exaggerated opinion of himself, he never dreamed that the other saw him mainly as the unworthy husband of an admirable wife.

On his departure, the two women exchanged a smile of relief; and Claire slipped a hand through her friend's arm.

'Now we can talk,' she said. 'What's all this about Sir Roy Sinclair getting mislaid? I've heard of him, of course. But what's he doing out here? Just a tourist?'

'Far from it. He's a great friend of mine. And I sincerely hope he isn't mislaid,' Grace said with feeling. 'Have another cigarette, and I'll tell you what I can before John comes back with the news — if there *is* any news.'

[1] Indian Civil Service.

Chapter II

The bond that holds people in love is their own; neither prose nor poetry can define it.

HECTOR BOLITHO

GRACE pulled their chairs into a moon-flooded space between two pillars, lit a cigarette and asked in her direct fashion, 'What have you heard about Roy Sinclair?'

'Well ——' Claire hesitated palpably.

'Well —— ?'

The smile and the note of challenge encouraged her.

'I heard that his father, Sir Nevil, married a beautiful Rajput girl. Probably fiction. Rajputs don't ——'

'No — they don't. But, for a wonder, this one did. I've had it all from Roy. She was taken home at seventeen, by a father with advanced ideas, to save her from marrying an elderly, priest-chosen suitor. At Antibes she met Sir Nevil, an unconventional specimen of an English county family, and something of an artist. He painted her portrait. They fell in love; and between them, they carried it through, in the face of every known obstacle.'

'But good Heavens —— ! His people?'

'Yes. County to the bone. The pair were happy enough in Italy. But when his father died suddenly, the fat was in the fire. Picture a Hindu Lady Sinclair facing an English family, as custom- and caste-ridden as any out here. She didn't have a gay time of it, I gather. But she had the courage and devotion of her race. She inspired Sir Nevil to paint a series of Indian pictures that made his name as an artist. And my friend, Sir Roy, was the first child of that amazing marriage.'

'Plucky of him,' remarked Claire, 'to come out here and face the stigma.'

'Oh, he faced all that when he came out after the War. Rightly proud of his Rajput heritage, he suffered more than his parents ever guessed.'

'Not married, I hope?'

'Twelve years married to a charming wife. She's at Home with three children, running the estate in his absence. He came out to see and hear things for himself; to get in touch with non-political India. Thanks to his fine traditions on both sides, he can *think* with the English and *feel* with the Indian. As I'm rather that way myself, we became great friends. He hopes, after all this, to write a book on the subject, that may do a real service to both countries.'

Claire sighed. '*If* anyone in authority can be induced to read it — and heed it. Those who glance through it — because of Sir Roy's reputation — will say "How remarkable!" "How true! But not practical politics," — and return to their tinkering at the White Paper.'

Grace laid a hand on her friend's knee.

'You're a pessimist, Claire.'

'Not fundamentally. But, for some of us, life is too discouraging.'

Grace, who understood, could only say, 'There's always a stubborn fragment inside one that refuses to be discouraged.'

'You're a brave woman,' Claire stated in her deep-toned voice.

'I'm not feeling very brave at this moment. For, in a sense, I feel responsible. It was I that put Roy in touch with the Guru, a remarkable man, who recognised his two-fold genius and India's need of it. Through his spiritual influence over the East in Roy, he induced him to break with his personal life — for a time; to remain alone up there, working on the material he had gathered, and seeking illumination from those heavenly hills — "Abode of the Gods."'

'And every hot weather,' murmured Claire, 'we desecrate them with our infinite littleness.'

'Dear, we can't desecrate them, any more than the buzzing of flies in summer can desecrate a cathedral. And they often bring peace or healing to those who are after quite other things. I wonder what they have brought to Roy. We've not heard of him since last September; though the favoured Lance did get a line at Christmas.'

'It's a strange thing,' mused Claire — more intent on the story than on the man — 'how many young Englishmen, whom one wouldn't credit with spiritual tendencies, are being attracted to Yoga thought and practice. Is it a natural reaction from lost faith? Or is it a portent?'

'Roy believes it's a possible prelude to a new era of the spirit. There are signs everywhere of such an awakening. If — when — it really comes to pass, I believe India would be its natural birthplace; Radhakrishnan its major prophet.'

Claire looked intently at her friend's moonlit face.

'You don't talk like a missionary, Grace.'

'I never was one, in the narrow sense; or I would never have married John. I'm at loggerheads with them more often than not — the kind that spend half a lifetime in this astounding country almost blind and deaf to its realities. So busy teaching India, that they never discover what India has to teach them.'

'That,' said Claire, 'is because India doesn't dogmatise. She permeates.'

Grace nodded. 'Permeates is the word. There's an indefinable strangeness in the very air of India. Things can be done and believed out here which would be unthinkable elsewhere. But even India can't permeate a lacquered surface. — Heavens!' She checked herself with a short laugh. 'If the elect at the Club could hear us talking like this.'

Claire sighed. 'Elect? It depresses me sometimes to realise that, for many Indians, they and their kind do represent England. I'm proud of my race and all it has done out here. I always stand up for "the snob community" — as they unkindly call us. But I'm afraid most of them do run in blinkers. Even intelligent men ——'

Her pause suggested a reluctant thought of Jasper; and Grace deftly shifted the issue.

'Even intelligent men, like my John,' she said, 'must needs look askance at a man of genius, like Sir Roy, because of the Rajput strain in his blood.'

'Well —' Claire hesitated — 'even the best of us have an instinctive distaste for mixed breeding. Haven't you?'

'No. I've worked with and liked too many of them. Not that I favour intermarriage. But as we can't prevent or control it, we do no good by penalising those who are brave enough to make the venture. I'm sorry, though, that it's on the increase nowadays.'

'Is it?'

'Yes — in a one-sided way: the Indian man and English girl. Within the last ten years it has almost become a mass movement. In Lahore, I'm told, there are at least a hundred white women married to Indians. In Hyderabad about fifty. Probably far more in cities like Bombay and Calcutta.'

Claire wrinkled her nose. 'Surely not of our class?'

'Not many. But they aren't all typists or landladies' daughters. And they aren't all sorry for themselves either.'

'That's a mercy, anyhow. And what about these young Brindians? Educated men of good caste, but — Indians for all that. Mostly not married; not wanting to marry their own backward women.'

Grace glanced at her sidelong, guessing her thought.

'They *are* a problem. Such fine fellows, many of them; and it's the best ones who may have to pay the longest price for their new privilege. John specially likes that young Pathan, Sher Afzul.'

'Is he married?' Claire asked with sudden urgency.

'No. His father is a man of broad ideas. But his family want him to marry the daughter of a fellow-chief. He spoke of it once to John.' This time she looked straight at her friend. 'Are you afraid — for Chrystal?'

'Not seriously. But still — the man's handsome and intelligent. And I've no real hold over her. Yet I'm responsible to Esther and Malcolm. To me, of course, it's unthinkable. And Jasper would have a fit. But really, nowadays, anything seems possible. And Chrystal, if she set her heart on such madness, would take her own line. Nothing would frighten her out of it.'

'I like her the better for that,' said Grace Lynch, most headstrong of women; 'I've done much the same all my life. Even with my *zubberdust*[1] man, I still take my own line, in certain ways — sometimes at a fearful risk. — Ah, there he is!'

Claire Inglis heard, with a prick of envy, the quiet content in her voice. 'I'll leave you two to your talk,' she said, 'if John will let his man run me home?'

'Man and car are at your service,' said Lynch himself, stepping into the verandah. 'Must you be running away at once?'

'I ought to, or Jasper will get fussed. Then he won't sleep.'

'Won't he?' — Lynch raised a sceptical eyebrow at her. 'You're a model wife. You demoralise him — as models do. I had the good sense not to marry one, so I've kept my spine intact. Come on then — if you positively must.'

He took her by the arm in a friendly fashion reserved for herself and Eve Desmond; settled her into his car and returned to find his wife lying back in the long chair she had assigned to her friend.

'Poor soul,' he said with unusual feeling. 'She's worth fifty of her lath-and-plaster husband.'

Grace laughed softly. 'Lath and plaster! You're as good as Eve sometimes, with your epithets. A woman like Claire! It's deplorable. But just now —' she put up a hand, drawing him round to confront her — 'I want news of Roy.'

'There *is* no news of the damned man. That's where the worry comes in.' He sat down near her, leaning forward, elbows on knees. 'Sir Vinx has heard from your Guru friend, with whom Sinclair was supposed to keep in touch. Not a line from him for more than two months.'

[1] High-handed.

'Oh, what *can* have happened?'

John's hand closed firmly on one of hers. 'Don't *you* get worrying. The fellow's not worth it.'

'He *is* worth it.'

Lynch frowned. It was an old quarrel between them.

'Well, we won't wrangle over *him* again.'

'We don't wrangle, John.'

'No. We contradict each other flat. A more robust and satisfying form of argument.'

'But I want to know about Roy,' she persisted, serious again.

'My darling, I can't tell you what the Holy One himself doesn't know. Sinclair's probably gone Yogi — cast off all human obligations, including his wretched family. Much book *he*'ll write about India. I've no use for the type — say what you will. Going off and playing a fancy game. Causing more trouble than he's worth to hard-worked officials — harder worked than ever, in these enlightened days.'

He was obviously letting off steam, as he seldom allowed himself to do: and his wife asked with an amused look, 'Did you say all that to Sir Vinx?'

'Not likely. Bottled it up for you! He and Lady Leigh are taking it to heart.'

'Of course they are. So will everyone who loves Roy. And oh, his poor wife — !'

'Hard luck on her. But if he's swallowed the renunciation microbe, that won't worry him.'

'It strikes me,' she said crisply, 'that it's you who are playing a fancy game: inventing fairy tales about a man you don't really know or understand.'

'I make no claim to do either,' he bluntly agreed. 'But I'm let in for trying to unearth him with the help of my two famous trackers; find out when and where he was last seen — that sort of thing.'

'Are you going?'

At the note of anxiety in her voice, he regarded her quizzically.

'Am I? There's the rub. I told Sir Vincent straight that,

because I pulled off a miracle, when Lance went astray in the Hindu Khush on my business, I couldn't guarantee to find any sort of needle in a Himalayan haystack.'

'But you didn't refuse?'

'Couldn't very well; though I've a lot more important work on hand. Let alone seeing you safe to Kashmir.'

His vague light eyes dwelt on her with a thinking look. The knowledge that in the autumn a child would be coming to them, after more than two years of marriage, was still fresh enough to make even his unimaginative mind see her in a new light.

'Yes,' she agreed, 'I was looking forward to that. But the finding of Roy is a far more important consideration.'

'That's as may be,' he grudgingly admitted. '*I'm* only concerned to set your mind at rest. You'll worry over that wretched Sinclair till I've dragged him to light. And you ought *not* to be worried just now. I can't feel easy about you till you're safely through this tricky business.'

The deep note in his voice so moved her that she leaned forward and kissed him. Both were 'tongue-bound' in matters of the heart: and her kiss tacitly shelved the subject.

Lynch spoke of Sir Vincent Leigh, a man whom he could sincerely admire in spite of diverse views, temperament, and character. For five years, as Chief Commissioner of the Province, Leigh had devoted all his energy, wisdom, and understanding to the people's welfare; had followed the light of his own convictions, often in the teeth of official disapproval; and had now — amazedly — reaped his reward. It might be a crown of thorns, but it remained a high tribute that he had been chosen as first Governor of the last Province admitted into the fold of the India Act. The delay — resented by advanced Moslems — had been justified on the whole by the danger zone of Afghanistan and the Free Country of the Tribes running all along its border. But at last, the proud day had dawned: the 'backward Province' could stand 'head erect' with the rest of them. Better still, their first Governor was to be no strange Burra

Sahib, but a true friend of the Border, known and loved for years.

'The Khans haven't yet finished wondering,' Lynch told his wife, 'at the marvel of Government having actually chosen the right peg for this difficult hole. Sir Vincent, having no conceit of himself, is surprised and deeply moved by the letters, flowing in from all over the district. As for Lady Leigh — well —— ! You don't need telling.'

'I do *not!*'

The two had been friends for years; had done more, between them, for India's women, high and low, than those who ran in blinkers would be likely to conceive.

'She's all over herself — charming creature. Wants you round there tomorrow. Longing to show you those letters from the Khans, blessing Government for the wise choice of "our most loved and respected Administrator." They're in luck, and they know it, to have Leigh's guidance along the thorny path of provincial self-government. Thorny they'll find it, even so.'

He pushed back his chair and stood up, smiling down at her.

'Bedtime for you, my dear, study table for me. I've a whole sheaf of reports to tackle.'

As she rose and stood beside him the thought of Claire returned irrelevantly to her mind.

'John,' she said, laying a hand on him, 'I'm bothered to find that Claire is rather concerned over Chrystal's friendliness with young Sher Afzul. Do you think — ? Is there any likelihood — ?'

He narrowed his gaze. 'On which side?'

'Either, or both? I discouraged the idea. But one can't deny the possibility.'

'One can't,' he gravely agreed. 'Sher Afzul, I should say, is too purely Pathan — for all his English training — to think seriously of an English wife. But I wouldn't guarantee a Hottentot against succumbing to the charms of that particular young woman. Sex appeal — what?'

'No: just *not* that,' she countered with decision. 'Hideous phrase.'

'Inelegant, I own. But there's no getting away from the damned thing,' mused the man for whom woman had been little more than sex till he loved and married Grace Yolande. 'That girl's no common charmer. She's got breeding written all over her; and there's nothing an Asiatic spots quicker than breeding — which doesn't mean he'll want to marry her. But it may mean hell for the poor beggar. The devil's in it when the races begin to mix socially.'

Grace looked thoughtful. 'It used to be said that the trouble came from not mixing socially. But where *is* one to draw the line?'

'Ask me another. We're up against creation. Male and female created he them.' A quizzical glance lightened his pale eyes. 'You and I, Madam, did our devil utmost to draw the line at marriage between a devout Christian missionary and a rank heathen policeman. And we didn't manage it — did we?'

He pulled her close and kissed her with quiet fervour.

'You get to bed — and to sleep. Don't damage your own chances by bearing another woman's burdens.'

Wise counsel; but so much of her earlier life had been spent in bearing other people's burdens that Grace could not shed the habit, even at John's command. It pained her to think of Claire, so mated and so shadowed by natural concern for her sister's child, while her own heart was steeped in something more profound than personal happiness; an anchored tranquillity foreign to her vivid temperament. During these months of inner creative activity, she was content to stand aside. But afterwards — even John's child could not be allowed to hamper their companionable way of life.

Chapter III

Do we move ourselves, or are moved
By an Unseen Hand at a game?

TENNYSON

THE Club dance was 'going with a swing,' in Miss Gugglesby's well-worn phrase. Most of her phrases were so well worn as to be almost out at elbows. The neat flick was Eve Desmond's — not unkindly meant: for her humour was never spiced with malice. It was not she, but an impertinent subaltern, had christened Miss Gugglesby, 'Goggles': a blend of her impossible name and her astonished eyes, magnified by pink-rimmed glasses.

No novice to India, she had been out five years with her brother, a Major in the Supply and Transport Service. Vainly he had hoped that she might marry: she was the neuter woman of her period; the born Honourable Secretary, the devotee of Public Spirit. Capably and zealously she ran the Peshawar Girl Guides, the Club dances, and any other social activity designed to keep alive 'the good old friendly traditions of Anglo-India.'

But, for all her zeal, traditions crumbled, cliques multiplied. New-comers — deaf to the call of Public Spirit — were intent on saving money for their children's education, or the cost of their next flight Home. The non-public-spirited — even while they made fun of her — were privately grateful to her for relieving them of those tiresome odd jobs that must be done by some tiresome, good-natured busybody, if the wheels of station life were to be kept whirling.

Chrystal Adair, pounced on as a new-comer, had tactfully

evaded hopeful attempts to entangle her in local concerns about which she knew nothing and cared less. In their life, yet not of it, she watched and appraised these Peshawar people with the critical, detached interest of her artist nature. Water-colour work — studied under a first-rate man — was her 'secret bread'; for which reason, she seldom spoke of it in this official-minded world, where the arts seemed to be regarded merely as social assets, if regarded at all. But if she said little, she noticed much; and tonight she knew that 'Goggles' had her eye on Sher Afzul Khan, tall and conspicuous — a sheep not of her fold. In theory, she favoured a friendly spirit towards advanced Indians. In theory she favoured these newfangled officers, admitted their skill at tennis, cricket, and bridge. But, of course, 'one must draw the line ——'

Chrystal knew that she drew her line at these small Club dances, where they seldom, if ever, put in an appearance. Lance probably knew it also; and had deliberately cut the line. More and more she liked Lance Desmond; the smiling, resolute way he had with him, the lightness of true strength. Without any patronising babble, he would stand fairly by these men, who had earned the right to be treated as British officers. No matter who followed, he would give a clear lead, according to the light that was in him.

They had arrived late. The second dance was over; the room almost empty. Peter Grant had been delayed outside over his car; and Sher Afzul turned to Chrystal, with his mixture of shyness and pride.

'Is Desmond right — that you *will* give me a dance, because I've come with his party?'

'I would give you one, if you hadn't,' she said.

'That's because *you* are kinder than the others.'

'Or because you are too proud to ask them?'

A light flashed in his tawny eyes. 'Yes, I *am* too proud. If they refused, it would make me angry. In England I would ask any of them. But here — well ——' He looked away from her. 'Some of these English in India seem hardly the same people as those in England.'

'You notice that? So do I sometimes.' She lowered her voice; and the smile they exchanged gave her an odd sense of fellowship. Both of them—from a different angle, could see the English in India as beings outside their ken.

She could feel him watching her; perhaps wondering how soon she would become like those others; and as the opening bars of a tango swelled louder, he said with repressed eagerness, 'Which dance, Miss Adair? — This one?'

'Yes, this one.' (Peter would be furious, but if he came late he must take his chance.)

'You *will* dance it — really? Not just sitting out?'

'Of course I will.'

'I am proud that you honour me.'

His grave tone stirred in her a glow of friendly feeling. 'Can you tango?' she asked, smiling.

'Try me.'

With shy deliberation he put an arm round her, holding her carefully as if she might break, guiding her skilfully, dancing with ease and precision. As they swung round, she saw Peter skidding towards them, plainly staggered at sight of her purloined by a Pathan, whom he had not yet seen dancing with an English woman. His look and gesture spurred her to resistance. She smiled back at him, shook her head — and danced on. Preference apart, she was upholding a principle; and Lance Desmond's approval was good enough for her. If she did scarify a few hide-bound Anglo-Indians, she was no permanent pigeon in their pigeon-hole world. Twice she caught the Goggles glaring; and hoped that Sher Afzul might be looking the other way. She had given him his dance partly because she liked him, partly in a spirit of challenge, and now she had her reward. He was neither stiff nor clumsy. He danced with the ingrained Eastern sense of rhythm. If only he would not hold her as though she were made of glass.

When the music stopped, she again became aware of Peter — waiting to pounce. But everyone clapped and the mournful tune began again.

This time Sher Afzul held her less cautiously, and she

forgot all but her natural delight in dancing; forgot Peter and disapproving Peshawar....

When it was over, she said, smiling, 'You *can* dance.'

'Yes, I can,' he quaintly agreed, 'but I get no practice now. Another time — perhaps? You wouldn't be afraid?'

'Certainly not.'

His pleasure was evident. 'Not to be afraid,' he said, 'is the first law, for men and women, in our hills.'

'In ours too,' she told him. 'I come from the Scottish Highlands, where the clans were once as wild and free as your own.'

'A grand country,' he said with sudden warmth. 'I went there twice for my leave. But there is no land now, in the West, so free as ours. Some people say we are lawless: but we have our own laws, though no law courts; our own leaders, though no kings.'

While he spoke, the two Desmonds halted near them, and he said in a lower tone: 'Would Mrs. Desmond be afraid?'

'No. Ask her and see.'

As he went forward, Lance joined Chrystal, drawing her a little apart from the other two.

'Well done,' he said in his quick way. 'He's a damn good fellow. You've given him a lift. Trust Eve to back you up.'

'Trust Peter to dress me down!'

From a distant doorway he was coming to claim her.

'You'll soon bring him to heel. Easy to see what's the matter with him, poor devil. Give me the third, after this. Will Afzul get another — if he dares?'

He has dared. He asked — would I be afraid?'

'Not you!'

She liked the implied tribute; yet instinctively she discounted it.

'Oh, I'm not cadging for credit. He's patently a gentleman. — Heavens! Here comes Peter. Stay and uphold me — in case he says impossible things.'

'Hullo, Peter! What's bitten you?' Lance innocently asked.

Grant's blue eyes flashed reproach at Chrystal.

'Dancing with those fellows is the limit. Hell's bells! What's India coming to?'

'Coming into her own, maybe,' Lance ventured to suggest; and Grant flung him a puzzled look. But as the music began, he turned to Chrystal.

'Ours,' he said: and Lance faded away.

It was no dream-dance this time: the quick, fussy fox-trot, Peter hopping round her like a grasshopper, or buzzing like a mosquito at her ear. And when it was over — when he had her safe outside — he did begin to say impossible things; piling on all the stark objections to white women dancing with Indians. She took it coolly, making allowance for the fact that he was more hurt than angry; his peppery temper on a hair trigger. So she let his volleys of blank cartridge go harmlessly over her head, which annoyed him more than ever.

After the next, which was a valse, he lured her out into the Club compound: and there urgently begged her to marry him — for the 'second time of asking.' On the whole she preferred the volleys of blank cartridge. It seemed impossible to convince him, without brutality, that her 'No' meant no.

'*I* don't want my life to run all on rubber tyres,' she told him; 'I'd prefer a bit of rough going, *if* — ?'

'If —— ?' Convulsively he caught at her hand.

'Don't you care a damn for me, Chrystal?' he insanely persisted; and, because of the pain in his eyes, she gave him the truth.

'I care about half a damn: which is just not half enough to marry on.'

And she saw that he simply did not believe her. In some men, there seemed to be a core of natural conceit that fire would not burn out of them. It was a positive relief to hear the opening bars of another dance.

'Mine?' he asked eagerly.

'No — it's Lance this time.' She hurried on to the nearest door; but he was still beside her.

'The next then?'

She shook her head and signalled with her fan to Lance, who had sighted them.

'The next,' she said, with deliberation, 'I think I'm dancing with — Sher Afzul Khan.'

He flared up, red with rage.

'*Again* — ? That damned Brindian. Chrystal, for God's sake — !'

She checked him with a lifted hand.

'Don't let's bring God into such a trivial affair. I really must be allowed to choose my own partners.'

'Hear, hear!' Lance slid up and clicked his heels. 'Trying to oust me, Peter? That's asking for trouble.'

But Grant's parting shot was for Chrystal.

'*She*'s asking for trouble,' he said; and turning away, he sauntered off to the bar.

'Still harping on Sher Afzul?' Desmond queried.

She nodded. 'I said I might be dancing with him again. That tore it.'

'Poor old Pete! He'll now go and fuddle his brain with drinking more than he can carry or pay for.' He eyed her a moment: 'You are giving Afzul another?'

'Yes. Will they all be popping their eyes at me — and at your Eve — tomorrow?'

He twinkled.

'Likely as not.'

She regarded him with her vivid look of intelligence, liking the man she saw behind his smiling eyes; a man to whom one could speak one's thought without reservation.

'These English, out here,' she said — 'what makes most of them so frightfully narrow in certain ways? Are they forced to run in a groove? Or are they instinctively hanging on by their eyelids to something that's slipping away from them — something they didn't have to clutch at before?'

He met her question with a straight answer.

'Likely as not, again. You're a thinking young woman. And if we *do* hang on to the tail end of a very great inheritance — can you blame us?'

'I don't blame anybody, ever. I just notice things, being made that way. I'm sorry for these Brindians — and I'm interested.'

'So I perceive. It's a treat, out here, to find anyone actively interested in anything outside the three P.'s — pay, promotion, and personalities. But we have our few bright exceptions ——'

'Your Eve,' she suggested: and his sudden smile told her more than he realised.

'Eve's unique,' he said. 'And a genius at that. — There's Afzul watching us. Shall we carry on?'

They carried on. Lance not only moved with athletic ease and grace, he had music in him. And his dancing was the least of his merits. What a man to make a life with. She hoped, one day, to make a real life with a real man. But she did not see herself consenting to marry out here, to spend her best years in this cheerful, Philistine world that seemed to her critical half-knowledge neither England, nor India. It would need a man like Lance to work the miracle....

Later on, Sher Afzul dared again. It was a valse this time; and he seemed more at ease. Probably Eve had helped. She had a spontaneous way with her, once you got past her shyness, that would conjure the stiffness out of a poker.

After the dance, they wandered out, at her suggestion, into the Club garden, lantern-lit and pencilled with moonlight. Across the centre lawn they strolled; and she drew him, by casual questions, into telling her of his home; a fortified stronghold in the Yusufzai country beyond the Khyber Pass; of his father, the fine old chieftain, who had encouraged his early dream of becoming a commissioned British officer in a Frontier Cavalry regiment. Many of the family had been against it. He did not specify them: probably mother or sisters, who were never mentioned. One might suppose, from his talk, that he had no female relations. Their hidden women were obviously a bar to making friends with these people; but, according to Grace Lynch, they would not be hidden much longer.

He confessed that, at first, he had been miserable at school across the sea, away from his own people and his 'Free Land.' England seemed so little and green, tied up in bunches of dumpy hills and woods; palings everywhere, even in open country. But gradually he had become bitten with English ways of life and thought; had worked hard and gained the coveted commission. His family were proud of him. He could spend part of his leave with them every year. Further encouraged, he told her tales of blood feuds that might have come straight out of old Scottish history. Strange how often men of the hills, for all their courage, were marred by a racial taint of cruelty and cunning; raiders all; careless of life, their own or other people's.

Her frank interest seemed to loosen his tongue. Never yet had their talk taken so personal a turn. And when at last a familiar air drew them back to the ballroom, they discovered — to her amusement and his concern — that they had skipped a dance. Deliberately she treated their 'little lapse' as a joke; and when Dixon Verney, of the Police, lamented his lost dance, she only said, 'Take this one,' without troubling to explain.

Verney was a clever man, thin and dark; not a ready talker, but a superb dancer. He merely alluded in passing to Sher Afzul Khan.

'He's a good sort — our tamed Yusufzai.'

'Tamed?' she queried, wondering.

'Supposed to be. Heaven knows how many inches deep it goes. I haven't seen him dancing before. You giving the women a lead?'

She laughed. 'I wouldn't presume! Eve danced with him too. Lance encouraged us.'

He twitched an eyebrow at her; and again she wondered — does he disapprove? But he only said, 'Mrs. Peel had her lorgnette on you just now.'

'Admiring my new frock?' she asked demurely. 'I'm not to be overawed by a local Burra Mem. I'll dance with whom I please, as often as I please.'

Again he glanced at her. 'Will you dance another with me — though I'm *not* a Pathan?'

'Of course I will,' she said, adding to herself, 'I don't believe he disapproves.'

For some undefined reason, she hoped he did not. He was a queer detached kind of man, a good deal older than herself, and obviously friends with Claire. Yet she liked him better than some of the younger men. She liked his cool, ironic manner; his interest in the people and the country, not mushed up with sentiment, nor tainted with superiority. And his dancing was supreme.

It was her favourite tango again; but this time her mind was distracted a trifle by the sight of Mrs. Peel in her flame-coloured velvet. The Candid Peel they called her; and, being one of Jasper's flattering specials, she might work him up into a state of righteous protest that would mainly worry Claire, who had quite enough to endure in that line. How they fumed and fussed over nothing, these local-minded people. Sex and marriage seemed fastened, like barnacles, on their brains. Because of a few dances, she had given to a harmless Pathan, they would picture her committing a mixed marriage or some such impossibility.

Once, while dancing, she looked round to see what had become of Sher Afzul. There he stood alone in one of the doorways, watching the room full of dancers. What did he really think of all this in his reserved Eastern mind? If her own and Eve's simple act of courtesy did set the hide-bound buzzing like bees, she hoped no comment would reach his ears. He seemed so genuinely to like and admire the right kind of English; and this was the way they encouraged the Better Understanding cult. Between them all, they were largely responsible for the fact that she now felt a good deal more interested in him, as a person, than she had done earlier in the evening.

Chapter IV

It is we ourselves, acting through others,
that are the instruments of our own fate.

ROBERT SPEIAGHT

NEXT afternoon, Social Peshawar of all grades was present in force at one of the last big gymkhanas of the winter season; non-social elements packed together on the outskirts: British Tommies, Indian sepoys and sowars, and horse-loving Pathans from the city — gamblers all. The band blared cheerfully at intervals; horses went scampering past in a stream of rainbow colours; Indian cavalry units vied with each other at tent-pegging and every conceivable mounted gymnastic.

In the great *shamianah*, the *élite* of the station were gathered together: an impressive phalanx of tradition, prestige, and crystallised opinion. No sign of Sir Vincent Leigh in the Government House group. He left social ceremonies mainly to his wife, a gracious and beautiful woman; no taint in her of the prevailing snob mentality, or of the sweepingly derided Anglo-Indian Memsahib. Yet inherently she was Anglo-Indian to the bone; a Desmond by birth and temperament, love of the Frontier in her blood, its few familiar stations hardly less 'Home' to her than England itself. Her four brothers, all born on the Frontier, had returned there as a matter of course, only excepting John, the Royal Engineer. Even the younger generation — notably Lance — had followed the Desmond tradition, that dated back to the very first Punjab Cavalry regiments, raised by Sir Henry Lawrence, for his famous Irregular Frontier Force.

The 'Border Clan'—as Vincent called them—were fairly well in evidence this afternoon. There was her brother—now General Sir Paul Desmond, Commanding the Northern Division—up from Pindi for a week; and her own Theo, still Political Officer at Malakand, had come in on business connected with these first unbelievable Frontier Province elections. There was John's son Lance, her favourite nephew—Lance, who had deserted the Family Regiment for Frontier Political Service; had done fine work in Chitral, and was earning fresh credit as Assistant Commissioner of Peshawar. Neil, a few years younger, was the born cavalry officer, never likely to desert the Regiment; winning laurels for it today by steeple-chasing and feats of horsemanship that were the delight of his life.

Very soon, now, she would be welcoming yet another of the Clan—her youngest boy Vernon, not seen for three years, coming out to join the R.A.F. And now that their term in Peshawar was prolonged, Phyllis—her baby—must come out in the autumn when she would be turned seventeen. But in spite of those five grown-up children, and a visibly sprouting grandson, she could not yet manage to feel other than young in mind and heart. For her, these early middle years brought with them a sense of fuller flowering, a less convulsive clutch on life. More ambitious always for her man than he had ever been for himself, her pride and delight in this crowning tribute knew no bounds.

But at present she was less immediately concerned with her own happiness than with anxiety over Roy Sinclair, who should by rights—in her soldierly opinion—have gone straight back to his home duties and that much-enduring wife. Yet she loved him no less for a decision that was really none of his; and she could not doubt that, finally, the West in him would prevail—the high-minded, sensitive, lovable Roy, whom she had known since prep school and Marlborough years, when he and her lost brother, Lance, had sown the seeds of a close friendship, cut short by the death of Lance in those dreadful Lahore riots, more than twelve years ago.

She could still hardly bear to think of those terrible days, when she and Roy had been drawn so close together by shared grief and love. He was a finer man now than he had been then. With his blend of soldier and poet, of East and West, he had a gift of endearing himself to many and varied human beings of both races. He had even got under the skin of her own shy, critical Vinx. Lance and Eve loved him as dearly as did either of his Rajput cousins, Aruna and Surāj Mul. And there was Grace Lynch, also, attracted by another facet of his complex nature, deeply concerned for his possible fate. Would she persuade that formidable husband of hers to go personally in search of him? Thea had expected to see her at the gymkhana and ask her about it: but social functions were no more in her line, as Mrs. John Lynch, than they had been as Doctor Grace Yolande. She still remained, at heart, a 'doctor-mish,' caring more for the welfare of Indian women and children than for anything in life, except the *zubberdasti* Lynch, whom she had so amazingly married.

Ah, here she was after all; late, as usual. A smile and a gesture drew her at once into the Government House group. A chair was vacated for her — after protests — by a talkative General's wife in the smallest of hats and the smartest of frocks. It was Lady Leigh who noted, with amusement, her pained glance at the Police Officer's wife, in last summer's coat and a simple straw hat. Grace herself, completely unaware, unimpressed by the smallest hat and the smartest frock, nodded her thanks and sat down — not by the wife of a Governor-to-be, but by the woman who was her friend.

'What have we arrived at?' she asked in her brisk fashion, accepting a programme of events from Captain Creagh, Private Secretary to Sir Vincent Leigh. His finger politely indicated 'Frontier Cavalry Sports,' as a dozen young officers went galloping past, bareback, to a line of saddles and bridles dumped on the ground. There they dismounted, seized their saddles, girthed them on, and dashed back helter-skelter to the winning post — Neil Desmond leading, Sher Afzul half a length behind.

Thea and Grace clapped with the rest: but the thoughts of both were elsewhere.

'You've not heard any more?' Grace asked, with John at the back of her mind.

'Not a word. I'm cursing your friend the Guru. Why can't they turn their magic powers to practical account? We must send a search party at once. I hope your "John" can arrange to get away.'

'I know he's trying to,' Grace answered the implied question. 'He'll be seeing Sir Vincent again about it, tonight or tomorrow. 'Have you written to his wife?'

'Yes. By air mail. But it's all so horribly vague. If she *has* heard from him —— we've asked her to wire. It wasn't fair to *her* — his going off like that at the eleventh hour.'

Grace smiled pensively at a line of racing horses. 'I wonder — if *she* saw it that way? When a man has hitched his wagon to a star, there are bound to be times when his wife can only serve by standing aside.'

Thea smiled. 'Tara [1] herself being a star! That, I imagine, will be her attitude to Roy's exalted form of truancy.'

'You know her?'

'I met her as a small girl when I first met Roy, a lovely creature, steeped in his mother's tales of heroic Rajput wives and very jealous of Roy's devotion to my brother Lance——.'

She was interrupted by a masculine voice at her elbow: 'Good God! A near thing. See that, Lady Leigh?'

It was Colonel Brereton, commanding Neil's battalion. The near thing referred to Neil himself — and she had not seen, her mind having wandered years away.

Eight officers were competing now in the hair-raising feat of snatching a handkerchief off the ground at full gallop. Bareback they rode, legs gripping the animal's body, as they swung head downwards to whisk up the trophy and carry it to the goal. If the upward swing were delayed by a fraction, the rider might have his head kicked open by the hind legs of his own horse. Neil, it seemed, had been within

[1] *Tara*, Indian for 'star.'

an ace of that mortal danger; and his narrow escape evoked yells of applause as he swung upright, waving his flag. He was a popular youngster; keen soldier and sportsman, an ace at polo and all feats of horsemanship; only dividing the honours in that line with Sher Afzul Khan, who now went thundering past. Lean and muscular, a very Centaur, the upward swing of his body suggested the spring of a steel blade released from tension.

'Fine fellow of ours that,' remarked Brereton, with his slightly possessive C.O. air.

'One of the *few* bright exceptions,' added a pessimistic Major. 'The experiment's right enough — in theory. But in practice, on a large scale, it's not going to work.'

The lurking note of satisfaction in his tone was not lost on Thea Leigh, who fixed him with a disapproving eye.

'Of course not, if people are convinced it won't. So much depends on the attitude of our own officers. And most of them seem friendly.'

'Oh, rather — up to a point. We're lucky with our lot; and our chaps put a good face on it, because they must. But, stands to reason, even one Indian at Mess makes a fellow's talk less easy, more guarded. Must play up to the theory, even if we don't half like it, or them, under our skins.'

The said 'chaps' were doing their loyal best, at the moment, to applaud Sher Afzul as heartily as they had applauded Neil. Yells from his fellow Pathans followed him as he passed; and at the far end of the tent, one English girl was clapping as she seldom clapped, being little given to random bursts of enthusiasm.

Chrystal Adair had come early with the Desmonds, leaving Claire to finish her mail and follow on later, if she felt like it. She seemed a martyr to headaches, funked the strong sun of early afternoon; and Chrystal jumped at any excuse to go anywhere with the Desmonds. She had spent two weeks with them in camp, and Lance, as administrator, had impressed her mightily. She had done some unusual and successful sketches of his camp and his crowd; had enjoyed the freedom of mind and body, after the 'barbed-wire internment' life of Peshawar—its ceaseless gaiety and gossip and personal jealousies; its blank indifference to the many and strange realities of India. The men, on the whole, seemed more knowledgeable than the women, especially officers in the Indian Army. Quick to detect minds congenial to her own, she had very soon singled out Lance and Eve — worker and artist, her favourite types of human being. They were artists in life, also, those two — an enviable thing to be.

She was sitting beside Eve now; Lance behind them with a group of men. He had ridden in two races and carried off the prize for lemon-slicing. Peter had been pestering her, like any mosquito, backing all the wrong horses and generally damning his luck in terms more picturesque than polite. At least, she had the grace to feel genuinely sorry for him; but she wearied of his vain dangling, without having the heart to be consistently unkind. The Verney man — who would have been more welcome — never 'dangled.' Except in the ballroom, he favoured his own sex. She could hear his curious flat voice behind her now, talking to Lance about that vanished Sinclair man. Sher Afzul, taken up with various events, had hardly entered the *shamianah*, which was just as well, in the circumstances. For, this morning, Jasper had been thoroughly Jasperious; trotting out, like Peter, all the stale stuff about Indians and their muffled-up wives, who were emerging from purdah by the score; and Sher Afzul, not possessing a wife, was obviously outside that argument. Claire vainly had tried to calm him down; and she herself had not mended matters by remarking that it seemed a pity to waste nervous energy and risk a heart attack on account of a few dances given to a man who was, after all, in the position of a British officer and danced very well. He had told her sharply not to be impertinent. She had given him one eloquent look and gone out of the room, leaving poor Claire to tackle the fretful porcupine. It was hard on her. She had a thin time at best. But if she would spoil her impossible husband, she must accept the consequences.

And this afternoon, of course, the Goggles had ventured a mild protest, in her rôle as Club Secretary; her washy blue eyes rounder than ever, the busy tip of her tongue nervously moistening her lips. The line she took was not Indian wives in purdah, but 'English women and girls making themselves cheap.' Of course she admitted that dancing with the right sort of Indian was no longer taboo. At big balls, and in mixed stations, it was all very well. But at these intimate little Club dances—out popped the inevitable platitude—'one *had* to draw the line.'

'"East is East and West is West," as Kipling rightly insists. Though I can't quite see where the genius comes in. So glaringly obvious. What else *could* East be? It couldn't be West—if you see what I mean?'

And Chrystal had not dared to look at Eve, or to venture a retort that might have started another hare: the lucid query 'What else *could* East be?' was too priceless to be mangled by argument.

Was East going to be the winner at this hair-raising handkerchief trick? she wondered—as Afzul Khan dashed past in splendid style. The fact that everyone else in the tent was probably favouring Neil gave her sympathy a perverse tilt the other way. With a new undersense of excitement, she clapped and clapped so vigorously that Eve glanced at her sidelong, a twinkle in her serious eyes, as if she understood. Perhaps she, too, was liking him better because she had done him a good turn?

But was it the good turn that accounted for her own quickened interest? Or was it the difference of race—the sense of something insidious, yet potent, in the very air of India? What did it do to one, this mysterious country, with its blazing sun and passionate blue heavens, its intoxicating nights of full moon and flashing stars? At first she had not liked it at all. The fascination of its toneless landscape, its endless plains, and those fierce, magnetic hills had penetrated slowly. Now it seemed to be laying a spell upon her.

It was the voice of Lance that broke the thread of her musings, telling her and Eve: 'Those two have tied. Just a question of pace. But they're not content with "Honours easy." Death on trying it again. Rank vanity, I tell Neil. Here he comes.'

Shouts of applause greeted his passing at a pace that no rival, it seemed, could challenge. But Lance — who was timing them — had an eye out for Afzul Khan.

'Lord! His Arab's going like the wind,' Chrystal heard him say.

And, like the wind, they came. A long arm whisked up the handkerchief — and they were gone, almost before the applause broke out again. No friendly shouts this time: no '*Shahbāsh,*' as before, except from Lance. Wilder yells from the outer circle, deep-throated shouts from regimental Pathans. In the clapping, with its subtle difference — to Chrystal's fancy — in the Pathans' shouts of triumph, one could feel the underlying clash of race conflict.

'*We* ought to show them we are above it,' she thought, with her young sententiousness. 'But we aren't — that's the trouble.'

And now Lance was back again, announcing that Afzul had done it this time by a shave.

'Nothing proved either way. But his Pathans'll be sky-high. Here come the dead-heat rivals.'

A few subalterns sang out 'Cheerio,' and 'Are we down-hearted?' as the two approached, Neil grasping Afzul's arm, calling him 'Son of Lightning,' insisting that the loser must stand him a drink. And there was Dixon Verney strolling up to congratulate. Nice man —

Followed a general move to the refreshment table: a ten minutes' interval between two halves of the programme, for tea or cocktails, with selections from *Ruddigore* hammered out by the British Infantry band.

'Come on, you two,' said Lance, 'and comfort old Neil.'

'He doesn't look heart-broken,' remarked Chrystal with her serious air.

'No cause to be. Anyhow — he brought it on himself.'

Neil came forward grinning cheerfully, and escorted them to the table, where Afzul Khan received, with his most courteous air, their genuine congratulations, their praise of his victorious Arab, '*Badshah Pasund.*'

'Beloved of Kings,' he translated for Chrystal's benefit.

'I'm not surprised at the Kings!' she said; and Lance gave her a smile of approval. He himself had a soft spot in his Irish heart for Afzul's Arab, though the sinner had outpaced Neil's Devil-May-Care.

Afzul, himself, patently pleased, asked leave to fetch her a drink — tea, coffee, a cocktail?

She chose iced coffee; and as he moved off to waylay a wandering *kit*, Peter Grant sauntered up to the table.

'Luck — to find you unattached. Backed a winner last race, thanks be. But I lost on Desmond. Damned shame! It was *his* "win" by rights. Pity he didn't knock the stuffing out of that conceited Pathan ——'

'He's not conceited. He rode splendidly,' she retorted; and he made round eyes at her.

'Lucky dog, to have you for a champion. All *I* have to say is — *Kubberdar!*[1] A King's commission can't conjure a Yusufzai Pathan into a Sahib. The Ethiopian can't change his skin to order, which is Bible truth, my Chrys — though *I* say it.'

'I'm not your Chrys,' she told him with a touch of asperity.

'Another unpalatable truth!' His flippant tone belied the pain in his eyes. 'Let's comfort ourselves with cocktails. Hullo, what's that?' It was Afzul Khan returning from his quest. 'Iced coffee? No thanks. Beastly stuff.'

His tone — unconsciously perhaps — was that of the less-than-average white man to his bearer; and the Pathan's face hardened.

'It's *not* for you,' he said stiffly. 'It is for Miss Adair.'

'Oh, quite. But she wants a cocktail. *I*'m seeing after Miss Adair.'

'If you'll give me a chance, Peter, that's *my* coffee you're waving away.' The girl's brisk tone implicitly called him to order. 'I asked for it. Thank you so much.'

She put out a hand for the slim frosted glass, with its

[1] Take care.

crown of whipped cream, and Grant — ignoring Afzul Khan — strolled off with a casual air. Chrystal, looking up quickly to make amends, was startled by Sher Afzul's changed aspect.

He was staring fixedly after the unsuspecting Peter, a glint like a steel blade in his eyes; a sudden revealing of the vindictive, untamed Border Pathan that lurked beneath the contained manner of his class and English training. In that startled moment she knew that the disgruntled Peter — unaware of offending a mere Brindian — was lucky to leave the tent alive. It was he who needed the warning that a Pathan could not change his skin to order.

The whole brief affair seemed so trifling in itself — so far from trifling the passions it called into play. That murderous look and her own thrill of fear passed in a few seconds; and her impulse to atone was checked by Afzul asking in his normal voice, 'Would you really prefer a cocktail?'

'Of course not. Iced coffee's my pet weakness. May I have a small pastry? Yes — one of those ——'

Peter and his ill-manners were tacitly ignored; but their obvious effect on Sher Afzul moved Chrystal to spend the whole ten minutes' interval talking to him. Once she caught the disapproving eye of Mrs. Pedley-Burne, tall and slimmed and smart, strolling by, with Jasper in tow, as usual.

'A peacock of a woman,' was Chrystal's irreverent thought, 'pecking grain out of any male hand that offers it. *She* can't cast a stone.'

Let her think what she would; let hopeful young officers hover; a spirit of challenge, abetted by personal liking, kept Chrystal firmly attached to the favoured Pathan. If she liked him the better for his awkward position, it was their doing, and Peter's doing, rather than her own.

Chapter V

How came you to me
Opening timeless skies,
Like a heaven within me
That is all sunrise?

LAURENCE BINYON

LIEUTENANT SHER AFZUL KHAN, son of a warrior chief, whose house was his fortress, whose women folk wore garments woven from threads of pure gold, wondered at times what his people would say to the outward signs of his rise in life. The colourless khaki uniform, the regulation Mess kit and *mufti* would seem a poor exchange for the gold-peaked turban, the brocaded waistcoat, and the tasselled girdle of a well-born Pathan: the shabby bungalow, an even poorer exchange for the rough comfort and dignity of the Khan Bahadur's fort among the hard-faced hills.

But in modern Anglo-India bungalows of any sort were becoming a luxury for the few. Even married officers were herded together in Army Mansions designed for mass habitation. On the whole he and his fellows — three Cavalry subalterns and one in the Frontier Rifles — had considered their shabby dwelling a 'find,' though, in places, it leaked generously; no single door fitted its frame, and the blotched outer walls cried aloud for a fresh coat of colour wash, promised anon by their Hindu shopkeeper landlord. Every month it would 'infallibly be done.' Every month it was infallibly left undone. Finally, two wrathful Pathan subalterns had threatened a raid on the sinner's 'emporium' of very mixed goods, ranging from braces to binoculars, from patent 'cure-alls' to silk pyjamas from Japan. But they knew — and he knew — that any attempt at direct action would recoil on their own heads. So the blotched bungalow continued to affront their eyes.

Their one large living-room betrayed the Asiatic's curious indifference to surroundings: bare walls except for a few personal photographs hung up anyhow; the broad mantel-shelf adorned with tobacco jars, cigarette tins, and a few stray books. Corners were stacked untidily with polo-sticks, racquets, and golf-clubs. Only two out of the six doors were curtained with Bokhara hangings, the property of Afzul Khan: and a fine Kashmir carpet was laid down over the former owner's matting, that showed unevenly round the edge.

Here sat three of them on the evening after the sports — Pathan, Sikh, and Brahmin, strangely united in the service of the new India; conjured, by Army training, into brother officers and good friends — up to a point. All were in Mess dress. Sher Afzul stood with his back to the gaping Indian fireplace, lighting a pipe. Gopāl Singh, taller and handsomer, sprawled on the shabby Chesterfield, his waistcoat buttons open, his Sikh beard parted, the ends vanishing under his turban.

A keen soldier, liked by his British officers, he seemed, at sight, one of the more fortunate specimens of the changing Indian Army; but he alone knew where the shoe pinched — and pinched hard. An early, arranged marriage to a Zemindar's daughter had saddled him with a young wife of little or no education; a plump and smiling creature, mother of two sons, happy in her narrow round of home and village life. A few phrases of broken English had been learnt from the 'doctor-Mem' to please her officer husband; but these would scarcely serve as passport to life in a station bungalow. She was his destiny and he had fathered her sons; but there were times when he envied Siri Nath, Brahmin, the educated wife who was completing a course at the Kinnaird College at Lahore, hoping to join her husband next cold weather. At four and twenty this goodly young man saw himself wedged between two impossibles: the impossibility of a permanently divided house; and the equal impossibility of transferring his Chyria[1] and her nestlings to this aggressively

[1] Bird.

Moslem Border region. The double expense fretted his money-loving soul; but at present there seemed no practical way out.

Neither of the Pathans had yet taken a wife; but marriage being the ordained fate of man, they could not for long evade the problem of finding wives, among their backward people, to suit their own educated thoughts and ways.

This evening, as usual, the Brahmin sat apart at the littered writing-table; a small, spare man, alert in mind and body, his undistinguished features redeemed by a wide brow and expressive dark eyes. Shoulders hunched, head bowed, he was writing at great length to his student wife, telling her of his hopes and plans and daily doings. But of one recent episode, that still rankled, he could not write, even to her. For his private difficulties were not domestic, but regimental. A young man of culture and breeding, son of a Divisional Judge, he had chosen the Army rather than 'the Civil,' because British officers were reputed to be friendly and less exclusive than the 'White Brahmins' of the I.C.S. And so, on the whole, he had found them to be.

It was the men of his Sikh platoon who had given him trouble from the start. Too soon they had perceived that, for all his training and zeal, he was no true soldier. He could not even give them a word of command or a simple order as one to the manner born; nor would the Indian officers take from him what they would take from their pink-faced British subaltern two years his junior. More: his housemates — pleasant enough in some ways — were so arrogantly race-proud, especially the Pathans, that they forced on him an unwilling sense of inferiority, though he reckoned himself their out-and-out superior in the depths of his Brahminical soul. That acute sense of race and creed was the crux of the whole Indian Army problem; and today's rankling incident was typical of the troubles that would multiply with the progress of Indianising on a large scale.

It had arisen out of a shooting competition at the butts between two companies, Rajput and Pathan, for whom he had been detailed to keep the score. But, at the last moment, his fellow subaltern had turned up, looking sheepish, to announce that Captain Hayes had sent him to take over the scoring. Pressed for a reason, it came out that the company Jemadars had privately pleaded for a '*pukka* British officer.'

Vainly Captain Hayes had told them that Lieutenant Siri Nath, a man of highest caste, was officially as *pukka* as himself. A Brahmin British officer — the Pathans had insisted — must inevitably favour Rajputs in scoring. Only from a white officer could his men accept the given score, if it went against them.

'But how will it be,' Hayes had queried, only half in joke, 'when there are no more white officers, as decreed, in twenty years' time?'

And the Pathan had laughed aloud.

'Twenty years? Stop in India, Captain Sahib, and see.'

So Hayes had reluctantly ordered a change-over, leaving Siri Nath — with a detested hockey match on his hands — wondering seriously how things would go, if ever there were no more white officers in the Indian Army?

For all the progress achieved in the last ten years, there were too many Indians still incapable of working together for one end.

The Sikh and Pathan behind him were talking, now, of the gymkhana and Sher Afzul's hairbreadth victory: of race feelings too easily stirred up, like mud from the depths of a river.

He had hoped for a game of bridge to distract his thoughts from that nagging incident. For they were apt to leave Mess early, being happier in the unbuttoned ease of their own bungalow. But tonight Abdul Jān Afridi had gone off to the pictures, where he could get vicarious excitement from the knifings and shootings of American gangsters. Afzul had voted against 'cut-throat bridge'; and now those two were distracting his mind in another fashion with their talk on the never-ending theme.

From the gymkhana they had drifted on to speak of their Colonel, a man of quite another *jāt* than his own; one who made none of those trifling distinctions, that Indians were no doubt over-ready to detect or imagine. They gave him, in consequence, loyal, unstinted service, while Siri Nath would do no more than he positively must for a Colonel who saw him as an unpromising item in an unworkable experiment. For the East instinctively gives allegiance to the leader, rather than to any abstract sense of duty.

'Desmond says we make a god of the Colonel.'—It was Afzul speaking. 'What harm? The others make a god of the regiment.'

'We honour our regiment also.' The Sikh leaned forward, elbows on knees. 'But work for the leader is in our blood. Only so can we learn the ropes. And afterwards—?'

'Yes, afterwards—?' Sher Afzul echoed with a significant look. 'What then? We of the North are willing to lead. Whom would we follow, except a white man, or a blood-brother of our own faith? A Bengali or Madrassi Colonel—? *Istagh far Ullah!*[1] I can't see, yet, an all-India Army without British leaders, men who never tire and never take bribes.'

The Sikh chuckled. 'It remains to be seen if those who are shouting loudest for a National Army would send their own sons to the Indian Sandhurst? Not many, I think. But we live in strange times, with all this talkie-talkie in London about Federal India and responsibility at the centre.'

'So it should *be*.' Siri Nath swung round in his swivel chair, confronting the two men of the North—farther removed from him, in many ways, than from the average army Englishman.

'So *let* it *be*,' agreed Sher Afzul with his truculent air. 'If such weakening of British power should ever come about, we Moslems know what would happen next. Perhaps you two have heard of the Pakistān Plan.'

'What's that?' Siri Nath eyed him with instinctive suspicion.

'Aha! You prick up your ears.' Sher Afzul laid his pipe on the mantelpiece and thrust long sinewy hands into his trouser pockets. 'It is a plan talked of among all Moslems of the North for more than twenty years. Now we are watch-

[1] God forbid.

ing how the wind blows. The first sign of weakness in British rule will be the signal for a great Moslem rising that will make a clean cut across India. All the South below Jumma and Aravallis for the Hindu; all the North for us, from Kabul and Kashmir to Delhi; worshipping one God, acknowledging full sovereignty of our great King Emperor. Let the heavens fall, Punjabi-Moslem, and Pathan will never be ruled by Bengali or Madrassi...'

'My dear chap, you go too fast.' Gopāl Singh flung out a protesting hand. 'All the North is *not* Moslem. You won't work your proud plan, unless you can make terms with the brotherhood of the Khalsa.'[1]

It was the voice of Communal India, foe to the best-laid schemes for Federation; a goal that can only be reached when the prevailing spirit of intolerance has been transcended by an agreed loyalty, British and Indian, to the Aryan ideal of life and thought — primal source of all culture, the one basic harmonising influence in a faction-ridden land.

Not yet had the clash of creeds been transcended in the minds of this English-trained Sikh and Pathan.

'That will be seen, Gopāl, when the time arrives,' said Afzul, his arrogance tempered by friendly feeling. 'We may yet find some bond of the spirit with those who are at least no idolators, worshippers of one God ——'

'We Hindus also,' the Brahmin quietly reminded him, 'worship the One — unheard, unseen, behind the changing aspects of the Many: "The Inward Ruler, the Deathless."'

There spoke Aryan India of the Vedas, earliest and most profound source of spiritual truth.

Sher Afzul eyed the small, cultured man, whom he privately held in no particular esteem. 'You Brahmins have the pull with your high-flown talk. But it will cut no ice with us, till you clear India of caste tyranny of gods and goddesses and idol worship.'

Siri Nath's gesture deprecated argument.

'Idols are for the ignorant, as all who know the higher Hinduism understand. But questions of spiritual belief are

[1] Sikhs.

not matter for discussion. Your faith is fanatical, seeing no merit in other forms that meet other needs. Ours — oldest of all — is not so much a faith as a code of conduct, a form of philosophy, admitting that truth may flow through other channels, that the streams are many, but the Source is One.'

On that unanswerable conclusion, he picked up his writing-case and went out, leaving Sikh and Pathan curiously drawn to each other by a vague sense of relief at his departure.

Sher Afzul picked up his pipe and began refilling it.

'Education, I suppose,' he remarked, sinking into the largest armchair, 'is our only cure-all. Look what it's done for you and me. Five or six years ago I couldn't have conceived sharing a bungalow with that Brahmin and his bookish talk. What will it do, I wonder, for the mixed lot of boys in the Doon School with their English masters and English games? And this Indian Sandhurst they will soon be starting. After twenty years of all that — how will it be?'

Gopāl Singh shook his head. 'I can see no Army of all India, any more than of all Europe. For a *pukka* weapon of defence, it would be hard to beat what we have now, with perhaps a higher percentage of *our* sort, picked from the fighting races.'

'Right. You've hit it. South India need not apply. But that would not suit the Congress wallahs or the talking shop at Delhi.'

The Sikh grunted dubiously and smoothed his beard.

'*We* have become a talking shop this evening! What would our Messmates think of such speculations from a pair of sporting subs who seldom utter a thought?'

'What do they utter, I wonder,' mused Afzul, 'when we are not there? Sport — shop — gup? The English never speak their thought. For better understanding, we need a more equal mixing of men and women — both races. And I think it is coming now.' In his mind's eye he saw the fair face of Chrystal Adair, who had said she was not afraid. 'Look at our schools and colleges, chock-full of girls who have left the curtain. Good for them and for us. We want wives who can and will live as we do ——'

He broke off, recalling his friend's dilemma; but the Sikh gave no sign. With a mighty yawn, he rose and stretched himself, revealing his full six feet three inches: a splendid figure of manhood and a soldier in the grain; yet fundamentally unsatisfied.

'I'm for bed,' he remarked. 'Abdul's making a night of it.'

He dragged at an ill-fitting door; cursed it when it jerked open; slammed it behind him and could be heard shouting for his bearer in approved British style.

Sher Afzul Khan, left alone, pulled out a letter from his father that he had found awaiting him on his return from the sports; a letter that concerned the crucial subject of his marriage. Last summer his mother had urgently begged him to consider the particular wife they desired for him; daughter of a fellow-chief, a playmate of early days. He himself had not forgotten Selima, a tall, spirited girl, fair-skinned, with liquid dark eyes. She often had come to the fort on feast days with her parents till purdah restrictions put an end to their meetings.

Last year he had evaded the issue, without completely crushing his mother's hope. Now his father, who was no scribe, wrote again of the proposed marriage that would link their two houses in lasting friendship. Selima, he said, would be willing to break purdah. She could read and talk some English, and could soon learn more. It was her father's belief that such a marriage would fulfil the secret wish of her heart.

> *My Son* — his own father concluded — *the peace of Allah be with you. We count the weeks to your coming. I am unskilled with a pen, but I have tried to put in your lap our distress of mind over the uncertainty of your consent to a formal betrothal when you come again on leave. If you have other thoughts in your heart, we do not wish to stand between you and the sun. I know you have learnt many English ways, but in blood you are still Yusufzai Pathan. And you know it is not our custom for a young man merely to gratify his own desires, shirking his natural duty to the family and the race. Let us have no cause to reproach ourselves — your mother and I — that we permitted a mountain*

eagle to be half converted into a college crow. Let us not look in vain for a favourable reply to this matter that is so near our hearts. The blessing of Allah be upon you. His peace be with you, is the prayer of your father, Khan Zemān Khan.

Twice over he read that moving letter, sitting alone in the lofty whitewashed room, its three verandah doors flung open; only the wired frames closed to foil the insects who buzzed and bumped against them, seeking the fatal light. Idly watching, a thought smote him: Was he like one of those winged creatures, seeking the flame that would destroy him? Could the faith of his people and his Pathan heritage prevent him, like those wire screens, from singeing his wings?

For weeks his mind had been haunted by the face of that young girl from another Free Land of the North — a country of hill men, worshippers of clans and courage and one God. Now she had danced with him. He had felt her slim hand in his own, like a captured bird. The sense of her so near him, though so carefully held apart, had stirred his blood. And this afternoon in the *shamianah*, she had shown him favour, even to the discomfiting of that speckle-faced R.A.F. cad. It was a pity that, too often now, the English sent their second-best to India. He himself had been startled by the lust of murder that blazed up in him as he watched Grant leaving the tent. Impossible to quell racial instinct by a few years of discipline and mental schooling. These were good; and the soldier's life was good; but at times he wondered whether he and his fellows might not have to pay too high a price for their new privilege.

What could come of his desire but frustration? Passion he had known from early manhood: never yet this more exalted urge of a love that demanded marriage — to what end? So many forces were arrayed against it: race-prejudice and religion, the tradition of his own clan; the probability that he might be obliged to leave the regiment and fling overboard all that he had won. Impossible to tell his father that indeed he had other thoughts in his heart: seed of fire that could only burn and not bear fruit.

What then?

Marry Selima, for the simple duty of carrying on his family and clan? To that question his half-civilised heart prompted one answer, his Pathan blood and heritage another. The streak of fatalism in him argued, 'As it must be, so it will be.' But belief in *Kismet* could not quiet his conflict of heart and mind.

Half the night he lay wakeful under his mosquito net, till weariness lulled him into unrefreshing sleep.

Chapter VI

In my heart of hearts, through dark and bright,
The violins of passion swirl a tune
As brave as morning and as fond as night.

GERALD GOULD

SHER AFZUL was dragged out of sleep by the voice of his servant waking him for early parade. Within the hour he was up and dressed, mounted on Badshah, youth and health tingling in his veins; problems of marriage shaken off, as a bird shakes water from its feathers.

The wide Peshawar Valley, on an April morning, was a scene to rejoice the heart: everywhere blossoming orchards — apple, almond, and peach — young leaves and cornfields almost sickle-high. Even here, in the ordered station, gardens of the larger bungalows and borders along the Mall were gay with English flowers. And there, along the skyline, beyond the fruitful valley, north and west, ranged the barrier of gaunt, unfruitful hills, rising to snowy giants of the Safed Koh Range. Northward, towered the dark mass of Mount Tartara; eastward, the snow peaks tumbled into rocky spurs and ravines of his own Yusufzai mountain region; fit breeding-ground for the raiders and marksmen of his tribe.

Often, looking that way, as now, he would be troubled, as by a hand tugging at his heart; a longing to shake himself free from the inhuman efficiency of this British Army life; its fetish of law and order expressed in terms of whitewash, pipeclay, and sanitation; in the dreary sameness of barrack blocks, in regulation clothes, carriage, and behaviour. Happily a fair percentage of men survived the steam-roller process that evolved, at its best, a terribly effective fighting machine. At its worst, it gave his lawless nature a tilt toward the works and ways of ancient India, the 'insanitary sanity' of an Akbar or a Ranjit Singh.

On the infantry square, rows and rows of little figures, emerging from a self-created dust-storm, ran and stopped, wheeled and turned, in response to barked-out words of command: more like marionettes than living men. Cavalry parade had, at least, the merit of massed horses; the gleam of their burnished coats, the rhythm of every movement; tossing of heads and manes, as the squadron went forward from trot to gallop. There was exhilaration in sheer pace, even if it only carried a man back again to the same old dusty square, to the 'Dismiss' that set him free, for an hour or so, to ride where he would, through the valley of orchards and cornfields; to cut loose from the dust and compulsion and organised sanity of cantonments.

Out towards Kohat he cantered, past the high ochreous walls of Peshawar, City of a Thousand and One Sins, where Mohmands, Yusufzais, and Afridis went armed, not for show; where life was a lawless, exciting affair of strong passions rather than cool brains: on through orchards in fullest flower, past cornfields already being reaped by tribal families; free unveiled Pathan women working beside their men, most of them able to shoulder a gun at need, or hold their fort against a raid. All wore scarlet trousers for protection from the sniper's bullet. For no Pathan brigand would dream of killing a woman — which could scarcely be said of those civilised murderers who assaulted harmless women of all ages in the quiet lanes or woods of England.

Peaceful enough they all looked in their rural occupation; but Sher Afzul knew that among the young bloods there were many who preferred the *jezail*[1] or knife to the sickle, who celebrated the 'Frontier Silly Season' by harassing the 'army of occupation' encamped on their sacred Kajauri plain.

[1] Pathan rifle.

And there was 'a certain liveliness' again among the Red Shirts, owing to these first elections and the Viceroy's coming visit to Peshawar. At Hoti Mardan and Charsadda, their picketing tactics had reduced voting to a farce: one vote recorded and more than one head broken to obtain it. No Hindus need apply. Personally, Sher Afzul deplored their methods, while he sympathised with their resolve to keep the locust plague of job-seeking Hindus out of the Prophet's Province — ninety-two per cent Moslem, and devil take the remainder.

Himself no politician, his eyes reverted to those magnetic hills, their subtle shades of ochre and indigo shadows, their crags and ridges more sharply defined as the sun rode higher; calling to him, tempting him to gallop on and on into the wild region of the Kohat Pass; thence into independent Afridi country, 'where a man was a man and a knife was a knife.'

And after that —?

Marry Selima Jān and breed strong sons and live in the lesser fort a few miles from his father; visit India when business or fancy took him: a free man in the Free Land of his own race.

There was nothing on earth to prevent him from obeying the sudden passionate urge in his blood; nothing except the invisible pull of all he had imbibed during his few years in England, and the stronger pull of this new fascination that might only be luring him to disaster. England had given him much that he valued; and his practical mind perceived the folly of flinging away all he had won at no small cost. They possessed one great quality, these British, capacity for working together: 'team-spirit' they called it. They knew how to be friends, as Asiatics did not, except through British influence. Loyalty they knew, to leader, family, or clan; but personal affection between man and man — such as he had known at Sandhurst and in the regiment — had no place in the typically Eastern mind. That spirit of friendship among the best British officers, their ingrained honesty and love of hard work, were strong ropes that bound him to life in their Army. And if he wanted to keep all that, he must submit to the iron hand of rules and regulations, while hanging on to the Pathan personality of Khan Sher Afzul Khan.

Instinctively he glanced at his wrist-watch. Punctuality was the hardest of all Western habits for the East to achieve. Since he was not out to play the deserter, he must hustle back to the routine of breakfast, 'stables,' 'water and feed,' 'durbar' — the perpetual daily round.

Turning the Arab's head towards Peshawar, he put him at his best pace along the dusty stretch of Frontier road; back past *betel* groves and orchards, past the city and the railway station to the edge of Sadar Bazaar. There on the roadside his attention was attracted by a lively group of urchins and an English white helmet in the midst: some tourist sketching the little mosque and collecting the usual crowd. Trotting nearer, he perceived that the artist was a woman seated on a camp-stool; and as the urchins crowded in too close, she turned to fling them a handful of small objects that sent them scrambling in the dust.

At sight of her face, his heart gave a jerk. It was Chrystal Adair. She had seen him. She smiled and waved her paint-brush. He dismounted and came forward, flicking at the boys, who scurried off, like rabbits, at sight of an officer.

'Poor little wretches!' she reproached him. 'Give them a chance to find their peppermint balls.'

'They'll come back. Little devils — pestering you.' And coming nearer, he asked, 'May I look?'

She laid the sketch-book open on her knee: and he stood close to her shoulder looking down at it, more acutely aware of her than of her work.

'It's a study in contrast,' she said. 'The mosque, so simple and serene, against that queer, distorted old tree. But I'm not satisfied. I must try again.'

He gazed at the picture, unable to criticise, fascinated by the sequence of strong, clear colours: vivid sky, indigo shadows, living green of a few young leaves on the lightning-smitten tree.

'I like it,' he said briefly. 'I didn't know you were so clever at this kind of thing.'

'I want to be more than clever,' she said, closing her book and snapping the elastic round it. 'I've done quite a lot since I came out. But I don't talk of it much. So few people are interested.'

'Do you often come here like this, without any escort? Does Mrs. Inglis allow it?'

'I'm afraid I take French leave. I bar escorts: a solemn *chaprassi* shadowing me; squatting at a respectful distance, coughing and spitting till I could murder the poor devil. I had to submit at first. But now I've struck!'

'You would *not* be afraid.' He reminded her of the little phrase that had so pleased him.

She looked amused.

'We often talk braver than we feel. But anyhow—"Safety first" isn't a *pukka* British motto either. The man who invented it ought to be shot!'

He laughed. 'I'd shoot him for you, on sight.'

'You'd never sight him. He'd be down some funk-hole, doing "Safety first"! I don't believe there's anything here to be afraid of; and I like the queer bazaar smells, the splashes of colour. Nobody bothers me, except those little demons. I bring lemon drops and bulls'-eyes to keep them off, just as I bring geranium oil for the flies. Mrs. Inglis says that these people are much more friendly than they were four or five years ago. And I *have* been told that a lone woman is safer out here than she would be in many English lanes, these dangerous days, because you Indians hold women in such respect——'

'*You Indians!*' he checked her sharply, his pride flaring up as if a match had been struck inside. '*I* am no Indian, Miss Adair. I am Afghāna Pathan.'

'Oh, I *am* sorry. How could I know—?'

Her swift penitence and startled tone shamed him into saying more quietly: 'Of course not. I didn't stop to think. But you see, Pathans don't belong to India. We are from Arabia—Ben-i-Israel; descendants of that lost Jewish tribe sent from Jerusalem by King Nebuchadnezzar, after he destroyed Solomon's temple. We Afghāna Pathans, and all

Afghans, are said to come direct from a so-named younger son of King Saul.'

'But then — are you all Jews?' she asked, only half enlightened.

'No — Moslems of Jewish origin. We have many of their names — Yakub, Ibrahim, Suleiman; many of their customs taken from the laws of Moses... Oh, damn those little brats!'

He was an English subaltern again, brandishing his whip at the half-naked small boys, who were pressing round hopeful of further largesse. His threatening gesture sent them scampering in earnest; and the interruption reminded him that he was supposed to be hurrying back for breakfast.

'Are you going along now?' he asked, reluctant to leave her.

'Yes, I ought to be.'

'May I see you home — though you do bar escorts?'

She laughed. 'I bar *chaprassis!* But the paces of my steed won't suit yours.' She indicated a bicycle, propped against a wall near the mosque. 'Half Peshawar on wheels now! Saving petrol because of these cuts in pay.'

'Well, it's not too hot to walk for a bit under those trees, and I can push your wheel. Badshah will follow me like a dog, if I give the word.'

So they set out together, as leisurely as if no breakfast hour existed for either; the man, hardly able to believe in his luck. Why had he never found her thus before?

The cold season was nearly over now, and the thought emboldened him to ask, 'Are you for Simla, when Social Peshawar fades out?'

'Simla? No, thank you! Eve Desmond calls it the "Snob's Paradise"! She and I are for Srinagar and Gulmarg later on.'

'Won't you be any more with Mrs. Inglis?'

'Oh, yes, afterwards. But I don't mark time in blazing Peshawar, while she does dutiful wife to a healthy man with a heart complex. I fearfully want to see — and paint — Kashmir. I suppose *you* mostly stay in the wilds, for *shikar*?'

And it cost him an effort to say: 'I go first to the Yusufzai, to see my own people. After that' — he hesitated palpably — 'perhaps Gulmarg. But my Afridi friend, mad for *shikar*, is after luring me into the higher hills.'

'I expect *shikar* will have it,' she said, in her cool, level tone. 'The one irresistible magnet for all you men — to hunt and kill some beautiful wild thing that wouldn't do you any harm.'

Words and tone spurred him to reckless retort.

'We don't always want to *kill* beautiful things. And there will be a strong magnet in Gulmarg.'

Whatever she made of his bold move, she merely smiled at the station landscape — leaving him as much as ever in the dark, more than ever enamoured of her unassailable charm.

'When d'you go?' she asked, nodding to a smart woman on horseback, who stared hard at her companion and ignored his salute.

'I've got first leave,' he said, looking after the offender with fury in his heart. 'But sometimes — when your women behave like that, knowing I am an officer — I feel more like taking French leave (as you said) and returning for good to a land where a man may kill his enemies but will never be ill-mannered to unoffending people.'

'If *you* feel angry, *I* feel ashamed,' she said; and the pain in her tone was balm to his hurt pride. 'Mrs. Pedley-Burne is one of the world's worst snobs. Hear her talk about the Viceroy's visit, and you'd suppose the King Emperor was coming in his glory to baptise the Frontier Province. A new frock ordered for every occasion, because she flatters herself that the Great Lady would notice if she wore the same one twice running.'

'I'd like a chance to *ruin* a few of her fine frocks,' he said, so viciously that she laughed it off.

'You sound terribly fierce!'

'I'm fiercer than I sound.'

'Giving place to the devil,' she gently reproved him. 'You should be too proud to bother about bad manners from a woman like that.'

'Pride doesn't always take such a sensible form,' he excused himself. 'And some things do wake the devil in a man. I wanted to floor that staring woman. I wanted to kill that speckled R.A.F. cub at the gymkhana.' His bold glance challenged her astonished gaze. 'Yes. That's the sort of half-tamed Pathan you're being so gracious to.'

Unexpectedly, she smiled at him with softened eyes.

'I don't like you any the less for being honest about it.'

'Then I shall continue to be honest — with you. The real Sher Afzul, so carefully chained up, sometimes gets out of hand. Sher means Tiger, you know.'

They were turning now into the flower-bordered Mall, a more frequented thoroughfare; cars and bicycles and mounted officers passing this way and that. Friends exchanged greetings. A pink-faced sub, on the chronic bicycle, waved a cane at them.

From Mess buildings, farther down the road, bugles rang out in a cheerful pattern of sound.

'Breakfast,' said Chrystal Adair. 'You'd better mount. The bugles are calling. *I'm* dead late, anyhow. My ill-used Aunt will think I've been kidnapped!'

'I'll probably cut breakfast,' he said, and she opened her eyes at him.

'All my fault.'

'All through my streak of luck.'

He was reckless now; and, as before, she left it at that.

'I must scoot,' she said, 'as best I can. I'm not a star performer.'

She mounted; he fixed her painting satchel behind her, steadied the wheel, and gave it a gentle push.

'Thank you,' she said. 'I daren't turn and wave farewell!'

'I don't want any farewell,' he answered in an odd voice.

He stood watching her as she went, a confused turmoil in his heart; and in his mind the distracting question, What could or would come out of it all?

Chapter VII

What place for dreams is here,
Save nightmare loss of what, in dreams, was dear?

GERALD GOULD

Claire Inglis, the ill-used aunt, had a good deal more on her mind that morning than the vagaries of her independent niece. She still wished that the girl would let Hari Singh go with her, especially towards the bazaar, but refrained from the futility of pressing the point. The modern young knew what they wanted — and went for it, regardless of superfluous elders. If Chrystal did go her own way, it was in pursuit of art, not of men. On the whole, she was a fine and lovable creature, even if she had proved a trifle disappointing in the way of daughterly companionship and the sharing of artistic tastes.

Water-colour was her medium; and she took little interest in the black-and-white work with which Claire had saved her soul alive during endless hot-weather days. Her frank, critical moments were not calculated to encourage one who had never set a high value on herself or her own activities. But, impelled by a genuine gift, she carried on as before, dreaming of a book that her etchings might one day embellish, and meeting Chrystal's few friendly advances more than halfway. For the girl had her father's withdrawn, critical make of mind, his flashes of insight and sympathy that suggested hidden depths of feeling. Independent in her comings and goings, she had soon attached herself to those delightful young Desmonds: a proof of discernment if it did take her a good deal away from home. They were also partly responsible for her friendship with Sher Afzul Khan; an admirable young man, if she could be trusted to keep him at a safe distance. Their ideas of safety might not, perhaps, coincide: one could only hope for the stronger pull of her own race and kind.

This morning, in any case, she was less concerned with Chrystal's possible affair than with the news that her own Madge, at Cheltenham College, had developed measles — a sharp attack. Of course the Head wrote hopefully: but — did they tell one everything? Always that lurking doubt sharpened anxiety; and she had lain awake half the night, while Jasper snored in an adjoining room. She knew more than he supposed about his rotten nights. For his door was always ajar; and often, while she lay awake with a book, she would listen enviously to the sound of his regular breathing. Soon after five, she had waked for good and made her own bedside *chota hazri*. Nights and mornings were still cool; and the quiet of these very early hours was balm to her heart.

Softly she closed the door into Jasper's room, slipped on her blue silk kimono, brushing back the mop of short brown hair falling over her forehead. Her full-lidded eyes, under their straight brows, showed blue, green, or grey, in different lights. Broad cheekbones, a decided nose, and generous mouth had inclined her always to seem older than her age.

'Thirty-seven in July — and I look forty in this pitiless morning light,' she told the not uncomely woman who confronted her; a big woman, large-boned, large-natured, built for motherhood and friendship, not for the snaring of men. As companions, she preferred them to women; but, knowing herself emotionally unsatisfied, she discouraged the inevitable attaché in a society where almost every woman under fifty had some dangling boy in tow. Perhaps it was as well that she refrained, since Jasper did enough in that line for two. The flame of the moment was Pamela Pedley-Burne. But that either of them took the other seriously she was unwilling to believe.

With a sigh, that was not for Jasper's defection, she turned away and settled herself in the canvas chair at her open doorway that looked through the side verandah, out across the dusty back compound with its grey-green clumps of oleander, its mulberry tree a paradise for squirrels and chittering sparrows and fawn-coloured, sentimental doves; its blindfold bullock ambling round and round the Persian well that watered the thirsty garden. Now and then, the joyous shriek of a blue jay, the flash of small parrots, like winged emeralds. For nearly two hours she could lie there undisturbed, could imbibe large drafts of the peace and leisure that gave India its peculiar charm. Time, out here, did seem to lose some of its overwhelming importance; and the need for very early rising gave an illusion of spaciousness to the coming day; a chance to steady one's nerves against possible 'slings and arrows,' trivial or otherwise.

This morning it gave her a quiet hour for writing to Gerald, her first-born, at Charterhouse: for re-reading hastily scanned mail letters, that were apt to sharpen the persistent ache at her heart. She was not yet inured — would she ever be? — to a house empty of a child's laughter and footsteps and ceaseless demands; to the disjointed life of English mothers in India. Neither here nor there any settled sense of home. In England, where her heart was at peace, she herself was perforce a pilgrim; the golden days slipping too fast through her fingers. Here, in the semblance of home, heart and mind were for ever astray; her self-centred husband seeming only to need her for social purposes, or to take tiresome duties off his hands. And in spite of India's half-repellent fascination, its merry-go-round of social life was little to her taste: the incessant entertaining, the trivial bustle over trivial things that devoured one's days; and, underlying all, the hidden strain of a mistaken marriage, aggravated by those minor failings that do more to alienate an ill-matched pair than graver faults of character.

Too soon — yet too late — she had discovered the insincerity of Jasper's easy, surface charm, the deeper taint of his egoism. Blandly self-engrossed, he lived in a world that was instinctively planned for his own personal comfort, looking askance at whatever he did not wish to see, lest the winds of reality visit his mind too roughly; a kind of oblique vision that detracted from his very ability. For clever he was, within limits; fond of her, no doubt — also within limits. But whatever his conception of her might be, he knew nothing of the real woman who had lived with him for sixteen years; had borne him four children and made herself indispensable to his self-regarding way of life. It was she rather than he who endured the burden of his obscure form of heart trouble, which he preferred to leave conveniently vague. He would have 'no damned doctors messing about' with his inside. The 'groggy heart' tag served him too well as a plausible excuse for evading the undesired. He would go till he dropped in harness, was the heroic implication. And all the while India's climate was undermining her strength to an extent he would never realise till she — not he — dropped in harness, the more likely event of the two.

There were times when she almost wished that she could see him as other women presumably did; as she herself must have done in those distant days before her own mental honesty had forced her to recognise that she could not trust — in word or act — the man she had married. The pain of it had severed some vital link between them. Slowly the inner rift had widened, till it now seemed as if her real self stood apart from him, a spectator rather than a sharer; as if even his troubles were not her own. They approached every subject from a different angle. Their sensations never sprang from the same root. Like two parallel lines, moving side by side, they had never met, nor ever would.

In such moods of too clear-seeing she could almost wish that she had not been born so uncomfortably honest; that she could blind herself to the real Jasper, take him at his face value. But the real Claire could not, if she would, purchase comfort at the cost of truth.

And now here was still another hot weather closing in upon her, dreaded the more for the heavenly respite of a summer at Home. Most years she 'stuck it out' till he could get away for his month of leave, because the heat upset his digestion and his heart. Not that he pressed the point. He simply took her staying for granted, either not heeding or not perceiving the strain that Indian conditions were putting on her health and on her heart, in quite another sense than that which was his own monopoly.

India exacts a higher price for motherhood than any land on earth, though she had been luckier, on the whole, than many others. Out of four children she had lost but one; and Norman, her baby, she had managed to keep with her till Jasper's furlough was due. One radiant year she had spent with them all; and when it came to the final wrench — no child to return with her — she had found herself shrinking from the prospect of life alone with Jasper; hence the happy thought of bringing Chrystal out for a year or two. If the result had not been all her fancy painted it, the child's presence had saved her from loneliness unspeakable. And what hope of getting away to the hills? One feared the hot weather more and more each year ——

Her fountain pen, idly laid down, was making a blot on her kimono, while her thoughts played truant. Gerald's letter was not half written, and the sun was fast drinking up the shadows: flickering through the mulberry boughs, making lovely patterns on the dust. From the servants' quarter came shrill voices of women: and nearer by she heard Chrystal's door into the front verandah quietly opened and closed. Lucky child! She was off and away somewhere with her sketch-book. Claire had pictured outings together; but their objectives were different, and Chrystal mainly preferred to go alone. Heaven send she would not be late for breakfast; a privilege reserved for Jasper, by Jasper.

'Breakfast was made for man, not man for breakfast,' was his pet aphorism when flagrant lapses moved her to protest. Yet woman and breakfast alike must be ready whenever he chose to appear; eggs done to a turn, toast or *chupattis* piping hot. Mercifully Indian servants were not addicted to 'giving notice'; though the privileged Nussar Ali — head *kit* and old friend — did, at times, 'make *bobbery*'[1] over the Burra Sahib's unreasonable demands.

The mere thought of Jasper and breakfast recalled to mind her chief housewifely concern of the moment, a select dinner of twelve, not all of her selecting. There were times when she wearied of this constant call to feed in batches a perpetual stream of men and women, likable or unlikable; carefully parking them according to precedence, that no feelings might be injured. In India it was people, people all the way, mainly in their social aspect; the cards constantly shuffled, the game and the rules unvaried. The French aphorism, *Plus ça change, plus c'est la même chose*, might have been written for Anglo-India.

About the vast and various country, that flowed round its isolated cantonments like an uncharted ocean, most of its men and women — except the intelligent few — seemed content to remain abysmally ignorant. Indians, as a whole, they regarded at best with blank indifference; at worst with bored contempt; and how could a friendlier understanding hope to flourish on such stony ground? Jasper's fine Service had a bad name, on the whole, for complacent assumption of superiority, denounced by Dixon Verney as 'the sin against the Holy Ghost.' In the Army, especially the Indian Army, a better spirit prevailed; and in other Services there were men like Lynch and Dixon, who could reel off the blackest cases of murder, bride-stealing, and confession by torture, yet remained open-eyed to all the better elements of Indian character.

Dixon was one of her own 'select' this evening. Jasper vaguely disliked him, because he was no respecter of persons. Claire herself liked him greatly, for several other reasons. She liked his masculine mind, his clean-cut forehead, and jutting nose. Especially she liked the dry humour that often seemed to serve as a cloak for deep feeling. Her secret self knew by now that she could do more than like him, if she dared indulge in the luxury of letting go. But she did not dare. Life had too painfully taught her how devastating are the

[1] Trouble.

major passions, good or bad. Not for any man living would she lower her flag. Yet she was essentially a man's woman; not as coquette, but as companion. She frankly preferred talking to men, especially to Dixon Verney. One could count on him to give the dinner-table chatter a lift out of its rutted grooves—golf and gossip, 'cuts' in pay, Lord Lothian's franchise 'touring company,' and the Viceroy's visit to install Sir Vincent Leigh.

Tonight the talk would need all the lifting he could compass, Pamela Pedley-Burne being guest in chief, which meant that Jasper had been fussing inordinately over the menu. For Pamela, who gave perfect little dinners, was apt to pick holes in other people's; also he was eager to advertise the merits of an English cooking-range, lately installed, to Claire's dismay, in her windowless, mud-walled kitchen. Led astray by a gourmet bachelor, he had imported the wretched thing, at great expense, from Bombay, that his food might be better and more cleanly cooked than in the orthodox Indian mud shelf with holes in it. Her own private doubts on that score had, so far, been more than justified.

To begin with, on its arrival, her first-rate khansamah had promptly taken French leave, with twelve rupees 'advance' in his wallet: and to Claire his skill had been worth more than a dozen English ranges. His successor, a bustling person, not to be outfaced by any devil-machine, had boldly tackled it — with dire results. Breakfast had been a burnt offering; luncheon a hollow mockery, flavoured with kerosene. Jasper, blaming her for imperfect explanations, had not offered to do the explaining himself; but had mercifully dined at the Borderers' Mess. Nussar Ali had promised to unearth a more accomplished chef: and had been as good as his word. Ramzān's impressive bookful of chits might have been borrowed or stolen, for all one could tell; but at least he had taken an intelligent interest in the monster and listened with respect to her explanations. Whether he was actually cooking in it, or using it as a glory-hole, she had not yet ventured to ask. It was simpler to keep Jasper happy over the supposed success of his innovation. And this morning it basely chose her peaceful hour to thrust itself again on her attention.

For here came the good Nussar Ali, with a distressed countenance, regretting to report that Ramzān, moved by curiosity, had taken the devil-machine to pieces, hoping to discover how it worked. And, behold, the kitchen was strewn with fragments of iron that no persuasion could bring together again. Perhaps the Memsahib, knowing its ways, could give advice on the matter?

Outwardly unmoved, she replied that she would come in half an hour to examine the ruins. A kitchen range treated like a jigsaw puzzle could only be reasoned with by the Garrison Engineer; unless —? There sprang an inspiration: Why not leave the puzzle in pieces till her party was safely over? Better still, persuade Captain Earnley to remove the corpse, and offer a nominal sum for it as scrap iron. She now believed that Ramzān had never once used the oven; and had probably dismembered it, in the hope that it could not be brought to life again. If so, she sympathised from her heart.

Very soon she was hurrying across the sunlit compound to the row of mud huts that housed a small colony of servants and their families. There, on the threshold of his dingy cook-house, stood Ramzān, a small cock-eyed person with an ill-kept beard, the picture of puzzled innocence. It was '*burra taklif*' [1] for the Memsahib, he meekly apologised, indicating the corpse, that looked like a victim of bomb practice. Everything was in bits that could be in bits; and she privately marvelled how on earth he had managed to detach the dampers. Her suspicion of deliberate slaughter was confirmed by his dismayed surprise at mention of the Garrison Engineer, who could charm all devil-machines into working order again.

'But for tonight,' she suggested, watching the effect of her words, 'perhaps you could manage with the old friend and the old *degchis*?' [2]

Could he manage —? His face was a study.

'For the black men, Memsahib,' he ventured, his cock-eye

[1] Great trouble. [2] Cooking-pots.

bright as a bird's, 'the *desi*[1] oven and *degchis* make easier work; better work, too, perhaps?'

'That is my own opinion, Khansamah-*ji*. For each country its own ways of life and work are best.'

He acknowledged her pearl of wisdom with a profound salaam; and she departed in a glow of gratitude to the shrewdly sensible creature; fortified to hold her own against half a dozen Jaspers; strengthened in her resolve that all the King's horses and all the King's men should *not* put Humpty-Dumpty together again.

And so to breakfast.

[1] Country.

Chapter VIII

God made him, therefore let him pass for a man.
SHAKESPEARE

By the unwritten law of life, Jasper must needs be abnormally punctual because she was a trifle late, and Chrystal a good deal later. She found him settled at the table, a martyr confessed; his tea poured out, his plate piled with devilled kidneys, his *Pioneer* propped against the milk jug.

At her entrance, he merely twitched an eyebrow.

'Twenty to ten,' he remarked. 'Your watch out of gear?'

'Probably. It's apt to be.' Her normal impulse of penitence was chilled by his look and tone. 'But it meanly doesn't absolve me. I'm *ten* to ten. I was delayed. Ramzān wanted to see me — about tonight's menu.'

Hating the petty deception, she had promptly decided that this was not the acceptable moment for reporting the murder of his kitchen range. While she helped herself to scrambled eggs, he spoke again.

'Have you rubbed it in that the melons must be thoroughly iced? Lukewarm melon, in this weather, is the limit.'

'I'm not in the habit of treating my guests to lukewarm melon,' she answered in a sheathed voice; and he shamed her with his most disarming smile.

'No insult intended! Being a new man, I thought he might need a bit of coaching. He seems a pretty fair specimen. Hope the dinner will be worthy of the company.'

'I hope they'll be worthy of *my* dinner,' she retorted, only half mollified; but he had reverted to the *Pioneer*.

After a longish interval of munching and reading, he remarked impersonally: 'The way these Congress fellows are howling over H.E.'s emergency Ordinances, one might fancy India was a spring meadow full of newborn lambs, instead of a hotbed for young firebrands out to cripple British trade. Wholesome change for Gandhi and Company, being jailed *jut-put.*[1] This time we've *got* a Viceroy. I must have a talk with him — *if* Leigh gives me a look-in.'

His trick of implied disparagement set her teeth on edge. 'I can't see Sir Vincent,' she said, 'standing in anyone's light — except his own.'

''Course not. *You* see him as the *pukka* Philip Sydney, portrayed by Mrs. Lynch and the fair Thea. *She* knows the value of fitting her husband out with a home-made halo.'

And Claire could only say, without looking up, 'I'm sure you wouldn't feel comfortable in a halo.'

'Wouldn't I? Who knows? I've never been given the chance to try.'

The suggestion of unappreciated merit left her speechless; too honest to hand him an empty sugar plum, too sensitive to tell him outright that he lived in a halo not of her devising. Hampered by her lack of feminine instinct in dealing with men, she left his reproach in mid-air and finished her scrambled eggs.

Presently he handed her his cup, and asked in a suave tone, 'Where's your Chrys? On the no-breakfast tack?'

'Chrystal.' Claire amended the forbidden abbreviation. 'I heard her go out very early. She has a rather special picture on hand.'

'And doesn't trouble to look at her watch. Don't keep anything hot for the casual young woman. Let her have it cold.'

This time she treated him to a very straight look. 'Do *you* expect to have it cold when you happen to be late?'

He stared back at her, amazed.

'I fail to see the connection. You forget that I'm master in this house. It's run for my convenience. The girl's our guest; and she treats the place like a hotel.'

'She does *not!*' Claire flashed out the more sharply because

[1] At once.

it was not altogether a libel. 'When one's painting, one can't stop at any given moment, and perhaps spoil a picture.'

'What does she *do* with her precious pictures?' he inquired, unimpressed. 'Hoping to sell them?'

'I really don't know. She might, later on. Her work's very clever, and it means a lot to her.'

'Oh, quite. But what about *you*, and the sisterly daughter you reckoned on? A pity you brought her out, in my opinion.'

Claire, recalling the main reason, carefully pursed her lips. 'I don't agree with you. I'm very fond of Chrystal.'

'She knows it; and she takes advantage.'

'She does nothing of the kind —— Hush. Here she is!'

She came in hurriedly, glancing from one to the other, as if uncertain of her reception. Jasper ostentatiously folded up his paper and took a banana, indicating the end of his meal.

Chrystal nodded 'Good morning' towards him; but her apology was for Claire.

'Fearfully sorry, darling. My little mosque was giving trouble, and I clean forgot the time. But afterwards, I *did* scoot.'

Damp ringlets round her forehead affirmed the statement, which Jasper probably did not believe.

'Hungry?' he asked with a show of concern. 'I've left some nice cold remnants for you.'

'Not required, thanks. Hard luck!' Her glance challenged his.

'Chrystal — *behave!*' Claire called her to order; and she responded with a small grimace.

'Well, he *did* hope he'd got a nice bit of punishment up his sleeve. Mayn't I enjoy my little triumph?'

'More than you deserve,' he remarked to the back view of her slender shoulders, as she stood by the sideboard, helping herself to a generous curve of melon and a pile of Kabul grapes. Jasper sat watching her with a gleam in his eye that Claire knew only too well. In her absence he might criticise her; but he was pervious as any male of them all to her cool young aloofness and charm.

Leaving his banana half eaten, he rose and stood beside her, looking a good deal less than his forty years.

'Is *this* the way you triumph over your legitimate uncle?' he asked, in his silkiest voice. 'Doesn't it strike you that you're an extremely casual creature?'

'Am I? It isn't calculated.' She edged away from him. 'Claire treats me like a sister, and I never think of you as an uncle.'

'That's very gratifying. *My* little triumph!'

Almost in speaking he caught her round the waist and kissed her twice on her swiftly averted cheek.

With a small gasp, she pushed him from her. Claire, tingling at the sheer bad taste of it, dared not speak or stir.

'You don't like it, eh?' he chuckled, as if she were a petulant child. 'Any uncle to any niece — why not? That's your forfeit for being unpunctual. So *kubberdar!*[1] And mind you look your best this evening.'

She turned from him, ignoring his playful threat, and sat down at the table intent on her fruit.

Jasper winked at Claire like a peccant schoolboy.

'See you at the General's cocktail crowd, my dear,' he said; and strolled out, leaving her uncertain how to soothe her ruffled niece without apologising for her own husband. Any uncle, after all, might kiss any niece without offence. It was the manner of it that the child would resent, as she palpably did.

Before Claire could speak, she looked up from her plate of fruit, a hard light in her clear eyes.

'He'd better not take that line of being funny with me, Claire. Can you tell him so?'

'I can *advise*,' Claire cautiously amended the imperative verb.

'In very plain language, please. Because — if he does it again, he'll get a smart slap in the face. Then, I suppose, you'd have to bundle me Home. And I'd rather not, just as India's getting under my skin. But I can't stand being mauled; and he doesn't really like me. Why does he do it?'

[1] Take care.

They were so disconcertingly direct, these young things; and Claire herself was just old enough to be hampered by outmoded reserves, constrained by an instinctive loyalty to the man who had so little loyalty in him. Treating it lightly seemed the best line to take.

'Kissing doesn't always go by liking, or loving,' she said, an amused smile in her eyes. 'He's a man, and you're an attractive — rather provocative girl.'

Chrystal frowned at her empty plate. 'Yes, that's the sort he is,' she said as if to herself. Then she looked up with an air of decision. 'He *makes* me provocative. But do, please, give him a spot of plain English on my behalf. I suppose wives can?'

Claire smiled outright. 'It depends a good deal... on the husbands!'

Chrystal did not answer at once; and when she spoke, it was in a changed tone.

'Some of us *do* let ourselves down damnably over the marriage business, don't we?'

The personal allusion, tactfully veiled, pricked Claire's heart; but she replied in the same vein.

'Well, most of us have to choose young; and it seems the right choice, at the time. But life and character don't stand still.'

Chrystal was pensively spreading her toast with honey. 'Seems a wicked waste — all that fine flare-up, all those vows, beyond mortal power to keep; and then — it mayn't be a winner. Perhaps I oughtn't to be saying this to you. But you do like me to say what I think.'

'Yes. It's the only thing worth saying.'

'And with you, I can. You're such an understanding person.'

Compliments from Chrystal were so few and genuine that Claire's heart warmed to her sister's child.

'One ought to be fairly so, at my age,' was her modest disclaimer.

'One ought. But it's not age ——'

'No, it's not,' Claire agreed in a careful voice; 'understanding, like wisdom, has to be bought with a price.'

'You mean — being hurt?'

'Yes, wise child; being hurt by life, and reaching a certain distance beyond the hurt.'

The girl listened with her vivid, thinking look.

'I see,' she said. 'That makes being hurt rather important, in an uncomfortable way, for one's character. Also —' a sudden thought flashed — 'it accounts for Eve. Chock full of understanding — and not twenty-three. I believe she had a hell of a time over their first baby.'

Claire nodded. 'I've heard something of that from Grace. I'm glad you're friends with those two. They're quite outside the rut.'

'Oh, quite. So clever — and such fun. I must have a lot of camp with them next cold weather. It struck me, out there, that Lance knows tons more about India and the people than a good many older men. Do I libel — the older ones?'

They frankly smiled at each other, thinking of the same man; and Claire said cautiously: 'One can't damn them in the lump. There are so many fine exceptions. But the older men *are* more deeply rutted in the habit of not knowing Indians or wishing to know them, even when the Indians are more than willing to come halfway.'

'It's so *stupid*,' cried the girl with young impatience. 'Can't they *see* it puts our side all in the wrong? And I suppose the young men who do start without prejudice haven't a dog's chance till they toe the line? Lance won't. I know that much. He and Jasper don't seem to hit it off too well.'

'No — they don't. Lance is a difficult junior. His traditions are not I.C.S. He's had political experience, and he has his uncle's backing.'

'*And* he's after the friendly spirit all the time. He says there's more need of it now than there's ever been. And half our people out here don't seem to care a damn. — Shall we have to fight them in order to be friends?'

Claire smiled at the shrewd question. 'I hope not. India's the most incalculable country. And politics out here are curiously unreal. Not growth of the soil.' She pulled out her cigarette-case — 'What a conversation for the breakfast table!'

'Why not?' Wasn't there a Professor at the Breakfast Table in the year One? Why *should* it be doomed to daily papers and plans? I like airing my notions, when they crop up at any old time of day.'

'So do I,' Claire agreed, striking a match. This was one of the moments when she knew she had done well to purloin Esther's child. And suddenly she added: 'Have you talked Indian politics much with Sher Afzul Khan?'

'Not extensively. He says things in passing. And I take notice.' She was spreading her last strip of toast, and her pause had a deliberate air, as if more were coming.

Claire wisely held her peace: and it came.

'By the way, darling,' she looked sideways like a bird. 'The mosque wasn't the one and only cause of my lapse from grace. It was partly Sher Afzul, dropping out of the blue and walking a little way back with me, till I saw how late it was — and scooted. I only didn't mention it, because Jasper might have hinted at an assignation and I'd have snapped at him. Rough on you. — Oh, damn it all!' She sharply slapped the table. 'I clean forgot. We ran into the P.-B. woman. *She* won't keep it dark; and if Jasper tackles me about it, sparks will fly. She looked clean through Sher Afzul and out the other side. He felt like murder, and I didn't blame him. I suppose she fancied she was upholding British dignity, giving him "one" for presuming to escort a British damsel. I wish to glory someone could give it her hot and strong. Of course *you* can't.'

She left it at that; and Claire left it also.

'Thea could — and would, if she got the chance. But, at Government House, Pamela minds her *p*'s and *q*'s.'

'Trust *her*. That's what I hate about India.'

'I hate it, too. But it's a natural human weakness, only more noticeable in our official-minded world. Don't blame India, darling, for what we make of our life out here. It's often only India's large compensations that keep some of us going at all.'

'Yes — I understand that,' the girl said in a changed tone. 'I thought I didn't like it at first. But now I'm terribly interested — the wrong way round, of course, from the station point of view.'

Again Claire wondered what that might bode. Again, rightly or wrongly, she held her peace. A hovering figure in the verandah recalled her to Ramzān and the day's employ.

'Nearly eleven,' she said briskly. 'The clock won't stand still while we discuss matters of national importance!' And she added on impulse: 'I'm glad you told me about Afzul and the lateness. If Jasper makes Pam-inspired remarks about it, I'll do buffer state between you.'

At that Chrystal came over and kissed her with unusual warmth.

'You're beyond words,' she said softly, 'the way you put up with things and people — undeserving people. *I* won't force you to bundle me Home... if I can help it.'

Claire Inglis, moved by that surprising tribute, stood up and took the girl in her arms, kissing her, holding her close. It was as if some mute pact had been sealed between them; and Claire knew she had done well to withhold the trite word of warning.

After lunch and a short rest, they bicycled to the Club, where Chrystal was bound for a foursome at tennis, Claire for a book *shikar*; a 'smash-and-grab raid,' they called it, on the latest consignment from Home. To the library all keen readers flocked on such days, like birds to newly turned earth. Dixon was apt to be among the earliest raiders. But this afternoon there was no sign of him; and the faint prick of disappointment warned Claire that even a carefully guarded heart is a living organism, not to be sterilised by a diet of husks. No sign, either, of the special book she had come for, the first on her list: *India in Revolt.* Perhaps Grace had spotted it. But on enquiry she was told it had just been taken out by Mr. Verney. Mean of him, knowing it was her suggestion. She would tell him so tonight. She contented herself with a good novel, a new biography, and tea in the verandah, well away from a couple who patently regarded her as very much *de trop*. Then she carried off her trophies, resolved to cut the 'sherryfication' at the General's and enjoy the luxury of losing herself in a book.

Jasper — attached to one or other of his devotees — would not be worried by her defection; and Dixon was unlikely to be there.

Swerving through her own gateposts, she was confronted by the car, obviously awaiting Jasper, rather late. If he had not yet gone, she would lie low in her own back verandah till the coast was clear. But, at the sound of voices in the drawing-room, she moved cautiously nearer.

Outside one of the curtained open doorways she paused. Pamela, of course; no mistaking the soft, lazy drawl that men found so alluring. Claire stood still. Both voices were pitched low; a sort of human kuroo-koo-ing — with apologies to the doves. And she was glad of it. Eavesdropping was a despicable game, and she had not even jealousy for an excuse.

On the point of turning away, she was arrested by a low sound of protest from Pamela.

'Jasper — you sinner!' And Jasper's voice, urgent, as she never heard it now: 'Darling Dot, who *wouldn't* be a sinner, tempted by you?'

'Tempted?' Her low laugh acknowledged the facile compliment.

'Yes, in every way that a woman like you *can* tempt a decent-minded man. *You're* no saint, my sweet; nor am I. You can't deny me now.'

In the silence that followed, Claire held her breath; seeing it all; hearing unmistakable sounds of murmured endearments, of kisses given and returned.

Anger flamed in her; not the heart's anger of jealousy, but a cold anger against him for calmly making love to the creature in her room. And he called himself a decent-minded man. The actuality did not pain her, as the same sort of discovery had once done long ago. He had killed all that.

Should she startle them? Why not? They deserved it.

With a dull thud, she dropped her books and her bag; picked them up, and turned to find herself confronted by the barefaced couple, looking as cool as if they had merely been talking scandal.

'Well, of *all* the women!' Jasper's voice was amused and possessive. 'Hurling your books around, and no attendant swain to pick them up! You were supposed to be at the General's.'

'So were *you*,' she reminded him with a straight glance. And he took it smiling.

'I'm on my way there, as you perceive. Pam just looked in to suggest going along with us, P.-B. not being keen.'

She knew it for a lie — a deft, impromptu lie — judging from the faint stir of Pamela's raspberry-red lips. She herself said nothing, but even he could not mistake the flash of scorn in her eyes.

'You coming along, too?' he asked, with his jaunty air of a caught-out schoolboy. 'Time we were off. Can you don the wedding garment in two shakes?'

'No. I'm not coming.'

'But I thought —?'

'Well, I've changed my mind. So I needn't keep you waiting. I give you leave to escort Pam.'

The sarcasm would slide off him like water off a duck's wing; and she could hardly forbear a smile at his patent relief.

'There you are, Pam. Straight from the horse's mouth!' The less obtuse Pam was nibbling her lips. 'You're a wise woman, Claire,' he said; 'you'll come fresher to dinner for not blunting your appetite with Martinis and deadly delectable morsels.'

In speaking, he signalled to the chauffeur, and they went down the steps together, not looking at each other.

She remained where they left her, staring after the car; chiefly aware of a curiously impersonal disgust, as if his trivial sinning concerned her real self not at all. She seemed to stand apart, looking on at another woman's perplexity. What did wives do, in such a case, she wondered. If they loved — of course they suffered. Her own position was less tragic, more ironical. She simply did not care. What then? Did one, on principle, make a scene about it? Hateful thought. The thing was not worth the indignity of recriminations. She could not strip herself emotionally or physically in the prevailing fashion. Remained the dreary alternative — to ignore it, to go on indefinitely enduring the suffocation of marital intimacy unsanctified by love. It was no new story; but not till now had she cynically admitted the fact of a loss that she could not deplore. This was certainly not the first time he had made love to his woman-of-the-moment. Nor would it be the last. He had given her proof conclusive: that was all. He would not be likely to leave her for any of them. He valued his comfort too much; and she looked after him too well. Seduced by his charm, she had committed the folly of marrying him: and that was that. One was tied and bound by the chain of one's follies; the old Biblical word being out of fashion.

And suddenly she realised that she was standing there like a statue staring absently at the figure of a man, who came quickly forward waving a book at her; realised, with a tingling shock, that it was Dixon Verney.

'Cut me dead!' was his greeting, as he took the steps at a bound.

'I — I really didn't see you,' she stammered, half laughing. With this man one could speak the truth.

'That was obvious. Gone clean away into one of your brown studies?'

'Clean away. But why "brown," I wonder? What's the book? You've stolen my *India in Revolt*.'

'Stolen, indeed! I grabbed it for you, in case Mrs. Lynch might spot it. Brought it round, thinking you'd be at the General's, to put it on your table for a surprise, instead of handing it out at the dinner party. Bet you didn't think that of me, Claire?'

'How should I?'

The thoughtful kindness, the planned surprise, robbed her of words. She had not even the grace to thank him.

'I wanted it so,' was all she said: and he laughed.

'Well, now you've got it. Seeing the car, I stood by, thinking you'd be in it. And it was the wrong lady. Then I saw you; and I thought, "What luck!" And you stared clean through me.'

'Very ungrateful!' She was herself again, and he was here: that sufficed. 'I suddenly decided that I couldn't endure cocktails and scandal. So I let them go without me.'

'Must have been a brain wave. Where's your little Gem?'

'Playing tennis.'

'Good. Now we can have a spot of talk. Not much chance tonight.'

'No. Do come in. We'll explore the book together. I'll tell, *darwāza bund*.' [1]

And there, where Jasper had kissed his Pamela, they sat down to enjoy the stimulant of minds that could as happily march in unison as agree to differ. She was not even disturbed by the irony of the unplanned event. What, after all, did Jasper and his stolen kisses matter to the real Claire, whom he had probably never coveted, and certainly never possessed.

[1] The door is shut.

Chapter IX

The idealist is actually a power in the physical world; far more so than the proverb-making, platitude-mongers believe.

E. SIDGWICK

WHILE Claire Inglis enjoyed her peaceful hour, while more than half the station sipped and scrunched at the General's — discussing and rediscussing the threadbare topic of the Viceroy's visit — the man whom it chiefly concerned sat alone in his book-filled study, a pipe between his teeth, an open volume on his knee. Like many of his kind, he had proved from experience that the really busy man can always find time to think. At fifty-one he looked his age. The dark hair framing his brow was already noticeably powdered with grey, but the eyes had a lurking gleam in them that lit up his serious face when he talked and smiled.

The book was a new one, after his own heart: *An Idealist View of Life*, by Professor Radhakrishnan, one of the finest living exponents of the higher Hinduism. They had met in England. Leigh had heard him lecture, had keenly looked forward to receiving from him a promised copy of his latest work.

For nearly an hour he had been browsing on it: an hour of escape from immediate duties into the larger atmosphere of mental and spiritual issues of man's deep need to 'know the creative mystery and serve it to the best of his power.' But he was not reading now. The masterly prelude, 'Modern Challenge to Religion,' had set him turning the pages to catch the trend of later chapters. Here and there an arresting sentence caught his eye.

> *To know the truth we have to deepen ourselves, not merely widen the surface. Silence and quiet are necessary to the profound alteration of our being.*

That suggested the vanished Sinclair, who positively must be unearthed and restored to the world that had need of him. Lynch, for all his talk of Himalayan haystacks, was a miracle-worker in his own line. Having agreed to go, he would leave no 'haystack' unturned. In half an hour he would be round for a final talk. After that — weeks of suspense, unless any word came from Roy's plucky wife at Home.

He was turning the pages again, reading at random, this:

> *To keep one's balance in the face of a hostile, uncomprehending world, is no light affair. It is possible only if we get back constantly to the depths.*

The tale of Vincent Leigh in a nutshell: keeping his balance, more or less, against the pull of unconquerable shyness inherited from his mother; saved from himself by the courageous girl who had flatly refused to let him break her heart because a Zakka Khel bullet had broken his leg. To her, and her incomparable father, he owed, in his modest opinion, the better part of all that he had since achieved. And, in that chance phrase, he seemed almost to hear the voice of the Master, commending his years of ceaseless effort in negative terms that pleased his English love of understatement.

'No light affair': even he could admit as much. That it had often been a desperate affair, none but he had known, or would ever know.

Looking back across thirty years of it, he could recall, as if it were yesterday, how reluctantly he had faced the self-imposed ordeal of Army life, in the forlorn hope that enforced comradeship with men might demolish the barrier between himself and them.

In thought he followed that reluctant boy to India, to the Border, through painful weeks and months of trying to 'keep his balance in a hostile, uncomprehending world.' How hostile, how uncomprehending they had seemed to his cultured mind and oversensitive spirit, not one among those cheerful, athletic subalterns and captains could have believed.

Then, clear as dawn, the coming of Thea Desmond — a radiant nineteen; his surrender to the girl who had lit a flame in his heart, and banished the aching sense of severance from his kind. Through every ill-hap that could beset a man who was his own worst enemy, he had remained her unfailing lover; and the loss of his left leg from the knee — that transferred him to the Political Service — had proved the turning-point of his career. In that Service, his deep reading, his knowledge of the language and the people had conspired with Thea's belief in him to lift him, rung by rung, up to this unimagined height of responsibility and honour.

His crowning honour, it was true, had found him a tired man, dreaming of spring and summer in England, of leisure to complete his comprehensive book on *The Border and Its People*. Now it must continue to serve as solace during the intervals of lending a hand in the boldest experiment ever tried, even by a race given to achieving the impossible.

Happily he had acquired merit in high quarters on account of his firm handling of Red Shirt activities last autumn; his lightning arrest and deportation of Abdul Ghaffur Khan. For this new Viceroy had a working knowledge of India's response to the firm hand.

Hence his outcrop of Ordinances; the only effective retort to renewed threats of civil disobedience and picketing, far from peaceful: a sorry outcome of the second Round Table conferences: where Congress leaders, including Gandhi, had failed signally; had retired, in a fit of sulks, to scare the Indian Government with a revival of wrecking tactics that had hitherto served them well. But they soon found that the new Viceroy was 'another story.' Gandhi, landing in Bombay with his halo badly tarnished, had been whisked back into jail, while ordinance followed ordinance, till India seemed almost under martial law, and it began to look as if open conflict were inevitable. But in spite of sporadic resistance, the people, as a whole, were sick of Congress activities, disinclined for a serious clash with Government. Certain rosy-spectacled officials could even persuade themselves that the danger was over, that the strong hand could safely loosen its hold. Leigh expected some straight talk on the subject from Lynch, who had no use for pink spectacles in any walk of life. There was his voice in the verandah, his solid figure blocking the doorway.

'Hope I've not kept you waiting, Sir Vincent. I was delayed myself.' He pulled forward a chair and sat down. 'Our friends the Red Shirts are kicking up an unholy dust over these elections. Not a dog's chance for the Hindu voter. I don't blame them. I'd be doing the same in their shoes. But, officially, we've got to "learn" 'em the rules of the game. We can't afford to wink the other eye in *this* Province — eh?'

Sir Vincent did not answer at once. His own inner knowledge of the whole affair went deeper than the Policeman's; but he was not of those who speak peace where there is no peace, or he would never have won the respect and friendship of John Lynch.

'I'm no fire-eater, as you know,' he said. 'But emergency measures will not be withdrawn while I'm in charge up here.'

'Luck for us, then, that your arm is to be strengthened, and your stay prolonged.'

Leigh's tired face lit up at the frank tribute from one who seldom spoke so straight from his heart.

'I'd have welcomed a year at Home first,' he said. 'But I'd rather not be handing over just now, when the Border will be in much the same state as a crab changing its shell.'

'All India'll be pretty well in that state, if the new Act goes through,' muttered Lynch, pulling out his pipe. 'Politics have become the major curse of this country.'

Again Sir Vincent was silent, wondering how far Lynch would go along with his own wider view of England's changing relation to India.

'Politics ——? Yes,' he said at last. 'What we need is first principles and a drastic change of attitude. India can only be ruled by her lovers, by personal example, such as Henry Lawrence gave in his day. It takes nothing less to win and hold the East. That's half the present Viceroy's secret. He cares for India; and most Indians know it. There's principle, too, behind his policy. It almost amounts to a Yoga of action.'

Lynch thumped the arm of his chair.

'That form of Yoga is our best gift to India, *pace* her holy dreamers up in the clouds.'

'You know many of them?' Leigh asked casually.

'No, thanks. We don't talk the same language.'

'Well, I've known several: and I can tell you that their sane philosophy of life *includes* a Yoga of action — the dream and the business: a conjunction common to most of our own great men, even if they don't mention it. As a race, we're too bone lazy to articulate our thoughts; half suspicious of the man who can do it for us; the man of imagination and vision — like Sinclair, for example. If you'd read all the papers he left with me, you'd recognise, as I do, that he and his work are necessary to this changing India.'

'And I'm highly honoured as the chosen instrument for unearthing him?'

'More so, perhaps, than you're likely to believe.'

Lynch raised his level eyelids at that.

'You've a very high opinion of Sinclair?'

'I have. And you have not; though you're a sound judge of men. But in his case prejudice against mixed breeding warped your judgment.'

'A natural prejudice, you'll admit?

'Yes. But one can't sweepingly turn down a whole community. Many Eurasians have done good work out here with small recognition. They're the backbone of our Indian railways. Looking higher, when it comes to good breeding on both sides, there have been some notable results. Sir Roy is one of them, as your Grace was quick to perceive.'

'Oh, she would be.'

A light flickered in Leigh's serious eyes.

'If *she* had been a shade less discerning, perhaps you would have been a shade more so?'

Lynch looked hard at the man who was not given to trespassing.

'That I wouldn't vouch for,' said he, in a contained voice.

For it was a shrewd hit. Few men, knowing Lynch, would have risked so personal an implication. But Sir Vincent Leigh, being what he was, could speak his thought with impunity.

He spoke it now. 'I know what *I* would vouch for. When you find Sinclair up there — as you *must* — you'll see him in a new light that will confirm my view — and hers. Of course I've had the advantage of deeper knowledge, through gaining his friendship and soaking in his papers: an inspired survey from the heights.'

'Any practical conclusions?'

Sir Vincent smiled. 'The man of vision is not of necessity unpractical.'

''M — I take your word for it. The tables of stone brought down from the mountain were practical enough in a sledge-hammer fashion. But how would his hill-inspired conclusions work out on the dusty plains?'

'That would depend on the man — or men — who have the handling of them. They would demand a change of mental attitude in the Services, no less than in the Government — and an exceptional Viceroy. My own choice — you'll smile! — would be such a one as Sinclair himself, for this critical turn of the tide.'

At that amazing conclusion, Lynch laughed outright.

'My good sir! A half-breed? Whatever his gifts, he's that, in plain terms.'

'In terms equally plain,' Leigh retorted, 'he's a man with the best blood of East and West in his veins, a unique love and understanding of both in his heart. He has the strength of his handicap, which often counts far more than no handicap at all. Have you never heard of a lurking Indian belief that the successor of Buddha may prove to be, not impossibly, a man of double birthright, East and West, in whom will be revealed the hidden meaning of our long link with India? Is your British prejudice impervious to that thought-provoking idea?'

Lynch took a moment to consider a proposition that from any other man he would damn outright.

'*As* an idea,' he cautiously agreed, 'it has points. Personally, I've seldom found the best of both races, even in the most promising specimens of intermarriage.'

'How many of them spring from the best of both sides?' Sir Vincent urged, with unusual insistence. 'In Sinclair it's a clear case of double-caste, as he sees it himself. Through his father he is inherently artist and poet. Through his mother's father, he inherits a strain of the seer and thinker essential to leadership, which India must have — or perish. A man of that quality — in my unorthodox opinion — is better fitted to govern this changing India than even the most experienced administrator.'

'Yourself, for instance?' Lynch asked boldly, his disagreement being obvious.

'Myself, certainly,' Sir Vincent agreed in his level tone. 'I may be something of a thinker: I'm no leader.'

'You've given this Province as fine a lead, in these five years, as Sir Theo Desmond himself,' Lynch countered with a directness positively embarrassing to so modest a man.

'That needs a grain of salt ——' He lightly turned it off. 'At least I haven't sold my convictions for a mess of pottage. And any good I may have done for these people has sprung from my faith in the aristocratic principle — India's only hope of salvation from the octopus of industry or the poison of communism. No committee can do it; no paper constitution. It must be a *man* — a leader of men.'

'How about another Akbar?' Lynch queried in all seriousness; '*If* we could find him? There's the rub.'

'Yes, if ——,' Sir Vincent sighed and smiled. 'What a pair of wiseacres we are!'

'We are,' Lynch echoed, pocketing his pipe. 'If England would only give us a free hand in the North, with a backing from His Excellency, she might have the surprise of her life!' He glanced at his watch. 'Good Lord, it's after seven. My Inspector must be cooling his heels in the duftar.'

'While we usurp the throne! — But remember,' Leigh added, in the changed tone of authority, 'I'm trusting you to unearth Sir Roy Sinclair, if it's humanly possible.'

Lynch stood up, very square and dependable. 'Count on me, for all that man can do — and a bit over. If I am a realist I don't put the impossible quite outside my reckoning in this highly improbable country.'

So they parted, mighty opposites, who had never liked the other better in five years of working along different lines to the same end.

Chapter X

There is neither East nor West, Border nor breed nor birth,
When two strong men stand face to face, though they come from the ends of the earth.

KIPLING

NOWHERE on earth can April be lovelier than in the valley of Kashmir: silver lakes blurred with mirrored purple and mauve of wild iris, willows and poplars, walnut and mulberry, flecked with youngest leaves; wild peach trees everywhere in full bloom, like puffs of cloud flushed with coming dawn; snow on all the nearer heights; and beyond them, the silver frieze of the Pir Panjàl.

In the Residency garden, on this afternoon of early spring, it was almost England: daffodils in profusion, columbines already out; clumps of purple iris and scarlet Kashmir tulips flaunting their splendour. The vast lawn that swept up to the house was flanked by four great chenars, the glory of Kashmir, many of them over three hundred years old; none allowed to be felled without royal permission. Under one of them, afternoon tea had been set out for the Residency party, Sir Havelock and Lady Thorne, Lynch and his wife.

For Grace had not, after all, been allowed to stay behind and await the coming of Roy's devoted Rajput cousin, Aruna. Lynch rightly mistrusted the rattletrap, Indian-driven motors that hurled confiding passengers from Murree to Srinagar at the hourly risk of their lives. So Grace had travelled up with him, in his big, smooth-running car; and here he would leave her to enjoy a quiet spell with her friends, before Srinagar was converted into a replica of any Punjab station in an Arcadian setting. By early May, houseboats would be moored to lake or river banks as thick as punts at Henley, each with its calling box and label, '*Sans Souci*' or '*Mon Repos*,' like any suburban villa. There would be ukuleles throbbing, deck parties for morning coffee or Gin-and-It; a plague of shopkeepers afloat yelling for custom.

John, as usual, had done wisely, Grace reflected, while she sat under the chenars with two sleeping terriers and the deserted remains of tea. He had gone off with Sir Havelock on some last-minute business; and Vanessa had taken her two-year-old son indoors. A pity their time in Kashmir would so soon be over, and strangers would invade this house of cherished memories; the house where she and John had at last been driven to admit that even the work they lived by could no longer prevail against their very human need of each other. He and Sir Havelock were friends in a surface masculine fashion, very different from his firmly knit bond with Vincent Leigh.

Here he was back again, making Havelock laugh his deep, rumbling laugh. Both were big men, Lynch the tougher and harder of the two; Sir Havelock more obviously the type of Englishman who will never take his coat off till the ground opens underfoot, and then seize the first chance to put it on again.

They came and sat down by her. White-coated servants with scarlet cross-belts and gold badges carried away the tea. Lynch was not going far that evening, as the Guru Maharāj, Sri Samādhi, was camping in the Nishát Bagh.

'Can't say I relish the prospect,' he remarked with a grin at his wife, 'of an evening with the Holy One talking higher Hinduism, when I'm after practical information.'

'Pocket your prejudice for once,' Grace advised him, from her fuller knowledge. 'He has the finest mind of any Asiatic I know. I would dearly love to meet him again.'

'And I would gladly make you a present of my coming interview. No doubt he'd call on you, if invited.'

Grace turned eagerly to Thorne. 'Will you invite him?'

'No need. He'll be coming along. He is chief spiritual adviser to H. H., who appreciates his mixture of worldly knowledge and other-worldly wisdom.' He shook a warning finger at Lynch. 'No *zubberdust*, mind, in your dealings with His Holiness.'

'Not likely.' Lynch stiffened under the imperative tone he so freely bestowed on others. 'I wasn't born the day before yesterday. If I *am* a better hand with criminals than saints, you can rely on J. L. through all your "thicks and thins," as the inspired *babu* has it. If I bar saluting the Holy One's toe, I undertake to refrain from pulling his sacred nose!'

'Some concession!' Thorne mumbled, heaving himself out of his low chair. 'You're incurable. There's no reverence in you.'

'*Kubberdar* ——,' Lynch retorted with an odd lift of the eyelids that showed a gleam of white above the pale iris. 'There's a limit to my meekness. But no limit to what I'll dare for the satisfaction of this lady and the honour of the police force I command.'

Thorne nodded with a smile for Grace.

'That's good enough for me. Pitch in any news when you can, and bring Sir Roy back to us all in record time.'

Grace sat silent a moment, oppressed by the inadequacy of last words. John, equal to most occasions, hitched his chair closer to hers.

'Nice being here together again,' he remarked, and she heard in his changed tone the memory of those good days. 'You found you couldn't bear not to marry me — remember? You're bearing up under it pretty well, eh?'

For answer, she could only lay a hand over his that he had brought down on her knee. And he added in his more practical vein: 'I'm thankful to be leaving you here; I'll send a line whenever it's feasible. Getting a word from you will be a stiffer proposition. I'm cursing Sinclair root and branch.'

He sighed and stood up, pulling her with him; took her in

his arms and kissed her — a long, slow kiss. Then, deliberately, he put her from him.

'Damn it all, I must be moving on. For the love of God, take care of yourself, you feckless woman, if you know how it's done?'

She laughed. 'I don't. I never did. But Vanessa will do it for me.'

She and Havelock were coming down the verandah steps now; and in less than ten minutes John was gone, leaving her oppressed with a sense of emptiness in the midst of lavish beauty that would have satisfied even his demanding heart.

Lynch himself, very far from satisfied, was leaning back in his river-boat trying not to think of Grace and scanning Kashmir's familiar charm with a curiously indifferent eye. His traps had gone along to the Bagh by road, with his two Afridi trackers, Umra Khan and young Mahomed Akbar, while he enjoyed the slower transit by canal and lake. He wanted a quiet time alone to re-read a long report received that morning from Verney, acting D.I.G. in his absence: tackling very efficiently this fresh outcrop of Red Shirt activity and the extra precautions needed for the Viceregal visit, that was 'not all jam' for the Police. He himself was glad of a month or two away from the district in its present state of ferment. He had long known J. L. for a marked man. Communal sizzlings and his own strong hand on the Red Shirts had brought him many threatening letters of late; a chronic infliction that had never yet been allowed to rattle his nerves; but Lynch the benedick set a higher value on his own life than Lynch the bachelor had ever done. Marriage with Grace had so deeply satisfied the whole man that he viewed even the coming of a child with mixed sensations, though his faith in her was founded on a rock. She knew his needs and his limitations, knew the normal selfish man that was J. L. Whatever the counter-pull, she would not fail him. Recognizing her spiritual outlook as beyond his range, he yet knew himself her equal in other respects; knew that no clash of will or principle could ever trouble the depths of their reliance on each other.

Today he had found it harder to leave her than ever yet; nor was he upheld by any personal zeal for his quest, beyond the credit of pulling off a difficult task. Not for a moment did he doubt that he would find his needle in the haystack. An ingrained assurance that the thing which must be done would be done was not the least element in the success of his notable career. There was also at the back of his mind the pull of those stupendous mountains round Gilgit and Chitral, a region infinitely more to his taste than this pretty-pretty Vale of Kashmir.

His deftly paddled boat had carried him now beyond the open green spaces of the English quarter — the smart bungalows, the inescapable Club and banks and shops; a parsonage and an English church, intruding among ruins of temples and shrines. On his left rose the embankment with its avenue of poplars; on his right rocky spurs of the Takt-i-Suleiman, that lifts its temple-crowned head a thousand feet above the City of the Sun.

At this hour the river was thronged with boats large and small gracefully propelled by punt or paddle; a shifting pattern of many colours; and Lynch, who ignored mere 'scenery,' had an eye for the richly blended tones of the East. He liked Srinagar's golden domes, and roof gardens gay with spring flowers. He liked the walnut-brown *doonga* thatched with emerald-green rushes and a scarlet pile of chillies in the prow; the country boat heaped with pale gold, rifled from mustard fields that splashed the lower reaches of the valley like spilled sunshine. Bearing down upon them both came a bulky timber-laden barge, creaking and crashing its way towards India; a looming threat to all lesser craft. But these Kashmiris were as clever with their punt poles as the gondoliers of Venice. While the country boat and the barge were shrilling lurid abuse at each other, his own boat slid skilfully between them and joined a crowd that besieged the gateway entry to the lake.

The transit was apt to be an exciting affair, as now: the

water rushing through with all its force from the over-full lake; boatmen yelling to each other, clinging for dear life to the iron chains that alone saved them from being whirled like straws downstream. Lynch laughed as the boat heaved through waves that swirled and splashed in his face; shooting out, at last, into the silvery stillness of deep water that fell away from the prow in long, smooth ripples, shivering the dream-world of inverted trees and mountains, and galleons of white cloud. Already the late afternoon sun was changing the water into wine; but Lynch, frowning over his report, heeded none of these things.

He only looked up when the gentle movement ceased at the gateway of Nishát Bagh, flanked by masses of Persian lilac. Beyond them Jehanghir's lovely garden climbed the hillside in seven terraces. From the highest, a cascade of waterfalls came splashing down to the lake, escorted by statuesque chenars in youngest leafage. Everywhere sheets of purple iris, blossoms of peach and cherry and pear struck the authentic note of a Kashmir April, the loveliest on earth.

Here Lynch stepped ashore and sauntered up the hillside to the seventh terrace and the wide stretch of turf, where the Guru had pitched his modest camp. There he found his own little tent set up at a respectful distance, his canvas chair outside it inviting him to loaf and smoke in peace. Roundabout him lay blocks and throne-like seats, fragments of an old Moghul pavilion; and not far off, on a moss-grown slab, sat the Holy One he sought; an impressive figure, saffron-robed, still as a statue. There was power in the modelling of his close-cropped head and spacious forehead, in the firmly wrought features, more European than Indian; power in balance, every nerve and muscle under control. The closed eyes and abnormal stillness forbade intrusion on so complete a withdrawal; and Lynch waved aside an officious attendant.

'I will wait,' he said.

And he waited, motionless. That brooding presence had put a spell on him, till a ray stole through the young leaves and lingered on the Guru's face as if to dissolve its carven stillness. The lips parted on an indrawn breath. The eyes opened, and the finely modelled head turned slowly towards the intruder.

The deep voice greeted him without preamble: 'You have come.'

And Lynch answered simply: 'Yes. I have come.'

Implicit friendliness lurked in their unsmiling gaze, as the Guru rose, and they confronted each other.

'Did I keep you waiting long?'

'No matter.' Lynch dismissed his own unfamiliar sensations. 'We have all time.'

Sri Samādhi's answering smile transfigured his face.

'A fact,' he said, 'that so many of your people forget or overlook. For ever hurrying, to save time, they often lose that which no time can recapture. I am glad you were able to come yourself on this difficult errand. Sir Vincent Leigh wrote highly of your knowledge and skill.'

'His good opinion is worth having.'

'I agree. Sir Vincent is no ordinary man. It is only such as he who promote understanding between East and West. He and Sinclair seem, to my limited knowledge, two of the most remarkable men of your race at present in India.'

Lynch pondered that statement, perceiving that here was a man who spoke his mind and would respect the differing mind of another.

'I give you Sir Vincent,' he said; 'I don't know Sinclair well enough to pronounce an opinion.'

'Perhaps you will know him better before your search is ended. Then you will also "give" me Sir Roy.'

'I hope, at any rate,' said Lynch, evading the issue, 'that I may succeed in giving him back to his family and friends. He has let them all in for a very anxious time.'

Look and tone implied reproach, but Sri Samādhi remarked in his measured voice: 'That is unfortunate. When risks are taken for great ends, all cannot be foreseen.'

'You think the end justifies the means?'

'In this case, yes. Though you think otherwise, I know.'

'I'm not aware of having expressed an opinion,' Lynch

retorted, amazed to find this impressive Holy One answering a mental reservation that hardly amounted to a thought.

The other smiled. 'I have saved you the trouble. You would rather not doubt my word, but you are by nature a sceptic. I see behind your eyes those mists of unbelief that too often distort the vision of your people in India, even those who have lived and worked here, like yourself, for over twenty years.'

Lynch opened his eyes. 'Twenty-two years next month, Guru-*ji*. Where did you see *that* written?'

'In your mind,' the other answered, as coolly as if he had said, 'In the Police Service list.' 'It is a mind governed by power and hardness, and a strong will, but there is a limit of sympathy. By which I do *not* imply that indifference to my country and people, which too often blunts the edge of even keen intelligence. What I have to say, you will treat with respect; but most of it you will probably not believe. The unprepared mind, meeting unfamiliar truth, shies away like a pony from a blown piece of paper.'

Lynch chuckled at the apt simile; and the Guru added with a shrewd look, 'Your own mind, though enlightened by much strange experience, is not yet ready to travel off the rails, as you would say.'

'Right again. I don't take much stock in off-the-rail travelling. What *is* the unfamiliar truth you're asking me to believe?'

'I don't ask belief of any man, my friend. What I have just seen, I will tell you. What you will think of it is your affair.'

The clear brown eyes brooded on him with a more human look of interest. 'You are married, I think, to my friend of the Kohat Hospital, who was Doctor Grace Yolande?'

'I am,' Lynch stated simply.

'Ah, *that* is a woman,' the Holy One mused, as if to himself. 'The only woman of your race whom I have had the privilege to call friend. She is well?'

'She is well,' Lynch echoed, as reticent on that head as any Oriental. 'She awaits me at Srinagar.'

'Perhaps I may see her?'

'She hoped it would be possible.'

A gleam lightened the serious eyes. 'She, I think, would "give" me Sir Roy?'

'She *would*,' Lynch smiled to himself, recalling Sir Vincent, and shifted his ground. 'Does it concern Sinclair, what you have to tell me?'

'Yes. Shall we sit?'

He indicated the mossy slab; and there they sat together, that incongruous pair, looking down the stately avenue, past glittering fountains and cascades, to the quiet lake fringed with willow and poplar, to the fort of Hari Parbat and faintly flushed snows.

Sri Samādhi's voice took a deeper tone, rather as if he were thinking aloud.

'When you came and stood over there, my mind was far away among other mountains greater and more terrible than these.'

'You seemed — in a trance.'

'Not that exactly. But sometimes we, who have attained, can project our minds to a distance. Not always from choice. Today, during my evening quiet, all thought suspended, an intimation flashed like a comet across the night sky, drawing me in spirit far away from here. I saw, as clearly as I now behold this gentle scene, a narrow, broken road among rugged mountains; a river roaring far below; a heavy snowstorm swirling in the faces of muffled men. One tall figure walked apart from the others; muffled also, yet instantly known to me. No Guru can mistake his god-sent *chela*. It was Sinclair, no other, among those great mountains, with those unknown men. Perhaps in danger. They are evil men; intending evil towards him.'

His low monotone made the brief bald statements curiously arresting; though Lynch, on instinct, hardened his mind against facile impressions.

'Sounds like Gilgit or Chitral,' he mused. 'It might be a clue worth following up.'

The Guru turned to him and spoke with decision. 'It *is* a clue. It *must* be followed up.'

'Must —— ?' Lynch jibbed at the note of command.

'Yes. By all means. I understand that your chief concern is to find Sir Roy? I give you information ——'

'You call *that* information,' Lynch began — and checked himself, instantly regretting the discourtesy.

Sri Samādhi looked at him — a penetrating look that made him feel almost as if he had flouted royalty.

'Sorry, Guru-*ji*,' he apologised in abrupt Western fashion. 'I'm not used to getting my information along those lines.'

'Also you don't like travelling off the rails?' Sri Samādhi reminded him, tacitly dismissing his lapse from grace. 'And such things do not happen in your country. I have told you precisely what I saw. Your disbelief is of no consequence. It is for you to go there, to prove if I have seen true.'

'Go — where?' Lynch made bold to ask. 'There's a whole wilderness of naked hills around Gilgit and Chitral.'

For answer the Guru closed his eyes. Once more he became still as a statue; and, in spite of himself, Lynch wondered, 'How much of it all is pose — how much genuine?' As if to shame his scepticism, the Holy One opened his eyes and announced, 'It might be towards the Burzil Pass, or nearer to Astor.'

Lynch grunted. 'Within reasonable distance. That's a mercy. But why should Sinclair have got mixed up with evil men?'

'That we have to discover.'

'I thought a big dose of solitude was the programme.'

'For his work — yes. But man can no more command events than your Danish King could command the rising tide.'

Lynch looked amused. 'You know all about our early Kings?'

'I know English history more deeply, perhaps, than some of your own young men who come out to legislate India. I took a First in history at Oxford, a good many years ago.'

That utterly unexpected statement made a deeper impression on Lynch than any Asiatic mental gymnastics. To please His Holiness he would take the Gilgit road, though he still regarded the snowstorm and the evil men as figments of a dream. He preferred solid earth; and by this time he was craving for a pipe.

'Can a fellow smoke, Guru-*ji*?' he asked hopefully.

'Why not? An Englishman without a pipe is like a dog without a tail.'

Lynch laughed. This blend of saint and scholar was a man.

In the act of striking his match, he noticed a saffron-robed figure strolling farther along the avenue.

'Another Guru in camp?' he asked with a touch of apprehension. One could hardly hope for a second unique specimen.

'No Guru, yet, but a young *chela* of high attainment. Not of the East by birth. He is English. But he has chosen the Path; discarding all possessions, even his English name.'

'Good God!'

The note of dismay was so unfeigned that the Indian smiled; and Lynch laughed again.

'A tall order,' he excused himself.

'Too tall for one of little faith? Yet it is a fact that today more and more thoughtful young men of your race are looking towards the spiritual wisdom for the light that burns dim in the West. Once again the world's wise men may follow the star in the East. We turn to you for knowledge; you look to us for wisdom. The first is of little use, lacking the other. So there is virtue in such intermarriage of the spirit, not of the flesh.'

Lynch accepted without comment that illuminating conclusion. If he could not discuss these high matters, he could and did recognise an aristocracy of mind and character in this man of profound understanding and saintly life. Here was no woolliness of thought such as his Western mind was quick to detect and distrust in Eastern talk on higher levels.

The Guru was speaking again now in his modulated tone: 'Loyalties and ideals of the West have become riddled with scepticism; and to strip away these from a man's mind is like stripping the clothes from his body. Your people have become used to naked bodies over there, but they rightly fear a naked mind. We Hindus have many failings, but we have not quite lost hold of those spiritual values. This is the true bond between East and West. Each has something essential to give the other; and the men most needed today are those who can bring them closer together, like our philosopher, Radhakrishnan, and your Sir Roy Sinclair, builders of the Rainbow Bridge between our age-old wisdom and all the new knowledge of the West that, without wisdom, can only bring destruction. My young friend, now called Shivanàth, aspires to be such a builder; and for that purpose he has given up the promise of a fine career.'

'If he cuts himself off from his own race, how does he propose to benefit them?' Lynch wanted to know.

'He is not entirely cut off. He may visit England later on. He may write and build his bridge that way. He is well qualified, having taken his tripos in Mental and Moral Sciences. He sincerely believes there is no finer work for a modern thinking man than this. You may consider him deluded. That is a matter of opinion. He is only important for your purpose as the last man known to be in touch with Sir Roy.'

At the return to practical politics, Lynch was himself again.

'I'd be glad to hear anything he can tell me in that line.'

'*Not* off the rails?' Sri Samādhi reminded him, frankly amused. 'I will call him.'

His pursed lips emitted a long low note. The strolling figure turned and came towards them: a lean young man of ascetic aspect, with deep-set grey eyes and compressed lips, his skin tanned to the colour of ripe corn. No sign of the late graduate in dress, carriage, or formal greeting; but when they sat down together, he spoke of his meeting with Sinclair in the cultured tones of Cambridge.

It may have been early February, he said, that they had strangely met, as fellow Indians, on the border of Poonch

State. Sinclair, who had been ill, was in the rest-house as the Raja's guest; Shivanàth in his own small tent with two followers. Taking Sinclair for a cultured Hindu, he had not spoken in English; and they had spent several hours together, talking Hindu philosophy, without either realising that the other was of his own race.

'Quite an achievement in its way,' Lynch remarked, instinctively proffering his cigar case.

The translated Englishman shook his head.

'Never no more?' Lynch queried.

'That's a long word. I don't bind myself beyond the present.'

'And *that*'s a wise word,' Lynch commended him, lighting his own weed. 'I presume you didn't keep it up for long — your undesigned deception?'

'No. When I came next morning, Sinclair asked me outright, was I Indian or English; not revealing himself till afterwards. I was on a pilgrimage at the time; but he begged me to stay at the rest-house till he was well enough for marching on to Kashmir. He seemed to need me; so I stayed. And it was only then I discovered that he was Sir Roy Sinclair, the writer, whose two illuminating books on India had decided my own future. He was writing a great deal then; and he read me some very fine recent poems. We used to sit up half the night, building the Rainbow Bridge.'

'And when did you part company?' Lynch pursued his own aim.

The young man frowned. 'I'm not strong on dates. I use neither clock nor calendar. It may have been early in February.'

'He was returning to Kashmir?'

'Yes.'

'By what route?'

'He mentioned the Hàji Pir Pass.'

'And was he fit for marching?'

'He seemed so. He was keen to get on, to get Home.'

'Any severe weather about then? Heavy snow or rain?

Cast your mind back. I've a reason for asking. I've taken on an almost impossible job. Glad of any clue. And you seem to set a value on Sinclair.'

'I do — the highest.' He cast his mind back. 'Yes, I remember a big snowfall, soon after we left the lower hills. Then a sudden thaw and heavy rain.'

Lynch nodded. 'Nasty months in Kashmir, those two. Had he much with him?'

'No. He was travelling nearly as light as I do. Food from villages, as available. Only his Hindu bearer, and an all-round man for any cooking and so forth.'

'Turned *Yogi*, in fact?' the Policeman queried casually.

'I didn't get that impression,' was the cautious reply. 'A certain amount of *Yoga* practice — yes. He would pass anywhere as a hill-born high caste Indian.'

Lynch nodded. He knew all about that.

'Since then,' he asked, 'not a word?'

'Not a word. The impress of his mind, his personality, remains indelible. I hope I may meet him again.'

'It will be my endeavour to fulfil that hope,' Lynch concluded with formal courtesy, as the Guru joined them for their simple evening meal.

That night, at parting, he thanked his holy friend for the introduction, adding, 'Tomorrow, early, I'll be getting a move on. Hàji Pir Pass doesn't seem to link up with your naked mountains. But if you are definitely of opinion —— ?'

'I have seen,' the other answered with quiet finality.

'Very well, then. I and my two men will take the Gilgit road; but I'll send another prize tracker across that Pass, to sound the Poonch Rajah and make geographical enquiries. Might have been an avalanche, a landslide, or what not, from that sudden change of weather.'

'Quite possible. I noticed your question. You are a wise man.'

Lynch chuckled at the unexpected compliment.

'Wise enough to salute one who beats him at the game!'

That generous and honest conclusion would atone, he

hoped, for the earlier slip that had been so courteously ignored. For all his natural scepticism, he could not feel other than profoundly impressed by the personality of this Holy One who could say of Grace, '*That* is a woman,' with a conviction that almost matched his own.

Before turning in, he scribbled two close-written sheets crackling with pungent comment on the 'discarnate' youth, balanced by comments in quite another vein on Sri Samādhi, Lord of Bliss; not forgetting to pass on the high compliment he had paid to Grace herself. And because the thought of her stirred emotional deeps that few suspected in him, a sudden wish crossed his mind that the afternoon's talk had been fruitful enough to justify a hopeful message for Sinclair's deserted wife, seven thousand miles away, looking for bread and receiving a stone.

BOOK TWO

TRUMPETS OF DAWN

Chapter I

Soft and loving is her soul,
Swift and lofty-soaring;
Mixing with its dove-like dole
Passionate adoring.

MEREDITH

TARA SINCLAIR had waked far too early in her primrose-yellow bedroom, with its uncurtained eastern windows; waked with a dismally familiar sense of reluctance: the instinctive flicker of hope, quenched by an almost certainty that the dead weight of Roy's long silence would remain unbroken.

The first fine days of April had too soon been blotted out by clouds and rain. Gusts of wind from Iceland, sudden fierce showers lashing the windows, had a desolating effect on a heart full of unshed tears. Bravely and in silence she had combatted her inevitable moods of despair during these three months, more like three years, since Roy's last letters had reached her at Christmas-time, with the lovely sapphire pendant, pledge of his abiding love and promise of his return. But the coming of spring, without a sign that he still lived, was almost more than even her schooled courage could bear. There were days when she would fain have found relief in such a fury of tears as the April heavens could shed without shame. Tears were given after all for relief; but she feared the too discerning eyes of her mother, who would not say a word, never had said a word, since Roy's shattering wire from India announced that he could not return, as planned. She knew her daughter, which cannot be said of all mothers by any means. She could appreciate, with understanding, a simplicity quite unrelated to simpleness; a singleness of heart, a harmony of will and desire that could say with Saint Paul, 'This one thing I do.'

For Tara that one thing was to be, in the deepest sense, wife of Roy Sinclair. Her passion of loyalty to the vanished man would admit of no implication that he had laid on her a burden too heavy to be borne. In some undefined way, she had always feared India and Indian influence for him; had recognised, none the less, his need to go out there alone, for a time, as preparation for this big new book. It was his utterly unexpected non-return, when all was arranged, that had shaken her heart. But she would neither judge nor criticise a line of action that she could not yet fully understand. His wonderful letter from Kashmir had thrown a flood of light on her first bewilderment over the bald cable — that had killed at a stroke her hope of reunion after almost a year apart; and if ever he were allowed to return, he would surely be able to make her understand.

Already that difficult process had been eased by assiduous reading of his papers and endless notes, sent to her through Sir Vincent Leigh, by the hand of Aruna. If she could not always keep pace with his swallow-flights of thought, she had drawn from these vital fragments of himself a sense of closer contact with Roy, the poet and thinker, as distinct from the human Roy, her husband and lover.

And the unexpected coming of Aruna from India, her talk of his daily doings, had re-created the actual man, of whom she could tell so much and talk so freely, after the first half-hour together that had revealed, by chance, the hidden secret of Aruna's life. Not until then had Tara known how, as a girl-student at Oxford, Aruna had loved Roy; how deeply she loved him still, in a sublimated fashion. And that undesigned revealing had shown each to the other in a fresh light. Their brief times together had left Tara enriched, not only by what she had received, but by what she herself had given from the depth of her understanding heart.

To that very gift for understanding she owed — without fully realising it — the intrinsic unity of her marriage with a man who gave generously of himself and made large demands in return. There was much virtue also in the sharing of early lessons and games, the deeper sharing of his love for the gifted Indian mother, who had imbued him with his profound concern for the linked destinies of England and India. That concern had reft him from her for a time — only for a time. She had his own word for it: 'In you, in England, are all the personal roots of my being.... We must live for afterwards, you and I.' With those words printed on her mind, she was living for afterwards, in the rooted belief that his constant heart must draw him back again — if he lived — to all he loved best on earth. If he lived —— ? Neither courage, nor unshakeable faith in him, could still that haunting fear.

Meantime, life slipped through one's fingers. The hidden ache increasingly persisted, as a burden long carried seems to weigh heavier with every mile. Just as well, perhaps, that she was constrained to cheerfulness on account of her mother and the small, adoring Lilāmani, who counted so confidently on his coming in time for her eighth birthday. She had no heart to crush a hope, that might, by some strange chance, be fulfilled.

In Roy's deserted bed, beyond her narrow table, the creature lay sleeping peacefully. It felt less lonely having her there; and seven years old could be unashamedly sentimental about 'sleeping in Daddy's bed.' Her mind and her talk were full of him. She felt his long absence more deeply than Nevil seemed to do, though he was two years older; and Nell was too young to be actively concerned about things or persons unseen.

The dark head stirred. An arm was flung out. 'Daddy — Daddy!' Lilāmani murmured, as if he had just gone from her; a dream illusion that Tara knew too well.

'Mummy's here, darling.' She reached out across the table, quite aware that Mummy was not the same thing. 'Time for early tea. Come along.'

The child sat up, wide awake now — a true Lilāmani, except for Roy's blue-grey eyes: the nose delicately curved, the soft mouth and resolute lower lip. Her dark hair, with its natural wave, was brushed back and hung in a plait over one shoulder. Her skin had neither the cleanness of Nevil's, nor the duskiness of Nell's that revealed the Indian strain. Its creamy pallor and the neatly finished features suggested a miniature on ivory. Later she would be beautiful, as that other Lilāmani. In her fairy fashion, she was lovely enough now.

Springing out of bed, she crept in beside her mother, nestling close, while Tara lit the kettle.

'Mum, d'you often dream of Daddy?' she asked in a small voice.

'Not very often,' Tara admitted, spooning tea out of her pot.

'I do — rather. Sometimes it's lovely. Sometimes it muddles up into horrid nonsense. He was quite real in my dream. Oh, Mummy' — a sob broke in her throat — 'where *is* he now? Why doesn't he come home? He promised.'

The clinging hands seemed to close on Tara's heart. Turning in bed, she gathered the child in her arms, as if she would protect her from the ache of not knowing that she herself must endure.

'He's in India still, darling, in Kashmir. He *will* come as soon as ever he can. We must be patient.'

'I'm tired of being patient.'

And Tara's heart echoed the cry. But her lips said sagely: 'Often we have to keep on, even when we are tired.' And to escape from the subject, she asked, lightly, 'Are you too tired to pour out my tea?'

'No, no — please.' She wriggled up, eager for her own share in the daily rite; eager for sweet biscuits to scrunch — a particular weakness.

They were happily engrossed, when Hilda came in with letters; and Tara's quick eye caught the sight of the Indian stamp — but not his writing; and her lifted heart fell like a shot bird. From the envelope she pulled out a thin sheet, and read the letter written by Thea Leigh in Peshawar only a week ago; a letter full of sympathy, seasoned with hopeful assurance that failed to reassure Roy's wife.

'Vincent,' she wrote, 'has implicit confidence in Lynch, who will send you a cable direct, the moment he has any definite news. He is off to Kashmir, at once. Keep a brave heart, Tara. We have never known Lynch to fail in any big undertaking.'

Tara's thin hand instinctively crushed the paper she held; and the movement, the catch in her breath, drew Lilāmani's attention from the biscuit that she was neatly nibbling round and round in pursuance of a private game.

'Mummy, are you feeling rather sad?' she asked.

'No, not sad,' Tara resolutely denied her troubled heart; and to prove it, she added briskly, 'You never told me, darling, what Daddy was doing in your dream.'

'My dream?' Her eyes took on their pensive look, remembering. 'There was you and me with him, in those far big Indian hills. He wasn't our or'nery Daddy. He had a funny kind of coat on and a turban round his head like grandfather's picture. But it *was* him. You couldn' help knowing. And he was terribly pleased that we came.'

'We came?' Tara echoed, her heart shaken by a sudden idea. 'Did you know, in your dream, that we came?'

'Of course I knew. We flew on an eagle's back. And all among those hills, there was Daddy — Prithvi Rāj — terribly pleased ——' The small mouth quivered and was controlled. 'We sat on a rock and Daddy put me on his knee. It was lovely. Then — I don't know — something flapped in my face. And — he was *gone*....'

She broke down and sobbed, clinging to Tara. 'Oh, Mummy, I want him! I *want* him! Won't he ever come?'

'Yes, Lilāmani. He *will* come,' Tara mechanically assured her, because one dared not suppose otherwise.

At that, the child looked up eagerly.

'Why can't *we* go and find him, like my dream?'

And Tara held her close, not answering at once. For, in that crazy question, she heard an echo of her own swift resolve, her conviction that Roy *was* alive among those Kashmir hills. She ought to be out there — to have news of him sooner, to welcome him when — not 'if' ——?

And Lilāmani's 'Can't we go?' suggested another bold idea. She must come too. Impossible to leave her bereft of both parents; and she herself could hardly face that far flight, to an uncertain end, without some living fragment of home to comfort her heart. It would be hard enough to leave the other two: Nevil, her pride and treasure, already assuming protective masculine airs. Happily he and his Gran were very good friends; and she herself could thank Heaven for a mother capable of filling her place.

For her quick nature, to decide was to act; and here was practical comfort for the sobbing child.

'Listen, my sweet.' She turned the wet face up to hers. '*I've* got something to tell now; better than your dream, because it's real. I've had a letter from India about Daddy. He's wanting us, but he can't come to us. So I think — we *must* go out to him.'

Lilāmani gazed at her, taking it in. 'You and me?'

'Yes, you and me.' Tara also was taking it in.

'*This* Lilāmani — going to India,' she murmured in a voice of awe. She was little given to childish excitement: and for her there seemed to be some secret magic in the word. Pictures or stories of India seized and held her, as they never held Nevil.

Now she looked up, radiant.

'Why can't *we* go on an eagle — make it all true?'

More craziness, that flashed another inspiration. Why not? A mechanised eagle was at their service. And what was the cost of two air-line passages compared with the dazzling fact that, within a week of starting, they could land on Indian soil?

'Mummy, can we?' the child persisted; and, stooping, she kissed the upturned face.

'Yes, darling. We can go on an airship with wings.'

'A meechine eagle!'

She sparkled now with excitement; and Tara's quick brain sprang to meet the call for action. The age of speed, descried by Roy, had its advantages. Obstructions there might be; but she was keyed up now to override them all.

Chapter II

It belongs to the genius of this life to endure its uncertainties.

EDWARD SHILLITO

THEY were flying and flying and flying, eating up the miles at the rate of over a hundred an hour; a form of travel more romantic in prospect than in actual experience. A ship was bad enough, but here one was more cramped and confined. The cabin was chilly; the food uninviting to a squeamish inside. More than once Tara was unpleasantly reminded of Roy's apt phrase, 'the familiar gastric lurch.' But through it all ran an under-sense of achievement.

Overriding obstacles had proved no light affair: Nevil's unexpected outburst of wrath and dismay, that had almost shaken her resolve; Elinor's elder-sisterly disapproval of her 'costly craziness'; Aunt Jane — informed at the last moment — having the traditional 'fit.' As Lady Roscoe, titular head of the Sinclair clan, she deemed it unthinkable that any major event should be decided on at Bramleigh Beeches without giving her the rightful opportunity to 'register disapproval,' which could always be counted on where Roy was concerned. And Tara, safe out of England, could shamelessly rejoice at having defrauded her of her due; could thank Heaven for a mother who understood the passionate driving force behind her impulsive action. Without argument or sententious carpings, she had agreed to take over the home, the children, the estate, till such time as their rightful owners could return to claim them.

A cable to Thea had brought the cheering answer, 'Welcome. Fly straight to us.'

And here she was, obeying the royal command, trying to keep her mind away from the lurking question — What would she find at the end of the journey? At first she had been upheld by the thrill of swift action; but during the nights and days of travel, demons of doubt walked to and fro in her brain, tormenting her with cruel suggestions as to Roy's probable fate. Even this new wonder of flight could only distract her mind in snatches; though the sense of complete detachment from earth, the arresting beauty of sky and cloud appealed strongly to her imagination, in spite of protests from her much-enduring body.

Today, making for Gaza, they had been fifteen hours in the sky, intrigued by pancake glimpses of the Holy Land. She had wearied of endless going; but happily the child seemed content. It sufficed that they were 'flying to find Daddy': and she was full of half-terrified curiosity over the mysteries of the 'meechine eagle.' How it knew the way. How its wings were never tired. And 'how turrifically it kept on purring inside.'

On the first afternoon, her demure, confiding ways had beguiled the only young man among the few passengers making for India in April. He was an attractive boy, with a glint of humour in his hazel-grey eyes that gave her an odd sense of knowing and liking the man behind them. The child's interest in Silver Wing attracted him. There was nothing about her machine eagle that he could not tell her; and it was useless trying to detach her from him, lest he might be bored.

That evening, when they dined on shore, he told her he was in the Air Force, going out to join a squadron at Peshawar.

'My people are there,' he added. 'My father's bossing the Province.'

'Sir Vincent Leigh?' she exclaimed: and he smiled at her with those familiar eyes. She knew them now: the eyes of Thea and Roy's Lance.

'Good shot! My revered father. Out there, a Burra Sahib. At home, the shyest and nicest man ever. Terribly shy, even of his own offspring!'

Tara laughed. This was more Thea's boy than Vincent's;

and the shared background made one feel no longer a wandering atom in uncharted skies.

'Which one of them are you?' she asked.

'I'm Vernon. There's only Phyllis under me.'

'Vernon and Phyll,' she murmured, recalling Roy's tales of them when he had stayed with the Leighs after the war. 'D'you remember Jaipur?'

'Yes — in patches. I must have been about seven. I remember millions of fairy lights — Dewali festival: a big garden, and a sentry, who used to scare me stiff, pretending he'd shoot me. I remember Uncle Lance and a very kind man stopping there. I told him about my terror; and he gave Mr. Sentry what for.'

That sounded like Roy. 'Perhaps it was my husband,' she suggested. 'Not married then — Roy Sinclair.'

He stared at her, a puzzled, admiring look.

'*Your* husband? But that man was ——' An awkward pause; and Tara knew what it might bode. 'I seem to remember — Indian cousins. Perhaps I'm all wrong?' he queried hopefully.

'No. Roy has Indian cousins,' she said briskly. 'His mother was a Rajputni. Your mother loved her. So did Lance.'

Again he looked hard at her, still puzzled. 'That's queer — the way our families are mixed up,' he jerked out, as if it were not precisely what he had meant to say. 'And my — my little Fairy?'

'Your Fairy is called Lilāmani, after her. She's wonderfully like her. I hope she'll grow up like her, in all ways.'

Vernon accepted that without comment, and asked casually, 'Where is Sir Roy now?'

'He's in Kashmir on account of his work,' she answered in a schooled voice. 'We're going to join him. But first we go to your people in Peshawar.'

He cheered up at that. 'Great luck! I can do Cook's agent for you all the way.'

And he was as good as his word. From that evening, he attached himself to his new friends and won the heart of his

Fairy. But he did not again mention Roy; and Tara preferred it so. Increasingly she liked him: and the active personal interest kept her from dwelling overmuch on that haunting question mark at the end of her journey.

On and on they flew, through an ocean of blue air; over the desolate ranges of the Persian littoral and the war region, known to her through Roy's letters to his mother. There were dawns that she would never forget and unbelievable violet sunsets over the desert. It was — as Roy had said — an experience not to be missed. As for Lilāmani, she enjoyed even the longest days aloft. When she was not talking to Vernon or playing cards with him, or 'sketching,' she would sit curiously still, looking and looking at it all with her serious eyes: not chattering or asking the random questions of average childhood.

Vernon seemed surprised when he found she was nearly eight. For all her intelligence, imagination, and quick sympathy, people did seem to find her young for her age: no blemish, in this day of little premature grown-ups, reared on gramophones, cinemas, and children's newspapers of the trashiest. Tara discouraged all three, especially the last. But her Fairy devoured books, loved poetry, and had her grandfather's gift for drawing. In these lonely months, she had found the child more of a companion than many grown-ups; and she would be old enough for her age all too soon. This friendly young man was a novelty appreciated to the full.

So the long days and the evenings on shore passed pleasantly enough. Vernon was a blessing in his brotherly kindness to Lilāmani, who adored him; and she herself was grateful for the distraction of his intelligent talk; touched by his knack of forestalling her needs. But she was too deeply absorbed in her own hopes and fears to expend much thought on this charming stranger boy. It was only a week, though it seemed an unmeasured time, between the pang of parting with her mother on that final morning, and the blazing April afternoon when, at last, they hung poised above modernised Karachi, that was neither true East nor true West.

Lilāmani, peering over, protested ruefully: ''Tisn' India'; and Vernon laughed.

'Clever Fairy!' He never used her Indian name. 'It's nothing on earth. It's just Karachi.'

Even on shore, in spite of clamouring coolies, the real India eluded them. They drove down an asphalt road scored with tram-lines between blocks of standardised houses. They drew up before a lordly building labelled 'Carlton Hotel.'

'Back in London Town!' chaffed Vernon. 'And all the lovely journey to do over again.'

Tara could feel how his gaze lingered on her face; but her mind held only one thought — 'Any letters?'

Vernon, the perfect courier, enquired at the bureau, and returned with a large blue envelope. 'One for me, one for you. *She*'s written.'

A smart young woman ushered them into the lift. Lilāmani glanced at the envelope, but said nothing till they were alone in the bleak hotel bedroom. Then she asked, in a hushed voice, 'Is it from Prithvi Raj?'

Tara drew in her lip. 'No, darling. They've still got to find him. We must go on being patient.'

The child sighed and went over to the window. Tara sat down rather suddenly on a spring-cushioned chair and opened her letter. It was full of human kindness, but no word from Kashmir. Lynch himself, Thea said, had now vanished into the blue. And she ran on, as if to cover with lighter talk the sympathy it was so difficult to express:

> *Here we are fairly immersed in festivities: Vinx and the Province having taken a rise in life. Their Excellencies flew up from Delhi: and we've a big official dinner on to welcome them. Poor Vincent! He has no official instincts. But they* are *a charming pair. She and I hob-nob over Indian women.*
>
> *Tara, my dear, I wish we could have you and the child here, but I'm swamped. Every bedroom full. Almost every meal a party. So I'm lodging you with my Lance and Eve. Roy was*

with them, you remember, last autumn. They're delighted. Eve will be going up soon to Kashmir with her boy; and you might like to do that journey with a practised hand. Oh, and Aruna arrived last mail; amazed at the news of your winged journey, longing to see you again.

Talking of wings, Vincent is sending an R.A.F. 'plane, that will bring you here in three hours. He feels you mayn't appreciate the warmth of India's welcome in April. Better take a night at Karachi, and be early birds. My Vernon will come with you. Strange that you should meet so. I hope he's been useful. Be sure I'll run round the first snatchable minute to reintroduce myself.

Yours ever

THEA LEIGH

P.S. We look for a wire from Lynch any day; but——?

But——? The small, fatal word lodged like a bullet in Tara's heart. More than ever she felt grateful for Vernon's talk and laughter when they met in the lounge for tea.

Lilāmani, nibbling her sugared cake, heeded nothing but the Indian servants, watching and listening when they spoke to each other. Suddenly she said, in a voice of suppressed excitement, 'Mummy, I know their talk — what they say.'

Vernon stared; and Tara felt an odd prick of discomfiture.

'Nonsense, darling. You can't possibly understand them,' she dismissed the fantastic statement with more assurance in her tone than in her mind.

'Well, anyhow, I *do*,' Lilāmani insisted, uncrushed. 'Only some bits go all wrong. Isn' it funny?'

But Tara could not see it so.

'It might be scraps you remember from one of Daddy's fairy tales,' she lamely suggested. 'Finish your cake, and we'll go for a drive to find some real India.'

Lilāmani's reproachful gaze made Tara wish her words unsaid, lest the child might not speak of it again; but with Vernon at her elbow, patently puzzled, she had simply wanted to dismiss the subject.

He at once began talking to his Fairy; and she finished her own tea in silence, wondering... ? Might some streak of unconscious race memory enable Lilāmani to understand fragments of Hindustani? Any other supposition seemed, to her Anglo-Saxon sanity, too fantastic for serious consideration. And yet — knowing of Roy's uncanny intimations — it vaguely troubled her. Had she after all been unwise in bringing his favourite child to India?

Before dawn they were again on the wing, they three and two young R.A.F. officers, pilot and observer. The pilot, freckled and red-haired, introduced himself as Flight-Lieutenant Grant, very jovial, but not very likeable. Lilāmani regarded him with the clear, critical gaze of childhood; tightened her clutch on Vernon's hand, and snuggled close to him all through the journey; watching, watching, the vast expanse of real India that seemed to race backward as they raced forward. A strangely inhuman, formless land: mile on mile of dust, sand desert, the famous river Indus sprawling through it like a huge steel-grey snake, flashing back rays of the sun as he rose in unclouded splendour. In no time, they were crossing the Jhelum, a turmoil of yellowish waters set in a patchwork of mustard fields and young corn. And far off, in the utmost north, Tara could discern a tiara of peaks along a skyline of powdery azure; outliers of the mightier region that had engulfed Roy. She could not shift her eyes or mind from them; and the roar of the engine discouraged attempts at conversation.

Over Rawal Pindi they flew; then soared into cooler air above the desolate Salt Range. And here was the Indus once again, foaming through the defile near Attock, roaring under the double-decker steel bridge, with fortified gates at either end. For now they had reached the untamed, untameable Borderland. And all in a moment, it seemed, here was Peshawar City; young Grant sweeping low to show them the network of wide and narrow streets, the jumble of animals and humans, carts and cars, the flat roofs where women and children lived their lives apart. Lilāmani was roused to excitement now at the revealing of 'really truly India.' One would suppose the fanciful child was returning to some known country rather than seeing a new one for the first time.

In a flash they were over Cantonments, beflagged and gay

with bunting. Journey's end, for the moment: and Tara, intent on Kashmir, felt suddenly out of tune with the frivolous atmosphere of Viceroy-mad Peshawar. All this big political stir seemed to dwarf her passionate concern with one human being. Only the thought of Aruna cheered her heart; and it was much to feel that — unless Fate meant to mock at her utterly — she must now be within a few hundred miles of Roy.

Chapter III

Like threads making the pattern of a carpet, we are all mixed up with one another; and never can we get any idea what the pattern we are making is, in the end, to be.

ARVIND NEHRA

IT WAS the eighteenth of April: a day of triumph for the Pathan Province, a day of very mixed sensations for the Governor-to-be. In theory he approved the gradual transfer of Government machinery by a Power strong enough to keep the balance between rival communities aware of their own disability in that vital respect. Yet he could not fully approve the attempt to graft England's parliamentary system onto a so-called electorate, eighty per cent mediaeval and illiterate. Rightly or wrongly he believed that, without the realism of her aristocratic outlook, India could neither govern herself or be governed by others; that, of all countries, she was the most ill-adapted for 'government by counting of noses' — in the caustic phrase of John Lynch. Village India, the vast majority, still needed and welcomed personal administration, visible authority — a Sahib for choice — accessible to direct appeal. But unhappily, in these changed times, too few English officials would take the trouble to study peasant character and mentality; too many still justified the old-time diatribe on British rule — 'a despotism of despatch boxes, tempered by occasional loss of keys.' Proud of their racial common-sense, the English are apt to overlook the deeper need for a common heart, especially in the East. And pride begat complacence — the unforgivable sin.

He himself had, at least, been true to his private watchword, 'Let understanding be the law'; and among Indians a spirit of service, prompted by good feeling, never went unrecognised. It was the secret of their devotion to Henry Lawrence. It had won, for Vincent Leigh, the loyalty, confidence, and friendship of Khans and head men all over the Border. Their spontaneous tributes, in his hour of recognition, were the finest stimulant that a man could desire or deserve.

And he needed all of it to lift him through the coming ordeal of dinners and public ceremonies, as he sat in the big car with Thea and his personal staff, rolling through a double avenue of troops and trees to the Victoria Memorial Hall, where more troops formed a Guard of Honour. The Hall itself was packed with men in uniform, smartly dressed women, Nawabs and Khans in gold-embroidered coats and coloured turbans; all friends and well-wishers; most of them enjoying his great moment a good deal more than the Victim-Designate—Thea's happy thought.

Anchored at last in Government House front row, he stifled a yawn, and deliberately shifted his mind from the living audience to the dead and gone spectators of their transient glory: effigies in oils of seven Sikh rulers over this one-time Afghan city, wrested by force from Dost Mahomed Khan, the Great Amir, whose melancholy, bearded profile kept them unprotesting company. Gone were those ruthless rulers; gone the inspired Lawrences, makers of the Punjab and the Border. Some said that, before very long, the British themselves would be gone from this vote-infected India, largely of their own creation. A melancholy sense of walking in a vain shadow drifted through his brain, as he looked up at the beflagged dais with its gold and crimson throne, transported from Delhi for this high occasion.

And, as if to reprove his untimely mood, there came from without a burst of cheers. The Gordons were blaring the National Anthem. *They* had arrived.

In response to that familiar assault on the emotions, everyone stood up, and remained standing, while the Viceroy and Vicereine moved forward in solemn procession.

'The Aides go before, the Private Secs follow after!' whispered irrepressible Thea. 'But in the midst are *no* damsels playing on the timbrels.'

He loved the spirit that prompted her apt nonsense, but dared not risk more than a sidelong smile. For here came the processional pair, mounting the dais and seating themselves in the floodlight switched onto the throne, so that cinema agents might 'shoot' the brilliant scene.

His own limelight moment was mercifully brief. An oath, formally administered, installed him as first Governor of the Province, with a G.C.S.I. added to his Star of India. Then he also must mount the dais with Thea, who carried herself queenly like her mother. No speeches, by Heaven's mercy; and the ordeal was over. A mountain of pageantry, to bring forth a mouse, was his ungrateful view of the resplendent affair.

And up in the gallery, Tara Sinclair, a very new arrival, was thinking much the same in different words. Out here, they still invested this kind of thing with a pomp and circumstance almost mediaeval. She would be glad to have seen it all — afterwards; but it had come upon her too soon, tired as she was in body and mind, oppressed by the unaccustomed heat, unresponsive to the prevailing spirit of festivity. On this first morning she would fain have stayed at home in Eve Desmond's pleasant bungalow. But they would not hear of it, those two. In the kindness of their hearts they had pressed her to come with them. And of course they were right. She ought to be present. Roy himself would scold her, if she shirked it all. Even to be scolded by him would be luxury after his long, long silence, their first real separation in twelve years of marriage. The coming together again would be, for her, a new experience. Would she discern inner changes wrought by those months of work-engrossed isolation? With the instinctive wisdom of simple natures, she foresaw that at first there might be a strangeness, a need for patience, for adjustment: that was marriage — 'patience till the gleam returns.'...

A stir down the hall, the great ones rising from their

throne, while she had been far removed, dreaming of Roy. And there, beside her, sat Lilāmani, small hands clasped on each other, looking with all her eyes at those resplendent Khans and Nawabs, thinking—what? Beyond her sat Lance Desmond, a lively, yet impressive young man, the very twin (as Roy had said) of his uncle, that other schoolboy Lance, his friend of Marlborough days.

'Done finish,' he said, a hand on Lilāmani's shoulder.

And again the Hall was on its feet: again the band was commanding rather than beseeching that 'God Save the King.' Since the War years had drawn them all closer to their fine, lovable King and courageous Queen, those words had become more than a patriotic formula. People wished them personally, for the sake of England and for love of Those Two.

Tara's gaze followed Sir Vincent Leigh walking beside Thea, with his abstracted air, as if he were miles away from it all. She longed for an hour's talk with this man, who had sent her Roy's papers, and written such fine and true things of him. From every digression, her thoughts swung back to Roy, as the needle of a compass swings to the north.

The young Desmonds breakfasted in their wide verandah; Eve presiding, in a flowered green muslin, retailing plans for the day. This morning Tara must go and see Aruna. This afternoon, there would be tennis on their own court, when she would meet Chrystal Adair, 'a gem of a girl' and a keen player.

'Breather for us,' said Eve. 'But not for the poor dear Exes. Today they are doomed to the perpetual Khyber.'

'I thought the Khyber was one of your major thrills,' remarked Tara, between two luscious mouthfuls of iced melon.

'Nothing to beat it, at first sight. But even the Khyber palls with repetition. Relays of big-wigs and important travellers, all making much the same remarks. Same old peep into savage Afghanistan at the end of all things. Back again to same huge breakfast at Landi Kotal Brigade Mess, hungry and thirsty, their souls fainting in them. Heaven save Lance from becoming a Governor — the dream of his young life.'

'Dry up, you chatterbox,' cut in Lance, who was opening a sealed slip brought in by the bearer. 'Good Lord! Listen to this!' He looked up, addressing Tara. 'Last night, when we were all jubilating, a bomb exploded on the line. The Frontier Mail. You three might have been in it.'

Tara glanced at the child, and he changed his tone: 'Letting off a squib, in honour of the Viceroy; and a damp squib at that. Not even damaged the line. They've nabbed three students in the railway station. But it's the men behind we want to get at.'

'What *can* they hope to gain by this kind of thing?'

Lilāmini was busy now with her melon; and Lance looked thoughtful.

'That's a large question. There's a plan behind, Lynch says, to terrorise Government; a hidden sinister power, forcing infatuated boys to do the killing and pay the price. Thank goodness, they're beginning to revolt against it. They've started an Anti-Terrorist League at Ferōzpur. More power to them — and to the spreading influence of Scouts.'

Tara lit up. This young man was worth talking to.

'You're keen on Scouts?'

'Rather. Practical idealism. The thing India needs most and understands best.'

'And does the movement really catch on out here?'

'Ask B. P. or Tyndale Biscoe in Kashmir. Even I could a tale unfold — too long for now. We've got fifty thousand scouts in the Punjab alone. Four fifths of them Rovers, making hay all over the Province: cleaning up the villages, cutting down statistics of violent crime. And you have to know the Punjab to realise what *that* means. Good stuff on the Border too. I'm in it up to the neck.'

Lilāmani was listening again. Catching a familiar word, she put out a thin little hand and touched his.

'Mr. Desmond, please, I'm a Brownie, in Mummy's new pack.'

'Are you then?' he twinkled at her. 'I'm Chief Scoutmaster of all Peshawar. So be minding your *p*'s and your *q*'s.'

'What *are* those?' she gravely enquired.

'I've often wondered. — But I'm not Mr. Desmond, please. I'm Lance.'

'Yes. I heard. I like it. Now we're friends.'

'That's settled. Click little fingers.'

When they had solemnly clicked, he turned to Tara. 'Care to see the stables, Lady Sinclair?'

'Dearly I would. But please — if you say Roy, you must say Tara.'

'We always have. And we always will,' Eve assured her. 'If you two are game for pony worship, I'll go and worship the Chota Sahib. Then I'll come back and roll Lance to Kutcherry, roll you to Aruna, where you'll see Surāj Mul ——'

'Oh, come *on*, Mummy! Stables — stables —!' Lilāmani, clutching Desmond's hand, danced with impatience.

So they went, the three of them; and to Tara, the familiar stables atmosphere brought a whiff of Home. She liked the way Lance talked of the ponies as if they were his children. There was Grey Dawn, first favourite, a little Ladakhi mare, nuzzling into his pocket for half an apple, letting Lilāmani stroke her velvet nose. Next door was the Banshee: and his withered little *saïs* squatted outside the stall, whistling, whistling a soft tuneless trill, waggling his head, one eye cocked towards his charge.

'What *is* he doing?' asked Lilāmani, very much intrigued.

'He's whistling to amuse the pony,' Lance informed her; and she stared round-eyed at the happy minstrel.

'Does it eemuse the pony?'

'The little beggar won't tell me! Anyhow, he politely cocks an ear. Morning and evening Gulāb makes his musical offering. When he happens to be down with fever, he sends his naked little son to do a bit of yodelling, with apologies! Quite convinced that the Banshee won't be taken in.'

'Rather engaging,' murmured Tara.

'That's the way I see it. But some of our fellows here would treat the good little chap to a friendly kick in the pants he doesn't wear, and tell him not to be a damn fool.'

'*I* think he's rather a nice man,' Lilāmani decided, intent on the waggling head.

'One of the best. He sleeps in the Banshee's loose-box to guard him from night-prowling demons. If the pony died — which Heaven forbid — the little oddity, as like as not, would grieve himself to death.'

'Are many of them like that?' Tara asked.

'I've never met the whistling touch. But for any *pukka saīs*, the pony is his child — or his god.'

At this point Gulab sprang up and salaamed, grinning broadly. The Banshee was introduced; and Lilāmani was promised a bare-back ride one evening, when she would have on her breeches and Lance would be there to see.

'I must be off now,' he said. 'Here comes Eve. Only ten minutes behind time!'

She had been delayed, she told them, watching the *gwala* milk their private cow, that he might not squirt unclean water into his measure, and damage the youngest Desmond's inside.

'I'll be back in a flick,' she promised, as Lance sprang into the car, 'whisk you to Aruna's, and take the nestling under my wing.'

'Can't *I* see 'Runa, too?' asked Lilāmani, who had been first favourite at the Beeches.

'Not today, darling,' Tara said briskly. For some reason she felt averse from letting the child see too much of Indians.

And Lilāmani, with a rebellious *moue*, gave in, having discovered the futility of resistance. There was discipline, for herself and others, behind Tara's fervent love of her own; and her children responded to it unawares.

Now it was Aruna's house: quite a different Peshawar from the hall full of notables and the happy home life of the young Desmonds. In books about India one was sated with insistence on the Club and the gossip, the fetch-and-carry young men and British rudeness to Indians. One heard too little of that simple home happiness, the hot-weather trials, of the work for Indian women to which Thea and Vicereine and others gave much of their time and energy.

Now Tara saw the room in which Roy had read most of his novel to Aruna before he left for Kashmir: primrose-yellow walls and curtains, few pictures, many books in long, low shelves; her Indian musical instruments on a corner table. Above a bowl of yellow roses on the mantelpiece hung the two portraits left with her by Roy, both painted by his father: Tara of five and twenty, and the loveliest one of his mother. The whole atmosphere harmonised with Aruna's simple dress and *sari* in two tones of Rajput yellow.

They had only half an hour together, before they were joined by young Rajini, a vivid, beautiful creature, very intelligent and self-assured, looking more than her sixteen years, in purple dress and leaf-green *sari* like some tropical bird.

'Rajini — our kidnapped bride!' Aruna introduced her. 'Kidnapped by Grace Lynch, with help from Roy and me.'

'Very willing victim!' Rajini added with her flashing smile. 'Very grateful to bride-snatchers for studies at Kinnard College; and now — for this marriage about to be.'

'She really was a singing bird in a cage,' Aruna explained, as if to justify their high-handed abduction. 'Even before we released her from purdah village life, she was writing articles, self-taught, getting them placed in Hindu newspapers by a journalist cousin, who recognised her talent.'

'I was very unhappy,' Rajini chimed in. 'And now I am happy. Now I can help, with Aruna and others, to make the new India. No more Hindu-Moslem hatred; killing harmless people for quarrels about sacred cows or music near mosques. In the name of religion, they blacken their own faces, while shouting about India, one nation. It is for the *women* to teach them sense.'

'Can they?' asked Tara, half amused, half impressed by the assurance of Eastern sixteen.

'If they *will*, they can. Too long they have practised dancing in fetters. Already the men-folk have wondered at their courage in this time of civil disobedience and National Week. For the good cause every sect must unite. India first; one God for all. No breaking heads over mosques and cows.'

Tara glanced from the girl's eloquent face to Aruna, standing apart, her homely features lit by an inner grace of the spirit.

'Your singing bird ought one day to be a speaker,' she said.

'The woman's rôle!' laughed Rajini; 'one day she *will*— husband permitting——'

Sounds of arrival outside announced Surāj Mul, and a change flitted over her mobile face like a gleam of light on water.

'Listen! He is come. The *minah* must not chatter too much in the Presence!'

He came: a good-looking young man, with his Rajput grace and air of breeding, his cool dark coat, over wrinkled trousers; his orange-yellow turban worn with an air.

'As sure of himself as the girl,' thought Tara. 'No worshipping Hindu wife here. How *will* they combine?'

Unaware of her thought, he was bowing low above her hand.

'This is a feast day for me, when I meet the wife of Roy,' he said with genuine feeling; and she warmed to him as she had not done to the girl. 'It is thanks to Roy that I found this happiness; so we were waiting till his return — too long delayed. All is now arranged for next week. No wedding *tamasha* for us. Because we are a different caste, it must be civil marriage.'

'Civil marriage — in India?'

'Yes, even in India, now. You know our country?'

'We came out for a year, soon after our marriage. And I have known Indians in England. Aruna and Roy's grandfather and his mother.'

He looked up at the portrait over the mantelpiece. 'Very beautiful, true Rajputni. She was brave in early days, when it needed more courage to break purdah than it does now.'

'Not so easy, even now.' Rajini upheld her own generation. 'Lucky for India that her women *have* courage — even more than her men.'

'You say *that?* You forget — I am Rajput.'

The change of tone, the spark of temper in his fine eyes, set Tara wondering — would husband permit? Was Indian marriage itself undergoing transformation? But Surāj was asking her now if she would still be in Peshawar next week to grace their small gathering in Aruna's room, and stand for Roy?

Next week? By that time she hoped to be in Kashmir. He was desolate; but they also intended to go there after the ceremony: 'For English honeymoon,' he shyly explained. 'All who long for his return must be there to welcome Roy.'

His allegiance, his faith in the outcome fortified her spirit. She left that radiant pair and the loved Aruna with quickened interest in the young social India that was blossoming out of the old. Roy naturally believed in the women as India's light of inspiration, the core of her stability and strength. All roads led back again to him. No escape from the thought of him. No word from the man himself to comfort her heart.

In the afternoon there was tennis on the newly made grass court. Only three outsiders; Mr. Verney of the Police, a fine-looking Pathan subaltern, and Chrystal Adair, whom they called the Gem: an attractive girl, fresh to India.

Lance and Eve had challenged her and the Pathan, 'Desmonds against the World': Tara and Mr. Verney to cut in later when part of the court would be in shade. Tara was out of practice and feeling the heat; but she enjoyed watching people with her eyes and mind; in this case a very individual foursome. The Chrystal girl played with skill and precision. Her net-skimming strokes and deft back-handers were a pleasure to see. The Pathan, playing with force and fire, was more than a match for Lance, though he placed his balls unerringly. And there, on the outskirts, her Fairy was skipping about behind Lance, chasing his balls,' probably more hindrance than help, but he would not have her called to order.

The clever-looking man, who sat with Tara, talked well.

He had interesting things to say about Red Shirts and Congress and this wearisome Round Table Conference; but her mind was constantly deflected to those flying figures on the court.

Clearly that young Pathan was under the spell of his attractive partner. No mistaking the look in his eyes, when they lingered on her; and the girl obviously liked him, if no more.

'Are Lance and Eve encouraging this?' Tara mused with a faint prick of concern, for she had her private thoughts about mixed marriage, though the blend had given the world a Roy Sinclair; and changing Indian conditions were bound to increase the likelihood of such unions, for good or ill. Here were these young officers, often unmarried and intensely masculine, associating with English girls in free-and-easy modern fashion. They rode and danced and played tennis together. What was to prevent either side from falling in love? But marriage was a matter of more than love; a sharing of fundamentals, a passing-on to children of strains that might refuse to blend.

Presently a trifling incident threw fresh light on her intriguing speculation.

Lance, after a long rally, deliberately skied a ball to the far corner beyond Chrystal, daring her to an almost impossible feat. With a skidding run she reached the corner, sprang up to achieve a high back-hander, and sent the ball whizzing back to him. But even as he shouted 'Wimbledon style!' one foot slipped and she fell sprawling.

Sher Afzul, up to the net, turned and reached her in three strides. But Verney was nearer, quicker. As he grasped her bare arms and pulled her up, the two men almost collided, and again there was no mistaking the flash in Sher Afzul's eyes.

Chrystal, laughing, waved them both away.

'*I* can get on my feet without any kind assistance! Thanks very much all the same.' But Sher Afzul was not seeing the joke; and Verney's quick eyes had detected a slight wince, as her foot touched the ground.

'Can you *stand* on them?' he asked significantly; and she screwed up her nose at him.

'Don't fuss. We're winning the Conqueror. And we've got to beat that conceited pair!'

'Not at the cost of a game foot.'

'The foot *is* game!' she neatly retorted. But Tara thought otherwise. 'You'd be better sitting down for a little,' she said, 'and let me carry on for you. I'm not a crack player, but I'd do my best.'

Verney beamed at her. 'That's common sense. Drop it, Chrystal, and let Lady Sinclair carry your flag to victory!'

For a second Chrystal hesitated and glanced towards Sher Afzul, standing apart, twisting sinewy fingers on the handle of his racket as if they were closing on an enemy's throat. Then she turned smiling to Tara.

'It's very kind of you, Lady Sinclair. Will you play with my racket? She's a beauty. Then I can still count it my victory.'

Again she glanced at Afzul. '*Our* victory. It's for you to make it so.'

He gazed at her a moment; a strange, unsmiling look. Then he gravely inclined his head to the wrong partner and held out the balls.

'Your service, Lady Sinclair. Five — four.'

Tara, bent on winning, played better than she had hoped; and perhaps Lance was a shade more merciful to a less practised opponent. But she was aware of her partner distracted by the other pair, who were laughing a good deal, evidently enjoying themselves. The second time he missed an easy ball, she ventured a reminder — 'We've got to win her victory, you know.'

'We *will* win,' he replied, not looking at her. And after a spell of see-sawing, he scored the last point by a slashing stroke that made Eve jump a yard.

Chrystal sprang up to thank Tara and congratulate Afzul on failing to murder his hostess.

'I call that anyone's game,' said Lance.

'We call it *our* game,' she retorted. 'But we give full marks to the losers!'

The losers collapsed into canvas chairs. Lance invited the Fairy onto his knee. A *kit* was called to bring iced coffee and lemonade, sweet and savoury morsels. Sher Afzul sat down on the grass near Chrystal, speaking to her now and then in a low tone, while the others laughed and talked, and the sun freckled them all with patterns of light and shade.

'Hullo!' cried Lance suddenly. 'Here's the Babe.'

It was Vernon Leigh, in a smart flannel suit, come to 'pay respects'; and Lilāmani, deserting Lance, ran to him. He swung her off her feet; but he had eyes only for Tara.

'Oh, dear, what *have* I done to him?' she thought in dismay.

After greetings, it came out that he wanted to secure her and Lilāmani for a short flight in his Moth plane next day, out towards the Khyber and Jamrud. But Tara was non-committal, evading his reproachful gaze; wondering what Thea would think of Roy's tiresome wife if she caught her boy of twenty looking, in that tone of voice, at a woman just turned eight and thirty?

What Thea thought of it, Tara discovered next day, when the new Governor's wife 'blew in' after a second brilliant gathering, at which the Local Council had been warned to 'make haste slowly' if they desired full success for 'the most daring and momentous political experiment ever attempted by any branch of the human race.'

Thea quoted the Viceroy's memorable words in a platform voice; adding, in conversational tones, 'And of course we all sang out "Hear, hear!" to that.'

But she had come for a personal talk with Tara; and here she found her son paying more respects, obviously pleased with things in general.

'What are *you* doing out of school at this hour?' she asked, with mock severity.

'I'm enjoying myself,' he stated simply.

'That's fairly obvious! My turn now.'

He turned beseeching eyes on Tara. 'Have I *got* to go?'

And she felt grateful to Thea for saying briskly, 'Yes. This is my show. You run along and play with Lilāmani. She's flirting quite capably with your *sais*. And I'd rather it was you!'

'So would I,' echoed Tara.

He laughed at that, and took his dismissal with a good grace.

'This afternoon, then.' He tried to hold Tara's eyes, but she would not have it.

The curtain fell behind him, and the two women looked at each other. It was Thea who spoke.

'Tara, you sinner! You've bewitched my Babe, who has always doted on *me*.'

Tara looked distressed. 'At my age? — Impossible.'

'Dear innocent, when a man's a man and a woman has charm, all things are possible — if not expedient. Men and women are God's queerest invention. They've got to take themselves as He made them.'

'But your boy — of all people.'

'Lucky for my boy. At nineteen they've got to be smitten with someone. Better it should be you than one of our practised baby snatchers.' Her whimsical smile ended in a sigh. 'It's terrible the way we're all doomed to hurt each other with utter good will in our hearts.'

Tara caught a gleam of tears. 'It's lovely of you taking it like this. I feel I've been stupid. I've become such a home bird these last difficult years. I've lost my social instincts.'

'You've probably found better things. Social instincts overdevelop out here. What's on with him this afternoon?'

'Oh, he wants to take us up in his Moth plane, and I'm hoping to substitute Eve. But he would be pathetic and disappointed.'

'Better go with him. Treat it lightly. And tomorrow you come to me. With any luck, you may get a peep at Vinx.'

'I'm longing for that. And longing for the move on to Kashmir. When . . .?'

'As soon as we can detach Eve from Lance. You simply can't do that journey alone. She doesn't half like leaving so early. But Lance is one of the rare men who puts the health of his wife and child before his own need of them. Chrystal goes up with Eve. Can you wait?'

'I must. But — if a wire should come ——?'

'Then, of course, we would send you by air,' said the Governor's wife, to whom all things were possible. 'Heavens! Look at the time. My lunch party. Vinx will think I've evaporated. For twenty good minutes I'd actually forgotten their Excellent Exes. See you this evening. Be kind to the boy — but not too kind.'

Relieved and cheered, though not eased of her fundamental ache, Tara took up her weary task of waiting for the word that might come any day, yet never came.

Chapter IV

Greatness is the vision, not the deed,
Greatness is to be one with the vision and ensue it.

HUMBERT WOLFE

IN A WORLD of mountains, more stupendous and terrible than any he had yet seen, Roy Sinclair stood alone, so changed in aspect that few except his wife would have known him. Dress and appearance suggested a high-caste Hindu scholar: his Indian shirt hanging outside, his wrinkled cotton trousers, his orange-yellow turban and sheepskin coat, his face and hands browned with walnut juice, his dark moustache severely clipped. But no device could alter the fine grey-blue eyes under their long eyebrows, the clean modelling of forehead, chin, and jaw, the firm-lipped English mouth and proud Rajput curve of the nostril.

The grey-blue eye itself is not uncommon in the North; a heritage from the white race reputed to have invaded India before the dawn of history, leaving a legacy of more than fair skin and blue eyes: a legacy of thought, religion, and philosophy of life, linking all who derive from them — in Europe and Asia — mainly through a common root language — the supreme expression of man's spirit. In that basic language, Sanskrit, the *Rishis* [1] of old gave India her Vedic philosophy, her sense of spiritual values that may yet conceivably save from self-destruction a bewildered yet truth-seeking world. And from that same Aryan descent — using the word, Indian-fashion, to imply a heritage of nobility in thought and aspiration — the Anglo-Saxon race derives the

[1] Wise men.

strain of idealism and high purpose that has made its people, at their best, born leaders of men.

To that underlying kinship between England and India, Sinclair had given much thought during his enforced months of solitude. To it he ascribed his own belief in an ultimate working together for good, that could alone solve the problems of other than political India. But these must be seen as common problems—British, Hindu, Moslem. All-India being too complex for any one community to control her destiny.

Let each recognise and admit an identical seed of the spirit. Let the aristocratic ideal, shared by all three, prevail over alien growths of communism and vote-catching. Let his own people exchange aloofness and veiled contempt for a spirit of sympathy and understanding. Let Indians cleanse their minds of intransigeance, distrust, or open hostility. Then indeed might a willing union between Western science and Eastern wisdom beget, in time, a world spirit of civilisation that would shame this machine-ridden semblance of it and astonish posterity.

To become a bridge-builder between those mighty opposites, derived from the same root, had been his arrogant dream at Oxford, nearly twenty years ago. To that ambitious task he had again pledged himself in the meridian of manhood; his purpose deepened, his faculties quickened by all he had experienced in this most illuminating year of his life. Well for him that he possessed, in full measure, the faculty of seeing the end of a high project in its inception. Only so could he hold his vision like a torch to light him on his way.

The man who had left England sixteen months ago and the man who now walked solitary in this unknown mountain world were the same, yet not the same. An indefinable change had been wrought in him by that mysterious reality, the magnetic power of India; by months of lonely communing with her holy Himalayas, rightly named Abode of the Gods. They gave a man more than their incomparable beauty and terror. They transformed his scale values and coloured his attitude to all things. They lifted him, if only for a time, to the eternal snows of the spirit.

Absorbed, he walked on and on in the living dusk before dawn. Behind him, out of sight, lay the sleeping camp with which he had lived and moved since the day when his fellow travellers had found him, unconscious, in the débris of a land-slide, that had swept away the whole of his small party and possessions. He had lain a long while as one dead, they told him, for what their word was worth; but they would not enlighten him as to his whereabouts or their destination. He himself knew nothing of this vast Kashmir borderland, a mountain world of surpassing grandeur and desolation; and since they avoided the regular track, there was little chance of any human encounter outside the camp, where the 'honoured guest,' treated politely as a Hindu Swami and scholar, had become virtually a prisoner.

His two companions described themselves as traders from the United Provinces: one Rāmanand, a gross, good-humoured fellow, slippery as an eel; the other, Dinanāth, a Lucknow merchant, lean and pockmarked, with an aggressive nose and an evil mouth. His plausible tongue and shifty glance suggested an opaque glazed surface, covering depths of deceit. Sinclair himself had seldom encountered a pair of Indians whom he liked less and distrusted more. Their Moslem man-of-all-work, friendly but unintelligent, went in fear of Dinanāth, as did the two boys who worked under him. One of them, a low-caste Hindu lad of sixteen, had been told off to act as the Swami's personal servant. He rejoiced in the poetic name of Gulbaddan, Body of the Rose; and he was not ill-looking in his half-fledged fashion; the weak mouth atoned for by a pair of intelligent brown eyes. His few and simple duties for the supposed Swami were fulfilled with the zeal of a devotee; and by now, Sinclair knew that he could count on the boy to serve him, at a pinch, if ever his own in-genuity could devise some means of escape from this freedom.

So far he had been hampered by ignorance of the country and the uncertainties of a baffling situation. A perceptible change, of late, in Dinanāth's manner had awakened the disturbing question: What if these men suspected him to be a Sahib? Might they conceivably let the fact be made known in Peshawar, counting on the possible offer of a ransom from the British Government? In that case, the news would in time reach Vincent's ears, and the day of release might dawn at last. Had not the pair soon shown themselves to be frankly anti-British, he would have taken the risk of making himself known. They both spoke with great caution in his presence, if ever their talk strayed beyond the staple Indian topics — food, money, and trade; but they took his anti-British sympathies for granted. India, they would admit, needed contact with all foreigners. She needed fresh air, fresh ideas; but there could be no friendship with any race that came in this guise of an 'imperialistic tiger.' According to Pundit Nehru, their revolutionary leader, the British must leave India before there could be any hope of acting in concord; but doubtless they would always find some plausible reason to remain.

More and more Sinclair felt convinced that the pair were trading in other things than merchandise. More than once he had caught veiled allusions to Russian influence on the Border, where the independent tribes were now playing England's game of 'votes for all'; and again, certain remarks dropped by Rahim Bux, the Moslem, suggested the fearsome possibility that Central Asia might be the goal of their mysterious undertaking, which they obsequiously desired him to bless.

The lost Hari Lāl — who never let his Sahib be worried by the mosquitoes of life — would by some means have squeezed information out of that stupid, friendly Moslem; would have found some way of getting a letter to Kashmir by *dāk* runner, though none seemed ever to visit this shifting camp at the end of nowhere. Now and then Ramanand would vanish for a few days; and he probably then received or sent their few letters, if any. It was clear that they kept an unobtrusive watch on all his own movements; and even if he could elude their vigilance, he would be completely at sea, unable to replenish his small store of cash, physically unequal to long hill marches in broken weather.

One treasure alone remained to him from the landslide;

the waterproof knapsack, containing all his valuable papers, with Tara's letters and home photographs. It was fastened with a catch-lock of which he alone knew the trick; and his rescuers, regarding it as personal luggage, had given it over to him when his dazed mind emerged from the fog that blotted out all recent events. The distant past was clear, like a splash of sunlight on water behind a curtain of cloud, that hid the near past, for a time: and the mental effort of trying to remember was apt to bring back the deadly concussion headache that troubled him less often now. In this life-giving mountain air, mind and body were renewed. The cloud slowly dissolved. Details emerged.

Too clearly he could now recall his vain rebellion against the enforced renouncing of his plan to return home in the autumn.

> *I do not ask if you will come*, Sri Samādhi had written, in characteristic fashion, *I am sure of it, as I am sure the sun will rise tomorrow.... I am waiting. Come.*

For him, that fateful letter had amounted to a command from the man he had recognised at sight as Master of his spiritual life. He it was who had foreseen how the very discords of his own double nature might be fused, by a full awakening of his over-self, into a source of power and two-fold vision. To that end, he had bidden his *chela* renounce for a time all that his normal manhood most deeply loved and desired. Of the inner strife involved between his Eastern soul and his Western heart none would ever know the real truth, not even Tara herself. Yet now, looking back across six months of isolation, he could recognise that his Guru had done well not only for him, but for those whom he had, in common phrase, deserted. And some day Tara would know it also; would forgive and understand, as few wives could be trusted to do.

Never, while he lived, would he forget those autumn months in Kashmir: his underlying heartache subdued by daily *Yoga* practice of breath control and meditation; his absorbing study of ancient holy writ under the guidance of a master mind. Under that same guidance he had been led into the Way of Wisdom through the six first principles — silence, listening, remembering, understanding, judgment, and action; through closing the doors of physical busy-ness, that inner windows might open on to new vistas of the Path. Deep in talk of 'the Big Little Things,' they sat or strolled under mighty chenars, gold, crimson, and bronze, a harmony of rhythm and design, steeped in the all-pervading peace of these holy Himalayas. Day after day he had enjoyed the congenial march of mind with mind essential to fruitful intercourse. For this man of his mother's race possessed the key to his own complex nature; possessed also an Eastern brain of unusual clarity, precision, and humour, apt qualities for blazing a trail through the jungle of Hindu thought.

It had been a wrench having to leave Kashmir late in November, to put even this new-found human link behind him; and the Home letters, written to arrive at Christmas, had gone near to shatter all stoical resolves. But mind and body were already adjusting themselves to higher demands on them, answering to inner changes as a boat answers to the rudder. Over the Haji Pir Pass he had tramped, with his two servants and few belongings, down into the small Native State of Poonch, where the Rajah had made him hospitably welcome as friend and *chela* of the Guru Maharāj.

There in the State guest house and in camp he had lived a studious life of austerity. There the foundations of his book-to-be had been well and truly laid. Faithfully he had obeyed his Master's parting behest: 'Practise meditation daily, with love in your heart, at the hour of dawn or twilight, when the heavenly calm begets calm within you. Keep the Sun in your mind's heaven. Let him flood your whole being with light.'

So he had done. So he had proved. But no turning away from the world could weaken the link of a lifetime with Tara. Night after night, for one cherished hour, he would commune with her in a diary letter designed to tell her, afterwards, how intimately she had shared in the ordeal imposed on him of subduing all human desires to the greater end.

Clearly now he could recall the first spell of complete detachment, thought and sensation merged in the one commanding purpose of his book, that seemed at times to flow in upon him like light from another sphere; the revived mental impetus driving his thoughts onto paper with a swiftness and certainty that recalled his earlier weeks of isolation at Udaipur. Isolation — solitude: the eternal need for artist or thinker. Back to self and Nature, away from the pressure of crowd thoughts and emotions, from the insidious influence of other minds. Only so could sense and spirit lie open to intuitions that spring from deeper levels than the reasoning talkative brain; that come, like shy birds, in the silences between one urgent busy-ness and another. Much poetry also had resulted from his lonely communing with these hills in every changing aspect; poetry of a finer quality than any of his earlier work: imbued with the touch of austerity that had come into his life. To be writing it again, after many sterile years, was a sure sign of renewed spiritual health.

For an age beset with doubt and superstition, only the twin arts, poetry and music, could lead the soul to forget itself and find itself in wonder; could hasten the dawn of an era — not inconceivable — when the world's high priest would be the artist: Beethoven, Leonardo, and Shakespeare its major prophets: priests of a religion without dogma, confirming the creed of Plato that Truth and Beauty are one, that in unison they generate the Good.

A man must go solitary if he is to see beyond himself, to discover the hidden sources of his power; and a spell of solitude, absorbed in work and contemplation, had been good for mind and body: not so good when fever laid him low, and delirium brought distracting illusions of Tara's presence, distracting fears for her well being; and when severe inflammation of the eyes debarred him from attempting to read or write. For weeks he had lived in a semi-twilight, haunted by the dread of blindness, tantalised by flitting fragments of thought or of poems that sang themselves in the dark, like birds in a covered cage.

Then one restless, fevered night, as he lay wakeful towards

morning, there had stolen on his senses, faint and far, a wandering ghost of music, vaguely known to him. When? Where? As the familiar sound evoked pictures he remembered. It was the *bhairavi*, the dawn tune, played to him by Aruna one early morning at Udaipur. From her, sweet singer and player, he had learnt to appreciate the 'sound patterns' of Indian music, harmonising with certain times of the day and year; only to be played at such times, lest they clash with the unheard sound of life — the 'soundless ever sounding,' for those who have ears to hear. That blessing at least was not denied him: and as he lay there, soothed, entranced, the tuneless tune had wandered through his brain like a beam of light in darkness — till his troubled thoughts were stilled and the misery of his fevered body charmed away. Peace and healing flowed through his veins; and he sank into a profound sleep.

When at last he awoke, the fever had abated; and it did not return. He had discovered the true healer.

He commanded that the singer and player should be found; and they were found. They sang and played to him, at midnight, the dramatic chant that defies evil powers of darkness. They gave him at dusk the eerie song of twilight; reed-flute and voice and a little *tabla* [1] throbbing through them like a pulse of the dying day. The fascination of hearing that strange music, undistracted by sight, had evoked certain curious poems. Born in darkness and stamped on his brain, they had not been written till the Rajah's State doctor — a skilled herbalist — restored him to sunlight and books and the faces of his fellow men; allaying, with unguents and lotions, the inflammation that had blinded him.

It was the doctor who had suggested a change to higher hills on the Kashmir border; and there, as the Rajah's guest, Sinclair had spent an unspecified time, restored to the lost companionship of mountains, the inspiration of sunset and dawn, the stimulant of revived mental activity. He had seen no papers; had known nothing of events in the important outside world of new-born 1932, that seemed curiously of no

[1] Small drum.

account in this world of natural beauty, of simple needs and simple lives. Nor could he glean any accurate idea as to how long he had been ill, or what the date might be. Nature told him that spring was at hand; and in spring he had planned to be back with Tara, restored to the warmth of human love and understanding that had never failed him in all their married years. Remembrance of her evoked the constant, haunting question: Was all well with her, would they ever meet again?

India had enriched him beyond measure. To live among these incomparable mountains, to imbibe their lonely, listening beauty, was to experience an inner transfiguration, to remain for ever under their spell. And he himself had given to India the utmost that his conflicting needs and duties would permit. He had merged himself in the life of her people in the great northern provinces and Kashmir. He had sought and found illumination among her eternal hills, because to see clearly one must step far back. But there remained the counter-pull of his Western heritage. It was time now to return, bringing his sheaves with him; and there, isolated from India's potent influence — give the world such measure as he might of all he had gleaned from her; emphasising the need for an Indian renaissance based on Aryan ideals that alone could heal the discords of Hindu and Moslem, East and West.

Hard on that decision, he had despatched two letters, one to Sri Samādhi, the other to Tara announcing his freedom to move homeward at last, so soon as he was fit for rough marching. He had then been still further delayed by his encounter with young Shivanath, the Cambridge graduate, so completely Easternised that, for a few hours, he himself had been deceived. That many young Englishmen, bereft of faith, were looking for a star in the East, was common knowledge. It was no common event to meet, in the flesh, one who firmly believed — and acted on the belief — that there could be no leadership, no security, no peace or true happiness, till men could once again lose themselves in some Power greater than themselves; could admit, unashamed, their belief in a life beyond life. And Sinclair had been deeply moved to find that it was the most notable of his own earlier books, *This India*, which had inspired another to accomplish what he himself could not do, for all the Eastern blood in his veins. But that other was neither married nor steward of a great inheritance; and in his own view, *Yoga* practice should spell balance of mind in action; not the withdrawn, but the transfigured life.

Shivanath himself had refused to admit the imputation of selfishness levelled against the ascetic idea. There could not be very many, he argued, who would feel impelled, like himself, to discard personality and possessions; and it might be well for the world that a few men so-minded should withdraw from its unending activity for the sake of clearer vision. In the West, things dominated humanity. One could not see the wood for the trees. To realise man, one had need to escape from men. 'The jungle sage,' he had shrewdly opined, 'may not be inferior, after all, to the worldly fool.' And on that conclusion they had let the matter rest.

It had been a curious and interesting experience, that brief contact between two half-Indianised Englishmen among the eternal hills; a mental stimulant after long isolation. Sinclair would fain have prolonged it. But the other was bound for a shrine of peculiar sanctity: and his own face was turned towards wife and home.

When all was ready for the first march, a man from Hathu Pir had arrived with news of a *dāk* runner found dead, mauled by a leopard, his clothes and mail-bag torn, its contents scattered past retrieving. Among them must have been his own two letters, and his lifted heart had dropped like a stone. Useless to lament. He would be reaching Kashmir in a week: and thence he would write again to Tara.

But heavy rain, following on snowfalls high up, had moved Hari Lāl to suggest waiting another week or two, the road being in bad repair. It was as if all things conspired against him, at this eleventh hour; and even his disciplined spirit could brook no further delay. Useless to wait upon the weather, he argued, in this broken season; he would take his chance. And for Hari Lāl an order was an order, wise or otherwise; neither he nor his master guessing that this particular order amounted to a death-warrant for himself and several other harmless fellow men. Even now the remembrance was too painful to dwell upon. The brief delay, that he had girded at, was as nothing to that which had been laid upon him through overriding the wisdom of his lost bearer.

On the second day's march, his small party had been almost drowned by a sudden dense rain, as if a celestial tank had burst. In the midst of it — a rending roar; the earth slipping away from under his feet; yells of terror from his few coolies; and Hari Lāl seizing his arm in a futile, desperate impulse to drag him out of danger, when above and below and around them all was danger. He could remember now a nightmare sensation of tumbling headlong, down and down, clutching instinctively at fragments of loosened trees: one dazed thought before darkness fell, '*This* is the end of it all.'

And with the thought came a cruelly clear picture of Tara's face as he had seen it last; the carved blue beads, her blue eyes misted with tears, the controlled quiver of her sensitive lips. And as her arms went out to him, there came a stunning crash — the end indeed.

After that, a long, long darkness; how long he did not know. Time had been blotted out. A chasm in his memory so sharply divided 'then' from 'now,' that he seemed to have passed through a tunnel; to have emerged into another world.

He could recall only a confused lesser darkness, in which figures moved and handled him; a stunned head; a vain effort at coherent thought; an unknown face grinning at him when he opened his eyes; a voice assuring him that he had not been killed after all.

Instinctively remembering, his hand went to his head; but only a ghost of the deadly concussion ache troubled him now; a ghost revived by dwelling in thought on that terrible moment, as he seldom allowed himself to do. No thinking could call back yesterday or raise from the dead his lost Hari

Lāl, who would long ago have discovered some means of escape from an intolerable situation.

They were somewhere between Srinagar and Gilgit, though well off the regular road. That much he knew; and it meant that they were at least not outside the Kingdom of Kashmir. Yet, as to practical means of escape he might almost as well be in the Mountains of the Moon. If he could but manage to let Sir Havelock Thorne know that he was alive and in this region, the rest might be left to his sagacity. But how — but how?

The answer eluded him; and the spring days were slipping like pearls through his fingers. March or April it must be by now; the month of Tara's birthday and the child's, and he not with them, for all his haste that had resulted in less speed.

Baffled, yet refusing to admit defeat, he stood still, closed his eyes, gently slowed down the normal rhythm of his breathing, as in his daily exercise, and deliberately withdrew his mind from the outer atmosphere of personal distractions into the place of quiet 'where thoughts lie stilled like charmed serpents.'

For several minutes he stood so, breathing in that gentle fashion which so magically calmed the nerves. Then, as on an empty screen, there appeared a familiar face — the boy, Gulbaddan. The sensuous lips, the appealing eyes hovered on the verge of speech. 'Swami-Sahib, send *me*,' they seemed to say: and in that moment he knew the solution had been given him.

But details remained to be devised. Could he bear to banish — possibly to lose — his personal servant, the one human creature with whom he had achieved friendly relations? And the boy himself knew next to nothing of the country. Could he be persuaded to undertake the lonely trek of a hundred miles or so? There would have to be initial payment for road expenses from his own small hidden store; but more could surely be promised when the letter was delivered to the Resident of Kashmir in person.

The inner voice urged: 'There is no other hope. Take the risk. It will not fail.' And to that extent the matter was settled. He would plant the thought like a seed in his mind during his daily meditation. Afterwards he would find some means of speaking to the boy alone.

The living dusk had lightened perceptibly. Dawn was at hand.

Chapter V

The pain was great while the strings were being tuned, my Master.
Pour your heart into my life strings, in tunes that descend
From your stars.

RABINDRANATH TAGORE

ON THE edge of the narrow path he stood still and looked about him at a world of ghostly mountains emerging from a sea of mist that veiled the valley miles below, where the hidden river hurtled over rocks and boulders with a roar like breakers on a wild coast. Against the solemn sky — grey-violet, pricked with stars — rock profiles loomed, steadfast as a sworn purpose. Between films of dove-grey cloud, constellations of astonishing brilliance flashed low and clear. In the far South, dissolving mists revealed the twin peaks of Nanga Parbat; a mirage of a mountain outsoaring her peers.

And while Sinclair stood entranced, there drifted through his mind the words of Tagore:

Dawn sleeps behind the shadowy hills;
the stars are counting the hours.

Nothing on earth seemed real that did not match the sublimity, the desolation, and grandeur of these heights, half seen, half hidden, awaiting the first word of creation, 'Let there be light!'

On a flat rock he sat down cross-legged, hands lightly folded, body erect, his breath coming and going so gently that it could scarcely be perceived; his mind reaching out to the millions all over India, who awaited the dawn like himself, in prayer or meditation, or in the waters of some sacred river. Every morning, everywhere, an endless stream of worship rising, like invisible incense, from mountains and forests and cities; from holy and terrible Hindu temples, from austere mosques of Islam, from simple shrines and hermit caves. Everywhere the same unending ritual, the chanting of prayers and hymns sung, at that same hour, from the far-off beginning of days, when Aryan worshippers improvised their inspired paeans to the rising sun.

That was India. Her people's ingrained impulse of worship must be realised by all who aspired to know anything of this god-intoxicated country.

And he, sitting alone with closed eyes, drew his mind away from conscious thought, from frets and personal anxieties, to the secret Place of Quiet at the centre of his being; a centre not of darkness but of light. Bathed in that living radiance from the Self that transcended self, his becalmed mind rested in the words of his familiar ***mantra:***

I am thy Dawn, from darkness to release:
I am the Deep wherein thy sorrows cease.
Be still, be still, and know that I am God——

How long the spell lasted he never knew, nor was there any need to know. The intensity of the experience was all.

Roused by a sense of quickening outer light, he opened his eyes on a world that still hovered between night and day. Stars had vanished. Venus, rayless and silver-pale, kept watch in a sky that quivered with foreknowledge of dawn.

This morning it came almost unheralded: the veiled ghost of a sun slipping sideways from behind a dark and craggy peak. And at the same moment there rose, from the half-shrouded gorge below, a great lammergeier, the outspread wings so wide that the span of them seemed to measure an appreciable fraction of the ravine. Up out of the night he sailed, that kingly bird, the silent spirit of the wild; and below him, eight thousand feet down, the spectral river swirled and foamed through granite gateposts, between weather-scarred cliffs and shattered débris; a scene of savage grandeur only redeemed by flecks and flashes of young green.

By now the whole southward view was filled with the

majestic mass of Nanga Parbat; thirteen thousand feet of snow and glacier and stainless summit, like a throne set in heaven: the one familiar friend among these stranger giants of the Hindu Rāj and Hindu Khush. Profoundly he now knew that it was well for a man, at whatever cost, to have lived in daily communion with this glorious company of mountains, rooted in earth yet more nearly akin to heaven. From them he had drawn a new steadfastness of mind, an ability to see men and things in truer perspective — the first necessity of life and art. This morning he emerged from his baptism of light with a clearer brain, a more resolute will to face the long pause of not knowing, that must follow the despatch of Gulbaddan on his doubtful errand. Willing or unwilling, go he must.

And as if to clinch that desperate decision, there appeared round a bend in the path a familiar lanky figure in *dhoti* and shoulder blanket, dangling above the loose-jointed limbs of a young calf; unmistakably Gulbaddan, with his early offering of fruit and milk. Here was the chance of a talk that could not be overheard. The boy must be sworn to secrecy: and he must set out today — if he could be persuaded, bribed, or commanded to face the adventure.

With a seraphic smile, he ambled forward, laid on the rock his gourd of milk and leaf-dish of apricots, set his palms together, and made obeisance as to a holy image.

'The Swami-Sahib,' he murmured, 'walked far today; and this slave feared for his safety.'

The Swami-Sahib, emptying his gourd, looked very straight into a pair of adoring eyes.

'Do you know in your heart,' he asked, 'whether I am indeed a Swami or a Sahib?'

One moment the boy hesitated; then surprisingly he answered: 'To this slave it appears that Your Honour is indeed a Swami — and also a Sahib, not desiring to be known.'

Sinclair, taken aback, asked quickly, 'Have you said so to any in the camp?'

'*Na*, *na*, Sahib. This one speaks not till a word is given.'

Here was proof of intelligence and loyalty.

'The word is not given, because I do not desire to be known in the camp,' Sinclair stated, boldly taking his risk. 'My order is that nothing be said to those others.'

Again two hands were raised in reverence. 'Holiness, the order is obeyed.'

And Sinclair, reassured, went on: 'There is another order to be given for an errand of importance. I must have entire obedience; I must give entire trust. It is this. A secret letter must be taken quickly, from me to the Kashmir Burra Sahib at Srinagar. It can only be taken by you.'

'But *Hazúr*' — the expectant gaze changed to dismay. 'I belong to these men. I am a stranger here.'

'Yet it must be done. It is a matter of my life. You are a *hoshiar chokra*.[1] You know Kashmir. By asking you can soon find the Gilgit Road that leads to Srinagar. There are rest-houses by the way, and *dāk* runners with mail-bags. If you join one of these, you will have no more trouble.'

A happy thought flashed. 'I give him that letter?'

'No, you give it to none but the Burra Sahib himself. When he knows where I am, he will find means to remove me from these men. It is *you*, my faithful servant, who must bring them here: and great will be your reward.'

In spite of that magic word, tears welled up and overflowed. The boy knelt down and laid his forehead on Sinclair's foot.

'*Hazúr*, Holy One, from my heart I beg *do* not send me from the Presence. If Your Honour would come also —— ?'

'If that were possible I would have gone long ago, taking you with me. There is no way, Gulbaddan, for me to leave this camp except through obedience to my order. Now listen. I give you the sealed letter, with money for the road and extra for *baksheesh*. When you deliver it safe to the Burra Sahib, he will give you more money, by my request. Whoever he may send here, you will return to guide them, in case the camp has moved. If all goes well, and they take me back to Kashmir, you go with me in my service.'

[1] Clever boy.

'But *Hazúr*, if I return, these *badmàshes* ——' He lowered his voice as if the very hills might be their allies.

Sinclair laid a hand on his shoulder.

'Have no fear. I will see that no harm befalls one who has done me so great a service.'

'*Hazúr!*'

An uprush of adoration submerged his Eastern shrinking from responsibility and risk.

'I will go secretly, as bidden. But when they discover my absence — what then?'

'That will be my affair. You depart after placing the midday meal in my tent. Between that time and sunset I shall be absent on a long walk, and they may suppose you have gone with me. On my return I shall show no concern for your absence, except that I am inconvenienced. If they wish to seek you, I must baffle them and demand another servant, that suspicion be not aroused. They are not likely to make much trouble about one *chokra* more or less. Now all is clear; and my word is as sure as these hills. Will you do this service for your Swami-Sahib? If not, it is possible that I may never see my home or my own people again.'

He stated the fact without emphasis or emotional appeal. But the boy's lips quivered and he wept without shame.

Sinclair, hardening his heart of necessity, took his unpromising knight-errant by the shoulders, not ungently.

'Gulbaddan, what answer is this? I ask a man's work of you, and you give me a woman's tears. If you desire to get me away from this camp, there is only one proof to be given; face your journey and deliver my letter with all possible speed. Prove that you are now a man — and win a man's reward.'

Shamed by that straight appeal, the boy choked back his sobs and spoke with a valiant attempt at control.

'*Hazúr*, I go. My long legs are useful for trotting quickly. If I do not return, then these hills or some devil of the hills will have taken my life.'

'You *will* return,' Sinclair assured him, not merely to stiffen his courage. In the centre of his mind, he knew that his own hour of release was at hand. Swift decision and action had a tonic effect after unspecified weeks of resignation. He would promptly return to camp and write his letters. Gulbaddan had best not return till later; keep away from his fellows and not be seen near his master except when bringing the midday meal, which his sanctity preferred to eat in private.

So they parted, only to meet once again, when the meal was served, the secret letter written and sealed for despatch.

To the Resident, Sinclair wrote:

Dear Sir Havelock:

There has probably been some concern at Peshawar headquarters on account of my prolonged absence and silence. The cause, or causes, of my strange behaviour cannot be written here. All I can say now is that I am alive and more or less well; that I am, perforce, in camp with a pair of very fishy traders (so-called) somewhere between Kashmir Valley and Gilgit, a good way off the regular road. Ignorant of the country, lacking money and means of transport, I have been virtually held up by this precious pair for reasons of their own. They picked me out from the débris of a landslide, knocked silly with concussion, the only survivor of my small party; and they seem to be trekking for Central Asia. Only now I have been able to send word of my existence, by the boy who carries this. He can be trusted in any matter that concerns my safety. I have given him money for the road, and promised that you will give him twenty rupees on delivery of this, as from me.

Please send a party jut-put[1] *in this direction, police for choice, with a responsible officer qualified to take over mine hosts, if eligible for arrest. I can't be sure of this. So it's a case for the iron hand in a velvet glove. Let the boy, Gulbaddan, guide them. As I said, we are off the track, and these two have a way of suddenly shifting camp. So my final word is — the quicker the better; and I should be grateful if you or Sir Vincent would at once cable to my wife. Please also give the Guru Maharāj news of my dilemma. Respectful salaams from*

Yours very sincerely,

LE ROY SINCLAIR

[1] At once.

The sealed treasure — wrapped in a piece of old waterproof — he sewed inside Gulbaddan's shirt; and the boy, gulping down womanish tears, laid his forehead again on Sinclair's foot; vowing, in the name of his private god, that, unless death took him, he would infallibly return with those who could release his master from the snare of evil men. Leaving the tent unobserved, he slipped away from the camp, while his fellow-servant Nur-ud-din lay curled up, sleeping off his dinner like a dog.

And there descended on Sinclair an intensified loneliness, sharpened by the nagging ache of suspense.

His plan for being absent all the afternoon, his vexation at the disappearance of his attendant, worked well. Nur-ud-din could throw no light on the matter; and when next day brought no sign of the truant, he denounced Gulbaddan as 'one big fool: no eyes in his head.' He might have lost his balance mooning round and tumbled down the Khud. Rahim Bux seconded the bright idea. Nur-ud-din 'took on' the Swami-Sahib; and the lost youth vanished from the minds of all except the one man who counted the days to his return.

Chapter VI

The men who catch the gleam — they are the world's true leaders.

'NUMA'

TWELVE days later, on an unclouded morning of blue distance and shining summits, Sinclair sat outside his tent at a camp-table freely strewn with papers, half his mind intent on them, the other half tormented with vain fears for Gulbaddan, with dread of a sudden order to shift camp, a move that might hamper discovery. Rāmanand had returned only last night from a few days' absence. One never knew what these absences might signify, and the two had sat up late together.

By now, with any luck, the boy must have reached Srinagar. That meant yet another ten days crawling past, anxiety held aloof by concentration on the difficult task he had set himself to make his readers see India with understanding minds and hearts, as too few ever did, even Indians themselves; to emphasise the absolute need of an aristocratic basis for the latest London suggestion of creating a Federal India. With his princely heritage, his knowledge of Eastern thought and tradition, he could see only one acceptable and workable form of Federation: to convert all British Indian provinces into principalities, under a chosen ruler — Moslem, Hindu, or Sikh — with a Viceroy and Indian Council to keep a guiding hand on the reins. Even to the least perceptive it must be clear that India — a monarch country — tended naturally to respect the ruler rather than the figurehead, the voice from Sinai rather than the voice from the arena. Opposition from the political-minded, the Moscow-inspired, would surely yield to the prevailing spirit of the land.

Let him only succeed in firing the minds and imaginations of a few noteworthy men, English and Indian: the hardest task of all. He knew his father's people too well to indulge in any easy optimism on that score. But he also knew that England's tradition for achieving the impossible rested on no fantastic basis; witness that 'highest expression of national genius, the English administration of India.' Could she only add to her many real boons the crowning, coveted gift — a little genuine love and understanding of a people, who would prize, above all material blessings, a sincere impulse of the heart. For the Indian problem was more than political. It was social and racial; a matter of seeing through another man's eyes. And his own concern in the coming book was neither with politics nor with parliaments, but with the greater task of awakening both races to a spirit of fellowship, in working out their common destiny, that alone could bring mighty things to pass. 'Knowing the possible, see thou try beyond it': that must be the keynote of his call to the countries united within him.

As the credit for creating modern India belonged to the best brains and characters of both races, so the greater creation of a Federated India could only be achieved by Englishmen and Indians, who could rise to the height of such an opportunity as history has rarely offered to any two nations on earth. Without some fresh infusion of leadership and idealism, no success could spring from even the most generous measure of self-government. Given that new spirit, and the right men to foster it, a thousand years of hidebound convention might conceivably vanish in a few decades.

Given the right men; it came back always, the simple yet disregarded fact that the most important thing on earth is no abstract ideal of life or form of government, but the intelligent, balanced, high-minded human being. And for creating the new spirit, the finer type of man, one could rely on India's women, with their widening outlook, their new sense of responsibility balanced by their Indian ideals of loyalty, self-devotion, graciousness, and proud modesty. His own implicit reliance on them recalled the words spoken by his fine old grandfather in their last talk on the subject at Udaipur: 'Through women we are all born and shaped. Through our women we shall be saved...'

That memory of *Bapu* [1] deflected his thoughts into a more personal channel. It hurt him to think how the old man must have been grieved and worried by his long, unwilling silence. Meet once more they must, even if it delayed his journey to Bombay.

Restless again, and only half satisfied with his roughly written passages, he stowed away his papers, and decided to take a short walk, his only diversion, in the hope of quieting his disturbance of mind.

Absently he strolled on and on along the path taken by Gulbaddan ten or twelve days ago; oblivious, for once, of his surroundings, his midday meal forgotten. Dread of some imminent move weighed heavily on his mind; and his tiresome imagination was in perfect working order. One had to face the fact of possible failure in a dozen ways. By now, with any luck, the boy should have reached Srinagar. For him that meant dragging through another week or more of blank uncertainty: and then——? The longing for personal freedom had never so sharply beset him.

Suddenly he stood still and listened. Footsteps, voices were approaching round a sharp bend in the path. What now? Braced for any event, he confronted three strangers, who halted and stared at him: Moslems all, from the look of them. Two were broad bearded fellows, the third a young stalwart of Afridi type. The taller man, heavily bearded, wore his untidy turban down over one eyebrow. His vague pale eyes might be Afghan, but the blunt features were not Semitic like his companions'.

The elder one, a pockmarked son of Ben-i-Israel, took stock of Sinclair with a wary eye, and gave him the Pathan greeting, 'May you never be tired.'

The other, after emitting a deep-toned '*Salaam Aleikum*,'

[1] Grandfather.

spoke in Hindi. 'We have news, friend, of a small camp along this ridge. Two merchants travelling northward. We have urgent business with them. Can you direct us?'

'There *is* a camp,' Sinclair cautiously admitted, marvelling what business these Border folk could have with his unpleasant pair. 'You are expected?'

'We are *not* expected.'

The man's compelling gaze searched his face: and suddenly he wondered, 'Where *have* I seen those queer, pale eyes before?'

A lift of the lids, oddly familiar, answered him; and in a lightning flash he knew. By what marvel had this man, of all others, dropped from heaven?

He had need to steady himself before he ventured one word in a low tone: 'Lynch?'

A gleam in those unsmiling eyes answered his query before the deep voice said, without a flicker of surprise, 'Sinclair?'

'Yes.'

'Cute of you. I've never been caught out before.'

He turned with a gesture to the two Afridis, who fell back a few yards. Then he spoke again in the same low tone: 'I ought to have known you first, seeing I'm after you.'

'After me?' Sinclair echoed in a dazed voice.

'Didn't you send an S.O.S.?'

'I did. But only about ten days ago. A matter of a hundred miles. Man, it's impossible.'

Lynch smiled then for the first time. 'With the air arm,' he said, 'all things are possible. When Thorne got your note, I had just sent a line to my wife, who is at the Residency. So he had an inkling of my whereabouts. Not so sleepy as he looks, he promptly commandeered a plane from H. H., fired it off my way — not far from here — with two policemen and your *chokra* for guide. A *hoshiar baccha*,[1] in a blue funk at the machine and deathly sick, but hanging on to his wits. We were a bit off the track, but the pilot's no fool. And here we amazingly are.'

[1] Child.

Sinclair drew a deep breath. 'Of all the marvels! And where's my *chokra* now?'

'Back there with my police-*log* and the skittish little plane.'

'How the devil did you find a landing-place — here?'

'Natural intelligence raised to the *n*th degree! My unfailing ally "in tight corner." But I hand it to the pilot and your *chokra*, no less. The pilot vowed a landing was impossible. When I pointed out a clear space beside a gully, he asked — would I be responsible if we crashed? I said I would. My shoulders are fairly broad, and H. H. is a sportsman. That fetched him, and he brought it off slick. Extra luck running into you like this. You can give me the ropes. My knowledge of these wandering rogues is extensive and peculiar. Are they from Lucknow?'

'Yes. Nehru men, out and out.'

'What names — at the moment? I've a list of half a dozen aliases against one firebrand, whom I've been after for years.'

'They call themselves Rāmanand and Dinanāth.'

'Dinanāth?' Lynch raised his level eyelids in the odd way that had revealed him. 'Pockmarked on the forehead? A high nose, shifty eyes, and a mouth that shuts like a trap?'

'You've sketched him to a T. A personal friend?'

'A personal enemy would be nearer the mark. Talk of luck! Devadās was his last, but Dinanāth also runs. The fellow is one of the main links in a chain of liaison workers between the Soviet nest of serpents in Central Asia and Northern India. Frustrating their little game is one of my keenest interests in life. Lance was nearly snuffed out, two years ago, in a plucky attempt to nab this very scoundrel for me. And I lost the finest detective that I've ever had, for which I owe Mr. Dinanāth a knife-thrust. And I've got him — *so*. My God!'

He clenched his square fist and a steely light gleamed in his eyes. Sinclair had never seen his equanimity so nearly shaken. But he righted himself and remarked in his dryly humorous vein: 'I congratulate you, Sinclair, on your choice of a kidnapper — if it amounted to that? A beastly experience, but you've done Government and the Police a valuable service. The Bear is very efficiently at work beyond the Hindu Khush. All that region swarming with agitators against anything and anybody, especially British India. But it's my private opinion that the Soviets have about shot their bolt in that line. They've the world's job to control their own millions. And the way we're slackening hold on India may give 'em a notion that it's not worth so much as they supposed. — But Lord, I'm forgetting. I've got news for you. A letter' — he unearthed it and held it out — 'from Lady Sinclair.'

'My — wife?' Sinclair queried in a strange voice. 'From Home?'

'No: from Srinagar. She's at the Residency.'

'In *India?* Good God!' For one dizzying moment the whole scene swam before his eyes. Then, sharply, he righted himself. 'How —? Since when?'

'The air arm again. She arrived a few weeks ago. She's there, now, waiting for you.'

Behind that last astounding statement, Sinclair divined an unspoken, 'More than you deserve'; but to this man he could never justify himself. And he needed all his wits to compass a brief reply.

His pause, that was longer than he knew, moved Lynch to a show of fellow feeling.

'Shaken you up a bit?' he said, his hand closing on Sinclair's elbow. 'You stay and read your letter. I'll take my fellows along to the camp. Will you tell my policemen I'll whistle when I need them.'

Practical injunctions brought Sinclair to earth.

'How about my luggage?' he asked. 'My papers ——'

'Trust me. We'll be there for tiffin.'

'Tiffin ——?' At Sinclair's dazed voice, Lynch smiled.

'You've lost the habit? You'll soon pick it up now. My wife's there too. She'll be glad to see you again. Been worrying a bit.'

'Grace?'

Lynch looked amused. 'That's her name!'

Their eyes met in a frank friendliness new to Sinclair; and Lynch beckoned his Afridis, who came forward primed with curiosity.

'Now I'm going to enjoy myself,' he said, with a twitch of his left eyelid. 'Just as well for you to keep out of the picture. Come on, Umra Khan. Allah has delivered two *badmāshes* into our hands. You and Akbar stay outside, till you hear me cough. Then you come straight in and each *pukkerāo* one.'

Umra Khan grinned, showing both rows of teeth like a wolf; and the two Afridis went along with the man whom they would cheerfully have followed into hell's mouth had he given the word.

Arrived at the small camp, Lynch went on alone. Stepping with his curiously light tread, he came upon the uncomely pair seated in earnest confab over proof-like strips of paper, that were hastily thrust into a bag by the pockmarked villain, obviously his elusive quarry, given at last into his hands by Roy Sinclair, of all men on earth.

As he approached with *Salaam Aleikum*, they rose and stood before him, visibly disconcerted at sight of a stranger; but custom, and possibly caution, impelled them to the courtesy of asking him to sit down. They offered refreshment. They enquired if he were seeking any particular spot. He told them he had found the spot he sought. He had heard of two worthy travellers, who had done good work in India for the Tashkent people, and were returning to report progress. By good fortune it seemed that he had the pleasure to address those very men. He was romancing boldly, on the chance of hitting the mark; and a gleam in the suspicious eye of Dinanāth assured him that his shot had taken effect.

'I myself come from the Khyber country,' he stated, with intent to draw them out. 'Great *tamāsha* there with this new madness of votes.'

'Fools! Let them wait,' chuckled Rāmanand. 'Red Shirts are in the hands of Congress, acting as grit in the wheels of Government's motor car. They have done well at Charsadda and Mardān.'

Lynch nodded. 'I have heard of intimidation through ill-treating wives and children of men who went to record their votes.'

Rāmanand rubbed his hands.

'Those men will not easily be drawn away again for this fool's game of scratching marks on paper.'

Dinanāth shot a dagger glance at him, and he subsided into generalities.

They were clever enough to be cautious; but in Lynch they had met their match. With a question here, a morsel of inside knowledge there, he very soon satisfied himself that they were ripe for arrest. Putting up a hand, he coughed vigorously: once, twice.

Umra Khan and Akbar stepped into the tent.

Lynch stood up, a change in his whole bearing. And as the startled pair scrambled to their feet, each found himself grasped from behind; elbows pinioned and deftly roped together. The ingratiating Rāmanand became a plump and quivering jelly. His brown skin showed blotches of greenish pallor. Dinanāth's trap of a mouth snapped viciously, as if he would bite the hands that prisoned him; and his eyes looked murder at Lynch, who had whisked off the oppressive false beard, revealing a moustached and sunburnt Englishman.

'I am the Police Burra Sahib of Peshawar,' he said, without aggression. 'I know more about you than you fancy, Dinanāth, Devadās, Tulsi Ram, and all the rest of them. I know you are working with a chosen gang to shake the foundations of British rule in Northern India. You have — or had — in your camp a Sahib of high caste, from England, whom you have held by invisible chains against his will ——'

'We found him as one dead,' Rāmanand eagerly intervened. Neither hate nor dignity could override the one necessity — to save his own skin. 'But for our skilful care of him, he would now be dead indeed.'

'*Alive* he might be of higher value?' Lynch retorted with

a shrewd look. 'For instance, if a word were sent to Peshawar?'

Rāmanand looked blank, but ventured a last word.

'If the Swami-Sahib is a great one from England, surely some reward is our due.'

'The reward that is your due,' Lynch incisively assured him, 'will be paid in full when your account with the Sirkar has been made up. Meantime you will be handed over to the police-*lōg*; and I take charge of all papers that will doubtless be of use in settling your account.'

Again Dinanāth's eyes darted murder at Lynch, whose professional glow of satisfaction was deepened by his knowledge that the present Government could be relied on to give these devils their due. From his own secret records, he knew that they deserved the full rigour of the law; knew that Calcutta was still seething with inflammable material; and if these men were only two among thousands, their arrest might lead to the capture of others in the same line. On the whole, he found himself blessing Roy Sinclair, whom he had cursed root and branch in the hour of parting from Grace.

A shrill whistle summoned the policemen, who took over and handcuffed the pinioned pair, releasing the detectives for more responsible work. With their sullen charges, they must march back to Srinagar by road.

Lynch returned to find the great bird precariously tilted on its ledge, the pilot smoking in his cockpit; Gulbaddan on his haunches, gazing like a dog at his recovered master.

Sinclair sat apart on a jutting rock, turban removed, looking straight before him at the mighty wall of mountains that he would probably never see again. His complete stillness, his profound yet unseeing gaze reminded Lynch of that other abstracted figure at Nishāt Bagh. Instinctively, as before, he paused: and, for the first time since their long ago introduction, he saw the face of Roy Sinclair as a stranger might see it; not through the distorting glass of his instinctive bias against mixed breeding, and his no less instinctive male jealousy of the man who had so swiftly won the friendship and admiration of his own critical wife.

Today he perceived, as never before, signs of strength and fineness in the bone formation, of nobility in the brow and the firm set of the lips. More: he could vouch for some quality in the face that had not been there before: an impression of balance and poise, such as even his prejudiced eye could scarcely have overlooked. For he possessed an almost Eastern skill in reading men's faces and minds; a faculty dulled in the West by overmuch reading of newspapers and books. He had chosen to regard this special friend of Grace and Lance and Sir Vincent — good judges all — as a handsome, overestimated semi-Rajput idealist, likely to be as little reliable as most half-and-halfs in his own varied experience. Now, he looked with detached curiosity at a face that unmistakably revealed rare qualities of mind and character. And in that moment he recalled an unheeded remark made by Sri Samādhi about this very man: 'Perhaps you will know him better before your search is ended. Then you will also "give" me Sir Roy.'

It was at least conceivable, he admitted, as this newly perceived Sinclair drew a quick breath and rose to his feet.

At sight of Lynch, he smiled, more like his remembered self. 'Done the unpleasant job?'

'Done it neatly, thanks to you. Rank revolutionaries both. They ought to get a stiff sentence.'

'You've done *me* an unrepayable service,' Sinclair said, with sudden feeling.

Lynch raised his brows. 'Such service as I've rendered repays itself. I welcome any form of *shikar* that gives me a sight of Hindu Khush and Hindu Rāj.'

Sinclair looked again towards the mountains. 'There's a terrible splendour about them, a wildness and desolation that eclipse the obvious beauties of Kashmir.'

'*You* think that?' A fellow feeling for the Hindu Khush was a passport to the heart of John Lynch. 'It's my own private opinion. But it's heresy. So I never utter it. Precious few, except climbers, appreciate mountains in the nude.'

Sinclair laughed abruptly, as if it was long since he had indulged in that barbarous yet friendly sound.

'I'm no climber; but I like the austerity of line, a sense of mighty lives moving in their own orbit.'

Lynch nodded feelingly, though he could not have expressed it so.

'*I* like the uncompromising strength of naked precipice and crags. I've tramped through this region in Moslem kit, summer after summer; through the Dorah Pass, and beyond. I could many strange tales unfold. But in the Police — we don't. Only Sir Vincent gets the pick of my gleanings.'

'Vinx —— ? It'll be good to see *him* again.'

'Translated into first Governor of the N.W.F.P.'

'*Never!* They chose him?'

'To their everlasting credit they did, instead of shoving on us some favoured outsider from Delhi. He's been worried over your vanishing trick. Thorne has wired. You've a lot of dropped threads to pick up.'

Again Sinclair drew that quick breath. 'Can we be getting a move on?' He glanced at the plane. 'I don't like these machines; but I was never more grateful for anything in my life.'

Once they were well up among billows of cloud, bumping and tossing in air-pockets like a boat in a heavy swell, he felt additionally grateful that their journey would be brief. He was pure English in his stoical endurance of major hardships, his impatience over minor discomforts; and at the moment he needed all his faculties to grasp this unlooked-for turn of events. Tara in Kashmir — with Lilāmani, his two best treasures: and a lurking thought at the back of his mind: no urgent reason, now, for leaving India yet awhile. Tara by coming out here had given him his two deepest needs in conjunction; and to himself he could admit a secret sense of reprieve. She would surely be willing to stay for the summer, at least, give him a chance to see Bàpu once again, to show him the grandchild of his favourite daughter.

Seeing Lynch absorbed in thought, he drew out his letter and read it a third time.

Roy, my best beloved:

This is news beyond price, beyond belief, that you are alive and well, that tomorrow we meet, after this lifetime of waiting and not knowing. Thank God, I boldly came out, in defiance of prudent counsels. A terrible expense, but I know you'll approve. We have never lived by money values or by bread alone, you and I. We have also to thank Mother, who was an angel. Backed me through thick and thin.

But one desperate thing I have *done. I've brought the Darling with me. Unwise—? I don't know. I only know that I couldn't have left her behind. In feeling, she's ahead of her years, and she has kept* on *wanting you all the time. Superfluous to add that the same applies to your ever and always awaiting you,*

TARA

'Always awaiting you': and never a hint of reproach, nor ever would be——

A sudden bump and lurch flung him half out of his seat and tumbled him against the less abstracted Lynch, who hung on to his chair with one hand and grasped Sinclair's arm with the other.

'Damned uneasy sailing over mountains,' he shouted against the dull roar of the plane. 'Feel a bit squeamish? Hard luck. I've the stomach of an ostrich myself — the one that swallowed a bunch of keys. If you feel bad — heave it up. Don't mind me!'

But Sinclair minded the indignity for himself, in the eyes of Gulbaddan, who was pea-green, but holding out so far. A queer dizziness almost overcame him; and only now he realised that he had eaten nothing since his early morning fruit and milk; the coming of Lynch and the air journey having wiped out his midday meal. Better divert his mind by taking a last look at these mightiest mountains on earth.

Even seen from the air, there was no dwarfing them. Range on range they piled themselves to the limit of vision. As cloud billows rolled and parted, mountain after mountain reared its head, snow-fields like powder of diamonds, stark rock-faces, and craggy peaks in silhouette. The plane, keeping well away from them, seemed to be droning over an abyss; the Indus, far seen, hurtling between naked cliffs, a look of terror in its haste.

As they approached the Kashmir Valley, the whole scale of things seemed reduced. Here were flashes of lake and stream and the curving river Jhelum; the steadfast beauty of upward-marching pines; and beyond them, a shimmer of peaks guarding unknown mysteries. Lower still they swooped over the misted silver of the Dal Lake and its Moghul gardens: a riot of spring blossom and young green that stirred in Roy's veins a thrill of life renewed, of return to human levels.

But when it came to houseboats and a glimpse of the Srinagar Residency among stately trees, a sudden sense of strangeness came over him at the thought of his darkened skin, his Indian dress, his mind ill-equipped for the small change of surface talk. It was Tara he wanted—Tara only; and he must face a probable house-party of well-dressed men and women. Lynch, no doubt, had his English clothes handy, and could transform himself in half an hour. Those vague eyes were resting on him now, as if they read his thought.

'Where *are* your togs and other things?' he asked.

'Stored in Srinagar. I can't unearth them till tomorrow. Today these kind people must accept me as I am.'

'I gather they'll be glad enough to accept you in any guise or disguise—— Look out, he's nosing down. We'll be there in two two's.'

Near the landing-stage a car awaited them, two figures standing beside it. Roy recognised with relief Sir Havelock and Grace Lynch, with whom he could not feel other than at ease, in any guise or disguise.

There were greetings and congratulations; a short drive along the river road, past the familiar line of poplars; a swerving in at the Residency gateway.

They had arrived.

Chapter VII

This separate, sovereign loveliness can rhyme
Only with its own moment.

GERALD GOULD

LADY THORNE was in the verandah to welcome him. No sign of Tara: and he was thankful.

'She's waiting for you in her room,' Vanessa told him. 'She thought you'd prefer it. First on the left upstairs. You look played out.'

'I'm all right, thanks,' he assured her; but, as he mounted the stairs, a return of dizziness and hammering pulses unsteadied him.

Bracing himself to meet the shock of joy, he entered Tara's room very softly; and there she actually was, over near the window, in her blue frock, a ray of light waking gleams in her fawn-gold hair.

As the door opened, she turned and faced him. Colour flooded her cheeks.

'*Roy!*' she cried — and ran straight into his open arms.

Close and long he held her, loath to let her go. But suddenly his overtaxed body betrayed him. His brain reeled. Vainly he tried to speak her name. Still clinging to her, he slid sideways — and fainted outright.

Slowly light and sensation returned: a damp coolness on his forehead; a dazed wonder, 'What *is* it? Where am I?'

Then, in a rush of exquisite relief — he knew.

With a slow sigh, he opened his eyes and looked deep into hers, that were filled with consternation and alarm.

'Darling,' she breathed, 'why *did* you? Are you ill?'

'Not I — only empty, knocked out of time.' He took one

of her hands and cherished it. 'I've had nothing but a little milk and fruit since dawn.'

'Heavens! And it's after one o'clock.'

'Is it? I've no watch. I usually feed at midday. But what with bumping into Lynch and his staggering news and all, I never gave a thought to it, till I felt so queer up aloft.'

'That's you all over.'

She smiled at him through sudden tears; and he pressed her hand against his lips, as if to make sure that she was real. Half guessing his thought, she kneeled down beside him, laying her wet cheek against his. Simply to be near him, to watch the lines of his face, the familiar movement of his hands, set her heart soaring. The snail-paced year and four months without him seemed now no more than a watch in the night.

He stirred in sheer contentment; and she was her practical self again. Kneeling up, she stroked his hair.

'Darling, I *must* get you something. Tiffin's not till two. Another drop of brandy?'

He waved away the medicine glass. 'No more of *that* on my emptiness. I've not touched alcohol for six months. A cup of warm milk — if you can get it?'

'Of course I can. Ayah's in the next room.'

She called to the woman; and the milk was brought.

'Just let me lace it,' she pleaded, 'with this last drop.'

No resisting her; and he drank it slowly, with a sense of luxury more than physical.

For a few moments he lay there, letting the feel of her presence permeate him; then, suddenly he remembered his child.

'What have you done with the Darling?' he asked, sitting upright and discarding his *poshteen*, as she had already removed his turban. 'Nice sort of parent I am.'

'Didn't you think of her till now?'

'Honest I didn't. I was filled to the brim with you.'

Her eyes softened. She came and sat close to him on the sofa, her cheek against his shirt-sleeve.

'I practised guile. Not quite sure when you might arrive,

I said tiffin-time, and sent her out with little Kaye's ayah. I wanted first innings.'

'You got them — and you knocked me senseless.' His arms were round her again, for the joy of holding her.

'I suppose we're in for a tiffin party? Me, in this kit, sitting through an endless meal. I've lost the habit, as Lynch said, after months of simple Indian living; not a white face, not a word from the outer world. Of course I'm keen to see them all again. But I won't be wanting to eat their messed-up food. Nor I won't know what to talk about; but if I sit *choop* they'll think me unfriendly.'

'Look here, Roy, why *should* you?' She turned and laid both hands on him. 'I can easily make your excuses. Lady Thorne would understand.'

'Well, I won't have it.' He smiled into her eyes. 'At your old trick of spoiling me! I'd far sooner face the lot, than have any sort of fuss.' He raised his head, listening. 'There's the child.'

A small, clear voice in the next room was asking the ayah, '*Humara Daddy argya?*'[1]

'Talks it already?'

'Yes. She's queer about everything out here.'

'Is she? No matter. We three are together in India. And it's your doing. — Here she is.'

She had pushed aside the curtain. She was standing in the doorway; a slip of a thing in her creamy yellow frock that set off her ivory skin and dark hair, with its soft natural wave like Tara's. Utterly still she stood, gazing at him in his Indian shirt and wrinkled trousers, immense reserves of emotion in her serious eyes.

'Prithvi — ? Prithvi Rāj?' There was awe and delight in her voice.

'Lilāmani,' he said and opened his arms.

In a silent rush she came and nestled to him. He could feel her heart fluttering under his hand like a captured bird. Closer she pressed, not looking up for a kiss. A small shiver ran through her; and as he lifted her face with one hand, he found she was crying.

[1] Has my Daddy come?

Deeply moved, he stroked her hair, kissing the tears on her lashes and cheeks, while Tara stood watching them; marvelling, as often, at the child who seemed so curiously apart from the other two.

'Not a smile for Prithvi Rāj?' Roy gently reproached her. 'Aren't you happy that he's found at last?'

'I'm too happy. I'm loving him *too* much. It hurts.'

'Yes. It hurts,' he gravely agreed, and kissed her again. 'But it's grand — we three together in India.'

'Yes, it's *grand*,' she echoed, clutching him with sudden fervour. Then her gaze wandered to the discarded turban. 'Put it on,' she commanded. 'Really truly Prithvi Rāj.'

He glanced at Tara, caught a remembered look in her eyes, and said quickly: 'Mummy likes me better with it off. Really truly Roy Sinclair! — Hark! Civilisation's call to feed.'

The musical sequence of a Burmese gong went softly booming through the house.

'I must tidy up quick. Find my waistcoat, my camel's-hair *choga*.' He glanced down at the small head resting against him. 'Is she allowed?'

'Yes. Rather spoiled by Lady Thorne.'

'Come on, then. Three frightened people! We'll face the music.'

In the drawing-room they found Vanessa with Eve Desmond, an arm round the girl who seemed almost her own daughter — the girl whose father she had so tragically loved.

At sight of Roy, Eve ran to him and kissed him.

'First offence!' She turned laughing to Tara. 'Couldn't help meself. — Roy, you *are* a wonder. Coming down like manna from heaven and all!' She looked him up and down in frank approval. 'Terribly becoming. Why don't most of our men dress like that out here? Lynch, the Moslem, is quite impressive.'

As she spoke, he entered from the verandah, in greenish-brown coat and red cummerbund. Only his turban had been discarded. He hailed Sinclair with the '*Salaam Aleikum*' of their strange meeting, and shook hands with Tara, his level glance appraising her charm.

'Congratulations, Lady Sinclair. We saved him neatly from a pleasure trip to Central Asia.'

'Central Asia?' she echoed, turning startled eyes on her husband, who said quickly, 'Don't heed him, Tara. He's romancing. I *was* in the hands of two bad specimens ——'

'Now enjoying leisure,' Lynch cut in, 'to think over their sins, while we are privileged to enjoy one of Lady Thorne's famous tiffins.'

After him came Grace with Sir Havelock, putting on flesh in his comfortable appointment. He introduced Sinclair casually to Mr. Shane, Assistant Resident, a suave-mannered Civilian looking askance at Sahibs who lowered the prestige of their country by wearing 'native kit.'

Sinclair mentally dismissed him in favour of a singularly attractive girl introduced by Eve as 'Chrystal Adair, great friend of mine. And — here is an older friend.' She indicated Roy. 'Come along, both of you — Tiffin *tyar*.'[1] I'm sort of secondary hostess in this house, where my father Colonel Challoner was Resident when I'd just turned eleven.' In a lower tone she added, 'It was then that I lost him.' She looked down at Lilāmani, standing close to Roy, and lightly stroked the dark head. 'Lucky little scrap. *She*'s got her Daddy back again.'

'Lucky little scrap,' Lilāmani quaintly echoed in a soft contented voice.

Eve smiled at Roy; and they all moved on into the dining-room, Lilāmani holding the edge of his *choga* as if she feared that he might silently vanish away.

As guest of honour he found himself placed beside Vanessa, Grace assigned to the chair on his right. But a murmured 'Oh, Daddy!' from Lilāmani, moved her to put the small thing between them; and he smiled at her over his daughter's head.

To him, the whole affair, formerly so familiar, seemed an unreal spectacle, at one remove from his normal conscious-

[1] Lunch is ready.

ness: the dark, polished table, dimly reflecting bowls of early yellow roses, ferns and columbines, the glass and silver, the popping of champagne corks in his honour, hovering servants with scarlet belts and badges. After months of Spartan surroundings, the beauty of it all fascinated his senses; the women's frocks, the living charm of their faces. Lady Thorne, at forty-five, was almost beautiful; Eve a creature of radiant intelligence. Grace had personality, and the Chrystal Adair girl — in a dull yellow frock that toned with her honey-coloured hair — had charm of an intriguing quality. She watched and listened more than she talked. Watching her himself, he hazarded a guess that she was wise as well as young, more friendly than withholding, if one could find the key that fitted.

Once he encountered her eyes, clear as sea-water, yet suggesting depth. For a few seconds they looked steadily at each other. Then her serious gaze lightened, and he smiled back at her with an oddly unfamiliar sense of pleasure. Young Shane, sitting by her, deflected her attention; and a thought crept into his mind, 'I shall see a good deal of her. Perhaps through Eve. What is she doing out here?'

Beyond, between Lynch and Thorne, sat Tara, looking radiant, as if lit from within; the one point of escape from his bewilderment. Already she seemed quite at home with these former friends of his, listening with intelligent interest to Lynch, who deserved a special tribute of gratitude from them both.

At this abstracted moment, Vanessa leaned towards him, charmingly anxious that he should not feel left out of their local and personal talk.

'Don't *you* think so, Roy?' she asked, with a smile that invited agreement.

Startled and astray, he answered boldly, 'Yes, I do,' wondering what manner of opinion he had let loose on the world.

It was useless attempting to catch on. They were talking of people and events outside his ken; talking, it seemed to him, as if their lives depended on preventing a lapse into merciful silence. It set him wondering — how many months it might be since he had last even scanned a newspaper; wondering if he were any the worse for the hiatus, except that it unfitted him for table-talk. So strange, so objectless it seemed, this perpetual wagging of tongues, after months of comparative silence, of reading and writing and deep thought. It disturbed his accustomed inner quiet like gusts of wind ruffling a still pool. It made him feel oddly remote from them all. Yet no — not from them all. For there sat Tara, the closest being to him on earth; and here was a small hand creeping onto his knee under the table, not for the first time, and Lilāmani smiling up at him, as if they shared some happy secret. Whenever her hand crept onto his knee, he put his own down to meet it. This time he gave it a gentle squeeze; and her eyes danced.

'How d'you do, Mr. Prithvi Rāj!' she whispered demurely; and Grace, who had been talking to her, smiled at him again over her head.

'You were lost?' she said, with the frankness of an old friend.

'Yes. I'm feeling rather lost.'

'When you ought to be feeling found! Readjustment is an uncomfortable process, as I discovered when I changed over from being a "mish" doctor to being Mrs. John Lynch. I expect we all seem very far away.'

'*Miles* away,' he agreed; and the glance they exchanged carried him back to a shared experience — was it only a year ago? — in village India; an experience that had started their friendship, and had brought him up against the jealousy of her husband.

He was holding the table now, and Sinclair forced his mind to attention. Lynch, he remembered, was apt to be worth listening to whether one agreed with him or no. One could not easily resist the impact of a mind at once so able yet unimaginative, so impervious to all fine shades, yet capable of deeper feeling, in a few directions, than he would ever be likely to admit.

He was talking now of his 'precious pair,' of the damage

they and their kind had been doing, with partial success, in the Indian Army, in the Police, and among Border tribes — more restive, inflammable material, always a virtual powder magazine.

'I've a young friend up there now, on leave,' he said. 'A Pathan cavalry sub, sending me scraps of information that may come in handy against our two friends.'

Thorne chuckled. 'A Brindian sub! You *are* the *pukka* C.I.D. You'll get the stuff you want by any old means.'

'That's what I'm paid for,' Lynch reminded him. 'It's often undesigned; but my eyes and ears are never off duty. I liked young Sher Afzul from the start. Drew him out; and found him useful afterwards. Some of these officer Pathans have promising stuff in them.'

That shifted the talk to Army Indianisation, its value in theory, its enormous wastage in practice; the tendency of too many good starters to drift away into branch services or Native States.

'The main trouble is,' said Thorne, 'that most Indians begin to love ease before they're thirty.'

'Not the martial races,' Sinclair cut in, and Lynch replied:

'They are the salt of the earth. But most of 'em have too few brains for passing stiff promotion exams; and the brainier sort haven't got the grit. However, the new Indian Sandhurst seems to be turning out some good specimens. Our own officers are playing up, on the whole — like it or not. And the coach rolls on. To what destination, God Himself can't foresee.'

Sinclair, watching Chrystal Adair, was struck by the attentive interest with which she followed talk that seemed unlikely to attract the average girl fresh from Home. Decidedly an unusual young woman. He would ask Eve about her.

His wandering thought was checked by the entrance of a scarlet *chāprassi*, who salaamed deeply and handed a telegram to the strangely clad guest of honour. Vincent, of course. Sinclair opened it and read: 'Welcome and sincerest greetings from Thea and Vincent Leigh.'

Without a word, he handed the slip to Vanessa, who read it aloud.

'Hear, hear!' from Lynch and Thorne, with a drumming of knife-handles echoed by Eve and Grace; Lilāmani following suit from a vague sense of some excitement in the air.

And of course Thorne must get upon his feet, lifting his glass, though speeches had been forbidden.

'Health and happiness, in bumper measure, to Sir Roy and Lady Sinclair.'

The rest stood up. All round the table glasses were raised. Grace clinked hers with Roy, who could only bow his acknowledgements, and feel thankful for the timely arrival of *kitmutgars* with coffee.

The women preferred theirs in the drawing-room; and when the men joined them, Eve boldly took possession of Roy. The garden invited them. Formalities were over. But the realities hovered still beyond his grasp; still his detached self poised above it all, watched another self moving and speaking in a dream among dream people.

Keenly as he appreciated the manner of his welcome, the sense of human contact renewed, his real self was ungratefully plotting to elope with Tara; to escape from them all till readjustment had accomplished its difficult work.

Only when he could get away alone with her would he indeed feel as one risen from the dead.

Chapter VIII

Feel, where my life broke off from thine,
How fresh the splinters keep and fine,
Only a touch and we combine!

BROWNING

A CHANCE to reveal his secret plan did not arrive till after dinner, when the child, who clung to him like his shadow, was in bed and asleep, unaware of his treacherous intent.

The second civilised meal proved easier, in some ways, than the first; a smaller party, only Grace and Lynch, the Thornes, and themselves. But physically he was hampered by dinner jacket and trousers, evening shirt and hard shoes, after months of Eastern garb, the most sane and comfortable ever devised by man. Vigorously though he had scoured face and hands, the sunburn remained, giving him the air of a princely Rajput in evening dress. Lynch also was deeply tanned, the tone of his skin contrasting curiously with his lightish brown hair and pale eyes. Frankly he cursed the ugliness and discomfort of civilised male attire.

'If you can *call* it civilised?' he queried, with a grin at his own fine proportions cased in stiff black and white. 'I sometimes wonder whether we might have done better out here — in other ways than comfort — if we'd all adopted some modified form of Eastern dress.'

Thorne shook his head. 'No, thanks. None of that.'

Vanessa laughed.

'Havelock's been rather overdosed lately with that form of heresy. A clever man we've had staying here, full of ideas about our men adopting Indian dress by way of showing a friendlier spirit, making a more direct appeal to India's imagination.'

Lynch regarded her quizzically.

'We're treated to a lot of tall talk about Indian imagination and spirituality,' he remarked, with a wary glance at Sinclair. 'I venture to submit that on the whole they are credited with a good deal more in that line than they possess. The Moslem has both feet firmly planted on earth; and the spiritual Hindu mostly talks and thinks about food, money, or crops.'

'That rather depends' — Sinclair answered his look — 'on the man he's talking to. Any intelligent Hindu, in my experience, will talk by the hour about God and the soul and unseen realities to any man who shows a live interest in those subjects.'

'Well — no doubt I'm poorly equipped in that line,' Lynch surprisingly admitted, 'and no doubt you've associated with a better class of Indian. Grace would back you up; and I bow to the conclusions of first-hand experience, even when they differ from my own.'

He stated the fact without a hint of the old ironical undernote. Decidedly this unofficial Lynch was a more likeable man than the D.I.G. of Peshawar.

'But how did your fanciful friend' — he appealed to Vanessa — 'mix up dress and imagination?'

She smiled at his way of putting it.

'Be prepared for a shock! He argued that our state-occasion swallow-tails and tall hats are quite out of tune with the Indian setting and Indian taste for the splendiferous. They don't appeal to the eye like the gala dress of even a small Rajāh. He would have the Viceroy and Governors, on important occasions, wear embroidered coats and coloured turbans, that need not detract from dignity, and would be far more impressive to the mass of Indians.'

'Impressive? The white man would feel a fool and look it,' Thorne stoutly insisted. 'Imagine poor Sir Vincent and the Viceroy masquerading in fancy dress at Peshawar the other day.'

'It would irk those two less than most,' Sinclair hazarded. 'I'd like to meet this original man ——' He turned to Vanessa. 'Was it to be only Viceroys and Governors?'

'No. He suggested some kind of Indian uniform, in keeping with their regiment, for officers of the Indian Army. He would even advocate it for the I.C.S., both races ——'

Lynch shouted with laughter. 'The heaven-born! It would scare 'em stiff. They'd resign in shoals. Finest recipe out for Indianising the whole Service overnight — if that's the notion.'

'Are things as bad as all that?' Sinclair asked, with a direct look.

'Well — I was piling it on a bit. But, take it all round, I'd be with them, spite of my first remark. We've not only to consider the eye of the Indian, but the mind of the transferred Englishman. Dress can have a queer effect on a man's mind. I've experienced it. And no one can accuse *me* of imagination.'

It was his wife's turn to laugh softly; and Sinclair ventured to laugh with her. Lynch merely shook a square fist at them; and Vanessa deftly turned the talk into another channel.

Not until after coffee and cigars could Roy at last carry Tara off into the garden, reputed to be one of the loveliest in India. There light still lingered on spring blossom and new leafage; and just above the highest tree-tops a pearl-white half moon drifted in a sky exquisitely clear and remote.

Close together they walked, like new-made lovers, without the inner ferment of young passion that needs constant reassurance of itself. They were known to each other. They were proving in their lives that the happiness peculiar to marriage was not a function of love alone or even of youth alone. It was much that they had been young together. It was more that they could delight in growing old together, could wonder at themselves and this mysterious content in simple physical nearness. Enough for each that the other was there; that now they would again begin to live — with their peculiar capacity for shared experience — one satisfying life.

Through that very capacity, Tara was aware of some unseizable change in Roy that lifted her above ordinary things, even above ordinary happiness. So vital, so awake she felt all through, that she marvelled afresh at the depth and fervour of her mature love for him: she who believed she had fathomed the unfathomable. The fact that love was only a part of life's infinite variety could not lessen the wonder of its intensity, its hidden power of renewal, of obliterating time. For her, these few hours of overwhelming happiness more than equalised the strain and anxiety of sixteen endless months. Life had a singular balancing quality, discernible only as one grew old enough to look back and catch glimpses of the design that its ups and downs had woven unawares.

Turning her head, she let her gaze linger on Roy's face — thinner and more thought-graven — with a brimming content and quiet at her heart.

Suddenly he turned also, drawn by her gaze out of some abstracted mood.

'Tara —!' he said, his low tone charged with feeling; and blissfully she yielded to his arms, to the fervour of his kisses.

Then they moved on to the end of the lawn, scarcely heeding the moon and the stars, that flickered like fireflies among the leaves of brooding trees patterned on a pale sky.

Presently he stopped and spoke again.

'You angel woman, I can't find words to tell you all that is surging up in my heart; how I reproach myself for the strain and bitter disappointment I put upon you last autumn ——'

'Darling' — she laid both hands on him — 'you shall *not* reproach yourself. Think of the strain you suffered, held back by the power of that strange Guru and the East in your blood. We've both suffered, Roy; but some things are worth paying for. If we didn't know it then, we do know now that this has been the biggest thing that ever came into your life.'

'And *you*,' he said with sudden passion, 'the loveliest thing ——'

He caught her to him again, telling her from his heart. Gladly she would have endured the worst that Fate could do, to have her lover thus given back to her, almost as if twelve years of marriage had not been.

'Tara,' he said at last, 'listen. I want to carry you off somewhere.'

'Yes — where?' she murmured, in blissful surrender to any plan, any demand.

'Somewhere right away from all these kind people — rather superfluous just now.'

'Yes,' she agreed again, so meekly that he glanced at her, wondering ——

'What surprise plan have *you* got up your sleeve?'

She held out a shapely bare arm in the moonlight. 'No sleeve!'

His fingers closed lightly on it; and he kissed its inner softness.

'Under your skin, then,' he said. 'What is it?'

'How d'you know it *is* anything?'

'Because "each is both." You know the Persian saying?'

'No, I don't. For that beautiful answer, you shall be told! It's not a plan. It's an inspiration just arrived, because I've been exploring Moghul gardens with Lady Thorne. They fascinate me: the symbolism and all the history behind them. She has lent me a book about them. What a deeply understanding woman she is. One feels she must have suffered a great deal and always kept her head up.'

'It's true. She *has* suffered. She loved Eve's father, a fine man with a rotten wife, and he loved her. When he died in Gulmarg, she practically took over Eve; a proper little devil of eleven, who adored her father and her "Vanessa," but couldn't abide her mother. Eve herself told me. But that's by the way. — Let's have your inspiration.'

'We *will* have it, I do believe,' she murmured in a contented voice. 'Lady Thorne and I spent a whole day there last week; a hidden corner above this very lake, not yet infested with tourists and Americans — who arrive with the mosquitoes! — and all the plains people, who swarm to Srinagar chiefly because a house-boat is cheaper than a hotel. Why is it that human beings can't come together and enjoy a beautiful place without robbing it of something one can only call its soul?'

'It's because their noisy presence scares away the spirits of the wild, survivals of the old earth gods.'

She opened her eyes at him. 'Do *you* believe in those old earth gods?'

'I don't readily disbelieve in any hidden possibilities where Nature is concerned. There must be some age-old form of life in the earth to account for the way all primitive folk instinctively people woods and streams and hills with some kind of elemental — dryads or djinns or fairies. The local folk here believe that these hills are full of queer spirits, good or evil, not yet scared away by man.' He smiled at her absorbed, moonlit face. 'We've wandered off the track again. Where do we find *our* sanctuary of beauty that hasn't yet given up its ghost?'

'We find it in a gem of a Moghul garden and pavilion with pools and fountains and a live stream. I *think* the Rajāh might lend it to us for a week or two. Its ghosts are the spirits of Shah Jehan and his Mumtaz Mahāl. He built it as a refuge from crowds and court ceremonies, where he could be at peace alone with his Light of the World.'

'Wise man. There we'll go, Light of *my* World, if I can work it through Thorne.'

'And' — she looked full into his eyes — 'the Darling?'

'No,' he said, with surprising decision. 'Not the Darling. A shame to leave her; but it's you I want, not the mother bird, with half her mind straying away on "What's happening to the child?"'

'And it's you *I* want,' she said, very low. 'But what *will* be happening to the child?'

'I leave that to your resource. Can't the fragile flower be bedded out — here or with Eve?'

'Yes, I'm sure she can. I'd rather Eve. Lady Thorne has so much on her hands. Lilāmani's quite smitten with little Ian; and there would be the fun of living on a house-boat. But all the same — if you vanish again, she'll break her heart.'

'We won't vanish and she shan't break her heart. I'll explain. We could let Eve bring her once on a visit. But first we must celebrate her birthday. Also I must see the doctor about my demnition headaches; and introduce you to the Guru Maharāj.'

'My enemy!' she said, with a flash of her young fierceness. '*How* I've hated him!'

'You won't, when you see him, when I tell you —— Oh, there's no end to tell you; and there's a letter waiting for you about five months long!'

'A letter — to me?'

'So surprising? D'you suppose I could live in utter isolation without sometimes talking to the other half of my heart?'

'Roy! You *are* the loveliest person.'

'Am I?' His eyes searched hers. 'I always supposed I was the unworthy husband of the best wife on earth.'

She laughed softly. 'You didn't! That sounds like Aunt Jane. She labelled *me* the biggest fool on earth, when she heard of my wild proceedings. Oh, thank Heaven, I didn't let prudence have her perfect work.'

'Thank Heaven!' he echoed gravely. 'You've a streak of the divine folly in you that confounds the wisdom of the wise.'

A burst of deep, masculine laughter came out to them through the open doors.

'Hark at them in there. It's one of Lynch's *pukka* merits, the way he can make men laugh, brown or white. Not at mere broad stories; though he can tell the worst of those with the best of them. He has the real stuff of British humour in him.'

'Yes, he has. I like him.'

'I saw you liking him! I used almost to hate him in Peshawar. Always felt him spurning the Rajput in me. And Rajputs don't put up with being spurned. But I like him better now. And look here, we've got to thank him properly, somehow, for all the trouble he took on account of a man he didn't like overmuch; putting aside important work of his own. Thorne told me. He's a difficult man to thank. I've tried. We must give him some token of remembrance between us; and you shall write him a charming letter. He'd take the grateful touch from you; and it would please Grace no end.'

He made a move to continue their stroll.

'Oughtn't we to go in again?' she demurred.

'Perhaps we ought. But there's the moon lighting up. One more turn under these royal trees — our first evening.'

One more turn they took, not speaking, letting the beauty of the night fall on them like dew.

More than ever Roy was aware of the profound understanding between them — of his heightened perceptions permeating her; giving her, through some finer medium than words, a measure of what he had gained during his time apart.

And as the quiet of evening deepened, as the rising moon filled the garden with shadows of coming night, they took with both hands their golden hour, that must pass, but would never die.

Chapter IX

Incredulous world, be far, and tongues profane!
For the marvel that was most marvellous is most true.
To the music that moves the universe moves my heart
And the song of the starry worlds I sing apart.

LAURENCE BINYON

CHASMA SHAHI, Garden of the Royal Spring, is a gem of its kind; small only by comparison with the more frequented Moghul gardens already known to Tara: Nasim Bagh, Garden of Breezes, and the many-terraced Nishāt Bagh, Garden of Bliss. Few things pleased her more in Roy's mother country than the music and meaning of Indian names; the names of these royal retreats, the name of Roy's quaint, adoring servant, Gulbaddan, Body of the Rose — with them now as personal attendant; the name of their own Lilāmani, Jewel of Delight.

The mere thought of her started a dozen questions. What was her fanciful brain making of their strange desertion hard on the thrill of her Kashmir birthday? Dearly she loved Eve, who had proved a treasure when the bad moment came. How pluckily she had stood on the shore and watched them set out in their country boat; one hand clutching Eve, the other waving frantically. Tara had seen her lashes wet with tears, and her unchildish control had made the pang of parting sharper than if she had wept and clung to them.

'Only five days: then a visit in a boat!' That promise, given by Prithvi Raj, would be the star on her horizon.

Three of those days had already slipped past in this earthly paradise, planned three hundred years ago by the Emperor-lover Shah Jehan for his Crown of the Palace, Mumtaz Mahal.

Unchanged through passing centuries, it seemed consecrated still to those vanished lovers, who knew not that their love — and its abiding expression in the Taj Mahal — would cause their names to live for ever.

Now, as then, the Royal Spring still bubbled up in its carved stone vase. Still the garden glowed with the same colour harmonies, still the orchards bloomed and scattered their fallen petals like snow. A stone *chabutra* [1] invited them to meals in the open. A tiny carved water-chute cascaded the stream to a lower terrace, and on through another pavilion at the far end, where a tank with five fountain jets was set in gay flower borders — every shade of rose in this month of roses — and bounded by a hedge of Persian lilac. Everywhere, over trees and balustrades, billowed dense masses of wistaria; everywhere the wild roses of Kashmir flowered so profusely that no leaves could be seen. Nor was iris time yet over. Blue as distant hills they flowed between reefs of green meadowland, or crowded down to the lake as if enamoured of their own reflection.

On this third day, Tara sat alone in a cushioned chair by the black marble balustrade overlooking the lower terrace, where Roy — returned from his morning meditation — paced to and fro, hands behind his back, lost in thought. He was wearing his camel's-hair *choga* over the Indian shirt and orange-yellow cummerbund. He loved his Eastern dress; and she, by now, had conquered her inner distaste for it. She who had so deeply and secretly feared India for him would never now fear it again; and there are few forms of liberation comparable to release from a secret fear. Each day of their new life proved to her more clearly all that had been wrought in him by those months of solitude, thought, and self-discipline, as if in some way the basis of his character had been reinforced. And it had all been wrongfully the spirit of India working through the influence of that noble Guru Maharaj, whom she had so fiercely hated in her ignorance and dread. Now she had met him, had spent an unforgettable hour with him on the high terrace of Nishāt

[1] Raised platform.

Bagh; had felt drawn to him not only by his impressive personality, but by the look in his eyes when they rested on Roy — his thought disciple, the son of his spirit. Seeing them together, she could no longer wonder at the vital change in Roy. No sign, so far, of his dark moods, of his impatience and irritability; though he still maintained that there was virtue in an occasional explosive; life in it, also.

'"You don't say damn when your vitality is low,"' he would quote with his twinkle. '"You trail about among water-blooded words like regrettable and deplorable."'

She could find nothing water-blooded about this new Roy; could feel him all through more than ever a man. Without reserve she could glory in his high endeavour; for the grasping spirit of jealousy was not in her, and they two were one in the belief that love is enriched by the sharing of larger interests beyond its immediate delights and demands. His unposted letter nearly 'five months long,' bound in limp cloth, lay open on her knee; a revealing so personal that it was as if he had indeed given her the freedom of his spirit. She was reading it slowly in these early hours of his absence; re-living his life — his illness and semi-blindness, his longing for her and home; all their chances and changes leading them — to this. During these first days quite alone with him, there were strangely beautiful moments when she seemed almost to be entering a new life, with a new husband, known and loved long before.

In the upper story of their pavilion they slept almost *al fresco*. Arched openings gave free access to the night sky and astonishing Indian moon. Though at first they could hardly sleep for the penetrating beauty of it all, they woke with a sense of renewal never experienced in any mere bedroom. Today she had been waked before dawn by the piping of two yellow-breasted bulbuls — nightingales of Kashmir — the music of soaring larks, and a love duet between two golden orioles; but already Roy's bed was empty and he away on his early, early trek to some high point for sunrise meditation. Half drowsy she had lain there, listening to the murmur of the crystal spring that gave the place its name, to the song of birds and rustling of trees in the wind of dawn.

As light quickened, she had sprung up and stood at one of the arched openings, barefoot in her blue nightgown, looking out over the lake, that shimmered far below in misty beauty. Presently a few shreds of cloud caught fire. Pigeons wheeled and cooed. A wandering line of small birds flickered along the sky as the sun rose resplendent, staining the waters with faint primrose light, caressing the far snows of the Pir Panjal.

One could scarcely believe in the not-so-distant colony of houseboats and bungalows, the inescapable round of Station life; the constant new arrivals, the rush of endless cars; the perpetual sequence of games and gossip, dances and drinks. It seemed a pity that this should be the prevalent impression produced by the English in India. Though there were among them, as she knew, many jewels of price, the tinsel glitter — social and official — was more apt to catch the eye. To a woman like herself, with her heart and life deep-rooted in England's countryside — fighting against odds to save one among her stately homes from extinction — this froth of aimless activity seemed a rootless form of existence. For all her many new interests in Peshawar, she had soon begun to miss the daily bread of home duties and responsibilities, her pride in holding the fort for Roy, while he pursued his adventure of the spirit. Detached from it all, she had felt like a cut flower in a vase, longing for rain and soil; wondering how the estate fared in her absence, how Nevil was faring in his uncompanioned holidays. His bald, boyish letter, just received, revealed little; but his postscript told her much: 'I want you terribly. Come back soon.' How soon? That was the question troubling her heart. Now that Roy's coming had made her whole, there awoke the natural longing to return and take up their real, many-sided life again.

Roy himself, profoundly satisfied, had so far said nothing; and she had decided not to speak of home-going till he gave her the cue. The fragile texture of life's loveliest moments needed more delicate handling than moods of simple content. And for her it sufficed to be with him again, in these fairy-tale surroundings that only India could still produce.

At this moment she was sitting utterly still, all her senses pervious to the early morning lights on lake and mountain; all direct seeing and questing purpose lulled; mind and body at rest in the simple satisfaction of being alive, with the shared life of earth and sky. Only so could one experience the truth of Nietzsche's quaint phrase: 'The body is a big sagacity.... 'Saith not Ego. But doeth it.' And here, in Roy's long letter, she discovered how, in her own small sphere, she had been following the same path; preparing her mind, as it were, for the changed perspective that springs from a deepening of the inner life. Instead of giving place to the devils of disapproval or self-pity, she had followed the kindlier light of her own heart's guidance, climbed her own ladder to the stars...

He had halted now in his pacing and raised a hand, saluting her.

'Got it!' he called. 'Coming soon.'

'It' was the third stanza of a symbolic ode, that had been vaguely haunting him for some time without result. But the changed atmosphere, the stimulant of understanding companionship, had rekindled his poetic imagination. And she was in it. That was all she asked. Last night on the moon-splashed terrace he had given her a vivid picture of the original idea: the birth of holy Ganges, from Valmiki's opening scene of *The Ramayāna*.

First, the Immortals appearing among billows of cloud flooded with the light of their splendour. Then, at their word, the clouds dissolving into a great cataract, descending from heaven onto the snow-fields of Himalaya, silvering them with crests of foam as a royal lake might be silvered by the descent of a thousand swans. From valley to valley the cascade went leaping; gods in their chariots going on before, dolphins and nymphs at play among the waves. Down and down flowed the rush of water, till it spread into a mighty river, worshipped by all as a gift from the Gods;

branching into lesser streams, ever seeking its goal — the Indian Ocean. Even there its sacred waters plunged on through ocean depths, till they reached the nethermost hell, bringing life and refreshment to spirits in torment.

For the Hindu poet that wealth of imagery signified more than the birth of a great river. It symbolised the fount of heavenly wisdom descending to enrich the children of men; the immanence of spirit throughout the whole created world, from the teeming dust to the aspiring mind of man. And Roy had set his heart on capturing — as far as might be — the movement and the depth of his majestic theme.

Two opening stanzas Tara had heard. The third she would hear as soon as he could work it out on paper. Meantime she would be unpoetically glad of breakfast, laid in the pavilion by Gulbaddan, who asked for nothing better in life than thus to serve his Swami-Sahib and the Lady-Mem.

On her plate she found a small pile of letters, and her heart leaped at sight of Eve's handwriting. She gave a lively account of the child, surviving base desertion, enjoying life on a houseboat, helping her and ayah in a dozen ways. And here was a neatly printed scrap from the creature herself.

> *I am longing badly for you and Daddy to come back*, she wrote. *Eve is very cruel to me! She whips me with a cat of nine tails and spoils me terribly! I* do *like her fiddle calling birds and I like living in her funny houseboat. This Ian Baby loves me a lot. But I mostly love Prithvi and Tara. I will bring you tons of kisses when I come. Here are some. Please don't forget your Darling,*
>
> LILĀMANI

Her kisses were not crosses, 'because kisses couldn't make you cross.' They were full moons, worshipped by her secret Indian spirit with a fervour revealed only to Prithvi Rāj; and, of late, to her mother, whose loneliness she had divined by some uncanny perception of things far beyond the ken of eight years old.

'She *is* a jewel,' said Roy. 'We named her well.'

But Tara was deep in mail letters; one from Helen and one from Russell, their all-round man for the estate. He had reports to make and questions to pose that led the talk naturally towards home affairs. Over Russell's practical questions and problems, Roy seemed a trifle distrait, having lost touch with minor details during his long absence and isolation.

'Shall I tell him,' Tara ventured, 'that we will settle the question of re-roofing those cottages ourselves when we get back?'

'Get back?' he echoed, suddenly alive to the import of her question. 'A longish time for the cottagers to wait. I seem to remember that old Thingammy — forgotten his name — was apt to expect my landlordly attentions at once, if not sooner!'

'He could surely wait a month or two?' she suggested; and he gazed at her, taken aback.

'Beloved — you've only just arrived. Isn't this earthly paradise good enough for you?'

'It's perfect — for our coming together again. But it isn't home.'

'Seems home enough to me, having you two. Are you pining to hurry off *ek dum?*'

'N-no; not when you put it that way. But you said nothing; and I naturally thought ——'

'And *I* naturally thought,' he echoed, 'that you were sharing my content to rest, for the time being, in this unique bit of life — a gift from the blue. Am I utterly mistaken, Star Lady?'

At the bare hint that she was failing him now, after rising to the far larger demand he had made on her, tears started.

'You shouldn't need to ask that, Roy.'

'No, I shouldn't,' he agreed, in an odd voice. 'But you suddenly made me feel not sure; and I'm unused to that sensation with you. It's like the earth giving way under one. Having got you both out here, by an inspired move, I thought you'd enjoy a summer in these grand hills — higher than this, of course. I've been more or less held up, and there's a lot I'd like to do. People I want to see ——'

Not all at once could she readjust her mind to that unexpected plan of action.

'But darling,' she temporised, 'you *were* coming home at once.'

'Yes, I were,' he quaintly admitted. 'But I didn't dream of this angelic attention on your part! That we should once more be together out here. A chance we'll never get again.'

And she, only longing now to reassure him, felt those idiotic tears trickling down her nose. If she looked up, he would see them — he *had* seen them.

'*Tara!*' he cried in dismay. 'Are you heart-broken from sheer happiness?'

'Yes, from sheer happiness.' She caught at the grain of truth in his nonsense. But a sob escaped; and he sprang up, letting his fruit knife rattle onto the floor.

'My precious, what's happened to you this morning? Don't tell me you're regretting the loveliest thing you ever did.'

His hand closed on her shoulder with the slow, firm pressure that was new to her; and she looked up at him, ignoring her wet lashes.

'Darling — dear, as if I could?'

'Of course you couldn't.' His eyes darkened with love. 'And I wouldn't lay another ounce of weight on your shoulders. Not one wife in hundreds would have taken all this in the way you've taken it. They promise for better, for worse; but when it comes to "worse"' — an expressive shrug and smile — 'some do — and some do not! You are of those who do. For a man to feel dead sure of his wife in any emergency, good or bad: that's real marriage.'

With a slow sigh she leaned her head against his arm. 'It's worth all I've wrestled with, over and over, to hear you say that.'

'It's the simple truth. I counted on you before. I'm counting on you again. It's a big thing, this book of mine, though I say it. We've both made big sacrifices for it. Yours have been a free gift. And, by God's mercy, the long strain hasn't broken either of us. In a sense, it has lifted things. You feel that, Tara?'

'Very deeply I feel that.'

The vibration in her low voice brought him down on one knee, in the more impetuous way of an earlier Roy. Passionately he kissed her and kissed her, as if he would convey to her direct all that could not be told; give her, in full measure, the natural desire of her woman's heart.

'You will stay?' he whispered at last. 'A few months in this life-giving air would be the very thing to set you up again. But if you terribly mind being away till the autumn — ?'

'Darling Roy' — she pressed closer to him — 'how could I? It's not me myself I was thinking of.'

'It never is.'

'It's Helen and — the boy. I've never been so long away from him. And the summer holidays too.'

'Hard luck. It's always hard luck for someone in this difficult game of life. But he might spend part of them at Avonleigh. And he loves that.'

'Yes. But *you* must write and make him see it your way. It nearly broke me, dealing with him last time. And the dear Mother — everything on her shoulders.'

'Yes. A good deal to ask of her. But if I write frankly of it all, I believe she'll rise to the occasion, and not make a song about it either.'

'Oh, she will. She's been upholding me all the time. She'll squelch Elinor and tackle Aunt Jane.'

The last words lit a flicker in his eyes. 'I don't seem able to believe in Aunt Jane, here in this Moghul paradise, that she would call "heathen." She's *the* perfect anachronism! — Well, I'll write to Helen and to Nevil. Take that much off your shoulders. We'll be leaving this place soon. Shifting to higher ground — Gulmarg. We can do some fine trips from there, Darling and all. So no more tears, Star Lady. This Garden of Eden is sufficiently well watered without them!'

He stood up with a sigh of pure pleasure at the thought

of their Himalayan summer; and she stood up also, smiling and opening her arms to him. Again he held her close and long without a kiss or a word; lifting more than her heart by an inner sense of support, as new as it was welcome, while the music of mating birds and of the crystal spring matched the music in her heart.

Gravely he released her and set her down on the chair.

'After all that, I'll graciously permit you to finish your breakfast. Then you shall hear my new stanza. *Then* I will lend an attentive ear to the business of our deserted estate, seven thousand miles away.'

Chapter X

> *. . . All this scope*
> *Of happy courage and insurgent hope . . .*
> *. . . This careless trust*
> *In the divine occasion of our dust —*
> *This is the strength that love to beauty gave.*
>
> GERALD GOULD

LETTERS for breakfast heralded visitors for tea — the Guru Mahārāj, with young Shivanāth, eager to meet once again the author of *This India* before he set out with his Master on the yearly pilgrimage to Amarnath. Last spring the Guru's companion had been Roy, his new-found *chela*: an experience that neither would ever forget.

In a shaded corner of the lower terrace, tea was laid on a narrow table; sugared biscuits, cakes, and strawberries from the Residency garden. The afternoon heat was tempered by the plash of falling water; by spray of fountains, caught by the light, and conjured into a shower of jewels. The hills across the lake were half veiled in the luminous mist of Kashmir Valley; silver peaks rising out of it, faint yet clear.

The two holy ones in their yellow draperies, with cropped heads and shaven faces, were harmoniously in the picture; and Roy himself might be a Rajput noble, in his *choga* with orange cummerbund and jodhpurs. Tara felt entirely at ease presiding over her Eastern tea party. Yet only one of the three men was actual India; and he the most remarkable in all ways. His clear mind, his dignity and ease of manner, would be equal to any human contact, East or West. Even his silence had an impressive quality. One felt that he could say much, if he chose, but he knew when to listen without aimless interruption.

He was appraising now, in his mellow tones, an early rough chapter of Roy's book, recently read; commending his avoidance of political panaceas, his insistence on loyalty to the Aryan ideal as the only solvent of race-conflict, the only hope for a real Indian renaissance in art and life and religion.

'For our supreme struggle, if it comes,' he said, 'will not be between the two countries you so love, but between the *true* India and the *new* India, inoculated with foreign ideas that can never take root in her soil.'

Roy, leaning forward, an elbow on his knee, said pensively, 'If any poor word of mine can enlighten or stimulate the true India, I shall not have striven in vain.'

The Guru, a man of few gestures, laid a hand on his shoulder.

'Rest assured, my *chela*, that there will be no striving in vain. Whatever destiny God may have in store for our two countries, your work, and the spirit that inspires it, will live. In these months of solitude and deep thinking you have found, sooner than most, the true centre of gravity. "Thyself, the Inward Ruler." By the very writing of this book, so finely begun, you will become inwardly another man. For it is truth, not fantasy, that a man's work creates him in a deeper sense than he creates it.'

To Tara, woman of the West, it seemed strange that a statement so personal should be addressed to Roy before herself and this attentive stranger, who looked up now and said with conviction, 'I myself feel it will be Sir Roy Sinclair's privilege to convince our Western thinkers that they have sinned through failing to recognise or admit the spiritual essence of their being; through confusing culture, an affair of mind and spirit, with civilisation, an affair of luxury and comfort.'

And it was Roy who answered him, 'True talk, Shivanāth. If our ideals were right, if we could conquer the craze for blinding speed and deafening noise, even machinery could be rightly used. The devil is not in the machine, but in the man who lets it master him. The real merit of India's philosophy lies in her stress on things not seen.'

'In the words of your own Master, "Seek ye first the Kingdom of God,"' the Guru surprisingly quoted Scripture, in which he was more deeply versed than many Christians. Then, turning to Roy, he intimated that Shivanāth would much appreciate half an hour's talk with him, if Lady Sinclair was in no hurry to be rid of them.

Permission given, Roy strolled off with his young admirer into the orchard beyond the terrace; while Tara sat alone with her former enemy, feeling equally at ease whether he spoke to her of Roy and England, or sat beside her thinking his own thoughts; neither expecting talk nor proffering it unless he had something worth saying. She saw it as entirely his doing that they two could sit silent thus, in a curious content, steeped in the radiation of his serenity, while the fountains plashed and the stream gurgled and birds in the orchard uttered their happy tuneless cries. Roy would be pleased when she told him of this.

Suddenly their calm was dispelled by a sound of voices on the higher terrace, Indian voices, unmistakably. And there, at the top of the steps, appeared three unmistakable figures — Rajini, Surāj Mul, and Aruna, uninvited, yet sure of their welcome. The younger pair would deem themselves privileged; and Aruna had no doubt been persuaded to keep them in countenance, Surāj being well aware that, in Roy's eyes, she could do no wrong. Handsomer than ever he looked in his green coat and coppery pink turban; Rajini a gleaming vision in golden dress and *sari* that clung limply to her rounded slenderness.

Seeing Tara with a stranger, they halted; and as she stood up waving a welcome, the Guru rose also.

'Should we go? The ladies might prefer ——'

'No. Please stay,' she said quickly. 'Aruna is Roy's cousin. She would wish to meet you. The man, Surāj Mul, is also a connection, with his young wife.'

'I stay gladly.'

He remained standing while she went to meet them at the foot of the steps, kissed Aruna, and exclaimed at sight of Rajini's damp, clinging finery.

'What *has* happened to your lovely frock and *sari*?'

'She thought she would try a swim in the lake!' Surāj answered for her; but his bedraggled bird of paradise was in no mood for joking.

'*He* knocked me into the water ——' She flung an angry look at him.

'*Her* version!' he retorted, unabashed. 'We came in a light *shikara*. She foolishly stood up too near the edge when I was already standing. The boatman shouted. I tried to hold her — but too late. She was lucky not to be drowned.'

'Not lucky at all,' she pouted. 'My lovely new dress all so damp. Such a long walk up that horrid path in my best shoes.'

She held out one small foot shod in fawn-coloured kid.

'Poor Rajini,' Tara consoled her. 'Very pretty, but not suitable for hill walking.'

'I didn't expect hill walking. Surāj was so impatient to see his friend, he didn't find out.'

Aruna laid an arm round her damp shoulders, while Surāj made obeisance to the Guru and looked round for Roy.

'Never mind, *piari*.[1] We'll soon get your frock dried.'

'The sooner the better,' said practical Tara. 'You must be wet all though. Come with me.'

But Rajini — mainly concerned for damage to vanity — had caught sight of Roy. 'Presently,' she said, with decision. 'First I wish to greet my deliverer.'

It was Aruna who went towards him, with the grace and poise of movement that still astonished Tara in these Indian women, high or low.

'Aruna-*bai* — welcome!' He flung out both hands; but she halted and bowed her head, finger-tips touching her forehead.

'No, not that way, sister of my heart.' Gently taking down

[1] Darling.

both her hands, he held them between his own. 'Did you think — we were never to meet again?'

'Sometimes I feared ——' she admitted, very low. 'But always a voice within me said — that could not be. Tara also knew.'

'More than I did, lately. It was touch and go.'

Turning, he indicated the tall figure a few paces behind him, Shivanāth having slipped aside into a shadowed corner.

'You have come just in time to meet my Master, the Guru Mah-arāj of Kashmir.'

Again she touched her forehead; and while she spoke quietly with the Holy One, Surāj came forward, in high delight.

'Roy, brother and friend, it is like new life to see you again; and wearing our dress — just as I saw you first.'

They embraced Eastern fashion, shoulder pressed to shoulder. 'Rajini also is glad' — he turned to his bride. No pulling forward her *sari* now, as at their first meeting. Boldly she held out her hand.

'See all I have to thank you for, Sir... Sir Roy.'

And he, smiling at her hesitation, bowed over her hand. 'We did a good day's work — not only for you, but for Surāj!'

His glance appraised her golden dress and *sari*. 'You wanted to outshine the sun. But he was envious, and tried to extinguish you.'

'It was not the sun who tried ——' she flashed out; and Surāj retorted with a frown of reproof, 'See what comes from behaving carelessly in a boat.'

'I don't know about boats. Very queer things.'

'Aren't you living in one, like all Srinagar?' Roy asked, amused at the clash between them.

'Oh, yes — a tame, tied-up one. I don't like them running about loose on this dangerous lake. My beautiful frock — see!'

She pouted again like a child, and squeezed a trickle of water from her *sari*.

'A sad pity,' he sympathised. 'But don't hang about in damp clothes.'

'I am going, only — I wished to greet you first.'

'Now, that's done. You go with Lady Sinclair,' Surāj commanded with his husbandly air; and Roy promised strawberries on her return. 'We'll make fresh tea, if you take it?'

She brightened at that. 'Only strawberries, please. Don't let *him* eat all before I come back.'

'Not I,' Roy gravely assured her, with a wink at Surāj, who was not heeding her, cherishing his dignity.

And at last Tara was allowed to draw her away from male magnets to the upper story of their pavilion.

'I'm afraid we haven't any shut-in place,' she apologised for their arcaded bedroom; and Rajini noted with mild surprise the two camp-beds and chairs, the courtesy dressing-table, and a large fourfold screen.

'You'll find water and a bath behind there.' Tara proffered a coat-shaped towel. 'Slip into this, while ayah dries your dress on our cane hen-coop over the charcoal stove.'

'Not too long?' she queried, unfastening a brooch or two; and Tara smiled, guessing her thought.

'You're afraid the strawberries may melt away?'

'Yes — I *am* afraid,' she said, simply as a child. 'Surāj is lord of me; but he is a greedy man. Not satisfied if I don't cook him tastesome dinners. I think — Sir Roy will protect the fruit for me.'

'I'm sure of it. We'll be quick all the same.'

Divested of dress and *sari*, she peeled off her wet pink stockings and stood up — a creature of unconscious grace — in her primrose silk combined garment, the golden-brown limbs lovely in form and colour. Not yet seventeen, and looking little more than a child, she was clearly in herself complete woman, as Tara had certainly not been at that age.

Smiling, she patted her silken thighs. 'Aruna made these for me. Not so damp. But I will take off everything behind there and rub my body with your queer nice towel.'

Presently she reappeared, lost in the large garment, a child again, full of fun and astonishingly beautiful. But when ayah brought her gleaming frock, she swiftly transformed herself: drew oddments out of her bag; reddened her lips, darkened the smudge under her eyes, and slipped a hand through Tara's arm.

'*Now* we will see if any strawberries are left for the bird they tried to drown!'

They found that fresh tea had arrived, and Surāj had raided the sweet biscuits and cakes, the fruit being 'protected' by Roy.

'Berries for the Bird of Paradise!' he sinfully flattered Rajini; and she glowed, sitting between him and Surāj, who adored her with his eyes, but said nothing.

And here was Tara presiding over a second tea party of not very mixable elements. But they were friendly together, in courteous Indian fashion. Only Shivanāth seemed still inclined to hold aloof. Not so the Guru, a greater and holier man. No trace in him of that 'get-thee-behind-me' air, which Tara detected in the younger man's eyes when they were drawn to the lovely, laughing bride. Sri Samādhi, she decided — watching him with Aruna — had known the love of woman. Shivanāth, with his curiously remote face, was the born celibate. He had come to talk of deep things with Roy, and had been interrupted, too soon, by unbidden intruders.

Aruna spoke little, but had clearly found some link with the Guru; and her eyes were more eloquent than she knew when they rested on Roy. Surāj — introduced as the coming epic poet of Rajasthan — was so full of a long ballad lately written that it needed all Roy's tact and courtesy to ward off an impromptu recitation without hurting his friend's naïve vanity. Skilfully he linked Surāj up with Shivanāth, not revealing his race, interested always in diverse types. For here, the Englishman was ascetic, the Rajput a man of masculine fibre, living through his senses and sensibilities.

Tara, who was watching and listening more than she talked, perceived with pride and pleasure how the focal point for all was Roy and the glad fact of his return; how effortless was his response to a burning of incense that might have embarrassed or over-elated another make of man. Contact with his Indian friends brought out all that was best in his Rajput heritage; a dignity and courtesy of bearing, especially to the women, that set her wondering how he would readjust himself to the mannerless manners of the modern West? Mentally also she was contrasting this Indian welcome, so eager and informal, so palpably from the heart, with his English welcome at the Residency; not a shade less genuine, yet expressed in a champagne lunch and drinking of healths; deeper feeling veiled by casual talk.

She herself fully approved the emotional reticence of her race; yet, as wife of Roy, her romantic temperament warmed towards these Indians, who loved him with fervour and thought no shame of letting it be seen.

Presently Aruna came to sit by her and talked of the child, of her unforgettable visits to their English home, that seemed centuries away in this terraced garden of Shah Jehān and his Mumtāz Mahal.

Slowly lengthening shadows crept across the terrace; but the Indians took no note of time. Probably none but she wore a watch, unless Surāj wore one for show — not wound up. It was Aruna who, reluctantly, suggested that they ought to be moving back, having far to go; and Tara said, in a low voice, 'You must come again one afternoon, without them, and have some real talk with Roy.'

'Oh, if I may ——' She caught her breath on the word. 'He does look wonderful. The same — yet different.'

'*You* see that?'

'I *feel* it.' One hand lightly covered her heart.

And now the Guru came up to them, expressing a wish to meet Aruna again, for further talk about her work. There were leave-takings long drawn out; Rajini's brightness a trifle dimmed at the prospect of another journey in the boat that ran loose about the lake.

And Roy went with them a little way, keeping close to Aruna, talking specially to her, as he had not been able to do.

While Tara stood watching them, the Guru said, with quiet emphasis, '*That* is a woman of rare simplicity, farther advanced in holiness than she knows. She has obtained release through suffering. Her path is the path of *Bhakti Yoga* — the *Yoga* of devotion.'

And Tara, knowing much of Aruna's tragic story, gazed at him in wonder.

'She is deeply interested in everything that concerns Indian women.'

'So she told me. All her work is lit by the clear flame of the spirit. Through that she has found the true *Yoga*, which is not a matter of sitting cross-legged, squinting down the nose; but attainment of union with the divine, of stillness in the midst of action; a life enriched, not narrowed, by spiritual experience, as my *chela* will find when he returns to his ordained task in England.'

So simply and impressively he spoke his thought that there was no hint of sermonising; and Tara, after this fresh contact with him, could no longer wonder at his influence on Roy, who presently returned with the lighted look in his eyes that she would always associate with their renewed marriage. And she owed it all to the man whom she had once hated as heartily as she now admired him. The whole afternoon had given her a fuller sense of entering into Roy's Indian life, of realising that she need not fear it for him any more.

When at last they were left alone, they stood by the black balustrade in a blaze of light, as the sun streamed out from under a bank of purple cloud; and Roy said, with a sigh of content, 'It's worth letting the world break in, if only for the sake of getting back — to this. They harmonised with it all. Nice genuine people; my Guru something more than that.'

'Yes — a wonderful man.' She looked out across the lake, remembering his words. 'I think most Indians *are* nice genuine people.'

At that, he pulled her close and kissed her.

'I felt sure you'd find the best in them if you could only see and know the right sort. It was a God-sent chance, Aruna meeting the Guru. One could trust *him* to perceive her quality at sight. He will mean much to her. He won't lose hold of her.'

'And *we* mustn't either, Roy. She cares so deeply.'

He gazed at her in astonishment. 'Tara — you *know?*'

'Yes,' she said, 'I know. It came out by chance at Home. In our anxiety, it drew us very close together.'

'It wouldn't have worked so with most women,' was his masculine comment on that.

'Well, I'm glad it did with us.' She tacitly shared the implied compliment with Aruna. 'And I'm more than glad to see her with that Rajini. How she loves her.'

He smiled 'A brilliant creature, needing all the ballast of Aruna's wisdom, if her gifts are to ripen and bear fruit, other than sons for Surāj! I wonder — will he burden her with his two small girls by the earlier, unloved wife?'

'Two girls, are there? I should think more likely he would trust Aruna. They would mean much to her; little to Rajini.'

'Quite so. You've sized up the Bird of Paradise! Hers will not be the way of *Bhakti Yoga* — like Aruna and like you. Having both of you so unexpectedly together — you, my England; she, my India — made me feel curiously complete, as I often did with you and the little Mother.'

'And I felt, in some way, accepted by your India, especially by your splendid Guru.'

'That was because you accepted it with your heart, the organ we English, for all our practical cleverness, so often strangely misprize. It was the Hindu *bhakti* [1] that strengthened Akbar's throne. But how many of our own people out here have been even aware of India's unspoken appeal — "Masters of the Seven Seas, oh, love and understand"? The few that have heard and heeded have been our salvation.'

'It's a thousand pities,' she murmured feelingly: and from behind them came the voice of a very humble India; the voice of Gulbaddan announcing that dinner — delayed by the holy ones — was now served.

[1] Devotion.

'I hope they haven't spoilt some delectable dish,' remarked Roy, coming completely back to earth.

'I could forgive your Guru a lot more than that,' said Tara; thus intimating to her percipient husband how completely India had carried the day.

Chapter XI

Here, with an eye made quiet by the power
Of harmony and the deep power of joy,
We see into the heart of things.

WORDSWORTH

Two days later, they were welcoming Eve with Lilāmani, Chrystal Adair, and more strawberries from Vanessa.

Lilāmani, running ahead of them, paused in the arched entrance, an elfin creature in her yellow frock, the hated sun-hat dangling by its strap.

'Good morning,' said Tara, and the child's face lit up.

'Oh, Mummy, Mummy!' she cried, flinging herself into her mother's arms. 'Now you truly *are!*'

'But I always truly am.' Tara kissed her again.

'Not yesterday. Your face wouldn' come right in my head — nor Daddy's.' She gazed at him in his Indian dress — fascinated. 'Truly Prithvi Rāj, now,' she murmured. And leaving her mother she went to him in a demure fashion, as if instinctively she knew the Indian woman's way with a man, even a father.

But when he lifted her and kissed her, she clung to him, still holding his *choga*, while he greeted Chrystal Adair, whom he had only met a few times since the Residency lunch. This girl was not one of those tiresome pretty-pretties, who dash out for the cold weather, and find India 'so mysterious, so thrill-making' — the kind that, to many Indians, fatally typify England. She had brains under her honey-coloured casque of hair.

'It was Eve,' she said, 'who told me I ought to make a

sketch of this little gem. And it *is* a gem. What marvels they were, those Moghuls. Such artists in all they did.'

'"They were dreamers, dreaming greatly,"' Roy quoted. 'Dreamers of action, who left their mark on seething, formless Hindu India.'

'Artist-rulers — that's why they interest me,' she said, with her swift look of intelligence. 'The artist should be the ruler, don't you think?'

'*Don't* I think? It's the artist who may yet save the world — *if* the dead hand of the machine doesn't flatten us all. And the Moghuls, loving Nature, left their mark here also. But I can't forgive Akbar for degrading the men of Kashmir because they made such a plucky stand against him.'

'Degrading them — how?' she asked.

'He made them all wear a shapeless smock, like women; and you have to know Moslems to realise how that would gall them. If the Kashmiri is a poor thing now, Akbar's partly to blame. But one can forgive a good deal to men who gave India the Taj and Fatehpur Sikri and old Delhi.'

'Yes, I long to see them. But I may never get the chance. I'm not touring. I'm with an aunt, in Peshawar.'

'Having a good time? Liking the country so far?'

'Yes. I'm liking it,' she said, a curious change in her tone. 'Real India — not just the life out here. It's an amazing land. Its very queerness gets under one's skin. But *you* know all that.'

He looked at her a moment, wondering, 'Does *she* know?' His new-born self had resolved never again to let the prejudice of others make him shrink from admitting his link with India.

'Yes,' he said, 'I know, because it's in my blood.'

Her look of frank interest was his reward.

'Rajput,' she stated. 'Eve told me. I wondered why that charming little thing had such a lovely Indian name.'

The little thing, by now, had drifted away to the marble balustrade 'to see over the edge.'

'We've quite made friends,' Chrystal went on. 'We have

drawing lessons. She's an artist in her bones. A fascinating bit of quicksilver; and full of quaint fancies about "When I used to be before." Was she out here very young?'

'No, never. Unless — in some other life?'

'You believe in that uncanny idea?'

'Belief is a word I don't use lightly. I've had strange intimations myself. I've heard of astonishing cases, not otherwise accountable. But don't encourage the child to talk that way. She might get weaving fairy tales without intent to deceive.'

'Yes. I'll be wary. But I'm interested.'

His eyes shifted to the small figure by the balustrade. 'It's an interesting Little Scrap. Encourage the drawing. She has it from my father.'

She was craning over now, and he called to her quickly: 'Look out, Lilāmani. Don't take a header into the tank.'

At his voice, she came running back to him.

'Oh, Prithvi, a black lamb down there, trotting after the little girl. Can I stroke it?'

'Yes. It's Mary's lamb. Follows her everywhere. That little girl, Lilāmani, is only six — and she's quite blind.'

'Blind?' With a gesture unconsciously tragic she covered her eyes with one hand. 'Always dark? Isn't it morning ever?'

Remembering her acute dread of darkness, he drew down her hand and held it closely.

'Not quite all dark,' he consoled her. 'She can feel the light and see shadows of people, not their faces. And she can almost see with her finger-tips. Think of that.'

'See — with fingers?' She gazed down at her own, half incredulous; and he saw that he had shifted her mind from dread to wonder.

'Come along and find her. She's the gardener's little girl. She knows the colours of flowers by touching them, and she carries her baby brother about everywhere, feeling with her toes.'

Down they all went to the lower terrace; and the wizened old gardener grinned at sight of them. Tara and he were friends already. He had told her how the flowers 'talked' to him, how trees in India were still full of natural divinity, worshipped for their gifts of fruit and shelter, their leafy mystery; how scented flowers were cherished as acceptable offerings to the gods. The unscented might be cut and placed in vases; but if scented ones were used, without first being 'offered,' the devout Hindu would feel that the flowers must have sinned.

His deep salaam was echoed by the blind child, with her sightless yet seraphic smile that hurt the heart.

Lilāmani promptly took her hand and laid it against her bare arm, as if to prove the strange power in her finger-tips.

'This is a little white girl,' she hopefully explained, adding a few words of her limited Hindustani.

The child at once began to chatter gaily; and Lilāmani, caressing the lamb, looked for help to her father.

He joined them as interpreter, while Tara drew Eve's attention to old Rāmanand, who seemed to be having a murmured conversation with an unhappy-looking rosebush. She was a young bush, he told them on enquiry — and a little sick. So he was giving her '*Meeta bāt*'[1] and each evening a jar of water from the sacred spring, that would soon make her happy inside.

'I want a lightning sketch of him,' whispered Chrystal.

To give her time, Tara encouraged further talk and asked for a favourite story of Krishna hiding from his wife in the forest, playfully deserting her, to see whether love would guide her steps to him. But while he vainly waited in the shade of a kindly tree, the god fell fast asleep.

'And all that while,' Rāmanand assured them, 'the poor goddess, bewildered, went seeking him through green glades, where trees and flowers were drooping sadly, like herself. "These," she thought, "have surely not been cheered by the presence of my lord." But at last she came to an open glade, where fawns were fearlessly grazing and flowers smiling; birds, overhead, singing songs of love. The boughs of a great tree beckoned to her, "Here, here"; and her heart knew that

[1] Sweet talk.

they were all happy because a god had come among them. So she quickened her steps; and there, under that friendly tree, the goddess found her sleeping lord.'

'Delicious person. He believes it all!' murmured Chrystal, adding a few deft touches to her sketch. 'I've caught him neatly, a possession for ever.' Strange movements on the higher terrace attracted her attention. 'Are we being summoned? Or is your boy up there having a fit?'

It was Gulbaddan by the balustrade, making a windmill of his arms, calling them to feed.

At tiffin — laid in the cool pavilion — Eve held the field, telling them how she and Chrystal had rescued a shamefully overloaded donkey.

'Bulging bundles on each side' — her hands described them in the air. 'You couldn't see anything of the poor little beast but match-stick legs, flapping ears, and mangy hindquarters; one with a horrid open sore. I paused a minute to collect my courage. Because, if I pounced, I'd have to carry it through; and the fat *dhobi* looked rather a truculent person.'

'I'd back you to pounce,' said Roy, 'with due discretion.'

She laughed. 'I haven't any of that. Never had. Ask Lance. He calls himself my Major Indiscretion! But I did save that deplorable donkey. When the *dhobi* prodded its open sore, I fairly shouted at him. He stared hard — and prodded again. I was furious; but I bridled my tongue, seeing a certain person look a bit scared ——'

'Which one was that?' asked Lilāmani, listening with all her ears.

'One that you didn't happen to notice,' Eve neatly retorted, with a glance at Tara. 'You hush, my chicken. I'm telling Daddy. The man wasn't impertinent ——' She reverted to Roy. 'He simply didn't see what on earth I was fussing about. As for healing that sore, *he* wasn't going to spend money on a mere donkey. Then I flung my trump card — the Animal Welfare dressing station, where the sore would be dressed gratis, and the donkey fed up to be fit for work. While he was taking it in, I suggested removing the bundles. I also casually mentioned my friend the Resident Sahib. That did the trick. He promptly found a *bhai* [1] to guard his precious bundles; and we got there somehow.'

'Good deed for you, Eve,' Sinclair commended her; and she gave her quick double nod.

'I did feel a bit uplifted, pulling off a job I hate, when I saw the look of peace on that donkey's meek face after they'd cleaned up his sore and given him a feed. Blessed be the stray visitors who made a fuss about ill-used pack ponies up here. Even Kashmiris are discovering the advantage — to themselves! When Lance is here, he's after them all the time; and he subscribes a lot more than he can afford. He's pony mad.'

'Pony mad!' echoed Lilāmani, pouncing on the new word, and looking up sidelong at Roy. 'Like you and me, Daddy! We saw the *well* ponies, too, in a field. We're going to-morrow with carrots and sugar for our donkey. Going to find more shops and temples for Chrystal and me to paint: temples — like I used to know,' she added, half to herself. 'Men blowing curly horns, but no monkeys, no peacocks.'

'There *are* no peacocks in the hills,' Roy said, ignoring the rest of it, but remembering peacocks in the hill jungles of Udaipur.

She looked at him gravely. 'In other kind of hills, there are.'

'You know too much — or you think you do,' he lightly chaffed her.

'I *don't* think.' She half suspected a rebuff, and her father patted her hand.

'Of course you don't. You eat strawberries, like all sensible little girls.'

He picked out six large ones and spilled so much cream over them that she gave a small gasp. Temples and peacocks were forgotten; and they talked of other things.

When it came to leaving, he had a word aside with Eve.

'Take her to the ponies,' he said, 'not to the shops or temples. Her fanciful idea bothers Tara.'

[1] Brother.

'I'll do my best,' she promised. 'It's a darling Scrap and gives no trouble; but it's very persistent over anything it really wants to do.'

He smiled. 'I know where she gets that from — and the other. But your best is good enough for me.'

That evening at dinner he said nothing about Lilāmani's talk and its queer implications. He waited till they were settled in their canvas chairs by the balustrade, with coffee and cigarettes to keep off mosquitoes, that began to be lively and voracious in this first thundery week of May.

The lake, dreaming far below them, had a misty sheen. Promontories loomed like heraldic beasts black on a silver shield. The breeze had fallen asleep. Only an ink-blue cloud in the south held a threat of storm.

Roy, savouring his last whiffs of cigarette, said without preamble, 'Tara, does it creep you when Lilāmani talks as if she remembered scraps of some other life?'

Her faint sigh admitted as much.

'It sometimes makes me wish I hadn't brought her out here.'

'Never wish that. She'd have pined at home. She's blossoming here. Listen, darling——' he leaned towards her. 'You've realised now that she has more of India in her than the other two, though she doesn't show it like Helen. And if she has these sleeping memories or intimations, it's better she should out with them. I speak from my own experience. In the past eighteen months all that is India in me has been given free play; the balance of East and West readjusted, as my Guru foretold a year ago. I believe, in a lesser way, the child's coming to India will release much that might later have caused hidden discords like my own. And after all, since we do believe in some form of "going on and still to be," why boggle at the idea of having been before?'

'I don't know,' she truthfully answered. 'It's instinctive. Where does one's personality go to?'

'That's a very large question. Hindus believe in a subtle body that survives this one, and lasts through all chances and changes, not altogether forgetting them — which accounts for fleeting intimations. In that way the inextinguishable Self may prove, through many life-experiences, what *are* the supreme values. And although their *Karma* means a reaping what we've sown in other lives, it also implies ability to sow what we wish to reap; to gain true freedom of the spirit, chiefly by one's own efforts during cycles of death and rebirth.'

He had spoken, looking straight before him, intent on the effort of expressing in simple terms the complexities of Hindu thought. Now he turned and looked deep into her eyes.

'Most long-suffering of women! Am I lifting you clean off your feet?'

At that she laughed softly.

'I like being lifted off my feet by you. I missed it sadly when you weren't there. But, Roy ——' her eyes were serious again. 'You've gone so deep into this complex philosophy that I can't help wondering — are you now, in your heart of hearts, a Hindu?'

He shook his head. 'I couldn't be that, if I wanted to. A Hindu is born, not made. In my heart of hearts I believe in the God behind all religions, with the unreasoning faith of the artist, who knows that reason can never have the last word. One can't become a Hindu.'

'But then — what would you call Shivanāth?'

'A thinking young man, attracted by the profound truths of ancient Hinduism. I doubt if he would be accepted by the orthodox. The newer Hinduism is more elastic. It offers a noble philosophy of thought and life to any thinking man of any creed. There is much in it that the world needs today. Radkakrishnan is perhaps its finest interpreter to the West. My Guru calls him chief liaison officer between the two worlds; and he does me the honour to believe that such is also my destiny. That was the main idea behind my Vedic studies. But no hard-and-fast religious label fits the real me — nor the real you either. Never did. You've always lived by some light of your own direct from heaven. That's why we're sitting here together in paradise regained —— Listen!' He raised a hand. 'Thunder.'

It was a warning rumble from the ink-blue cloud that now came surging over the hilltops, the edges ragged and blurred. A ghostly wind shivered through the trees like a passing soul. A sizzle of lightning, a growl of thunder, and the squall sprang out of heaven, whipping the lake into a ruffled sheet of water flecked with foam.

They had only just time to whisk their chairs into shelter, before a second flash and crash released a rush of wind-driven rain. Poplars along the shore bowed and shivered in flurried agitation. Willows tossed wild arms aloft.

'Indra, the storm god, in a terrible temper,' said Roy. 'Too violent to last.'

Even as he spoke, the flying raindrops became a shower of silver needles, smitten by a rapier shaft from the sun that had burnt a hole in the cloud, dissolving it and flinging a blaze of glory across the troubled waters.

Now the storm was swerving eastward. Mahadeo was lost in darkness. The wind subsided. Rain ceased. A few shivering sighs passed over the lake — and all was calm again, as though Indra's burst of fury had never been.

And now, through every gap in the western hills, day's final splendour flowed like liquid fire; storm clouds piled into high alps, soaring and gleaming in unearthly beauty, as the sun slipped behind Kashmir's mountain battlements and fired the cloud-flags waving above them.

Roy brought out the chairs again; and while they sat entranced by gradations of dimming and dissolving light, there came from the sky, faint and far off, a sound like the rustling of paper. Drawing nearer, it changed to the long vibration of a smitten violin string.

'What *is* it?' whispered Tara, as though they were in a cathedral.

'Homing wild duck,' said Roy in the same low tone. 'Here they come.'

High overhead they flew; a wavering line of long necks and wide wings against the rain-washed sky, passing over and on, till they became once more a faint, invisible sound.

Silence grew and prevailed. The lower garden filled with

shadows. From the hush of the lake's deep sleep came the squawk and splash of a water-bird, the cry of an owl, answered from the hillside. And there, where ebbing light still lingered, Venus hung like a lamp.

And still there they sat on, while deepening dusk veiled peak after peak, withdrawing the mountains till they loomed like shadowy presences, felt rather than seen. Only the snows gleamed ghostly, as dusk dissolved in darkness and the stars set their watch. It was night.

Then they rose and went in together; but the sky and the stars were with them in their arcaded upper room; a night almost too magical for sleep.

Chapter XII

Here, at the edge of ecstasy, the fringe
Of what we two are capable to feel,
Time stands, and turns.

GERALD GOULD

After the Indian tea party and the coming of the child, they slipped back, as if from long habit, into a way of life so idyllic that it needed an occasional dash of earth to keep them from floating right off it — as Roy remarked when Gulbaddan dumped down their large borrowed milk jug so vigorously that it came in half, and baptised their breakfast with the precious fluid. Abjectly mopping up the flood, he must have resigned himself to prompt dismissal, so naïve was his joy when the bolt failed to fall and he found himself patted on the shoulder by that incalculable being, the British Sahib. Untrained though he was, often clumsy from sheer zeal, his devotion covered many lapses and his youth won Tara's heart.

She herself, in these days of renewal, was drawing life from the sun and strong air of the heights, from a well-spring of happiness within her, more tonic than either. Their two golden weeks — that had seemed untold wealth in anticipation — had slipped through their fingers like seed pearls. This garden retreat, with its scent of roses, its music of birds and running water, had become a part of their inmost selves for ever. Time and the hour might pass. The imperishable essence would remain. Here also Roy had become more consciously aware of his own increased creative power, driving him, lifting him towards new heights that must be scaled — given time, given life. Meanwhile the sense of pause was strong upon him, the surrender to secret processes often more fruitful than any conscious mental activity, the deep response of his whole being — after long abstinence — to the love of wife and child.

Before the midday sun became a deterrent and mosquitoes a torment, they explored their hillside in every direction; day-long tramps in which Tara found renewal rather than fatigue. And Roy himself was a tireless walker. His months of camp life and hill marching had left him thinner yet tougher, nerves and muscles in effortless control.

Voices from the outer world came to them only through another good batch of mail letters, two notes from Eve reporting all well with the child, and a brief letter from Peshawar — signed 'Yours ever, Vernon' — that pricked Tara's heart. So far, he had only sent his Fairy a picture postcard of aircraft on the war-path; and she had hoped for a swift transfer of interest to the young things who shared his work and play. She had talked of him to Roy — who remembered the 'kid of seven' — as the Darling's first conquest; very attentive to her 'lone' mother; had regarded the whole episode in the past tense. And now she felt half annoyed with the dear tiresome boy for that 'Yours ever' and a postscript not quite so casual as it was probably meant to appear: 'D'you mind if I sometimes write? You needn't feel bothered to answer. V.'

As she sat frowning over that, Roy asked suddenly, 'Who's presuming to worry you, Star Lady?'

'Vernon,' she said, handing him the letter. 'He *is* a dear, but I'd hoped he wouldn't write.'

'Hard on Vernon,' Roy remarked, scanning the open sheet, while she watched his face. The earlier Roy had been given to flashes of jealousy on small provocation; and in this case it might be a help — she having little or no experience of such human tangles in her home-loving life.

But this new Roy looked up from the letter with a smile in his eyes. 'Why not?' he queried. 'Let him write — and answer him. No young man, at that difficult age, could fail to be the better for contact with you.'

He stated the fact in an odd, impersonal way that impressed her more than any show of feeling.

'Thea,' he added, 'would agree with me.'

'She does.'

He raised an eyebrow at that. 'Two infallible authorities on budding manhood,' he said; and she smiled.

'If you see it that way, of course I'll write to him.'

She wrote next day at some length, chiefly about his Fairy and their latest 'explore' — the ruins of Kashmir's ancient capital in her golden age, two thousand years ago; a ghost of vanished glory, tumbled walls and pillars smothered in roses, crowned with clumps of sky-blue iris: Nature, as always, having the last word.

It was on the eleventh day of their fortnight that Roy proposed a more ambitious climb than they had attempted yet, to a height nine thousand feet up, where snow would still be lying in sheltered corners, and views would be superb; an outing such as Tara loved. So they laid their plans in great pleasure of the small enterprise.

Before dawn they were dressed and mounted on sturdy Kashmir ponies that would carry them nearly halfway up; the world all silvered with dew; pale stars winking down at them; the ghost of an old moon fading out as the east brightened. The lake, far below them, was veiled in mist; and their upward path curved among forest trees, where birds were at their matins.

Higher and higher they climbed; the keen night air shot through with early light, the aroma of pines all about them; till they reached a level space of grass and shade, where two clear pools invited them to bathe and breakfast before the last stiff pull of six hundred feet. The ponies had been left lower down to await their return. Only a coolie, with lunch-basket and drink, came all the way, squatting discreetly out of sight.

After breakfast, resting in the shade, they fell asleep; and woke to find the sun well up, the pools blue as heaven, the grass patterned with shadows. Tall trees stood round them, calm and old, yet for ever young, lifting stately heads to greet the morning. A small breeze, from nowhere in particular, stirred the upper branches that seemed to be having a murmured conversation, as no doubt they were, if one had ears to hear.

The peace and beauty, the sense of completeness, too rare in a world of broken arcs, tempted the pair to remain among these friendly trees, and to forego the triumph of ascent, the hill-top vision. But the zealous coolie had set out already; and Roy's Spartan decree, 'No summit, no tiffin,' carried the day.

It was hard going, up those few hundred feet; but they had their reward. Veils of morning had been withdrawn from mountain and valley; streams and cataracts laced the dark hillsides. The glaciers of Mahādeo seemed only a stone's throw from their lesser height. And there, on a rock near a snowdrift, the tiffin basket awaited them, bottles of ginger beer plunged neck deep into the snow by the vanished coolie. No elaborate indoor meal could rival that simple repast on a Himalayan summit; and the cigarettes that followed were incense burned to the gods.

In those few hours of shared isolation and peace they seemed to be lifted above life's pressing claims and demands, admitted into the source of Nature's unseizable beauty. Side by side they lay on the sun-warmed grass in great content, their bodies close together, their minds ranging apart. Roy, sinking with practised ease into a mental quiet, stiller than the hushed wind, felt within him the stir of a new significance in tree and cloud, a quickened relation with all things seen. His body felt light, his mind luminous; the ear of his spirit tuned to catch inaudible voices of the living earth. His released imagination, working with power, was aware of windows opening onto that 'world invisible,' which only poetic vision can apprehend direct. And he who apprehends direct has bid farewell to argument.

To him it seemed clear that the world's future must lie with the artist and the poet, through faith in those eternal values that equip them for seeing deeper than their reason-ridden fellows into the mystery of both worlds. Everywhere — in all discovery and experience — revelation stopped short of truth; and among all truth-seekers it was the poet who came nearest to the elusive goal. Lifted in spirit above the battle, he was constrained, like those high glaciers, to feed the streams that flow into the valleys and keep them green. He himself, his ode accomplished, the glow still in his veins, was lifted into one of those rare moods when a man can see the world transfigured, can almost believe that the transfigured may be the true.

Each week of return to normal ways proved more fully how his life had been enriched rather than narrowed by closing the door for a time against the world's confused voices and demands; how the pores of his mind had been opened, so that familiar thoughts and actions were charged with a new significance, seen in truer perspective — the essence of life and art.

A sound that was barely a sound drew him back from far flights to Tara lying beside him, in cool blue shirt and breeches, absorbed like himself, the horizon light in her eyes. Aware of his movement, she turned to him; and they looked deeply at one another.

'Roy, what *did* you do to me?' she asked, in a hushed voice.

'Nothing that I know of. I was miles away.'

'You carried me with you. We almost did slip off the edge of the world. And it seemed hardly strange. We're immortals!'

'We're immortal,' he said, deleting one letter and adding a cubit to the word. 'In such clear flashes we know it, instead of believing that we believe it.'

She smiled at the apt phrase. 'How many would be honest enough to admit that?'

'There's more honesty in these days, if less faith,' he said, 'than there used to be. I believe this new decade — thirty to forty — will witness a quickening of the spirit in life and art. There are signs already that the flame is kindled in many unexpected places; and "a flame is flame, wherever you find it." I believe scores of ordinary people want to see deeper into things, and haven't a notion how to set about it.'

'We're all too close up against each other,' she murmured, her eyes on a shining peak.

'You've discovered that by coming out here; getting "sight beyond the smoke." That has been the best part of my recent experience. We'll be higher than this before long. Gulmarg is nine thousand; but a plague of huts and golf and perpetual people rather spoil the effect. We'll climb to the top of Apharwāt; and you shall see the "frozen lakes" where I brooded alone, last summer, on *Out of the Dust*, which is doing its bit for Bramleigh Beeches.'

'It's doing more than that. Will you write another novel?'

'I hope so, as grist for the mill. At present I can't see beyond *the* book.'

A pause, and she asked in a changed tone: 'Roy, do you believe, like your Guru, that through writing it and living it, you will become another man?'

'Not in any way that you need worry over, darling. But when a man puts the whole of himself into his work, it stands to reason that it leaves him other than he was before. One might almost call it a sort of earth-reincarnation.'

'Roy — how queer!'

'It sounds fanciful; but it's not only artists who experience at times a sense of dying to one phase of life and being born into another. You must have known it.'

'Have I? Yes. I think — I'm knowing it now.'

'So am I, though it's only to you that I could speak of the profound inner transformation due to setting free the suppressed Indian side of my nature; balance in place of discord. You've been aware of it, Tara, haven't you?'

'Yes' — she paused — 'in a curious, fanciful way.'

'How? Tell me.'

So commanded, she told him how often, in these days, she had a strange and lovely sensation of being newly married to a husband loved long before, yet not fully known to her till now.

That moving confession, from one who never exaggerated

her sensations, he could only accept in a glow of gratitude too deep for words.

And now the changed angle of light on the hills, a keener air from the snow-line, warned them that their wonderful day was drawing to an end. Neither wore a watch, but Roy's practised eye could tell the time to within half an hour; and Tara had left orders for a cold meal with bowls of soup, that they might feel free to return when they pleased.

'Time we were moving,' he said, suddenly alive to the unwelcome fact. 'We may be birds of the air, but we don't want to get be-darked, with no lantern and no moon. Pity to shadow our perfect day with any minor calamity.'

Springing up, he pulled her to her feet. One look round to imprint the scene on their minds; one long kiss, to link it all up with their joy in each other; and reluctantly they started on the downward trek that proved, as usual, stiffer than the climb.

On the level, where they had bathed and breakfasted, they halted briefly; then down and down again, more walking than riding, sunset conflagrations flashing at them through forest gaps, while they had still a great way to go. Colour faded, but twilight lingered; and now they could ride the last few miles, reaching Chasma Shahi tired and hungry, but just not 'be-darked.'

At the entrance, Gulbaddan met them with a deep salaam. 'The Sahib is late. And there is a Memsahib waiting a long time.'

'A Memsahib — who on earth . . .?'

Roy turned to lift Tara from her saddle. 'Hard luck. You're played out. Who *can* it be at this time of day?'

On the dinner table in the pavilion stood a hurricane lamp newly lit; and from the terrace a shadowy figure came hurrying towards them.

'Eve!' cried Roy; adding with a swift premonition, 'What's up?'

'Oh, I thought you would *never* come,' she answered with a catch in her voice. 'It's — it's Lilāmini. She's vanished — since this morning. We've hunted everywhere.'

'Lost?' He shot out the fatal word, trying to grasp it; and Tara, feeling her head swim, sat down suddenly on the nearest chair.

Eve stood before them, her face white and strained.

'We've hunted and hunted,' she said again, 'at our wits' end. Oh, Roy! *Don't* look at me like that.'

The tremor in her voice penetrated his blank dismay.

'My dear girl' — he put an arm round her shoulders — 'I wasn't looking at you, I was looking at — the ghastly fact. And you've waited hours —? Sit.' He pressed her down onto another chair. 'Have some sherry to steady you. Tara, too. Then tell me — everything.'

Deliberately he filled three glasses, emptied one himself, and sat down near the table, where dinner awaited them unheeded. Resting an arm on the table, he leaned towards her.

'Now — please. And don't imagine I blame anyone but myself. She should have been here with us, as Tara wished. Who saw her last? When — and where?'

Eve drew a deep breath and told her difficult tale with studied quietness.

'She went out early, as usual, with ayah and Ian. It's almost the only time she is not with me. They joined Kaye's ayah and when my Mirbutti had to come home, Lilāmani said she would go along with Kaye, who was screaming for her. Mirbutti shouldn't have allowed it, but you know how weak they are with children. She simply told me the Missy Sahib had gone to the Residency, where I knew she'd be safe and happy. She had begged to go out with Chrystal to sketch one of the temples. But we had put her off, because you said, "not temples." She had been rather difficult about it. So I wasn't sorry she had gone to Vanessa.'

'And she hadn't gone there?'

'No. I scolded Kaye's ayah till she wept; but she could only say that near the Munshi Bagh the child suddenly said, in her mixed Hindustani: "Missy Sahib going now — ayah *mut āo.*"[1] And she ran off among the trees waving to little

[1] Not to come.

Kaye. Ayah waited for her, thinking she had gone to skip round the Bagh. But she never came back.'

Again the flash in Roy's eyes checked her and she drew a startled breath: 'Oh, how *can* I go on? You look like murder.'

'I *feel* like it,' he said, in a voice of deadly quiet. And Tara, on her other side, was quietly crying. 'You *must* go on. All day — not a sign? Where have you looked?'

'Everywhere. Round the temples, the ponies, the shops. Havelock sent out *chāprassis* to make it known that a little English girl was lost, offering a big reward. Then Lance came out here ——'

'Lance?'

'Yes. He'd had a fall at polo, hurt his arm. Ten days' special leave. He came last night. I was so happy. And *now* — oh, it's been a nightmare ——'

She choked back a sob and carried on her tale.

'They told Lance you'd be back for dinner. And as we'd had no luck, I tore out then. I began to think *you* were lost.'

'It's damnable,' Roy said, still with his deadly calm, that hurt Eve more than any outward show of pain. 'Have you got the car?'

'Yes. And room for you both on the boat.'

'*I* shall go on looking all night. Have you had any food?'

'No' — she smiled wanly — 'I counted on having some here.'

'You shall. And Tara too.'

'I can't,' she murmured brokenly.

'You must. You won't get much sleep.' His hand closed on her shoulder, and he sat down near her.

Against the grain, talking little, they swallowed untasted morsels of cold chicken and cups of coffee. Roy shot out an occasional sharp question. He could hardly bear the thought of his precious little daughter at large in a very mixed Indian city, though he knew she might be safer there than at night in an English town. Not once did any of them voice the fear that haunted their minds — fear of the river, canal, and lake.

Fortified in body, they set out with a handful of luggage

down the rough path to find Eve's car on the lake road, their perfect day shadowed indeed. Swiftly Eve drove them round the lake to her houseboat, moored in a quiet corner; and there, on the front deck, they were met by Lance, in a silence that told its own tale.

To Eve's 'No news yet?' he shook his head, holding out a hand to Roy. 'Thank God, we've got *you* safe back,' he said gravely. 'I'd looked forward to this.'

And Sinclair forced himself to say, 'Perhaps we shall both be glad of it — tomorrow.'

Then he took Tara's arm and added in a low tone: 'You go with Eve, darling. Try to get some sleep. I'm off at once. And I don't come back — without the child.'

To her agonised heart those last words had an ominous sound. Till she saw that look in his eyes, she had not fully realised how intense was his feeling for the fairy daughter who seemed almost his mother come to life again. Obediently she went into the houseboat with Eve, moving and speaking with outward calm. Then she lay down, only half undressed, in Lilāmani's little room, and tried vainly to obey Roy's parting command.

Chapter XIII

There's no dream that mustn't be dared.

GEORGE MALLORY

AND what of Lilāmani herself, on this wildest day of her life? For all her venturesome spirit, she was incapable of causing serious anxiety to Eve by a deliberate day-long disappearance. But who can fathom the mind of a child with its confused mingling of impulse and design? And the mind of this particular child, since her coming to India, had been further confused by a host of strange recollections, a vague sense of familiarity with the dark faces round her, with the open shops and temples, the wailing rams' horns, and the throbbing of small drums that seemed to go on inside her body in a queer, exciting way.

Happy enough though she was, with Eve and the drawing lessons and the baby, she still often ached for the pair who had basely deserted her. By way of distraction, she had encouraged those secret rememberings that made her feel as if one half of her — 'the Indian Lilāmani' — was living in a fairy tale of long ago, when the real Prithvi Rāj and Tara were battling and spearing and riding among hills and lakes and palaces of Rajputana. Sometimes that other Tara seemed to be her. There were pictures in her head; and when she tried to draw them, Chrystal said she had 'quite a notion.' But when she wanted to go with her and sketch the temple in the city, Eve had said 'No.' That most hateful of words had made her feel cross with Eve, who must not be disobeyed. Yet, again and again, something inside had kept tugging at her. She would never rest till she had got into a temple somehow. If they wouldn't let her go to the one in the city, she would climb that rocky hill of Takht-i-Suleiman and explore the old temple that looked like a giant's thimble against the sky.

So she had laid her secret plans: secret, because she could not bear to be thwarted this time; and not a disobedience because no one had ever said that she mustn't go up there. It wasn't so terribly far. Chrystal had been there and back before breakfast. She herself had been a little way with ayah. Now she would go alone to the very top and make a surprise picture for Chrystal, who must not be called 'Chrys,' just as she must never be called 'Lil.' Daddy would bite anyone who tried it on. She would take something to eat, in case she couldn't do it so quickly. And she would surely manage to slip away from the ayah-people. They were easy to order about. Not like Annie at home. From her supper she had 'smuggled' four choc biscuits, also a banana from early tea. If she could only smuggle herself away at the right moment, that would be triumph ——!

And, after all, the ayah-people didn't give her much trouble. Mirbutti thought she was going with Kaye to the Residency; and Kaye's pretty Nalini perhaps thought she had gone back to the houseboat. So she slipped between the two of them, and found herself actually alone on the edge of adventure, free as a bird in the morning sky — the most exciting moment of her life.

Nothing now could prevent her from reaching the little temple, sitting up there so proudly, waiting for worshippers and pilgrims. She saw herself as a pilgrim coming to make *puja* as she used to do before. There was a gap, she remembered, beyond the big hospital. From there, to the corner where ayah turned back, she knew her way. After that, adventure would begin. But if she said 'Takht-i-Suleiman,' any chance coolie could direct her.

Now it was up and up, a steady climb; and the sun was climbing too, the higher the hotter, till she felt quite glad of the hated sun-hat. She stopped now and then to pick a scented flower for her offering, because the old gardener said that temple flowers must have scent. Always up and up; yet the top still seemed very far away. Sitting down on a rock, she munched half her banana, resolved to keep the rest till she reached the temple. How long could it be? Climbing a steeper, stonier path, she wished she had put on her important birthday watch from Mummy.

At last the temple began to look bigger and nearer. She would reach it soon now. And reach it she did, her roses half withered, her legs rather wobbly. But what matter? She was there.

On the shady side of the wall she ate the rest of her banana, with two biscuits, carefully saving the other two and longing for a cup of milk. Here she could take off her hat to let the wind play with her damp hair, while she drowsed a little, listening to happy birds, loving all the flowers among the rocks, especially those masses and masses of tall iris, blue as the sky.

Quickly refreshed, she sprang up again and ran round the base to look for steps, which she found on the sunny side; a short flight, then a long one, through a pointed archway, nice to draw — but not yet. Climbing the steps, she stood on the eight-sided terrace, a brave, lonely little figure, looking with all her eyes at the lake and the mountains, the flowers and the sky, fluffed with soft white clouds. Even the temple was forgotten in the delight of gazing at that far, far scene: the lake with its islands; the winding silver river with bridges and tumbly houses of Srinagar; the sun shining on that big golden dome and the mosque with the queer-shaped roof. She could even see the Munshi Bagh and a bit of the Residency garden, only a few miles away. A gauzy mist was making a *sari* for the mountains and floating over another lake among the far hills. Everywhere hills, prickly with pointed trees. Everywhere roses pink and crimson, so thick you could hardly see the leaves. And high above the mist, all those big snow mountains where Daddy came from.

Suddenly she longed to be a bird or a hill fairy that could travel everywhere on a bird's back, like Thumbelina in Hans Andersen. But instead, here she was, dumped down out of her dream on to a temple platform, and the next thing was to get inside.

Another pointed arch framed a very old wooden door — shut, tight shut. By no effort could she force it open. The unkind, horrid thing was locked. No priest, no shrine for her withered flowers.

In a rush of bitter disappointment, tears started; but she blinked them back. She was angry with the god who went purdah when pilgrims came to worship. She had run away from ayah. She couldn't get home to breakfast. Eve would be angry. And here she stood, hot, thirsty, and heart-broken, staring at a locked door.

Defeated, she must trudge all the way back and face a scolding such as her soul abhorred. At thought of it, her temper flared. Again and again she banged that heartless door with her small fist, not caring that she only hurt herself.

Suddenly she remembered the surprise picture for Chrystal; and sitting on the parapet, she made one quick little scribble of the temple and the unkind door. Then sadly she descended the steps that she had mounted, so full of curiosity and hope.

This time she tried a different path among the rocks, and found that it led to a hut where somebody must live. Indians were kind people. She would boldly ask for milk. And there, near the hut, sat a very naked man with straggly hair, cooking *chupattis* over his oven. At sight of her he flung out an arm, warding her off; but if she mustn't come near, she could speak.

'I want milk,' she said, in the imperative Hindustani of the ruling race — and it worked.

He laid his *chupatti* on a leaf, popped into the hut, and came out with a brass bowl of milk. She emptied it without pausing for breath. It tasted boiled and smoky, but it was milk; and she ought to pay for it. Rather late to think of that. '*Pica nahin hai*,'[1] she said, returning the bowl; and his gesture dismissed *pica*, to her huge relief.

'Missy Sahib hungry?' he asked.

[1] No pennies.

She nodded so vigorously that he went in again and brought her a big leaf full of sun-dried apricots, grapes, and nobbly bits of Indian sugar candy. Sitting down, well away from him, she emptied the leaf, pocketed the candy, and tried to say thank you in a language that couldn't. But she touched her forehead, because he was a holy one, and left him to his sacred rite.

Back again on the main path, a sudden thought popped in — too late — perhaps he guarded the temple, perhaps he could have opened it.

Tantalised, she stood still, longing to return and ask; but a tiresome whisper inside told her that she ought to hurry on. A more tempting whisper suggested that there might be a way down to the city where she could find the temple Chrystal was painting, with a glittering roof. It seemed to be always open; and if she must be scolded, she might as well do a deed worth a scolding.

Down and down she scrambled, the sun hotter than ever — *and* the flies! Worst of all, she now felt uncertain about the path. It had seemed quite easy coming up, but things looked different going down, and her head felt wuzzy with sleepiness. A patch of shade and grass under a rock a little way off the path tempted her to sit and eat the two choc biscuits that were melting away, spoiling her birthday bag from Eve. Thankfully she settled herself on the cool grass; forgot all about her biscuits, and fell fast asleep....

She was awakened — after how long? — by light playing on her eyelids and heat on her bare head. For the sun had eaten up her patch of shade, the *topi* had tilted off while she slept, and the top of her frock was open. But why? But where ?

She had fastened it, in her hurry, with the precious little topaz brooch that Prithvi gave her long ago. She ought to have used a safety-pin, but she did love to wear it: and this was her punishment. Another scolding, and a bitter loss. Poor Lilāmani! A wave of desolation and self-pity submerged her. She gave it up and wept in her quiet, heart-broken fashion — and none near to comfort her.

It must be tiffin time by now, and she had nothing but two half-melted biscuits to fill the emptiness inside. Miserably she ate them, gulping down her tears, because Mummy said, 'Crying never mended anything.'

It couldn't bring back her lost brooch; and she herself seemed to be lost, as she had often wanted to be. And it wasn't any fun at all. The lake, not misty now, looked as if you could jump right into it; but even down there she would still be far from home. Why couldn't someone drop out of the sky, like in a fairy tale, and tell her the right way to the glittering temple and the Munshi Bagh? Perhaps they might, if she waited? And here was a chance to make one real picture for Chrystal.

By shifting her ground she could get a peep at the proud little temple that wouldn't let her in. And once she began to draw, everything else — as usual — went out of her head. The picture seemed to come of itself. Such a beauty, that it made her feel all lovely inside. Not till it was finished did her dilemma wake up again.

The sun moving nearer to the hills where he set so alarmed her that she resolutely started afresh, hoping for the best; took the first turning along an easier road — that happened to be the wrong one — and trotted on, till she was cheered by the sound of voices and the plop-plop of hoofs. People at last!

Round the corner came a smiling Kashmiri woman, a naked baby on her hip, and a man beside her leading a mule. Oh, that mule! Hope leapt at sight of it. She would give anything for a ride.

Their smiles and salaams emboldened her to ask for Srinagar, English quarter. They were actually going there, while she had been hurrying in the opposite direction. Gladly she agreed to go along with them. The relief it was, the feeling of safety, after the uncomfortable thrill of being lost. But beyond everything she wanted a ride. Could she? The man was rough-looking and bearded, but his smile inspired confidence; and at last she ventured to point up at the mule.

'Missy Sahib very hot, very tired, walking far,' she explained, and his smile showed he understood.

'Aha! No fear, Missy Sahib?' he asked.

'No fear,' she echoed, overjoyed.

So he lifted her up, dumping her between two wobbly bundles that hung on either side. And she — feeling quite at home anywhere between the animal's head and tail — boldly wriggled along, ruckling up her skirt, till she could hang her legs almost over its shoulders. Leaning forward, she talked to it softly, as she had heard Lance talk in his 'pony voice,' stroking the long velvet ears, while the pretty woman laughed and lifted her baby up to see the joke of the bold white Miss showing her pink legs.

The man at the mule's head paid no heed to them. He walked solemnly on and on; oh, so slowly. She could get along faster herself, but she was too tired; and by now there was a very big emptiness where tiffin and tea ought to be. The sun near the hilltops was making sun fairies on the lake when at last they came, by a narrow way, into the city, and she found herself among certain open shops where she had been with Eve. Oh, joy! There was a fruit shop known to her. So now she must be lifted from her bundle throne, and open her bag to show there were no pennies for her ride.

The man only said, '*Wah, wah!*' and looked amused. The smiling woman salaamed, and made the baby waggle a doll's fist at her.

'Nice kind people,' she thought; and ran to the fruit shop, where she could mention Desmond Mem. and Houseboat '*Shahbash*'; and the man wouldn't worry about *pice*.

He didn't worry. He plied her with fruit and milk and native sweets made by his wife. When she ventured to ask for a temple offering, he looked rather puzzled; but he gave her two sweet pink roses from his little strip of back garden, and a scented iris. Clutching them, she scampered off, not heeding something that he called after her about the Residency *chudrassi*.

For now strange sounds were coming from the temple. Men were playing on those curly horns, queer tunes that went up and down in the wrong places.

'What *is* happening?' she asked a boy, who stood gaping at the *tamasha*.

'Priests are putting the god to bed,' he told her; and she gasped. Here was a piece of luck: a god being put to bed; and she alone, free from worrysome grown-ups telling her 'little girls can't go in there.' This pilgrim Lilāmani knew quite well that little girls can go anywhere, if they are brave enough, especially if they used to be before. She was going in this time, anyhow. The scolding could wait.

All her crushed sense of adventure bubbled up again when she found the temple door invitingly open; no one near it just then but a squatting fakir, his hands counting beads, his deep eyes staring at nothing, like a blind man.

Cautiously she crept up the steps with an excited sense of trespassing; and that holy terror never once looked round. From the threshold she peered into the smelly, dusky place. No light, except a ruby-red lamp hanging over the funny fat elephant god, Ganesh, known to her from Indian pictures at home. Now he sat there, on a sort of throne, his trunk curling down over his stomach; forelegs hugging a bowl; hinder ones cuddled under him with huge round feet like hassocks. And in front of him, she could just make out the stone slab for offerings.

Bolder than ever, she stepped inside and laid her three blossoms on it by several others, with the strangest quiver all through that she had ever known.

Then those weepsome horns began again outside and the little lovely drums that seemed to beat in her body. It was the bedtime of Ganesh. She positively must see that, now she had got here; but they mustn't find her trespassing — or what *would* they do to her? Dark corners were terrifying, but she screwed up courage to slip behind the open door.

There it was darker than ever, and she stood stark still, breathing carefully, seeing, unseen, three men with curly horns and a boy with a little drum. Two more men with torches, behind the god's throne, were holding them high, making wavering lights on ugly old Ganesh, on carved pillars and walls. The pilgrim Lilāmani seemed vaguely to know it all. The other one was eagerly devouring a picture such as she might never see again. Even if she had been a bad girl, she couldn't feel truly sorry for any misdeed that had given her this thrilling moment.

But the droning and the drumming went on and on and on——

It grew wearisome. Would they never stop and give the god a chance of going to sleep? Excitement subsided and fear crept in; fear of going home in the dark. Craning forward, she could discern just enough space between the boy and the door for her to slip cautiously out; but the torch men might see her — and courage failed. She must wait and wait; and streak out the moment this endless bed-putting *tamasha* was over.

Now — *now*, they were turning round at last. The torch men had turned also. Holding her breath, she stood as near the edge of the open door as she dared, waiting for her chance——

And it never came.

When all were out, the last man pulled the door to with a dull thud like a thump on her chest. The clang of a bolt let down told her that she was caught in the shrine she had risked so much to see.

Stunned with terror, she stood there, helpless as a trapped mouse, in outer darkness, except for the red light hanging over Ganesh, changing him from a jovial god into an ogre, who might be angry at her for daring to stay there, when he was supposed to be in bed.

And, as the stunned feeling passed, active terror of the dark sprang at her, as if a hand clutched her heart. For now all about her there were scuttlings and rustlings that might mean rats or scorpions, or some other hateful crawler of this crawling India. And here was she — all the fun of high adventure snuffed out by another cruel closed door. Worse, far worse, to be locked into a Hindu temple than to be locked out of it.

How to escape from the horror of darkness and snakes and the red light that seemed to watch her like an angry eye?

She could not possibly stay alone here all night, hungry, and terrified out of her wits. Carefully she crept back and back towards the door. If she could thump loud enough, somebody might hear and come. They couldn't all be in bed yet. Even offended priests would be less fearsome than darkness and snake-people.

Standing on the high threshold, she rattled the latch and thumped with her small fists.

Dead silence outside, and a dead weight of despair inside her. But she could not give it up till she had tried everything. Inspired by terror, she snatched off a shoe, though her unprotected stocking foot started a terror of its own. With the heel she banged and clattered, might and main. Stopping at last, she waited, listening ——

Plenty of noises now outside, but no steps coming her way. Then, in despair, she let go of her courage and screamed and screamed and screamed ——

Suddenly she stopped and caught her breath. At *last* — someone on the steps outside. A priest? No matter, if she could only get out.

Clang! The bolt was lifted and she staggered back off the lintel — 'one shoe off and one shoe on' — as the door swung open, showing the figure of a man in the half dusk. No priest, for he wore turban and *choga*. *Could* it be . . .?

Half dazed with relief, she flung herself at him, as he stepped into the temple: 'Prithvi — Prithvi Rāj!'

Her voice broke, and a comforting arm came round her.

'That's not my name,' said an unknown voice. 'I am Surāj Mul.'

'Surāj Mul?' she echoed, looking up at him. It was a name linked with many brave tales of far-off times. 'That Rajput hero?'

'Don't know about hero! But I *am* Rajput.'

'It's a nice thing to be,' she said; and he laughed, very pleased.

'But who is Prithvi Rāj? And who are you? Whatever were you doing to get shut up in here?'

'I crept in because I wanted — I wanted to see the god

put to bed. They didn't know. And before I could nip out, they shut the door on me——' She shivered and shrank closer. 'Take me away, *please*.'

'That's what I came for.' He patted her shoulder. 'But little English girls don't play about in Hindu temples.'

'No, they don't,' she gravely agreed. 'But you see — I'm not all English, and I think I used to be, before, in a different India. I'm called Lilāmani Sinclair. My father is called Sir Roy.'

'Sir Roy?' He seemed quite excited. '*You* are daughter of my friend Roy Sinclair? But he is up at Chasma Shahi.'

'Yes, for a little while. And I'm staying here with Mrs. Desmond, Houseboat *Shahbash*.'

He laughed again at that, put on her shoe, drew her outside, and bolted the hateful door. '*Shahbash*,[1] indeed, that I have the luck to find you! I was having some talk with a priest of this temple, when the old fakir came to us and said there was much noise going on inside, like many devils let loose. Also he had seen a little white girl go in there before *puja* time, and not come out again. So I ran here, not able to believe such a tale.'

'Oh, the *good* fakir!' She clasped her hands tightly. 'I thought he couldn't see me with those blind eyes.'

'Fakir people see a lot more than you'd think for. But how do I get you home, little Lilāmani? And why *do* they let you go alone in the city?'

'They don't let me. I was a bad girl. I ran away because of wanting to see inside a temple——'

'Ran away? Mrs. Desmond must be frightened.'

'I spec she is.' Lilāmani felt a sudden tweak of compunction. She had only thought of Eve as being angry. 'But not half so frightened as I was — shut up in there. Take me home, quick.'

'Can you show the way? I don't know all these houseboats.'

'I think I can; but it's getting rather dark.'

'Shall I carry you?'

[1] Well done.

'No, thank you. I'm a big girl now.' She wouldn't trouble him, though Lance did call her Featherweight Fairy, and she still felt shaky inside. 'Might there perhaps be a donkey or a pony?'

'Perhaps there might. Anyhow, we must be moving on, or my wife will be getting alarmed.'

'Have you got a wife?' she asked, her interest promptly diverted.

'Yes — a very pretty wife.'

'Then I mustn't keep you,' she said politely. 'But I don't much like this getting-dark time.'

'You *think I* would leave the daughter of Sir Roy? You forget I am Rajput.'

'No, I don't forget. I like it.'

'That's good. — Now we go.'

So they set out together, holding hands; and before they had gone far, a tall man came striding towards them.

'A Sahib,' said Surāj. 'He will tell us the way.'

But Lilāmani had bounded forward to the shadowy stranger.

'Oh, Prithvi — Daddy!' she cried in a shaken voice. And this time it was Prithvi who lifted her into his arms — she crying and shivering, now it was all over; he kissing her and stroking her hair.

'Who's the man?' he asked sharply.

'A very kind one,' she told him between two sobs, as Surāj himself came up and greeted his friend, telling his tale and getting all the thanks he deserved, but giving chief credit to the fakir.

'I'll have a word with that holy one tomorrow, if he hasn't melted away,' said Roy, caressing the dark head that lay contentedly against his own. 'Where does your boat hang out? Can I lift you? I've got Mrs. Desmond's car beyond the bridge.'

'Thanks. I'll come along, and find my own way after, because I like so much to be with you.'

'Good,' said Sinclair, liking also the frank Eastern expression of affection.

In the car, Lilāmani snuggled close to him, a hand through his arm. Now and then a small shiver convulsed her and his elbow would tighten on her fingers. They were spoiling her terribly. Would she be scolded by Mummy and Eve?

Now, here were all the twinkling lights on the water and very soon they came to Houseboat *Shahbash*. Somebody was on deck, and Daddy shouted, 'Lance, I've got her!'

Then they all came up, Mummy and Eve and Chrystal; not scolding her, but loving her; saying, 'Thank God!' and also thanking Surāj, her new friend; Mummy hugging her and crying, which made her feel, more than any scolding, what a sinner she had been. They didn't even worry her with 'Why?' or 'What?' They only asked if she was hungry: and *wasn't* she?

They gave her a lovely supper; and she simply had to tell them that she went right up to the temple of Takht-i-Suleiman. Lance called her a 'sporting Fairy'; and Prithvi said: 'She shall tell me everything before she goes to bed, and you people shall hear the tale tomorrow morning. Tonight it's enough that, by God's mercy, we've got her back at all.'

Chapter XIV

The moment ends: but like perpetual dawn
It lives thereafter . . .
With the continual morrow of the king
Returning to his kingdom.

LASCELLES ABERCROMBIE

BUT if those who loved the child refrained from scolding or punishment, not all their love could avert the inevitable. When tomorrow came, Lilāmani spent most of it sound asleep. Not till near tiffin time did she wake with a sharp little scream, 'Oh, the snake — the snake!'

'No, darling. No snake. Here's Mummy.'

Tara had come in a moment earlier, and had been watching her intently. The stillness and pallor of the small face had awakened a nameless fear, and that sharp little scream hurt her in a different fashion. But at sight and touch of her mother, Lilāmani's terror vanished. She sat up and smiled with 'screwed eyes,' a trick from very young years when she felt specially pleased with anything.

'I'm hungry,' she announced, pushing back a wave of hair that fell over her forehead. 'Silly hair. It does flop so.'

Tara stooped and kissed her, smoothed back the 'silly hair,' and tied it with a ribbon. And there in the doorway stood Prithvi Rāj, having caught the first sound of her voice.

A bowl of bread and milk made her feel 'happy inside.' Then her father took over charge; and together they settled down in a corner of the deck, for a 'carry on' of their talk last night, when she had half told the tale of her sins and joys and terrors. Sitting on his knee, in the safe circle of his arm, she was all 'on pins and hooks' to show him her picture — her one triumph in a day of defeat — and watch his face. She had the flat sketchbook squeezed under her arm for a surprise; but he noticed it at once.

'Am I going to see the picture that made you forget everything?' he asked in his casual voice; and she nodded, turning the pages very slowly, till she knew it was the next. Then she paused. It might not seem so lovely to him.

All a-quiver, she opened the book wide and laid it on his knee. He covered her hand and tilted the page, just looking and looking and saying nothing, till she caught her breath in a small gasp.

'Are you frightened?' he asked.

'Terribly!' She looked up under her lashes.

'Because you love it very much?'

'Yes, I did — when I made it.'

'Don't you, now?'

'Not quite so much, but very nearly.'

'Well, I do — quite.'

He said it in such an everyday voice that it took her a moment to grasp the shining fact.

'I *could* have made it nicer,' she hurried to explain, 'with my paint-box. But I took only three colours.'

'It's none the worse for that,' he surprisingly said. 'Chrystal is bringing you on. That's the best you've done.'

'O-oh ——' She let out a breath of ecstasy. 'I did fearfully want you to love it.'

He kissed her at that, to show he was loving her too.

'Chrystal will give you some tips for making it better still,' he said. 'I hope she can keep up the lessons in Gulmarg. She's a find.'

'Yes — a *find*,' she echoed, with a wriggle of joy.

He smiled at the echoing trick. Her happiness, her imagination and courage warmed his heart; but a word must be said to impress on her that — in spite of no scolding and praise for her picture — she had been a sinner to run off chasing temples, when she knew it would not be allowed. He must exact a promise — never again; though deeply he realised the impulse behind it all; how deeply it might not be well for her to guess.

Unobtrusively he led her to talk of the temple, having avoided it while the terror was fresh upon her; and she appealed to him in the certainty that he must understand.

'It *is* funny — isn't it? — the way I did seem to know how it would be, because of how it used to be before.' A pause; her gaze lingered on his face. 'Daddy, did *you* ever used to be before, like me?'

'I think I did,' he admitted, sooner than let her magnify the idea as peculiar to herself. 'People do sometimes feel like that, but nobody can tell for certain. It might only be a strange kind of dream.'

Again she looked at him; puzzled, but not convinced.

'I don't think it's a dream,' she gravely stated. 'Dreams are more muddle-puddle, aren't they?' She pushed him gently with her shoulder. '*You* know.'

'Yes, I know — about dreams; but not for sure about the other. And see here, my sweet' — he turned up her face, looking full into her eyes — 'I want *you* to know something else, very important.'

'Oh, what?' she gasped, still easily shaken.

'Only this' — he tightened his hold — 'that you *must not* go running off like that, frightening us all out of our wits, ever, ever again.'

'No — oh, *no* —' She flung her arms round him in swift remorse. 'Never again. Oh, I *have* been a bad girl! But truly, Daddy, I didn't know anyone was frightened out of wits except me. Nor I didn't know that you and my angel Mummy would be "misked" up in it — so far away.'

'Well, of course they came and told us. Poor Eve was terrified, not able to find you all day. Weren't you frightened when I was lost?'

That struck at her heart. She clung tighter, sobbing now. 'I was bitterly, bitterly frightened.'

'Of course you were. But we needn't cry about it.' He dabbed her eyes with his handkerchief. 'So was Mummy. And we don't want to give her any more worry between us.'

'No, we don't' — she liked that 'we' — 'and we won't, ever and ever, world without end.'

She received another kiss for that, which was all very wrong from the nursery-discipline point of view. But he knew his child: knew that her final terror, his grave command, and her inkling that he understood the 'why' of it all, would leave a deeper impress on her sensitive spirit than any parental lecture on the whole duty of good little girls.

As if she guessed his thought, she nestled closer to him and whispered in his ear, '*Will* we play "Sevens" tonight?'

'Well — there'll only be three of us. Lance is driving us all back to Chasma Shahi after tea.'

'Me, too?' O-oh ——' She sat upright, hands tightly clasped. 'To that lovely garden and the blind girl and the black lamb, with You Two?'

He slanted a look at her.

'That's the punishment! We don't want to lose our last three days there; and we think Eve has had trouble enough with this young lady. So we're going to carry her off.'

Her eyes danced. 'What a lovely fun! — Here comes Mummy. Does she know?'

'Of course she does,' Tara answered for herself, leaning over them both from behind and resting a cheek on Roy's hair.

'Tiffin calling,' she told him, 'when you've quite finished flirting with your runaway daughter!'

'She isn't runaway ever, ever again.' Lilāmani — bundled off her father's knee — secured the last word.

At tiffin Roy set himself to make much of Eve, who had done them a real service and endured acute anxiety on their account without making a song about it. That was Eve's way. Fresh contact with her, and her hold on the child, revealed the intrinsic Eve afresh to his clearer-seeing eyes: the high lights and deep shadows of her personality, the courage under her lightness that recalled two lines of Humbert Wolfe's 'Uncommon Woman':

She lifts her courage like a shield,
Lifts up her laughter like a sword.

Yesterday the courage, today the laughter. She was frankly delighted when he remarked on her gift for imprinting her personality even on transient surroundings, and praised her choice of a quiet corner for the *Shahbash*, where they could lunch on deck untroubled by outbursts of human hilarity or other noises less inviting.

'I was in luck through coming up early,' she said. 'I knew this peaceful corner — and pounced. Round the other side it's pandemonium.'

'Snappier to call it hell,' Lance remarked, and she tilted her head towards the child.

'Call it what you please, it's the limit: hundreds of house-boats, nose to nose, gramophones blaring, ukuleles throbbing, dogs fighting, ayahs and children yelling. Not a moment's privacy, morning to night. Personally, I'm not keen on hearing my neighbour brush his teeth, splash in his bath, curse his wife or bearer, and the rest of his daily diversions! But the station crowd seem to take it all as part of the fun. They start their elevenses with Gin-and-It and the latest gup; and often keep the ball rolling till tiffin comes along.'

'Who's practising "the greatest of these"?' Lance twitched an eyebrow at her. 'The poor devils have nothing on earth to do. They're not artists or gifted composers; and it's their simple notion of having a good time.'

'The tragic fact is,' cut in Roy, 'that human beings, male and female — especially male — aren't educated in the right use of leisure. So they can't be trusted with it.'

'They can't. Gospel truth. But I didn't mean to be actively uncharitable. I was only stating deplorable facts, as I tell Lance when he accuses me of grousing. But let's discard our neighbours. Plans are more to the point.'

It was arranged that she and Lance should drive out with them, stay for early dinner and one game of 'Sevens' as a 'punishment for the sinner,' who was deep in a private talk with Chrystal about her picture, cheeks flushed, eyes very bright.

Tara, watching her, casually took her hand, laying a

finger on her pulse. Directly lunch was over, she produced a glass tube that a very unwilling Lilāmani was made to suck; and because the mean thing said 'fever,' she was whisked to bed almost in tears. No drive out to the Chasma, no game of 'Sevens,' her treat of treats ——

And up on deck Roy was discussing with Lance and Eve the upset of their pleasant plan; sad as the child herself at the prospect of no return to the enchanted garden, but more deeply concerned for the reason. Lilāmani's head was burning, her body shivering, her temperature 101°, probably rising. A *sais* had gone for the doctor. It looked like a touch of the sun. Chasma was out of the question. There was not room for them all on the boat; nor would Roy hear of letting Eve in for more worry on their account. But it is one of the shining merits of Anglo-India, even in these changed times, that any human being in any kind of straits can count on an open door and a hand held out, whether by friends or strangers. And Eve's instant thought was — Vanessa.

'*She*'s not one of those who shy off you if you're ill. No visitors just now, except Grace; and no doctor could beat Grace, especially with a child. I'll scoot there in the car.'

Roy's face lightened. 'I'll come, too, and have a word with Grace. Nothing she wouldn't do for our child.'

'Nothing Vanessa wouldn't do for *this* one!'

And so it proved.

The doctor said 'sun fever.' It might pass within the week, if there were no complications. After that, Gulmarg, the sooner the better.

'We must find a hut double-quick,' said Roy; and Eve knew all about that. There was little that she did not know about Gulmarg, where she had reached the heights of happiness and plumbed the depths of sorrow — loss of the father she had worshipped and of her first child.

'There's quite a good little hut,' she told Roy, 'just above ours, that we call Stream Cottage. We'd be under your wing, too, when Lance goes down, if it hasn't been grabbed already by some obnoxious unknown.'

'How do we find out and make the *bundobust*?'

'Leave all that to me. You look after the Treasure.'

They moved her into the Residency that night. Grace took over charge, with Tara for head nurse. And the anxious days that followed darkened, for a time, the unclouded memory of Chasma Shahi, where Gulbaddan remained importantly in charge, the Kashmiri woman coming in to act as ayah.

Roy, reluctant to go back there alone, preferred to wait till they could all go together and collect their belongings.

Lilāmani's fever ran high; and there could be no peace for any of them till the lurking dread of typhoid had been dispelled; the child's haunting fear of snakes and darkness and the angry eye charmed away by Grace. She had learnt the art of banishing bogies in fifteen years of dealing with a bogy-ridden people. It warmed Roy's heart to perceive how she understood and loved the streak of East in the child. Steadily she combated the recurring temperature and quieted the shaken nerves. In a week she had her small patient purged of fever and fear, begging for Daddy, but in all things obedient to her least command.

And Roy, looking down at the ivory-pale face of his child, could find no words for his gratitude to this capable, deep-hearted doctor-woman, who had quietly put aside all her own concerns and given her whole mind to the exorcising of those twin demons.

'You're a wonder-worker,' he said, 'but I fancy John will disapprove.'

Her smile admitted as much.

'If he'd been here, he might have tried the high hand. As it is, he'll accept the accomplished fact—and say "*Shahbash*"!'

'It *is* accomplished——? She'll do?'

'With that wise mother, she'll do. I can't tell you how many adored Indian children I've lost simply because they hadn't a notion of doing what they were told. Get her quickly up to Gulmarg.'

'Sooner the better for all concerned,' said Roy.

Eve had secured the hut, its owner being at Home on long leave; and so soon as Lilāmani was fit for the transfer they would go up together, Lance included. In view of his injured arm, that was not right yet, he had skilfully secured his month of leave, to 'run on,' earlier than intended.

Before leaving Srinagar, Roy and Tara must have twenty-four hours out at Chasma Shahi, to collect their possessions and bid the place farewell. By favour of the Maharāj, the pavilion and upper terrace had remained inviolate till they could come again; but the garden and lower terrace could no longer be denied to tourists and artists, devotees of the perpetual picnic, or sportsmen, with whom it was a favourite spot for breakfast.

On a silvery afternoon of light cloud, they drove out with Lilāmani, a trifle subdued at thought of all the trouble she had caused, all the days they had missed in fairyland: a sharper punishment than any human parents could have found it in their hearts to inflict.

The thrill of arrival was more than a little damped by a babble of alien voices from the lower terrace. There, where Tara had held her Eastern tea party, a noisy picnic was in progress. Bursts of laughter, snatches of song, and the throbbing of ukuleles desecrated their shrine.

Turning to Roy in dismay, she expected a mild explosion; but he met her look with a wry smile.

'Damned nuisance they are. But they've as much right to be here as we have — if they *are* turning our shrine to base uses. *They* won't spend the night here. We will. And I dare say many of them are as decent as we are under their picnic skins.'

Lilāmani, looking up at him, echoed, 'Picnic skins!' treasuring that odd phrase for future translation.

No time yet; for here was their real welcome: Gulbaddan, almost prostrate before his Swami-Sahib; wizened old Rāmanand with a bouquet of his finest rosebuds for Tara; the little daughter, with her seraphic smile, offering flowers to Lilāmani. And behind her was the black lamb, who gambolled up when Lilāmani called '*Āo, āo*'[1] and beckoned invitingly.

'It knows me!' she cried. 'It loves me. Look!'

The little pink tongue was busy licking her hand; and the blind girl's finger-tips caressed her bare arm, 'seeing' her again.

There was tea in the pavilion, not outside — Gulbaddan explained — because of those *tamasha wallahs*, who would soon be gone. And in undue time they did go, trailing past, calling out jokes, casting curious glances at the pair in the pavilion.

Roy, wearing his Rajput dress, caught the remark: 'These black fellows everywhere now'; and it did not prickle his skin as it would once have done.

Tara thanked Heaven audibly as their voices died away and peace returned to the Garden of the Royal Spring. No sounds now but the music of mating birds and running water, voices and laughter of the two children from the upper story, where a camp-bed was being prepared for Lilāmani — elated at the prospect of sleeping with Those Two in their 'pretence bedroom' without windows or doors.

They dined early on the terrace, that she might share the treat without sitting up beyond hours: and there they sat on afterwards, late into the night — a moonless night of stars. Talking or silent, they were steeped in a content the more profound because the raven's wing of threatened tragedy had brushed across their sun-dazzled eyes.

It was near the smallest hour when at last they stood up by the balustrade, looking out across dark water to the ghostly snows.

Without a word they turned and clung together, as if bidding farewell to an enchantment they could never recapture, whatever hidden happiness the years might hold in store.

[1] Come, come.

BOOK THREE

PLUCK THE THORN

Chapter I

Actual life is full of false clues and signposts that lead nowhere.

E. M. FORSTER

GULMARG, Meadow of Flowers, is a meadow no more. It remains one of the largest open spaces in the forests of the Pir Panjāl, where shepherds graze their long-haired goats and wandering man sets up his tent. Not even the learned can tell why the forests refrain from encroaching on these favoured glades. In the case of Gulmarg, man has not refrained. From a sylvan camping ground it has been gradually changed into a flourishing hill station, unique of its kind. Residency and palace, hotel and club, and an increasing outcrop of chalet-like huts have scared away the carpet of flowers; though these still flourish by streams, like Scottish burns, and among the trees that have stepped out from the encircling woods. Most of the marg itself is given over to every conceivable 'madness of a ball,' that follows the white man as trade follows the flag. All have their devotees; but the bulk of summer invaders live for golf, first, last, and all the time.

The after-war decline of the Station Club, and all it stood for, had not so far affected Gulmarg. Club, and State hotel, with its theatre and ballroom, were the centre of all social activity. There the ultra-smart played bridge at all hours, when they did not happen to be playing golf. Blocks of hotel quarters would soon be packed to overflowing. Huts were filling up daily, many of them occupied by Indians and their families. No question, in a Native State, of debarring any who might wish to join the Club, where they played as good a game of bridge as those who deplored them behind their backs.

But in defiance of the prevailing golf ball, polo still held its own; and Lance Desmond, an ace at the game, was collecting a scratch team, with Sinclair for his forward, to start practice as soon as his arm was available. The Sinclair hut — christened Laughing Water by Eve — was the joy of Lilāmani's life. A real live hut, with planks for walls, mightily pleased a child reared in the spacious English home of Sinclair ancestors. The stream, with its nymphs and water fairies, became her secret companion. Masses of *primula rosea*, forget-me-nots, and a score of water plants offered new faces for her 'Flower Portrait Album.' Drawing lessons every other day kept them in close touch with Stream Cottage, and there were short daily lessons with her mother. But her joy of joys was riding with Those Two, on her brown pony Squirrel, whose unshod feet could scramble up or down any hill path.

Neither Sinclairs nor Desmonds intended to be drawn into the social whirl: but Eve was linked with the Residency; all five were keen dancers, and men would want to play games with Chrystal. The place was an odd mixture of sophistication and simplicity. At the Club and hotel one could meet the smartest of frocks, the latest in cocktails and scandal: a world of nicknames and '*chota* pegs' and 'Have you heard this one?' — of grass widows, willing or otherwise, with their attendant swains. And all day long the crowd that lived for golf went trailing round the links, flaying the grass from the Meadow of Flowers.

But Gulmarg of the 'strenuous life' was a mere caravanserai in a range singularly free from human habitations. From the rim of its green cup one looked out over the whole Kashmir Valley; the Jhelum winding through it like a silver serpent to Manasbāl and the Wular Lake at its western end; to far peaks culminating in the lifted throne of Nanga Parbat. In half an hour one could leave it all behind. On horseback one could escape farther still, as did the Inseparables almost daily: down to Ningal Glen or Babamarashi's tomb; a drop into Ferōzpur Nullah, with its rocky precipice and mountain torrent, famous for snow trout. Better still, there were long days on the higher margs towards Apharwāt, thirteen thousand feet up, where Roy would shortly take his pair, with light camp equipment, to sleep aloft and watch for the dawn.

Too soon it passed, this winged fortnight of living in close touch with Nature, while every day brought more invaders crawling up from Baramulla or Tangmarg. And if Chrystal's thoughts turned at times towards Sher Afzul Khan, she never mentioned him, even to Lance or Eve. He had written only twice from his Free Land, brief, bald letters curiously empty of the personality that had attracted her in Peshawar. How would it be when they met again?

The twin huts greeted June's advent with an all-day picnic up on Killanmarg, the high triple meadow under the shoulder of Apharwāt. Only three outsiders: Dixon Verney, lately arrived on leave, and a Lahore journalist, invited with Mrs. Hyder Ali, an Irishwoman married to a Moslem doctor of the Indian Medical Service, barred, in consequence, by the social set. Though Lady Thorne herself had given them a lead, few had followed suit, except Eve, in whom the good Samaritan would oust the Levite any day of the week.

A wonderful climb it was, through the forest belt of fir and maple and tall pines, till they reached Killanmarg — and had the world to themselves. Through a mantle of pines they looked down into Ferōzpur Nullah, cliff and glade and torrent in full spate. On the far side, blue mountains merged into the greater peaks of Kashmir.

They were all well armed with occupations; Eve with her fiddle, Lilāmani and Chrystal with their sketchbooks, Tara with needlework and a book of *Tree Legends* by Eve's father, with which she would presently beguile Lilāmani in a quiet corner, after much running round in the sun with Bijli, the Afghan greyhound, who haunted Lance like a shadow. Mrs. Hyder Ali and young Banks, strolling apart, seemed chiefly taken up with each other; and Verney, leaning on his elbow near Chrystal, jerked out spasmodic remarks, while she scribbled pencil portraits of the party.

At the moment it was Roy Sinclair, whose finely modelled features were easier to capture than the personality behind them. His lips in repose had unusual beauty of line; and the clear eyes, deeply set, had an absent look, as if he had drifted away from them all. To her he had the air of a man set apart by the secret strength of his vocation. She felt flattered by his interest in her work, glad of a chance to attempt a portrait sketch of him unbeknownst. Absorbed in it, she forgot about the others; forgot the two unopened letters that she had thrust into her coat pocket at starting.

Suddenly Verney's voice, close to her shoulder, said in an undertone: 'Didn't know you went in for portraits. That's a stunning likeness.'

'No, it isn't,' she contradicted, covering it with her hand.

'I keep my own opinion. D'you mind my seeing it?'

'I don't much like being watched at work. — But hush! Listen to Eve.'

She had started — to amuse Lilāmani — a duet with some strange bird, that shivered its wings and kept up a high and lonely clamour on the tip of a blue pine. Quite uncannily she caught the quality of the notes; and Lilāmani loved to screw up her eyes, to guess 'which was fiddle and which was bird.'

While they listened, Chrystal could feel Verney's eyes on her face, and half regretted snubbing him over the Roy sketch, when his praise had really pleased her, he not being given to superlatives. But that special portrait was to be a private treasure. Eve must be her next victim; a fascinating face full of character; those kinked eyebrows and the vital way her hair grew up from her forehead.

Now she was talking nonsense with Mrs. Hyder Ali and her friend, not to let them feel they were outsiders. She had a gift that way. She brought something lively and natural into the most sober company. Her interest in people was real and stimulating. She could never be indifferent. Perhaps that was half her secret. She had them all laughing now at themselves and each other. The early summer sunshine, the flowers, and that grand array of snow peaks gave a glory to this group of mere human beings, each with its own hidden significance of purpose or joy or potential tragedy.

After tiffin, Tara carried off Lilāmani in search of a shady corner. Banks and the Moslem's wife wandered away to explore the other margs. The three men lounged together, smoking and talking; while Eve sat apart making wild corrections on a page covered with musical hieroglyphics. And suddenly Chrystal remembered her unopened letter from Claire.

It was longer than usual, two close-written sheets; and it contained news that made Chrystal open her eyes.

> *I'm in a quandary,* she wrote. *I stupidly managed to faint outright the other morning. I've felt very near it several times lately, but have managed to stave it off; Jasper fortunately not being there to see. But the heat made my temperature jerky; and this fainting fit took me so suddenly that I fell and hit my head. When I came to, I had to send for Doctor Ewart, who tiresomely insisted on a thorough overhaul — with depressing results. Nerves overstrained, blood pressure too low, tired heart, and the rest of it: all of which I knew, more or less, and have been trying to ignore. Jasper's health is essential to his work, and both of us can't be crocks, as I told Doctor Ewart, who insists that I'm the crock; and I really felt too ill to rebel. Jasper was at* Kutcherri, *of course. But Doctor Ewart insisted on seeing him that evening: and ordered me out of Peshawar as soon as I had been normal for twenty-four hours.*
>
> *Poor Jasper! You can fancy he found it difficult to grasp all that. Only twice before have I ever deserted him in the hot weather. In his eyes it* is *desertion; and he makes me feel it so. But he admits that I'm precious little use to him in my present state, and I'd better get patched up, to be fit for August and September after his leave. I was just going to wire for a room at Nedou's, when John looked in for a talk, backed up Ewart, and promptly offered me his own room in their hut. The relief it was. I could have hugged him! But I sometimes wonder if even Grace ever dares to hug John! I'm afraid Gulmarg may be a bit too high for me, but I can take things quietly. Grace being a doctor will keep me in hand. I feel as if all ills will vanish in that air and that green paradise.*

Chrystal looked up at the flowery marg and the circle of the snows — taking it all in. What marriage meant for some women! And there was that incurable Claire making allowances.

'What *is* it?' Eve asked suddenly, not too lost in her music to have eyes for a friend's face.

'A letter from Claire, rather worrying.'

'What's that about Claire?' Verney asked sharply.

No doubt he knew, being such a friend; so she answered in plain terms: 'Fever and fainting, and Doctor Ewart putting his foot down. She's coming up almost at once.'

'Leaving the *pukka* invalid in capable hands,' was Verney's dry comment. 'Ewart must have done some straight hitting. When does she leave?'

'Tomorrow or next day.'

'I'll ride down to Baramulla,' he said in his flat, fascinating voice. 'See her safe up the hill. She's probably not fit for travelling alone.'

A wicked impulse moved the girl to ask, 'Can't you see Jasper tenderly escorting her up?'

Verney stared at her; an odd, thinking look. 'Have you got that on paper? *Is* he coming?'

The sharpened tone arrested Chrystal; and it was Eve who answered briskly: 'Not *he*. My mind's eye sees him lounging around and suffering, doing all he can to make her feel like a damned deserter.'

Chrystal nodded. 'Something of the sort, neatly wrapped up in polite language.'

'Trust Jasper. That man could give the Devil points in the noble art of lying like a gentleman.'

Lance, who was listening, raised a finger. '*Kubberdar!*'

She wriggled her shoulders as if he had touched them.

'I *can't kubberdar* when it's Jasper. I must have special license to explode! Do you never' — she reverted to Dixon — 'fall in hate at sight?'

'I've known it happen.'

'Well, I'm simply plagued with it: the way a man eats or a woman walks, the shape of a nose or long rabbit teeth, my pet abomination: and Jasper's one of my worst ever. It is quite as unreasonable as falling in love, but fiercer — and not so elevating.'

'*Are* you elevated when you fall in love?' Verney asked with a quizzical look.

'Are you?' Eve echoed, appealing to Lance, who retorted smartly, 'We'll leave him to find out for himself.'

'Happy thought!' She twinkled at Verney. 'When you *have* found out we'll give a special picnic for you to unfold the tale.'

Verney fixed her with an inscrutable stare.

'I'm your elder, if I'm not your better,' he said, 'and you're an impertinent minx.'

She laughed and salaamed. 'Got it in one! Impertinence and disobedience were the two sins for which I was always being sent early to bed. What price the moral effect of punishment? — But falling in hate is my theme. The real trouble is, when you're feeling comfortably justified of it, the victim has a mean way of trotting out some pathetic detail in its life or character that makes you feel a beast, and privately hate it the more! But dear Jasper won't let me down. Not one damning shred of the pathetic about him.'

'Are you cocksure of that?' asked Verney darkly. 'If Claire collapsed, he'd lose the one human prop he's been leaning on for nearly twenty years — a nasty cropper.'

'I'm afraid I'd only say "Serve him right. Do him good." If the dear thing does collapse, the blame will be on his fancy heart and his fancy women, though I privately doubt if she worries much about them.'

'I share your private doubt,' Verney stated in a tone that made Chrystal glance at him through her lashes.

'Queer man,' she thought, 'but very nice man. I wonder — *is* it her? — And am I only near the rose?'

Sinclair, no longer abstracted, and frankly enjoying Eve on the warpath, asked outright, 'Who is this luckless Jasper for whom you haven't a good word?'

She turned brightly to Verney. 'How would *you* describe Jasper?'

'As a regrettable lapse on the part of the Creator,' Verney answered in his dryest tone.

The two men laughed outright, and Eve clapped softly.

'Oh, I *wish* I'd said that!'

'You may, next time. I make you a present of it. But don't give me away, on account of Claire.'

'All very illuminating,' remarked Roy. 'But it doesn't tell me *who* he is.'

Eve jerked her head at Lance. 'Ask him.'

Lance grinned. 'She daren't confess that she's hurling half bricks at the Commissioner of Peshawar, my chief next but one.'

'Friend of yours?' asked Roy.

'No. But it's wiser not to advertise the fact. She admits that, but she carries on this way all the same.'

'I don't carry on, except among my friends,' Eve pointed out. 'Chrystal knows; but she's the pink of discretion. Claire hasn't an inkling; nor has he. I'm butter and sugar — positively cream toffee! — when I meet him, simply because of Lance. And *that's* all the thanks I get. Here comes Tara. Nearly tea-time. More food! What a relief — specially for housewives and artists — if we could sometimes cut out food for a few days.'

Dixon chuckled. 'Probably more of us would die of boredom than of starvation.' He looked round the empty marg. 'No sign of Banks and his purloined lady.'

'Excelsior?' suggested Eve. 'If they're climbing Apharwāt, I'm afraid they'll get left.'

'I'm sorry for the woman,' he said. 'Gulmarg won't look at her, except a few decent specimens like Lady Thorne and yourself. She must have some companionship. But I wonder how the Moslem husband sees it?'

'I was wondering also,' said Roy. 'I met him up here last year. A good sort. More cultured than most Englishmen in this country. But "East is East" — so they turn the cold shoulder. And there you are.'

'There *they* are,' said Chrystal, who had sighted them on the higher marg walking back very close together. She watched them with an odd twinge of sympathy. The men's remarks had made her feel vaguely uncomfortable. A warning? Nonsense. The thing was impossible, even if Afzul asked her; and she believed he never would. But she was glad when Tara and tea created a diversion.

After tea, most of them played 'Sevens' and became wildly hilarious over it, to the delight of Lilāmani, who snuggled close to her father and shared his hand.

Too soon that radiant day declined to an evening of amber and gold, and they must descend to earth, as Eve expressed it, 'to sophistication and more food.' The downward path was pleasanter, on the whole, for walking than riding; and Dixon Verney walked with Chrystal. He asked searching questions about Claire; talked of her in a serious vein that set the girl wondering, 'Is Claire blind to this? Or is she putting up a futile fight and collapsing under the strain?'

Realising that she herself could like Verney exceedingly, if encouraged, another thought crept in: 'Rather a pity he doesn't look this way. He'll only bark his shins against the conventions, while Claire will insanely break her heart sooner than break her vow to that worthless man.'

But the surface Chrystal went on talking to him in an ordinary voice, about ordinary things.

At the hotel, where he lodged, Verney left them.

'When I'm back,' he said, 'we must fix up some tennis. And keep some dances for me on the ninth, if the juveniles don't collar the lot.'

'They won't be allowed to,' she answered, with a look that seemed to please him.

He held her eyes a moment, before he turned aside, calling out good night to the rest, thanking Eve and Tara for a perfect day. More thanks from Mrs. Hyder Ali and her escort, who attended her to the house she shared with Mrs. Battacharya, a fellow backslider.

The rest rode on along the marg to their huts, that were set among pines raked with shafts of evening light, though sunset was still far off.

Under one of the trees near Stream Cottage stood a tall man, his back towards them.

'Some poor devil you've invited to dinner and clean forgotten?' Lance asked Eve, who was given that way, like her father.

But before the figure moved, Chrystal's heart seemed to turn over slowly inside her. She had recognised Sher Afzul Khan.

Chapter II

Not your own heart perhaps can know
The way your soul's adventures go:
Yet somehow soul and heart are wise,
Each with the other's harmonies.

GERALD GOULD

'HULLO, Afzul! Come to "join the glad throng"?' Lance called out as he dismounted.

The two women, following suit, shook hands; and the girl's fingers ached from the force of his grip that sent a queer tingling up her arm. Quite unprepared for these sensations at sight of him, she could think of nothing to say.

Mercifully Lance was introducing him to Roy, asking him to 'Come in and feed.'

His pleasure was evident; and as he was in flannels, the women changed only into simple day-frocks.

Chrystal chose a moon-yellow silk with green belt, green beads, and shoes. Afzul had once ventured a remark on it in Peshawar, and she liked giving him pleasure. It might be unwise, but vanity prevailed. And she could feel him being pleased with it, though he said nothing.

At dinner Lance drew him out, knowing that he had done good work for Lynch; and their masculine talk left Chrystal free to renew her impression of the man who had so attracted her in Peshawar. The mere look of him pleased her; his vigour and vitality, the physical ease and power that flowed from him, as if no Army discipline could stiffen his suppleness or block the right of way from impulse to action. Lance was vital enough; but in Afzul there burned a spark of the untamed savage that any strong wind of provocation might blow into a flame. In the very element of danger there lurked a fascination that was lacking in the casual manner and schooled impulses of the modern young man.

Tonight, fresh from his own land, his talk was racy of its soil — or rather its rocks and stony hills — of clan friendships, fights, and intrigues, of two men, in particular, whom he had tracked for Lynch with the help of his fellow sub, the Khyber Afridi, Abdul Jān. Talking of it all, with one who understood, he seemed to slip out of his officer skin into the skin of Sher Afzul Khan, son of natural fighters, who knew no other way of life.

The women talked little. An absent look in Eve's eyes told Chrystal that her mind had drifted away to an impromptu for violin and piano that had been haunting her for days; and she herself liked listening to the men.

Afzul spoke of his father's fort, of the kinsmen and clansmen herded there, as in ancient Highland strongholds: sons and grandsons, cousins, retainers, and the rest. One would almost suppose there were no women in the Free Land. Half fascinated, half repelled, she heard Afzul's proudly told tale of nabbing and unfrocking a bogus holy man; guile countered with unscrupulous guile that grated a trifle on her ear. More easily she could condone a savage impulse than deliberate deceit. Yet among Pathans, it seemed, a lie here or there was not of much more account than a corpse here or there. The holy one — according to Lynch — was a prize not to be let slip for a scruple or two; but Afzul seemed unaware of scruples. One used a lie to catch a liar, as one used poison for rats. Lance listened to it all with his straight look, and commended the capture without comment on the trick that brought it off.

'Just as well some of 'em should get properly shown up,' he remarked. 'Make your people more chary about trusting them wholesale.'

Afzul's tawny eye gleamed. 'It's more superstition than trust that gives the Moslem holy one his pull over the unholy. They know it's a common dodge, among robber spies, to gain a night's lodging and worm out information. They only fear to risk refusing bed and board to a true *pir*,[1] who would have power to call down the curse of God on them and theirs. So any *badmāsh* need only drape himself in a patchwork quilt, sport a wand and straws in his hair, play the giddy goat with blood-curdling prophecies to make the ignorant swallow him whole. Only afterwards they find *he* has been swallowing their property, while they gulped down his empty words.'

Eve came out of her dream and laughed at that.

'You're in form tonight, Afzul! But I must ask leave to bolt. Devils are jumping about in my head; and if I don't quickly fling them onto paper, they'll perish.'

Lance gave her hand a friendly squeeze. 'Run along, then. Don't mind us. We refuse to be responsible for a single devil's funeral!'

She gave him one of her looks and went out.

Chrystal, feeling bound to make a move, was invited to remain. 'Unless you're bored,' Lance said, 'with our Frontier gup.'

'Bored? I'm fearfully interested.'

'Sit you down, then, and lighten our darkness.'

'An insult to the sun!' she said, sitting down again in a flood of evening light that streamed through the open door.

'Perhaps Miss Adair would like to hear,' said Afzul, addressing her through Lance, 'about a part of our country not so wild and wicked as I may have been making it seem in her eyes.'

'Yes, I should like to hear,' she answered for herself, 'though I don't believe any of it is very virtuous — or wants to be!'

'People think that,' he said, 'because we have so many dare-devil brigands, who defame a race of brave men, making outsiders think we live entirely by taking each other's lives.'

Lance laughed. 'A trifle Irish, Afzul. That's the way they'd be dying entirely!'

Afzul's big laugh thrilled through her like the note of a trumpet.

[1] Saint.

'Well, they aren't all dead entirely, nor ever will be! Though it's true that we *have* only one form of argument in a quarrel — rifle or knife. The brigands are outside our control; and it's they who cause more than half the trouble with the British Government, raiding Peshawar for arms and ammunition. But it is our brave clansmen who get the knock. Forbidden to pass into the city. All their trade held up. No salt it was once. And what's food without salt? If they couldn't trade for it, they must raid — and blacken their faces. Then your people wonder why there's bad blood between them and the Tribes.'

'It's a big price we pay,' Lance admitted, 'and make others pay, because we can't or won't take the trouble to see inside the next man's head. But my uncle, Sir Vincent, isn't one of that kidney.'

'He's not; and *they* don't need telling when they're dealing with a man who knows. Look at Lynch and the Afridis. He's after all their *badmāshes*, but no Afridi would harm *him*. Look at Captain Leigh in the Malakand. How the tribesmen swear by him. Always a joke on his lips, such as my people love, but always the strong hand for evildoers. The Swatis themselves have such a ruler as they may never see again. Think of it' — he turned to Chrystal — 'our Vali of Swat, neither reading nor writing, keeps pace with all practical progress — flying, electricity, radio, schools, and hospitals. He has flown all over his country and linked it all up by telephone. Always in touch with his people. A fine sportsman too, like his son, great friend of mine, educated at Islamid College. He looks and talks and acts like an Englishman. It was he who designed his father's guest-house, a splendid grand building; electric light, running water, and marble bathrooms, every comfort as if you were in England, but more spacious; and such grand wild country ——'

At this point Eve reappeared outside the door haloed in sunset gold.

'*Such* a conflagration — "trailing clouds of glory,"' she told them. 'Come out and do *pujah* instead of wagging tongues at each other.'

Lance laughed. 'Sounds as if we were a pack of puppies!'

But Afzul, rising and facing the splendour, said gravely, 'This is the hour for *pujah*.'

On rocks by the stream they sat down, and there was no more wagging of tongues. They forgot even to light cigarettes, while the heavens declared the glory of God; and snow peaks changed colour from moment to moment. Increasingly Chrystal felt aware that the man sitting by her was not the same Afzul from whom she had parted in Peshawar. That frank talk of his country and people had made him seem more definitely Pathan under his half-civilised surface; and or instinct she felt a greater need for discretion in the matter of looks and tones. Yet how undeniably glad she was to see him again.

The sun vanished. Peak after peak caught fire. It was the hour of colour, of Kashmir's pride; solemn pines etched darkly on flushed snows and palpitating sky. While the wonder lasted, trivial talk seemed a profanity.

As the glory faded slowly, Lance began filling his pipe. From within the hut came sounds that drew Eve to the nursery.

Afzul politely rose also; and remained standing.

'I ought to be going,' he remarked without conviction; and Lance took him at his word.

'Well, good night,' he said. 'I enjoyed getting a breath of the Border. See you again soon. Like to join my scratch polo team?'

'Thanks. I'd like nothing better.'

'Good. We'll challenge God's Own Guides and give 'em the surprise of their life!'

The Pathan chuckled, and Lance went indoors.

As Chrystal stood up, Afzul moved nearer to her.

'I was waiting more than an hour under that tree,' he stated in a suppressed voice.

'I'm sorry,' she sympathised. 'But you shouldn't do that. You could have come tomorrow.'

'Not the same. I *had* to see you now.'

He looked her up and down, perhaps recognising the frock she ought not to have put on.

'How about tennis tomorrow? I've not played since Peshawar.'

But of course she was already engaged.

'Next day, then? Would the Desmonds make a foursome?'

She shook her head. 'I've been let in for a fool of a Treasure Hunt. It may be put off for a day or two. Not quite settled. Mrs. Phillips — you remember her in Peshawar — Flippity-flop?'

He smiled. 'Yes. She was a friendly Flop. Asked me to dinner- and sherry-parties. If I call, she might ask me to her show.'

'If she needs a man. It's all in couples.'

'Good. I might be your partner.'

'It doesn't go by choosing. Chosen couples might wander off on their own. They have dodges to make it go by lot.'

'We might dodge their dodges!'

The gleam in his eye recalled his tricking of the faked holy one. He was Pathan again.

'We'd have to play fair,' she said; and he grinned.

'The first motto of your people.'

'So it should be. What's yours?'

He looked pensive; then out flashed his brilliant smile.

'"None but the brave deserve the fair." In the Free Land almost anything is forgiven to courage.'

'And in our land,' she said, 'almost anything is forgiven to honesty — to the man who "has no deceit in his tongue, but speaketh the truth from his heart."'

'*Sedar admi*, in fact — straight man. That is what Easterns call the best brand of Sahib, whom they will follow anywhere; though privately they may think him half a fool.'

'"God's fool,"' she quoted, not sure if he had seen or heard of Parsifal. The spirit of the Ring would better suit his people.

As she spoke, Lance reappeared at the open door. 'Hullo, Afzul! Not gone yet?'

'Just going,' the other answered casually.

Lance vanished, and Afzul held out his hand.

'Tomorrow at the Club?' he asked, and again her fingers ached under his pressure.

'No. I'm riding with the Sinclairs.'

'Next day, then — if the skies fall!'

Under his lightness fire smouldered.

She stood alone watching his tall figure pass through the shadowy trees out onto the open marg. Then she wandered back to the stream, lit a fresh cigarette, and sat down on a mossy rock still warm with the last of the sun. Hard to go indoors at all on such a night. If Lance wanted her, he would come out again. Eve would soon be with him; and although they never let her feel an awkward third, they were sufficient to each other, that very individual pair.

After living with Claire and Jasper in a state of suppressed antagonism, they were refreshing beyond words. Eve said there was an art in being married, badly neglected even by those who recognised it; an art not neglected by these two. She had seen them at close quarters in camp; here she was seeing them closer still; absorbed in each other, yet keeping intact their so-different personalities. The way Lance respected his wife's art, even when it hampered him, impressed the artist in Chrystal; and she rightly guessed, young as she was, that men of such quality were hard to find.

She herself had, as yet, little real leaning towards marriage; and the rope that Claire gave her — as Jasper said, to hang herself — had increased her love of independence, her instinctive recoil from the possessive spirit of man. Yet beneath her cool, critical surface glowed a secret burning life of her own. She had not the trick of unpacking her heart even to one who might understand, like Eve. She knew herself capable of deep feeling, passionate yet inviolable; untroubled by the sex obsession of her day. Either her Puritan forbears or her Scottish pride inclined her to set a high value on herself as a woman; to wish that any man who loved her should do the same. And how could that be, if he knew that casual intimacy — in the divorce-court sense — might be taken for granted? Chastity was going to mean more for women, now that it was no longer enforced by public opinion, but was a matter of choice or principle, as with men. She wanted the core of love, the hard inner kernel that would endure; the kind of love that she divined in those two. And instead she was beset by perpetual, possessive young men.

Here was Peter popping up again — oh, curse him! — Peter, who couldn't grasp the meaning of 'No.' Her second letter had proved to be from him, announcing his arrival, when she had hoped he was miles away pursuing harmless birds and animals. Every word of his letter told her that he was coming to walk round the walls of Jericho, which would certainly not fall flat at the blast of his tin trumpet. Mentally she thrust him aside, wishing she could as easily be quit of the actual man.

At the moment, she found herself peculiarly attracted by Roy Sinclair; partly the blend of artist and East in him; partly something magnetic, though she felt shy of the cheapened word. He seemed to radiate happiness and calm. She could talk to him of her painting as she could talk to few. His detached yet sympathetic understanding of people and life made her want tremendously to read his novel. He understood that devotion to an art meant more than mooning around after 'inspiration.' It meant study and hard thinking; guts and determination to get there. Some day she would get there, unless she let herself be wrecked on a man. And at present her art eclipsed any man of them all.

This peaceful two weeks of work and companionship had intensified her instinct to keep men and even life at arm's length. And now — here was Peter; here was Afzul, a strangely disturbing element; here was Claire with her tired heart, in every meaning. Selfishly she thanked Heaven and John Lynch that Claire's coming would not break up her happy arrangement with Eve, who would be alone when Lance went down. But what was really wrong with the poor dear? Would she be told? Claire kept the door of her lips. There was a kind of stifled bravery about her, as if she were sometimes very near the edge of despair. Because of that worthless man, she might try to belittle serious symptoms. Wide awake to his failings, she would never exalt herself at his expense. There was nothing of the obnoxious female saviour or put-upon martyr about Claire. She was simply worn out with upholding him and aching for those far-away children. Even if the doctors insisted on Home, would she leave him if he pulled out the pathetic stop? He would not be obstructive. He was too clever by half; knew where to have her every time. If it came to the worst, one might put Verney onto her: Verney, whom she was now to call Dixon, because he didn't like being treated as a 'not so young.' He needn't worry. He was worth more than most of them. Very decent of him going down the hill for Claire. It would cheer her up after wrestling with Jasper, who would promptly console himself with his Priceless Pam——

Oh, Heavens! What sacrilege to be thinking of Pam and Jasper in this quiet end of evening among these solemn trees. The air was utterly still, the kind of stillness that comes before change. Vaguely it troubled her with a premonition of difficulties ahead.

'Oh, Chrystal-*ji*, have you evaporated?' Eve's voice from the doorway positively startled her.

'Not quite!' She sprang up and ran to her friend, feeling glad of the lights and companionship, the sense of safety that seemed to emanate from everyday things.

Chapter III

. . . The whole
Of life is mixed: the mocking past will stay.

MEREDITH

CHRYSTAL's unkindly thoughts of Jasper Inglis were, on the whole, no libel. He saw the tiresome upset chiefly as a personal grievance. That Claire should fail him, in the hot weather, made him feel so ill-used that he had little spare concern for the wife who was escaping unfairly soon from the furnace that tried him, the worker, more severely than it could possibly be trying her. If she didn't know, it was not for want of telling. She could be dense at times; but he could be plain spoken, though it was not his *métier*. He frankly cursed old Ewart for fussing over temperature and a faint or two, hustling Claire off before he could possibly arrange to get away. Surely she could put up with her intermittent fever till his leave was due. Pam, though a martyr to prickly heat, showed no sign of deserting her peppery old Colonel: and so he told Claire, in terms that provoked her to attempt a fresh protest against Ewart's decree. But the doctor, no weakling, had threatened to tackle Inglis himself, if she talked any more nonsense about cancelling Gulmarg.

The threat sufficed; and that same afternoon her heart was hardened afresh by Jasper's inordinate fussing over some trivial matter she had left undone, when she was palpably too exhausted to cope with her own packing. Towards all that, he seemed curiously yet quite pleasantly callous; nor could he be expected to conceive that her real need was less for change of climate than for one merciful month of release from his hot-weather fads, his moods and daily demands.

Her pride had been nettled also by a call from Pam, nominally helping her to pack, tacitly taking over charge of the 'poor dear deserted man.' Looking cool as an iced lettuce leaf, her skin unblemished by prickly heat, she seemed designed to show up Claire's faded aspect and lack of *métier de femme*. Claire, frankly hating her, without a glimmer of jealousy, carried on with her packing, while Pam did the talking and acquired merit.

One way of comfort had lightened those dismal days: a wire from Dixon stating that he would meet her at Rāmpore and see her up the hill; an act of kindness so utterly unexpected that it made her stupid heart beat in a thick, muffled way. It meant that, on her account, he proposed to ride down a matter of thirty-four miles, to travel back with her, at semi-invalid pace. How much else it might mean, she dared not even ask herself. And while she lay combating physical sensations, she decided not to mention that wire. The reservation was distasteful to her, but it is hard to deal straightly with the crooked. Jasper cared too little to be troubled by jealousy; but, in his deprecating fashion, he might make remarks that would sting her to unwise retort.

Later that afternoon — Pam and Jasper out riding — J. L. looked in to hear her news; and his concern at the idea of her going alone moved her to tell him of Dixon's offer.

'That's more like it,' he said, a lurking gleam in his vague eyes. 'Good man, Verney.'

Mercifully no word of Jasper. If John could be too blunt at need, he could walk delicately among one's sensibilities, and he had an immense respect for other people's reserve. He was rock to Jasper's sand, a man after her own heart. And, before leaving, he coolly suggested driving her himself to Pindi, seeing her started on the motor journey to Baramulla. Better still, he offered her the hospitality of his room in their Gulmarg hut.

'Not much leave for me, just now,' he said. 'Pleasant for Grace, and better for you than that rabbit warren of a hotel, with all the human rabbits shouting each other's heads off!'

When she tried to thank him he pooh-poohed the necessity.

'We're good friends, aren't we? Leave it at that.'

Gratefully, she left it at that; and one wire sped to Grace, another to Nedou's Hotel, cancelling the probably non-existent room. In this case, Jasper would have to be told.

'Lynch turning lady's-man!' was his brief comment, though he probably suspected Lynch of implying that he ought himself to be taking her down. His next remark confirmed her guess.

'You've jumped this business on me just when I've a heavy batch of cases impending. And you know, I'm bad at hot-weather travelling. Never do if I collapsed also. Lynch is a bullock of a man. Rackets all over the district. Never a day's fever.'

'He's also an extremely busy man,' she added, not merely in justice to Lynch. 'And I'm grateful to him.'

He glanced at her, surprisingly, without evasion.

'For that matter — so am I!'

The refreshing honesty of it was a positive relief. John would mightily enjoy the kudos of earning Jasper's gratitude; but loyalty constrained her not to share that particular joke. And she was glad of it when Jasper, next day, bade her an unusually affectionate farewell, though the thought would creep in that perhaps he was not sorry to have the coast clear.

Rawal Pindi: an inferno of heat and dust and flies and clamouring native car drivers: Lynch, solid and competent, securing a reliable car, thinking of everything, providing her with every comfort. He secured her also against the nerve strain of reckless driving by an arrangement for *baksheesh*, to be paid when he had the lady's report from Baramulla.

And now every mile was lifting her up above the blazing Punjab haloed in its own dust. Yet even these hills could not at once dispel the fog of nervous depression that made her feel dead to the changing scene unrolled before her eyes. There were dark moods when one could hardly see beauty, much less respond to its healing influence. She felt tired and stale, oppressed with a sense of futility in all she did. It was only a mood that would pass, but while it lasted, no star could pierce the gloom. Even her reviving sense of escape was deadened by the failure of her loyal attempt to preserve something adequate out of a singularly unsatisfying marriage, by the conviction that Jasper was frankly making love to Pam. A technically virtuous woman, dishonest to the extent of her virtue, she was capable of alluring him with her sensuous charm — and giving him precisely nothing. The idea of Jasper defrauded strangely troubled her mother instinct, but a stronger conviction was forcing itself upon her that she had reached the limit in her pursuit of the impossible.

And now, at last, looking deep into her own heart she discovered there the image of another man. Deliberately she refused to dwell upon the possible motive that impelled him to so much kindness. In her present state, the comfort of it sufficed, and the prospect of a peaceful month with Grace, who was taking things easily for a far happier reason.

And while her thoughts went astray, the car kept rattling on, mile after mile, through a tangle of mountain and valley, now enchanting, now weird and wild; round hairpin bends, or along rock cuttings that dropped a clear two hundred feet to the roaring, foaming river. Though the pace and the rattle stunned her head, the air was elixir, and the mental fog was lifting. She could see. She could feel. And slowly a conviction awoke that she was journeying towards some fateful crisis, happy or otherwise, she could not tell.

Gulmarg was too high for her tiresome heart; but she must take her chance — 'live dangerously' in Jasper's phrase. It seemed almost like trespassing on his preserves that she should presume to be troubled with a heart, except as the seat of emotion. But emotion for the wrong man — would that worry him at all? Again, she could not tell.

Now they were nearing Rāmpore; thirteen miles of mountain road as varied and dramatic as any in Kashmir. The familiar scene, its mingling of beauty and terror, smote her afresh. Mighty cliffs of limestone rock; precipice walls that dropped to the swirling river a giddy distance below;

a plunge into the forest belt of deodars, giants of their kind. Then an easier road above the rapids, thundering down, flinging their spray so high that the cool breath of it moistened her face.

Only a few miles on to the Rāmpore bungalow; more towering cliffs, and a world of mountain arrayed in early evening light. And there, on the steps, stood Dixon in drill coat and breeches, very lean and erect, looking more than his height.

'Good going,' he greeted her. 'You're up to time; but you look fagged out.'

'I feel it.' She admitted, without a qualm, the unflattering implication that she was probably looking more than her age. His straight speaking was one of his major attractions. He would never say one thing and mean another. He might be hard; he would never be slippery. In all essentials, he was her man: and she had found him too late. Life was like that.

Dust and weariness were soon washed away by a steaming bath and a *dāk* bungalow dinner, not too bad, of its unvarying kind, grey coffee thick with grounds. Yet Claire, a fastidious feeder, enjoyed that unappetising meal more than any she had eaten for weeks.

After coffee, they strolled outside under those mighty cliffs among noble trees, far snows gleaming and dreaming in the brief twilight: an evening so steeped in peace and beauty, after the dust and rattle of the road, that Claire already felt healed in spirit, though her body might lag a long way behind. Life had dealt hardly with her; but the gods could be moved, on occasion, to let fall a crumb of manna from heaven.

Speaking or silent, she was equally content, so penetrating was the pleasure of Dixon's mere presence. Only at moments, when they fell silent, the mocking spirit whispered — to what end, this late flowering heart and senses? Not now could she freely give him the kind of encouragement that might quicken his friendship into love. Deliberately she must stop short of that which she most desired——

Dixon was talking now of the picnic at which he had

heard her news; speaking of that Sir Roy Sinclair whose strange story Grace had told her, whose attractive wife she had met in Peshawar.

'You'll like those two,' he said. 'They're thick with the Desmonds and have caught on with Chrystal, as no doubt you've heard.'

'Yes. She enjoys the drawing lessons, and seems greatly taken with Sir Roy.'

'She has quite an eye for character, that girl. Sir Roy is a good bit more than a distinguished writer. He's a man of unusual quality, in spite of the double strain — perhaps because of it,' he added truthfully, 'though I've never felt like admitting as much before. One doesn't see the East in him. One only feels it at times, in a curious way.'

'Probably that's what attracts Chrystal,' Claire remarked. 'I never thought she would feel the spell of India as she seems to do.'

'Could she stick it — do you think — permanently?'

'I don't know. She doesn't seem inclined to think of marriage yet, as far as I can see — which isn't very far. She's candid as the day; but in all personal matters she keeps the door closed.'

'She's none the worse for that.'

'No. A fine creature; not easy or pliable, but genuine. One must accept people as they are — even if one wishes they weren't!'

'Suffering gladly, in fact,' he said, 'applies to more than fools.'

She sighed, thinking of Jasper.

'It must — if certain states of life are to be endurable.'

'Especially the unholy estate — ?' he queried with a shrewd look. 'Which is one reason why your not very humble servant remains unattached. I *don't* suffer gladly, in the simple or subtle meaning of the word. You do.'

'Not gladly always,' she admitted in a low tone. She could feel his eyes on her averted face. Had she spoken unwisely? At the thought her heart beat in muffled strokes.

Troubled by his nearness and possible discernment, she

moved a step away from him, felt her right foot slip on something that slithered from under it. A snake — ? The shock of fear made her head swim. She seemed to be falling through space — hearing her own stifled cry very far off and his changed voice, 'My dear — my dear — !'

That drew her back from the edge of darkness.

'What *was* it? I thought — I'm a fool about snakes.'

She stiffened, and he withdrew his arm.

'Don't call yourself names,' he said. 'It's your nerves and heart all out of gear.'

And she thought, with a twinge, 'My heart in the wrong sense.'

'I don't see you doing thirty miles tomorrow,' he went on. 'Better take it easy and sleep at Baramulla; I'll wire to Mrs. Lynch.'

For one delirious moment she clung to the thought of another twenty-four hours alone with him; but the very disturbance of her heart forbade.

'No, you won't wire to Grace,' she countered with decision. 'If we start early, I can get a good rest at Baramulla, and be carted up the hill in a hateful dandy. An unexplained wire might alarm Chrystal.'

'*Hazur ke kushi!*'[1] he said with a sidelong smile. 'You're a valuable person. I don't want to be responsible for a collapse.'

'Collapse? I'm not such a crock as all that.'

'I hope not,' he said gravely. 'But you've walked enough. Have a lounge in the verandah with me before you turn in?'

For half an hour and more they lounged in the verandah, smoking and talking of many things. That brief contact and his changed voice in her ear were as if they had not been. Only deep within her the effect remained — and would remain. Other days, other moments had claimed permanence, and vanished. This magical evening would abide with her while she lived.

[1] As Your Honour pleases.

Chapter IV

I would not love you — yet I love
All things that you are fashioned of . . .
I would not love you — yet on me
Your beauty thunders like the sea.

GERALD GOULD

CHRYSTAL's life in Gulmarg was subtly, if not actively, affected by the coming of Claire. It pained her to see the dear woman looking so weary and washed out; but Himalayan air and relief from Jasper would soon change all that. She went over fairly often to the Lynch hut; told Claire about Little Scrap's drawing lessons, for which Roy insisted on paying her, now that it was a regular arrangement. She took a livelier interest in Claire's etchings; and suggested a small joint book on the Pir Panjāl, colour plates by herself, black and white by Claire, letter press by Roy, if he would honour them? The idea pleased Claire mightily. Here was the leisure and peace of mind. Only energy was lacking, but that would revive the quicker for a definite end in view.

One morning Chrystal took Tara and Lilāmani with her. The child, since her illness, adored Grace; and Claire was charmed with Tara's refreshing personality. Compared with the smartly dressed 'perm-and-lipstick' crowd she seemed like a wild flower among hothouse plants; yet she probably knew more in her own soul than any worldling could tell her. She looked years younger than Claire, though they must be almost of an age. They were evidently drawn to each other, and Chrystal was glad of it, partly on Claire's account, partly on her own, her time and mind being a good deal taken up with Sher Afzul Khan.

Claire must not be allowed to start worrying over questions that might never arise. It was tiresome enough to find Dixon taking a sort of paternal interest, obviously vexed that Afzul had reappeared on the scene. For of course he would talk of it to Claire; though he, too, seemed anxious to save her from worry or fatigue, which was decent of him. Altogether she liked him better up here than in Peshawar. She was pleased that he seemed to admire her, in his critical way. But she saw him chiefly as Claire's friend — if no more. Her young shrewdness half suspected Claire of a secret smite; but if Dixon himself were involved, he kept his shutters up. In any case, she did not see him purloining another man's wife, however much it might be the fashion. He was fundamentally straight. She had liked him for that from the first. With a shade of encouragement, she could like him a good deal more. But he was Claire's 'one and only.' To detach him would be a mean act, and for Chrystal there were few more damning words in the language. Claire should not be cheated of her one human compensation for Jasper by the niece to whom she had given the best year of her life.

The little station had by now reached its zenith of social activity; seven hundred souls, fleeing from the wrath of Northern India, flung together in a forest glade two miles by one; most of them living in and for the diversion of the moment, heedless of any world outside their echoing trivialities, while hidden forces were leading many of them, to unlikely ends.

The treasure hunt had been deferred, enabling Afzul to secure his coveted invitation and an afternoon of tennis with Chrystal before it came off. The tennis had brought her up against Grant, whom she was trying to avoid. He also had his invitation; and he had wormed out the trivial secret of Mrs. Flip's latest device for pairing off her couples: a whistling match; the men to whistle, the women to guess.

By guessing rightly, they could claim their squire for the hunt. Chrystal felt him triumphing over the fact that he could whistle creditably and Afzul probably could not. To her, the Pathan admitted as much, and cursed the bright idea. He enjoyed martial airs and Eastern music; but he could not, for his life, whistle an English tune. She would never guess what he was after.

'I would do my intelligent best!' she encouraged him, and his teeth flashed in a sudden smile. But he would not impart his own bright idea.

'I have thought of a thing,' was all he said.

Verney — no musician — flatly refused to make a fool of himself for any damsel or grass widow in creation. Lance and Eve accepted chiefly for the fun of seeing what happened when Grant and Afzul contended for Chrystal's 'bright eyes.'

'There won't *be* any contending,' she told them. 'I'll see to that.'

Lance regarded her pensively.

'For your tender years, Chrystal-*ji*, you're a devilish competent creature. We'll see what we will see!'

Half the party met in Mrs. Flip's drawing-room — six breeched women; a fashion that makes for comfort, but kills the charm of contrast and variety. Chrystal and Eve stood talking to a smart young married woman, fresh from Home, tailored to perfection; eyed enviously by Phoebe Farrell, neither smart nor young, in a *dirzi*-made drill coat over a bright pink shirt, surmounted by a full-moon face and ginger-yellow hair. She was one of those tiresome, rather pathetic people who make poor jokes, and giggle furtively at them if no one else laughs. Remained Mrs. Ross and her sister, a pleasant, colourless pair, good riders both.

Their hostess at least provided contrast; her willowy form and floating garments; her beautiful helpless hands clutching at an unmanageable cape, while she talked and talked; pouring out a flood of broken sentences, hearing little and telling less; facts escaping through her cloud of words. She enjoyed her own parties, in spite of getting hopelessly mixed over people's names and faces. She never could remember whether Sher Afzul was Pathan or Sikh, though she had grasped that he wasn't the Brahmin. She rather flourished her sympathy for those nice Brindians; and invariably forgot that they disliked the hybrid word. But her many lapses were forgiven for her kindness of heart.

Volubly she welcomed the women, giving them incoherent clues as to the radius covered by her treasure-hiders, bidding them return punctually for her cocktail diversion.

Now enter the men: Lance, an accomplished performer, whistling very softly his favourite 'Londonderry Air,' slanting an eye towards Chrystal, but promptly snared by the smart young woman. Captain Jarrold of the Gunners advanced boldly, his low-comedy face screwed up, his tuneless attempt at the 'British Grenadiers' palpably aimed at Eve.

And here was Peter sidling up to Chrystal, daring her not to recognise 'Annie Laurie'; but she, flagrantly refusing to heed him, moved towards Afzul, who was hopefully emitting sounds like nothing on earth.

Lance clapped him on the shoulder. 'No takers!' Phoebe Farrel had a wild shot at 'The Campbells are Coming.'

He shook his head, 'Not friends of mine!' while Chrystal racked her brain for a possible clue. Phoebe had caught the discarded Peter. Eve had won Captain Jarrold; and while they were all talking nonsense, the girl did her intelligent best.

'"God save the King"?' she hazarded.

He nodded vigorously, with a wicked gleam in his eye, and ranged himself beside her, flinging a glance at Peter that missed its mark.

Now they were paired, Mrs. Phillips was wishing them luck with her formidably vague smile. And of course she must have a word or two for the handsome Brindian — 'Azfool Khan,' she engagingly called him.

'Not quite such as-fool as he looks,' Afzul retorted smartly; and she shook her head at him, not seeing the point.

'Very clever of you, anyhow, winning Miss Adair. I was afraid you Sikhs didn't know any English tunes.'

This time he was not amused.

'I can't answer for Sikh,' he said abruptly. 'I am Pathan.'

'Oh dear, oh dear! Of course' — her distress was genuine. 'And there's a sort of disagreeableness between you, isn't there? Oil and water — someone was telling me.'

'More cat and dog than oil and water,' he corrected 'someone.' 'Only a little matter of a hundred years or so —— But we are getting left behind in this hunt-the-thimble game!'

They found their ponies impatiently pawing the air, and Chrystal overheard a deep-toned '*Bismillah*' as Afzul settled himself in his saddle, the whole look of him very pleasing to her eye.

The rest had trotted off, according to the clues that might or might not lead to a find; but Sher Afzul was not hunting any form of thimble, if he knew it.

Turning in his saddle he looked hard at Chrystal. 'Done with that tom-fool show. Will you — please come for a ride along the Ridge?'

His compelling gaze and the urgency of his tone so stirred her that she hovered a moment between refusal and acceptance.

'But, Afzul, we are at her party,' she temporised; 'we're expected back. We must play the game.'

'I am *not* at her party now. I am not playing any game.'

His tone was unaggressive but unyielding. She said nothing, and he added at once, 'Of course it is only — if you would prefer a real ride?'

His eyes besought her. This was the manly, courteous Afzul, more potently attractive than she cared to recognise. She did want the real ride. Why not be honest about it?

'Yes, I prefer that,' she said in a carefully colourless tone. 'But still — we *are* at her party.'

'Well, we'll jolly soon be somewhere else,' he exulted. 'Lots more will come for her cocktail drinking. She won't even notice.'

'But Lance and Eve will.'

'To them you can explain my Pathan behaviour! Now — let's go along that glorious Circular Road and see out all over Kashmir.'

The impatient ponies were off at last, and she, cantering beside him, was again troubled by an under-sense of fatality, as if, in those few moments, she had stood at the parting of two ways. And the man himself — his Eastern face masking his passionate heart — knew that he desired one thing only, whatever the issue, to see her, to be with her, to hear the cool tones of her voice. In her exceeding fairness there seemed almost a quality of light. For him she contained all loveliness, within and without, that a man could desire in a woman.

The triumph of her deliberate choice lifted him into a reckless mood. While it prevailed, they were not East and West, they were man and woman, created in the beginning for each other.

Yet his face told nothing to the girl who cantered on with him, stride for stride, dimly aware of some vital change that she could not fathom. Dismissing tiresome sensations, she yielded herself to the simple pleasure of riding with this particular man through the sun and shadow of a forest road beyond compare. Birch, sycamore, maple in young leafage gleamed among majestic pines that sprang above and below the road two hundred feet and more, framing glimpses of snow-line and valley, of the distant Jhelum and the silver sheen of Wular Lake, all bathed in the bluish haze of early evening. And everywhere the forest was peopled with flowers: columbines, delphiniums, monkshood, and Jacob's-ladder — the whole gamut of blues and purples that the bees love.

'Let's go slow here. It's perfect,' she said, blessing the Flop party for giving her this unplanned delight; thanking her own intelligence also for the random guess that had hit the mark.

She deserved praise for that; and as they slowed down to a foot's pace, she spoke of it. One could trust him to see the joke. He knew he was no blackbird like Lance.

'Did you practise your whistling a lot beforehand?' she asked; and he chuckled.

'No. I hoped for luck and trusted in Allah.'

'Perhaps Allah helped. But *I* felt rather proud of guessing right on spec. I never heard anything less like "the King"!'

'Not surprising——' Again that wicked gleam. 'I was having a shot at our cavalry canter, "Bonnie Dundee," my favourite English tune.'

She laughed outright. 'It happens to be a Scottish tune.'

'Of course. Fool I am. I love it the better.'

She did not answer. She was realising that he had secured her by a trick, recalling the guile he had practised on the bogus *pir*.[1]

'But, Afzul,' she protested. 'If it was "Dundee," you shouldn't have said it was "the King."'

'I didn't say,' he quibbled, with a grin. 'And *you* didn't ask. You only asked, "God save the King"? And as that is my wish, I nodded — getting my other wish also. Two birds with one stone!'

'I'd rather a stone than a trick,' she said. 'You knew what your nod was telling me. It wasn't playing fair.'

'"All's fair —!"' Again his eyes were eloquent, but she would not have it.

'You always have a proverb handy. Do your people rule their lives by them?' she asked.

'They are coin of the realm in Eastern countries.'

She heard a shade of resentment in his tone; but the stubborn element in her insisted on making the point that mattered.

'You can slip round any awkward corner with tags of potted wisdom. I prefer principles to proverbs.'

Suddenly she felt that sounded priggish; and, with a small stab of fear, she saw that he was angry. She had pressed her point too far and pricked his Pathan pride. He had himself in hand because she was a woman, but twin flames leaped in his eyes.

'You think I have no principles? You think I learnt no-

[1] Saint.

thing but textbook stuff at English public school and college? I can tell you I learnt to play a straight game there; and I play it here also. But I didn't come to play the fool at that damn party to let myself be caught by the dried-up sister of Mrs. Ross or that spinster who neighs like a filly. I came because I am steel to your magnet; and you despise me because I only nodded my head to win you. If you have no more use for me, because I am Pathan, perhaps you would rather ride home alone?'

Anger and hurt pride were flaming fiercely in him, or he would not have said that in the same breath as the other. He pressed in his heels, gathered up his reins. In another moment he would canter away, and her own pride would never stoop to recall him. Perhaps she ought to let him go? But on impulse, she flung out her right hand. Instantly he dropped his reins and caught at it, crushing her fingers till she winced.

Then, as suddenly, he dropped them and rode closer to her.

'*Did* I hurt you?' he asked, in a smothered voice. 'I would cut off my hand sooner than hurt your smallest finger.'

Here again was the other Afzul, gentle and courteous, yet no less virile than in his fiercer vein.

'It was nothing,' she assured him, forced to ignore his revealing words.

'And you don't really think I am a horrid liar?'

'No, I don't. I never would.'

She could say that truthfully, because the word was too strong for the occasion. And, moved by the change in him, she added with feeling: 'I'm frightfully sorry if I hurt you by any careless word. But I do like truth between friends. Let's be good friends, Afzul.'

He was silent, and she could not meet his gaze.

Then, 'If you are sorry,' he said with a touch of his earlier shyness, 'will you do me one small kindness? You say "Afzul." Can I say — "Chrystal"?'

She felt vaguely relieved. 'Of course you can. All the others do.'

'To those others'—he waved them away—'it means nothing. To me it would mean—everything.'

The word, the look, smote her with a tingling shock; but this time her reasoning self prevailed.

'In that case,' she said, 'perhaps you'd better not.'

The light in his tawny eyes startled her.

'No better or worse for me. Whatever name I say with my lips, in my heart there is only the one thing——'

'No—no——'

Again she put out a hand, warding off the unspoken. 'Don't say any more if you want to ride or dance with me again.'

'Your command is to me as God's command,' he said in grave deep tones. 'But even Allah cannot cool a heart on fire. I will say no more—not yet. And I *will* ride and dance with you again.'

They returned late, having ridden far and talked little, Chrystal's inner disturbance quieted by the rhythm of riding, the spell of forest and mountain, the sense of a new understanding between them. She had fixed the condition of their continued friendship. Like Canute, she had said, in effect, 'Here shall thy proud waves be stayed'; and resolutely she tried to put from her those words of his that mocked at the vain command. She caught herself, in fact, nodding when it wasn't 'the King.'

At parting, he lifted his hat with a brief 'Good night. Thank you—for all'; not riding on with her to the hut, perhaps not wishing to encounter Lance.

There he was, standing outside, having just parted from Roy, who waved to her as he went.

'Where have *you* sprung from, my pretty maid?' he greeted the delinquent, as she dismounted and gave her pony to the *saïs*.

'I've sprung from the everywhere into the here,' she answered lightly; and he proceeded to scold her, only half in joke, for deserting the party and leading Afzul astray.

'I didn't lead. In this case, it wasn't Eve. It was Adam.

Afzul said no one would notice, in a cocktail crowd, if we came back or not. And I don't suppose they did.'

He twitched an eyelid at her. 'Your innocence is only exceeded by your good looks! You bet they noticed. They're all eyes and ears in these damn little stations.'

The truth of it spurred her to a flash of irritation. 'As far as I'm concerned, they can say what they please.'

'They mostly do.' He paused a moment, regarding her seriously. 'If I may say what I please, I would like to add that it might be wiser not to go riding too often with a certain cavalier.'

When Lance looked and spoke like that, no one could take it amiss; but her spirit of independence resented the Gulmarg attitude.

'I'll heed *you*,' she said, 'if I won't heed them. But I like him a lot. He's a change from the others, and a very attractive man.'

'Quite: but don't you go forgetting that you're a damned attractive girl.'

She laughed at that, but it gave her a thrill to be told so by Lance in a blunt voice of warning, not the silky voice of flattery.

'And remember this, my dear,' he added, emboldened by her friendliness, 'a Pathan in love is not a mere man like the rest of us. He's an elemental force — a volcano in eruption.'

She said nothing. It was probably exaggeration, but the words remained in her mind. Afzul himself had given her a hint of their truth; and, in doing so, had awakened something in her that no other man had yet done; something that would not be stayed, either by reason or command.

Chapter V

What magic is theirs for whom the little things
Have become the great things?

LAURENCE BINYON

A FEW days later, Roy Sinclair was riding alone along the road to the old sawmills in the southward corner of the marg. He had been lunching at the Residency by special request, to meet a shining light from Delhi and a distinguished American traveller, Professor Higham D. Chadwick, who knew him through his earlier books. With them he had found a certain Sir Ahmed Jung, a public man of high repute, whom he had met and greatly liked at Delhi last year.

Finding themselves neighbours at table, they had talked of their vanished American friend, Lewis Buchan Edom, who had brought them together. A millionaire, studying Eastern thought as a hobby, he had sought out Sir Roy in England, had been attracted by his father's famous Ramayāna pictures; had persuaded Sinclair to part with them for a sum that had spelt relief to the overtaxed landowner and had facilitated the Indian adventure. Together they had flown out and parted, each going his own way. Last autumn they had met in Kashmir, Edom transformed from a Western millionaire into a Brahmo Samāj theist, his fortune given over to an astonished nephew in California. All that was news to Sir Ahmed. More than ever he would like to meet again a man who had changed his whole way of life from conviction, in an age when conviction was as rare, among Westerners, as honesty among thieves.

But chiefly the general talk had turned on the unescapable

theme of India 'in transition': and the stock phrase had moved Sinclair to quote Radhakrishnan: 'No doubt the first words uttered by Adam to Eve as they stepped out of Eden were, "We live in a time of transition."'

The shrewd witticism had delighted Vanessa, the only woman present; so had Sir Ahmed's pungent comment on 'these talking Round Tables in Town, that go for ever round and round and seem to arrive nowhere. Plenty of clever men,' he added, 'in every group. But two things they can't do, with their much talking: they can't talk India into a united, independent nation, and they can't talk the British out of India.'

That last had drawn from Chadwick the frank remark, 'It might be a refreshing change from those giddy gyrations, if you English, for once, said straight that you have no intention, in any case, of quitting India; that you have as much right to the dominion you created as the Moghuls to their Empire or the Sikhs to the Punjab they took by force. It is your policy of small concessions and large promises dangled out of reach that raises false hopes and breeds distrust.'

'It is also a pity that your politicians talk so much, while knowing so little,' Sir Ahmed lamented, without rancour; and the Professor had glanced at Sinclair, with his tight-lipped smile.

'The old, old story — eh? Those that say, don't know. Those that know, won't say. I'll wager any money that Sir Roy, there, looking wise enough for twenty, knows volumes on this prickly subject. But he'll keep us guessing till he tells the world in the great book he has got up his sleeve.'

Sir Roy, having talked little, had met that friendly challenge with a modest disclaimer, merely adding that political problems were not his quarry; and the Professor, looking sceptical, had refrained from pressing the point.

On the whole, Sinclair had enjoyed meeting the three men and hearing their exchange of views, so long as they did not try to drag opinions out of him. He knew too much — as the Professor implied — to swell the torrent of talk abroad in both countries, that darkened counsel and led nowhither. 'Strength is not won by miracle,' should be inscribed over the main doorway of India's Talking House.

But at present he was letting all that sink into the subsoil of his mind; obeying the male-female rhythm of thought essential to all creative work that owes as much to relaxation as to hard thinking. The period of preparation, of deep purposeful questing and seeing, could bear no fruit without the hidden female process of gestation — mental quiet, prelude to the intuitive flash. The mind, at rest from its own activity, moved on to some fresh discovery, or idea, while the surface brain looked another way. Seeking one thing and finding another: that was the law. And, in order to find, or to interpret things found, an artist must surrender to the whole of life, 'accepting everything beneath the sun,' keeping his hands in the world, his head cool, as if in solitude.

The man himself, in these few months, only asked leisure to enjoy the regained happiness of living in unity with a woman as balanced as she was captivating, responsive to high matters, interested and amused by small ones, not the less captivating for her strain of practical common sense, necessary to those who live intimately with artists. 'Beauty of being expressed in unconsidered acts' — that was Tara: so fragile-seeming, so durable in essence, by virtue of her wife-mother quality, expressed in the Indian word *shakti* — the joy-giving, life-giving power of woman to convert a lover's dream into a satisfying adventure in reality.

But the man who has achieved is at the mercy of his own achievement. The pressure of people, and his interest in them, drew him among them more than he intended. The Residency pair had a claim on his gratitude and affection, and there one met the *élite*, interested in his dramatic reappearance. The rest were mainly divided between taking a snobbish interest in his title and looking askance at the reputed Indian strain. But chiefly he was beset by Indians, who turned up casually at all times, sure of a welcome. They would sit on and on, talking politics and again politics, till he wearied of the word; but he neither could nor would send them empty away. Grace knew several families, and he encouraged Tara to make friends with them; firmly believing that the women of both races, working together in the right spirit, could do more for India's true welfare than any machinery of votes for persons unknown and policies not understood.

Trotting briskly back from the sawmills, he noticed ahead of him an Indian in Western dress, recognised as the Brahmin District Judge, Arvind Ghose, whom he had visited in Peshawar; a man of high intelligence and melancholy temperament, too easily jarred by the rubs of a position that gave him good money but left him unsatisfied in spirit.

Sinclair thought: 'Poor devil! Doomed to walk alone. *She* probably can't or won't walk a mile on a hill road.'

The poor devil, hearing hoofs behind him, looked round hopefully and recognised Sinclair, who pulled up and moved on beside him at a foot's pace.

'I didn't know you were up here, Mr. Ghose,' he said.

'Lately arrived on leave, Sir Roy, like all the world and his wife. Delighted to hear of your safe return and Lady Sinclair coming to join you. I regretted not seeing you at the Sports Gymkhana this afternoon.'

'I was lunching at the Residency to meet an American traveller. Much talk afterwards, and a ride to blow it away.'

'You were better employed!'

'Bored with sports, are you?' Sinclair asked lightly, and was quite unprepared for the vehemence of the Indian's low rejoinder.

'I was bored to the bottom of my soul, to keep looking on at so much senseless activity.'

'They're young,' Sinclair reminded him. 'And it's a harmless way of letting off steam. But if it hurts your soul to watch them, what took you there?'

The Brahmin shrugged and turned out his yellowish hands. 'Where else to go? I never played much tennis. I prefer this dog-walk, even without dog, to golf. In fact I only came out'—he paused perceptibly—'to get away from the women. My wife and mother don't like these hill stations. They are complaining of water arrangements and servants' quarters, of feeling cramped in the small hut, after my big house down below.'

'Don't they go out much? Still in *purdah*?'

'My wife, not strictly so. But my mother makes trouble over caste prejudice and fear of being defiled. I shall perhaps not be able to stay here, though I have taken this nice hut for two months.'

'That would be a pity, my friend,' Sinclair sympathised, instinctively using the Eastern phrase.

'Yes, a great pity. I already feel so much better in this fine air. A man has little chance against the women. They go always on and on. Sometimes I *must* escape. So I drug my soul with staring at sports. Often I envy you Englishmen. If your wife goes on and on ——' (Roy tried to picture Tara in spate.) 'You always have your club for city of refuge. You can bring a friend back for "pot-luck" and change of conversation ——'

He looked up with a sad, courteous smile.

'Forgive my bad manners, talking of Inside troubles to you, almost a stranger. But I was rather upset in my mind. You have made me feel peaceful and at ease, letting the small things go. So, I spoke from my heart.'

And Sinclair, genuinely moved, said on impulse: 'A burden is often eased by unpacking some of it. And if you can't ask me, I can ask *you* to join us for dinner.'

Surprise and pleasure transformed the melancholy face.

'Sir Roy, you are too kind. Are you sure Lady Sinclair—?'

'I am very sure of Lady Sinclair.' Something in his tone made the Indian husband sigh; and he added conversationally: 'We have two other Peshawaris dining tonight. Mrs. Inglis, the Commissioner's wife. You know her?'

'I have met her. I know him — so far as one of *us* can ever know that kind of Englishman.'

And Sinclair, recalling Eve's 'licence to explode,' asked casually, 'He's that kind, is he?'

'Yes. Very competent official, but all the time hating the

"damn country," like too many since the Great War. He will correctly give Indians what he thinks they ought to have. If they don't happen to like it, well — the worse for them. Because the I.C.S. can do no wrong.'

It was the truth deflected a trifle by bitterness; and Sinclair could see both sides.

'Most of them,' he said placably, 'are overworked and disgruntled by changed conditions of their Service. They live mentally in a world that is neither England nor India.'

The other nodded. 'They don't know us. They don't want to know. Not even your Viceroys know all that goes on under the smooth salaaming surface. Only the District Officer can tell how quickly a harmless-looking trouble may ferment and boil over.— But I must not plague you also with the unending troubles of my poor country.'

For that relief Sinclair gave thanks, and hoped the Judge would continue to refrain. He had looked forward to an evening with Grace and her friend — especially Grace, too seldom seen; but the hapless husband must be saved from those women who went 'on and on.'

'If talk could make an end of India's troubles,' he said, with truth, 'I'd willingly talk till all was blue.'

The Judge shook his head. 'Too much talk. And the mountain brings forth a mouse. What time do I come?'

'We dine at eight.' Sinclair gave his reins a shake. 'See you later,' he said, and rode on, leaving the Brahmin to continue his dog-walk — a new word for Lilāmani.

The evening proved, after all, livelier than he had expected, an evening of surprises. It turned out that Grace knew all about the Judge and his hampering women; and he, on arrival, hailed her as the saviour of his 'smallest son,' a detail she had not troubled to mention. The boy had been half killed by drugs and voodoo magic, because Gandhi had barred English doctors, and the women would not let him go to hospital, to be cut open with English knives. Happily the distracted father had heard of Grace Lynch, who had succeeded in combating their fears. The boy had not gone to hospital; and he had not died. He was here in Gulmarg. She must come and see them all soon. And Sinclair, looking on, felt that his kindly impulse had borne good fruit.

Later, when they all sat outside with their coffee, Mrs. Inglis contrived a word aside with him about Chrystal and Afzul Khan, who was clearly in love with her; a distracting position for an aunt lacking parental appeal.

'I feel I ought to speak to her, but there's always the risk of swinging her towards him. Under her cool surface she has very deep feelings; and if she won't listen to reason ——'

'Have you ever known anyone in love listen to reason?' Roy gently interposed.

'No. But I'm hoping she's not yet in love. D'you think — a word from you —?'

'If you wish it, I'll try, with due caution.'

'Do try. You have a singular influence over her.'

'Influence? Surely you're mistaken.'

'I'm not. I know Chrystal. I know she wouldn't lightly do what you would think unwise or wrong. You do think — ?' She hesitated so painfully that he helped her out.

'Yes, I do think that, in most cases, any form of mixed marriage is always a big risk and nearly always unfair to the children. I have known several happy instances, where the couple could live in England or in real India. In a world that is neither, the position's almost impossible. Yet what's going to stop these young officers from falling in love with our girls out here, or *vice versa?* It's a human dilemma that may cut at the root of this Indianising plan, unless these marriages are soon going to be decently recognised and accepted. Chrystal's a gem of a girl, and I feel for him. I'll speak to him also if I can.'

The shadow lifted from her sad eyes. 'You give one such a feeling of safety and certainty. It's strange.'

To him it seemed still more strange. His genuine concern for others left him no room to be aware of his effect on them: and just then he became aware of two uninvited strangers walking up towards the hut — Indians both.

Ungraciously he wished them anywhere else on earth. The next moment he was on his feet. The shorter man had waved to him; and he had recognised, under the yellow turban, his translated American friend Buck Edom; the prominent nose, the lower lip thrust forward, and the slate-grey eyes.

This was another pair of sleeves. He went quickly forward and shook hands.

'Good luck! We talked of you at the Residency this morning.'

'Brought it on yourself, then,' said the familiar nasal voice. 'If you talk of the Devil, you must expect to smell sulphur! I *had* to seek you out, hearing you'd risen from the dead. Not that I'd buried you — not by a long way. And what do I see?' Tara had risen and come forward. 'Your very lovely lady?'

He took her hand, bowing courteously over it.

'And now,' he said, 'let me introduce my young friend Dayālanand — Joy-of-the-Lord. He has things to tell you about a u-nique Indian colony near Agra that will rejoice your heart. So I ventured to bring him along, though a stranger, hoping at this hour to find you at home.'

The young man, tall and slender, wearing fine white muslin and pale green turban, went serenely through the ordeal of a sixfold introduction. Edom, a plain man, loosely built, was redeemed by his fine head and shoulders. At ease in any company, he sat on the steps of the hut, refusing a cigarette and holding their attention by his vivid account of the colony that had captured his imagination.

The boy, a member of the sect — Radha Soāmis they called themselves — should talk later on, he said, to Sinclair, who positively must see the colony himself on his way home.

'Dayālbagh, Garden of the Lord, it is called,' he said; 'and the Sahib-ji Maharāj, head gardener, is a pioneer of the first order. The original colony was started seventy years back, on four acres of waste land across the Jumna with a matter of five hundred rupees. It is now a flourishing garden city, self-maintained, covering only four square miles. Out

West we'd look down our noses at such a doll's-house affair. We can only gape at the big thing, the Big Noise. The Sahib-ji is not a Big Noise. He's the simplest, quietest human item you ever struck. But a personality, a born leader; no mistake about that; an inspired dreamer, with an alert American mind housed in a Hindu body. By sheer force of personality and vision — no rich supporters, like friend Gandhi — he has created within those few miles a complete little world; a world that puts first emphasis on first things — the religious and emotional needs of the natural man.'

'Purely Indian — is it?' asked Sinclair, the flame alight in him again. Here was no dust-cloud of politics. Here was achievement on a small scale, the seed of greater things to be. Instantly his prophetic mind beheld other colonies on the same lines, were it only one in each province: the little leaven——

'Purely Indian,' he heard Edom confirming his question, 'inspiration *and* execution; model industries, factories, and colleges. Five thousand souls and only one white face: a gracious lady, Principal of the Woman's College. Let any-one who doubts if India can run her own affairs — with the right man and the right method — go and cast an eye round the Lord's Garden for himself.'

He paused and looked round at the listening faces, a gleam in his own eye under its bushy brow.

'I sincerely hope I'm not generating boredom?' he asked, so gravely that he raised a laugh and drew a prompt dis-claimer from his audience. He so clearly enjoyed holding forth; and the others enjoyed no less his piquant mixture of the Indian-American point of view.

Reassured, he went on to tell of exports increasing, of agents all over the land.

'Not a few Indian leaders,' he added, 'are on the alert, watching for the full result of this bold experiment by an idealist who leads his people in daily worship, yet never loses his grasp on realities. No cast distinctions. No politics.' ('Suit you, Sinclair,' he twinkled.) 'No Gandhi nonsense about spurning machines. But *they* don't run the men there, as ours do in God's own country. Getting science, getting money, we sneer at sentiment and ignore the simple things that are the big things all the time — which is one of the reasons' — he looked straight at Mrs. Lynch — 'why you see me in this get-up today. And it isn't skin deep. God has not yet been argued out of His universe. Those who have eyes can see Him at work in that God-inspired corner of India.'

'How on earth has it managed to remain so little known?' Sinclair marvelled; and this time he was answered by the boy, an exalted look in his great dark eyes.

'We Radha Soāmis have always been a semi-secret brotherhood. We do not draw attention to ourselves by riots and civil disturbances; nor prove our religious zeal by breaking other people's heads. Yet there is hardly a town where you will not find some of us — one hundred and fifty thousand now, scattered in groups and branches, all giving allegiance to him who created our Garden of God.' And he added shyly in a lower voice: 'Garden is a word of inspiration for India. With us it is part of religion, a temple without walls; yet God is there. Your people out here, through not seeing that, have nearly destroyed our true Indian gardening. It is a pity.'

The change of theme led to more general talk on the spirit of Indian garden craft, on the lovely moonlight gardens of Rajputana — paved pergolas in black-and-white marble, dark shrubs, and flowers that open to the moon; on the havoc wrought by early Victorian influence that disfigured gracious gardens and multiplied public parks — iron railings, platoons of trees, and acres of unhappy-looking grass, only green in the rains.

Then Grace drew Edom into closer talk, and Roy strolled with Dayālanand. The boy could say much to this Indian-Englishman when relieved from shyness of strange white women. He was bidden to come again with Edom when husband and wife were alone, and assured that Sinclair would not leave India without visiting the Garden of the Lord.

The last of daylight was vanishing, a moon nearly full gleaming through the pines, when Edom bethought him that they had stayed long enough for one while, and offered to escort the ladies back across the marg. The enlivened Judge took his leave, thanking Sinclair fervently for 'pot-luck of the luckiest'; not least, the good fortune of meeting Mrs. Lynch again.

The chance party had been welded into a congenial group mainly through Sinclair's gift for setting a sympathetic current even through a mixed human company, his capacity to appreciate men and things entirely different from himself, not by any mental process, but by understanding, that springs from fellow feeling and imagination.

When all were gone, he sat down by Tara on the wooden steps, with a sigh of pure content.

'Quite a good party after all,' he said, '*and* a discovery. But this is better. See that moon blossoming like a great night flower? She's telling us that it's time we three took up our beds and walked to the top of Apharwāt, while she still shines all night. Have you anything on tomorrow?'

'No. And if I had, I wouldn't have!'

'That's the proper spirit for adventure. Tomorrow it is. We'll give our Little Scrap the experience of her young life; and we'll have a week of real camping and tramping later, before we pay a call on the Vinxes at Natthia Gully.'

Chapter VI

A little space is allowed
To this loveliness
That is not ours nor anyone's.

HUMBERT WOLFE

'I CALL a halt. Here, for at least half an hour, shall our proud progress be stayed.'

Sinclair, in *choga* and *chuplis*,[1] waved his alpenstock towards the scene that had been unrolling as they climbed the rugged shoulder of Apharwāt — the Jhelum Valley from end to end, flanked north and east by mighty ranges: a galaxy of Great Ones, each with its resounding name, its differing glory; Mahādeo of the triple peaks, beyond Srinagar; Haramokh, a rugged Minotaur, guarding the glacier lake of pilgrimage; Kolahoi, a lifted spear; the lovely summit of Machai, above Wardwan. And outsoaring them all, by a clear nine thousand feet, Nanga Parbat, the Naked Mountain, gleamed through an opalescent scarf of cloud. Wandering mists veiled the Jhelum and the Wular Lake. A flight of small birds wavered past with their happy dipping of light, living atoms flung into the void. And far below, among the pines, clustered chalets of Gulmarg seemed a world of midgets — the last touch of unreality. It mattered not that they had climbed the mountain three times already. Today cloud and sunlight and dissolving mists clothed the familiar scene in loveliness unsurpassed.

Near the rock, where Tara sat lost in wonder, sprang a graceful group of sky-blue poppies, and Lilāmani, crouched

[1] Indian sandals.

below her, was painting them yet again; true artist in her return to the attack, her conviction that they 'must come better this time.'

Roy, sitting apart among mossy boulders, had melted into the landscape — and what a landscape! As he sat there — lost in his deep response to the beauty of the world — a steady river of quietness seemed to flow from him, a sense of enlargement lifting Tara above the scurrying minutes and hours that one was for ever chasing at home.

Others beside Tara were alive to that subtle radiation, the measure of the Light he had received in his time apart. They seemed drawn to him by no effort of his own. For herself, more domestic than social, she could feel happy in either atmosphere so long as they were together. In whatever company they might be, she was always aware of the hidden glow, like Stevenson's Lantern-Bearers, with lights buttoned under their coats. But here, among his mountains, the light could burn in the open, 'still as a lamp in a windless place.' At seven and thirty she had no vain illusions about life — she who had worked through the terrible war years, ministering to shattered men. But when one's good hour came, one must hold the brimming cup with both hands that no drop might be spilled.

Roy was scribbling something now. He had returned from far away, bringing sheaves with him. The Darling was looking up to tell her that the poppies *have* come better this time. And now they were ready for the last stiff pull up five hundred feet, through soft Kashmir heather, to the summit. Thither Gulbaddan — who loved not mountains — had gone on with coolies to prepare supper and their small tent. Tomorrow, the 'Frozen Lakes.' Lilāmani, Tara decreed, had done enough for one day, though she looked and felt as if she could go on for ever. Mountains and streams and flowers were filling her mind with memory-pictures that would colour all her days. And here were no puzzling intimations of 'used to be before.' Here she was 'Forest Fairy' in a true fairyland, a world that offered new wonders each returning day.

Supper on this noble hilltop was an enchanted meal with sunlit peaks for company; Nanga Parbat as guest in chief, a mere eighty miles away, her half-veiled splendour suggesting a majesty and aloofness more impressive than any clear revealing on cloudless blue.

Tonight there was no spectacular glory. The sun slipped away among ripples of pearl and umber. The sky reddened in a brief ecstasy of flame, fading like a long-drawn violin note, while all shapes took on a clearer outline, all blue shadows a deeper tone.

'Look!' said Roy under his breath. Eastward, over nameless peaks, the full moon was rising — unclouded, serene.

'Oh, Daddy,' the child breathed in ecstasy, 'she was simply *creeping* up, thinking we didn't notice, because of the sunset. But I *did* see the firstest twink behind the snow. D'you think she minds?'

He stooped and kissed the top of her head.

'She probably likes being noticed and admired as much as we all do.'

'Let's notice her, then!' She rested her head lower on his arm, lost in wonder, tired a little with her long day. 'When you lean sideways, it comes much more beautiful.'

Tara heard the sleepy note in her voice and decided that she had overstayed bedtime long enough. It would be a short night for them all if they were to catch a midsummer dawn, with the help of Gulbaddan, who would faithfully rouse them at any given hour.

Earth and sky were only half awake when his voice outside the tent roused them with a long-drawn, 'Sa-hib, Memsa-hib. Dawn is near. The heavens are clean.'

Cups of steaming cocoa completed their awakening: and outside their little tent they sat together in a silence that seemed infinite. No bird song, no flitter of small wings to greet the sun in this high solitude sacred to eagles and the gods.

Eastward, where moonlight trembled into false dawn, the mighty bluffs of Haramokh were crowned with stars.

Kolahoi lifted a ghostly spear; and the far slopes of Amarnath loomed sombre against a brightening sky. Only Nanga Parbat, with the moon for satellite, remained half veiled in her *sari* of cloud. And below them a sea of mist that obliterated all things. It was as if they had risen in the night not only above earth, but above the clouds of heaven.

Already these had knowledge of the coming day. Flakes like swan's-down flushed and faded in a sky full of primrose light, that rent the dissolving veil round Nanga Parbat — and behold, in highest heaven, an opal shimmered. The throne-like summit swam into view: the goddess granting a *darstran* [1] to an unheeding world.

And now, behind Haramokh, light blazed in sudden splendour; common daylight, gift of gifts, not regarded until it is lost. After that waiting stillness, movement everywhere: eagles rising out of the mist on widespread wings; endless, unseen creatures, in grass and moss and heather, aware that once more it was day. And three worshippers came out of their dream to enjoy an ambrosial breakfast. Then, unashamed, they crept back into their hut for another hour or two of sleep.

It was full day when they set out for the Frozen Lakes; a mile of rough downhill walking, that took nearly an hour with halts by the way. And the lake, seen from rising ground, caught Lilāmani's breath: deep and still, vivid green, a mirror for ochreous yellow cliffs and broken masses of rock; drifts of frozen snow afloat on it, like giant swans. And there was a surprise in store, Roy told her, that she could discover only by singing to the lake one verse of a song.

She looked puzzled and glanced across at the circling cliffs.

'I'm rather shy of the lake.' She spoke softly as if it might hear. 'Does it know I can't sing very well?'

'It won't worry. It can't sing any better than you do. Don't be shy. Sing a line — and wait.'

She wriggled her shoulders; then, in a clear, small voice, she sang her mother's bedtime song: 'Sleep little pigeon and fold your wings ——'

[1] A beholding.

'Fold your wings.' Her own voice came back in a ghostly echo from those forbidding cliffs; and her hands went up to her ears.

'What is it? *Who* is it?'

And the cliffs mocked her: 'Who is it?'

'I don't like it,' she said, in her decided way; but softly, so as not to be mocked again. 'It's bogies.'

'No. It's the cliffs talking. Never heard of an echo, little ignoramus?'

'Echo? Of course.' Her fears were stilled. 'It makes noises, but I didn't know it could talk like us.'

'It can't always. But those cliffs are shaped so that they reflect your voice, like a mirror reflects your face. Now we'll make them show off properly.'

He drew from his pocket a reed flute and picked out a few simple airs, answered by the cliffs; and Lilāmani clapped her hands to hear the noise come back, not shy of them any more.

When they had eaten their picnic lunch, she made a wild attempt at the cliffs, that refused to stand upright on paper; and it was nearly time to return when they sighted two figures against the sky, a tall man and a short-skirted woman.

Roy put up his field-glasses. 'Sher Afzul — and Chrystal. No getting the world to ourselves for long, even up here.'

He spoke lightly; but sight of them, thus isolated, recalled his promise to Claire Inglis, not yet fulfilled. He met the man often enough at polo, playing in Desmond's team; but it was not a subject to be dragged in by the heels; nor did he relish the prospect of intruding on another man's private affair.

'We'd better join them for a bit,' he said, low, to Tara. 'I promised Mrs. Inglis I'd speak to him. If you freeze on to her, casually, I might manage it.'

Tara nodded, 'I'll freeze! So will she.'

The child, waving frantically without result, turned to her father.

'Let's make the cliffs call her! P'haps she'll think it's bogies.'

Bounding forward, she called in high, clear tones, 'Chrys-*tull!* Chrys-*tull!* Here we all *are!*'

That startled the pair, who were evidently coming down their way. Recognising the party, they shouted back, and the five of them met on high ground above the lake. Roy explained the echo, and Lilāmani, squeezing Chrystal's hand, whispered, 'I hoped you'd think it was bogies.'

She laughed and nodded towards Afzul.

'*He* didn't give me time to think. He knows all about echoes among his own hills.'

'Yes, we have plenty there,' he said. 'A famous one, very popular with brigands, repeats a *jezail* shot a dozen times from rock to rock. So the traveller, not knowing, thinks he is ambushed! Bolts for his life, leaving half his goods, and one clever brigand gets the haul.'

While Sinclair listened, Tara invited Chrystal to come for an 'explore,' Lilāmani still clutching her hand.

The Pathan watched them as they went; the look in his eyes told Sinclair it was high time to attempt his difficult word in season.

'Those cliffs,' he said, 'are mightily intriguing to my little girl.'

'Most charming little girl.' Afzul's gaze softened on the child. He was true Pathan in his feeling for all young things. 'Children are Allah's best gift,' he added, with unembarrassed candour.

The child was a safe topic and might serve as a bridge.

'She had never heard an echo; this one is remarkable. We ought to have Eve here with her fiddle. Pity she didn't come too.'

Afzul shot a suspicious glance at him. 'I think,' he said, 'they've often been up here. This was my party. I didn't ask them.'

Sinclair left it at that, and proffered his cigarette-case. 'Have a smoke. Shall we sit while they explore?'

Afzul helped himself, and they sat, both remarking, almost in one breath, on a heavy stillness in the air that might be a presage of storm.

'Hope it holds off till this evening,' Sinclair added.

'I think it will. But I rather like a bit of a storm.' A pause. '*We* go back by Zerbal plain.'

The slight emphasis seemed to intimate that they wanted that route to themselves.

'*We* go back by Killan,' Sinclair capped him, an amused gleam in his eyes. 'We like having the world to ourselves!'

Afzul retorted, with an answering gleam, 'We like it also — and this is a large mountain.'

That 'we' seemed a tacit admission that he ought not to let slip.

'Sher Afzul ——' He looked very straight at the goodly young Pathan. 'Will you forgive a plain question, in a friendly spirit? I admire Chrystal. I think the man who wins her will be luckier than most of us deserve to be.'

'The luckiest devil alive,' the other agreed with smothered passion.

'Does that mean — are you seriously hoping — ?'

The direct question was answered by a flashing glance.

'We Pathans never play fast and loose with such a matter, as you English so often do. She has taken possession of me.'

'And on her account,' Sinclair pressed him, 'you would forego your country, and religion, if she would face the big risk of marrying outside her own race?'

'I — ? My country — my religion?' Twin sparks came alight in his eyes. 'Those are in a man's blood. He has no power to forego.'

'Precisely. Even for love of the loveliest, a man can't change his spirit of race. And — the children? Allah's best gifts, as you said. Is it fair to them?'

'No. It is *not* fair.' The words were forced out of him. 'Children are for more than their parents. I would never wish ——' He looked hard at Sinclair, as fine a blend of England and India as could well be conceived. 'You, yourself — I had forgotten ——'

It was the highest compliment, paid unaware.

'Your own mother,' he added, 'pure Rajput?'

'Pure Rajput,' Sinclair echoed, and his pride in it was of her bestowing. 'That alone gives me some right to speak.'

'True. I felt angry at first, resenting English prejudice. But there is power in your voice and look to calm anger. And no prejudice. You can understand.'

'Yes, I *can* understand.' His tone gave the words a deeper meaning. 'I am well born on both sides. Yet I have suffered from the handicap more than my parents ever knew. Theirs was a marriage successful out of the common. But they lived in England. Could you live always in England?'

'I don't know. I loved your country for those few years of my youth. But — for always? Too tame and tied up. I am a soldier. What would I do over there? I had not looked so far.'

Sinclair smiled. 'You would leap first and look afterwards! Hard on her. Were you expecting her to give up country and belief on your account? Would she — could she — put everything behind her for what you have to give?'

That searching question troubled Sher Afzul to the depths of his courageous yet primitive soul. For a few moments he was silent, looking across the lake, where Chrystal and Lilāmani were waking the echoes with lovely flute calls. Then he turned to Sinclair, a shadow in his eyes.

'That — only she can answer. We have not yet spoken of such things. The great force, that none can resist, is pulling us together. But God knows if she would give up all in return for my heart, that I would cut out of my body at her wish. There is a coldness in your women, hard for us to understand. You understand them. Can *you* tell?'

The simplicity of that appeal moved Sinclair to wish he could sweep away all barriers with a few words of unqualified assurance.

'I wouldn't presume to say I understand them! Chrystal has many fine qualities; but I couldn't venture to say which would have the stronger pull for her — head or heart.'

'That,' said Afzul, 'is what I must discover — perhaps today?'

'Wouldn't it be wiser — to refrain?' Sinclair suggested,

more from an inner compulsion than from any hope of staying an elemental force.

'Wiser?' Youth and passion scorned the cold-blooded word. 'I have read in your sacred Book that Wisdom cries in vain from the housetops. Whatever may come after for me — or for her — I *must* know.'

That cry from his heart none but Chrystal could answer. And the women were returning now, Lilāmani running ahead, full of new marvels to tell the father who shared her pristine wonder even over the least of things.

Together they climbed to the summit, enjoyed a picnic tea, and parted in great good-will: Chrystal and Afzul crossing back to the right head of the moraine and disappearing down the south face of the hill; the Sinclairs returning to Killan by the heather track.

'Any impression?' Tara asked.

'Yes — so far as I could judge. But the heart, like the tongue, can no man tame. It lies with her.'

'Perhaps a pity you didn't try speaking to her.'

'I may try it yet if she doesn't give in today all along the line.'

Chapter VII

Their love is intense with longing; yet they can never fly wing to wing.

RABINDRANATH TAGORE

THE other pair — with all their ecstasies, ardours, and defeats ahead of them — were also tramping down through heather, making for a gap where the mountain's western shoulder dropped to the Zerbal plain: the man convinced that this day must surely bring him his heart's desire; the girl still hoping to ward off a crisis that might involve a surrender for which she was not prepared yet, if ever.

Not lightly had she consented to this day-long outing, in defiance of their small world and its prejudices. Having steeled herself against his urgency, something within her had suddenly rebelled at losing an expedition she craved and many hours of his good company, simply because her consent might raise false hopes. To herself, she could no longer deny an increasing fascination that might or might not amount to falling in love — a condition not yet fully experienced to her knowledge, unless one could reckon a crude smite for an unsuspecting schoolboy at the ripe age of fifteen. Two years later she had been besought to marry a shy learned man nearly double her age; but his nervous attempts at love-making had only hardened her conviction that she wanted to belong to herself, not to any man of them all: a conviction reaffirmed by the full awakening of her art.

Inhuman? Not altogether; though some vital part of her still shrank from the idea of being possessed; and even fascination could not blind her to the fact that Sher Afzul, under his half-civilised surface, was as primitive and possessive as any of his Pathan ancestors. The sun had stored up its strength in him, the mountains their hardness. He was a carrier of mysterious forces. He held some of her now; but could he hold all of her, always? The forces he kept in leash half frightened her, half tempted her to rouse them; not less because she knew it might be dangerous. Their effect on her might prove a test. She seemed to have reached a point at which she could neither let him go altogether, nor let him advance beyond their present semblance of friendship, with its underlying thrill. Yet instinct, if not experience, warned her that no human relation can ever remain static. A sense of adventuring along strange paths — half afraid, yet wholly daring — enhanced the fascination and the fear. A long day alone with him might show her which way she was leaning.

So she had consented to come in her coolest manner. With equal coolness she had told Eve, Lance not being present. One could trust Eve to respect one's independence, daughter of Scotland that she was.

She had simply remarked: 'That sounds decisive. Is it meant to be?'

And Chrystal had answered frankly, 'No, it's not.'

'Well, I leave the foster-mother touch to Claire,' was Eve's comment on that. 'You know what you're after.'

'I don't. I'm out to discover.'

Eve had raised a kinked eyebrow: but no more was said.

And now that the day was half over, had she discovered anything?

She had enjoyed the climb and the grand unfolding scene the more for sharing it with him. He lacked her artist's eye for natural beauty, but mountains were his breath of life — real mountains. These in Kashmir were too much 'fussed up' for his taste. He preferred the wild setting of the 'Frozen Lakes,' where he had been before. But obviously, today, the human attraction prevailed. Never had she seen him in such high spirits. Normally reserved, she had touched a spring in him that opened inner doors. When his rough Pathan humour flashed out, their happy laughter mingled, like streams tumbling down a hillside. Tales of his country and his people he told with a natural sense of the dramatic, instinctively choosing episodes that showed Pathan character in its best light.

And today, for the first time, he spoke of his mother and sisters, of the romance that had led to his younger sister's marriage — a story that might have served for one of Scott's Border tales: the boy and girl attraction before purdah fell between them; the girl's refusal to marry a chosen suitor, and the secret of her love revealed to her mother; hope darkened by a fatal rumour of cowardice, wrongfully imputed to a gallant young man, who had disproved it in dramatic fashion during a raid on his father's fort, and thereafter came proudly to claim his bride.

Afzul himself had been present at the wedding *tamasha*: clansmen, kinsmen, and retainers filling the great outer courtyard with joviality and gusts of laughter; the presents without number, jewels and furs, horses, carpets and cloth of gold. No thanks were looked for. The bride's acceptance sufficed. In most cases, even the giver's names were not revealed. His vivid phrases made pictures in her brain. And the dresses worn by his two sisters were like a fairy tale: loose Moslem trousers from cloth of woven gold; tunics of ruby and sapphire velvet embroidered in gold, filmy veils all sprinkled with sequins, like stars.

'Oh, if I could give *you* a dress like that!' he cried; and Chrystal's heart echoed the wish, but her lips refrained.

'And the food — !' His eyes shone, recalling curries and pillaus, sweets and puddings that must be tasted to be believed. 'In the Free Land appetites *are* appetites. Butter and sugar, no end! Yet your tiresome indigestion unknown. Not a dentist nearer than Peshawar; and I've never met a Pathan who needed his horrid attentions.'

'I suppose teeth are pulled out with tongs,' she laughed; and he grimaced.

'They come out easily, when old. We give them good stuff to chew. Only those who know us in our own country come to understand how we are a race apart, how we resent ignorant talk of "Indians." And that ugly half-caste word "Brindian," worst insult of all.'

'I think I can understand that,' she said, 'through knowing you, without seeing you in your country.'

'You would like to see me there — *pukka* Pathan?'

His eager question sent a thrill along her nerves.

'Part of me would. But I might feel rather afraid of *pukka* Pathan!'

'Never that. *You* would not be afraid.'

His gaze recalled their first dance — an age away. It reminded her, too, how much nearer they were being drawn to each other; and mentally she withdrew a trifle from his compelling personality.

'I'm just an ordinary girl,' she said, 'who might scream at a mouse! You mustn't glorify me.'

He looked away from her then, and said, with smothered fervour: 'You speak a few months too late. I glorify you, rightly, from the depths of my heart.'

'Oh, no — no,' she protested, like a child pushing away something secretly feared. For the first time it came over her that here they were alone, four thousand feet above their little world. By virtue of her own coolness — if she could remain cool — and the sincerity of his feeling for her, she must manage to retain command of the situation.

They had halted now in the rocky stretch of moraine crossing to the lake; and it was then that Lilāmani's call and its ghostly echo rang out, startling at first, then welcome as a voice from heaven. It was astonishing how she loved that child. Most children attracted or amused her in a purely detached way. This one curled soft fingers round her heart.

Not heeding an impatient sound from Afzul, she had bounded forward: and follow he must.

She had enjoyed the break-away with Tara and Lilāmani, the tea party on Apharwāt; Afzul at his liveliest, Roy imparting an atmosphere of calm and well-being that seemed to surround him like an aura. It steadied her for the possible assault on her emotions. He was one of those rare people who gain advantage by the simple fact of being there. She had felt half reluctant to leave those three: and very soon she perceived that she would need all the inner steadying Roy could give.

This was a changed Afzul; grave and thoughtful, his looks and tones charged with a stifled intensity of feeling that threatened the very crisis she hoped to evade.

The storm that brooded in the valley was impending also; clouds rolling up, little gusts of wind.

'We must put on a spurt,' said Afzul. 'There are some Gujar huts not far ahead, if we can get there in time.'

A shiver of lightning, a growl of thunder, still far off, seemed to confirm his doubt; but by now, the huts were in sight.

'Let's run for it,' he said. 'You must not get a soaking on my account.'

Surprisingly he took her left hand in his right, and they ran to the rough log hut that offered shelter, if no more. A few needle-points of rain whipped their cheeks as they dashed into the smelly place, empty of Gujars or goats.

'Well run!' Afzul triumphed, without releasing her hand.

'I'm glad we'll see it all among these grand hills,' she said. 'I love a big storm beyond everything.'

She was talking hurriedly, at random, pretending she was not aware how he still held her hand so hard that it would be undignified trying to retrieve it.

And suddenly she realised that he was not hearing a word. He was trembling. He clung harder to her hand. She could feel the fever in his blood. It set her own pulses throbbing with a strange excitement, so that she longed to give him what he craved and dared not ask.

It was a positive relief when the storm broke in fury almost overhead. On a scale of symphonic grandeur the heavens darkened and flashed and thundered. Forked lightning, almost continuous, darted among the clouds like fiery serpents run mad.

Suddenly — flash and crash in one, right overhead; a

flash that leaped out of heaven and struck the ground not a hundred yards from their shelter.

Chrystal gasped and jerked backwards, freeing herself—only for a moment. Alarm for her had released the passion he held in control. The raging heavens seemed to echo the storm within him.

And now, at last, he had her in his arms. Now she could not escape his eyes; and part of her would not, if she could. The intensity of his gaze roused all her senses as never yet. Speechless she gazed back at him: and in that unguarded moment, her defences were down indeed.

Triumphant, he held her close against him, she no longer resisting or wishing to resist, though the thought shivered through her: Where will this madness end?

He was kissing her and kissing her: a long, hard kiss that seemed to draw the heart out of her body, while the heavens raged above them, and the half-exhausted storm rolled on over Apharwāt, leaving the earth lightly sprinkled with snow.

'Look—look! how lovely!' she cried, gently pushing him from her, that he might not kiss her again.

And she saw with amazement how his face was transfigured by a startled happiness at his own achievement, at her response.

'Don't ask *me* to look anywhere but here,' he said. 'I can see no loveliness but in your face.' The faint tremor of his hand, that gently smoothed back her hair, brought sudden tears to her eyes. 'My lovely, tell me now in words that you have given me your heart, as I have given you mine.'

The simplicity and dignity of his own words, the fact that she had kissed him from her heart, yet could not give all, made no answer possible. Her limbs were shaking, as no fear of the storm could shake them.

Gently he led her to the back of the hut where two logs among the straw offered a rough seat. She had never felt more thankful to sit down. And he sat near her, not touching her, his restraint appealing to her more strongly than he could have conceived possible.

'I am asking,' he said, 'not only for your heart, but for your whole self — your life joined to mine.'

It took her a moment to grasp the full implication of that simple statement; the wonder of it, the utter impossibility.

'You mean that I should marry you. But Afzul, think ——'

'I cannot think. I *feel*. And you —?'

'Yes,' she softly admitted, 'I do — care. But this is a matter of other lives than our own. What of my people — and yours?'

'My people,' he said — but the exultation had gone from his tone — 'would, in the end, accept and love any woman I brought to them as my wife.'

'But they are Moslem.'

'And you?' he repeated, holding her eyes. 'Could you not bring yourself —? Our faith is not, after all, so far removed from your Old Testament. We have nearly all the same prophets; but not the God-man.'

She looked thoughtful at that; loving him — yes, loving him — longing to bridge the unbridgeable gulf; yet thankful, for the moment, to let emotion subside.

'With us,' she said, 'it is the God-man and his Testament that mean most, though our faith is not fanatical like yours. I could *call* myself Moslem. Could you call yourself Christian? *Could* you —' she suddenly pressed him, 'if that were the only barrier between us?'

'I?' he exclaimed in startled amazement. '*Lā hāol! Wā lā quatta illah Billah!*'

The torrent of guttural Pushtu seemed to set him leagues away from her; and he, perceiving it, ventured an arm round her shoulders.

'My beautiful one, do I seem to you utterly savage? Believe me, I was only speaking sacred words that we often use when taken aback.'

'What words? They sounded rather terrible.'

'I only said, "No power or might, except with God." And because of that power and might, I must always, in heart and life, be Moslem.'

'And I must always be Christian,' she quietly insisted. 'But that's only one stumbling-block. Others must be recognised. If we could live our own lives in a world of our own —? But we couldn't. We should have to live in this Anglo-Indian world that wouldn't have us at any price. Look at poor Mrs. Hyder Ali and her friend. Would you condemn me to the indignity of isolation, like them?'

'I would *not*. Nor would others. I am Pathan. There are those, even in Anglo-India, who recognise the difference.'

'Some of them — yes. Not all. Oh, Afzul, forgive me. I ought not to have let it go as far as this.'

'Forgive *you?* Ask me to forgive an angel in heaven for shedding light on earth. There are things too strong to be let or hindered. Now you have said — you care, no power on earth can come between us.'

His tawny eyes shone with a strange splendour; and the deeps in her responded as they could not have done half an hour ago.

'Don't press me, Afzul,' she pleaded. 'I can't see clear, think clear. And I can't, on impulse, say "yes" or "no" to anything so big as you are.'

'But,' he urged, 'if you consult with your mind, your heart will become cool.'

'That need not be. I only know that I *must* consult with my mind; or I must say "No" to you straightaway.'

Flames leaped in his eyes.

'I will not take "No" straightaway. I will give you time to consider this big thing — if you *will* do so.'

'I will,' she said, very low, with a sense of fatality, as if she were speaking the words at the altar rails. Then, with an effort, she recaptured her sanity.

'And now,' she said briskly, 'we have delayed too long up here already. The storm is over. Please take me home.'

The confiding simplicity of her request affected him like a caress. Her mere physical presence laid an enchantment on him; and the shining fact that she also cared, that she would actually consider the possibility of marriage, so exalted him that as yet he asked no more.

They smiled at each other, a sudden intimate smile, that calmed his heart. Gravely, without speaking, he followed her out of the hut, as if completing an action foreordained by Fate.

Chapter VIII

We two have taken up a lifeless vow
To rob a living passion: dust for fire.

MEREDITH

LANCE DESMOND had spoken with knowledge of the 'damn little station' all ears and eyes. Though Gulmarg had gaiety enough to keep the idlest out of mischief, there are human groups everywhere who live mainly at second-hand. Starved of first-hand emotion, they extract it from the doings — and above all the misdoings — of their livelier neighbours. And by now ears were being pricked, eyebrows raised over 'this Brindian affair.' The girl — they admitted — naturally didn't realise —— But the man must know that such a marriage would not be accepted either socially or by his regiment. He was taking advantage of her ignorance, of the fact that too many white women lately had been 'letting down the race.' What was Mrs. Inglis about, allowing things to go so far without exerting her semi-parental influence?

That significant question drew steel-tipped comments from a shrewd lady who could see more than a church by daylight. Mrs. Inglis — she broadly hinted — was too much taken up with 'a certain Police Officer' to keep an eye on her niece, whom she had so conveniently boarded out with the young Desmonds: an unkind thrust that had not yet reached the victim's ears. And in any case the libel would not have troubled her unduly. Her aching anxiety over Chrystal was no one else's affair. She could only trust Sir Roy to say things that the girl would be far readier to heed, if they came from him, than from herself. Shelved by order, and glad of it, she was paying no heed to the small world that loomed so large in its own eyes. The full days of a hill-station summer rushed aimlessly past her, like a crowd running to see a spectacle that might or might not be worth watching. None stayed to ask. Where one ran they all ran: and she, no longer compelled to run with them, could at least thank her tiresome heart for this brief respite, for leisure to enjoy long days with Grace, the discovery of Tara Sinclair, the stimulus given by Chrystal to her modest art.

Not for a moment did she suppose that Gulmarg would notice her and Dixon Verney, an established friend, with as clean a reputation as any man on the Border; though to her this peaceful fortnight had by now revealed how far her guarded heart had gone astray from an allegiance long since undermined by Jasper himself.

For years she had lived the complex, dual, unsatisfied life of the ill-mated woman, doing her loyal best to make bricks without straw. The fact had been less glaring while she could live mainly in and for her children, contending against the faults he had transferred to them, especially to Madge. But now they were removed from her daily life, she could not but recognise that marriage — with all its drags and difficulties — had neither meaning nor reality unless it satisfied more than the so-called natural needs. 'The unholy estate' Dixon had named it; and marriage with Jasper on their present lines seemed, to her clear seeing, unholy indeed.

The fact had been sharply brought home to her by a letter, announcing the good news that he had managed to alter the date of his leave so as to escape a week earlier from the fiery furnace. And the sudden news had so shaken her that she had refrained from telling Grace lest the shrewd woman should put two and two together.

Jasper wrote gaily of his good luck, his assurance that he would find her 'completely bucked up'; and towards the end he casually mentioned that Pam was on strike. It was a punishing June. He would be glad of the chance to travel up with her. In his state of heart, and pulled down by the heat, he rather funked travelling alone, though Khudar Bux was an adept at oiling the wheels.

The old tag about his heart moved her no longer to doubt, but to faint contempt. For Doctor Ewart, in their last talk, had opened her eyes, unaware, to the true nature of Jasper's 'trouble.' He had told her flatly that she must not dream of returning for August and September; had threatened her with the drastic prescription of two years at Home unless she took more care of herself; to which she had replied that he might as well prescribe a trip to the moon. Her husband's obscure heart weakness made it impossible to leave him.

And Ewart had said with grave kindliness: 'My dear Mrs. Inglis, as your doctor I can't allow you to worry unduly on that score. Worry is the worst thing possible for *your* heart, which needs much greater care just now than your husband's.'

'But Jasper,' she had protested in amazement, 'saw a specialist in Town.'

And Doctor Ewart had smiled outright. 'Ah, those London specialists have got to earn their guineas! I know Inglis suffers discomfort when he smokes too much, or plays too much tennis, or eats unwisely. But I can assure you, for your comfort, that there is no organic trouble. It's what we call a nervous heart. If he stopped thinking about it and took reasonable precautions, he'd be no more aware of his heart than I am.'

'Have you ever told him that?' she had asked in a careful voice; and he too had answered carefully.

'I tried to once, for the good of his heart! But he pinned his faith on the specialist. I'm afraid he now only thinks me rather a rotten doctor.'

She had kept her countenance: and he had kept his. He had once more insisted that she should not return till October: and there an end.

But the inner effect of that disclosure did not pass. Her mild anxiety had given place to a deadlier doubt. Was Jasper deliberately letting her worry and overtax herself on account of a trouble so slight that it could hardly be said to exist?

Or did he really believe in the specialist, who had probably read him like a book? With Jasper one never could tell whether he was deceiver or self-deceived! Too well she knew how skilfully he could slip and slide round the truth believing he had told it. Strange to remember how deeply all that had hurt her once, how little it hurt her now. She could not even manage to care whether or no he travelled up with Pam, or even if she had shared his bedroom. It was the fact of his coming that lay like lead on her heart: the move into the noisy crowded hotel; an end of her peaceful days with Grace, though no doubt she could come over often. Pam and Jasper would live for tennis and bridge. But the reviving sense of freedom would be gone. He would start worrying Chrystal and antagonise the girl, which would be deadlier than all. The trick of living ahead, the curse of imagination, made her feel positively ill; and physical sensations warned her how slender still were her reserves of strength.

She was sitting alone over her tea, combating these wretched sensations to the best of her ability: she had cried off going with Grace to see the Judge's family, shirking the mental effort of talk with Indian women, and she had yet to answer Jasper's letter in a spirit of wifely welcome: the kind of hypocrisy that was smoke to her eyes and vinegar to her teeth. Years of it should have hardened her by now. But truth, for her, was the A B C of conduct; and this urge of her whole being towards another man so acutely falsified their relation that she felt as if her married life had come to a sudden full stop. And she could not tell him so. That was the curse of the situation. They must keep up the eternal pretence, for decency's sake. It seemed as if her present life chiefly amounted to keeping up pretences.

In justice to herself ought she to keep them up any longer? Her sane mind perceived less harm in her natural feeling for Dixon than in the hypocrisies forced upon her by social convention, by the entangling love of her children, and a mild affection for Jasper that made her reluctant to hurt him — as a permanent break would presumably do.

It was the affections that complicated life more than

physical love, with its impersonal element of passion. But no fondness, no reluctance to hurt, could quiet the longing to escape. And if Dixon ever allowed her to see that he cared, beneath his unrevealing semblance of friendship — what then? Since that astonishing moment at Rāmpore, he had given no sign. But if he did — again, what then?

The possibility of having to face that tragic question brought home to her the peculiar crux of these modern days when all bonds were loosened and personal freedom easier to attain. There was now no accepted code or standard to which one must conform or be damned. Fires of hell and damnation had been damped down. There were too many pots that could not afford to call kettles black. Even fifty years ago a question of that kind would have been answered in advance by the 'Mighty Must' of convention, if not conviction. Now the man or woman faced with a tragic choice must decide by personal conscience, not by code. That was the dilemma of the moderns — even the more or less moderns, like herself. They lived in a disjointed way; and at times of crisis they must do hard thinking, straight thinking; learn by their own mistakes. A code might be cramping, but it built up men and women. Right or wrong, it gave them a technique in living. If the average modern woman owned a technique, it amounted to 'Take all you can get and give next to nothing in return.' Her own overwhelming desire was to save what remained of her life from misery and waste; to break off a personal relation that was no relation. Admit her own mistake — confess it, if needs must: and act on the admission...

From her desperate mental excursion she was recalled by the *kit* bringing in her lone afternoon tea. She had looked up to tell him, *Darwāza bund*, when she was arrested by a man's voice in the verandah asking if she were at home — Dixon.

Her inner flutter was half physical.

'*Sahib kō salaam dō*,' she said at once. But he must have heard her voice and he waited for no 'salaam.'

'Glad to find you alone,' he said: and something explosive

under his abrupt manner flashed the thought, 'Has it come at last?'

To quiet her tremor she asked politely, 'Will you share my tea? I'll send for another cup.'

'No, thanks. Nothing for me. Get on with your own picnic.'

He was wasting no words on politeness.

'I've something to say — something serious. And I don't readily express myself on such occasions.'

Deliberately she measured out her milk, her teaspoon of sugar, though teapot and tray seemed suddenly miles away from her. And his voice came from a distance.

'I wonder if you guess? I've said nothing; not pestered her. It seemed useless. But now — if she's heading for that Pathan —?'

'*She* —?' Her voice trailed off. The teaspoon rattled onto her saucer. Chrystal! She had never thought of that. Her senses seemed to be slipping from her, when the feel of his arm round her shoulders dragged her back to acute consciousness, and his voice of concern as at Rāmpore: 'My dear, my dear! Is it worrying you all that? I thought — you seemed so much better. Here: sniff this.'

He had picked up her lavender salts and thrust them under her nose, cold and hard, the stopper not removed.

'Oh, damn!' He frowned at his slip, opened the bottle, and handed it to her. A swift sense of the ludicrous restored her balance, but she dared not laugh. He was terribly in earnest; and laughter might tremble into self-betraying tears.

'Thank you, thank you.'

She took it and sniffed the strong salts so violently that it set her sneezing, which made her feel more than ever a fool.

Filling her cup, he held it out to her.

'Drink that,' he said. 'Make you feel better.'

Obediently she swallowed half the tea and her brain felt clearer, which only made the shock of discovery hurt the more.

'You mean,' she asked, 'that you — that Chrystal —?'

'Oh, not Chrystal.' She was hurt afresh by the pain in his tone. '*She* hasn't a glimmer.' He paused, his gaze searching her face. 'Hasn't it ever occurred to you?'

'To me? No. I could see you admired her. But I thought you didn't want — to marry.'

'I didn't, till she knocked me over. I bottled it all up in Peshawar. Seventeen years is too big a gap. But directly I saw her up here again, I knew nothing would stop me but her flat refusal. I soon found, however, she had eyes only for that damned Pathan. A shame to crab him. He's a fine fellow enough, but he can't have Chrystal Adair. Hasn't it worried you?'

'Yes. I've spoken to Sir Roy. They see more of her than I do. He promised he would speak to her.'

'He did? Decent of him. A word from him might give her to think — if it's not too late.'

'Too late?' she echoed in dismay.

'Well, I suppose you known of their Apharwāt adventure? Whole day up there, I believe.'

She caught her breath. 'Oh, Dixon! I didn't know. I haven't seen her since Monday. The whole day — are you sure?'

'Well, that's the gup. The Club's buzzing with it. They'd probably say the whole night if that Goggles woman hadn't met them coming back in the evening. Of course, she trumpeted an imminent engagement; and they're all up on their hind legs, demanding his head on a charger — or the polite equivalent. I'm sorry for him, poor devil. But we can't give these young Brindians the pick of our girls. My God! if there's any real risk of *that* catastrophe, I'll move heaven and earth to pull her my way.'

Claire, not venturing to look at him, heard him draw a deep breath. Her silence seemed to puzzle him.

'What d'*you* think of my chances, Claire?' he asked, with an eagerness that hurt. 'I've no taste for being spurned.'

'I haven't noticed — not thinking of it. I really don't know.'

The constraint she put upon herself made her sound so

colourless that his next words hurt her in quite another fashion.

'And you'd rather not have her marry your friend? Too old, am I? Not good enough? I'm with you there.'

She could stand no more.

'My *dear* Dixon ——' Her voice was alive again; her own pain thrust aside by the womanly impulse to heal the hurt she had unwittingly inflicted. 'How could I — knowing you as I do — think any such thing? If you can only make her care — as you care' (she thought the words would choke her) 'she'll be a lucky, lucky woman.'

He let out an audible breath of relief.

'That's more like it, more what I hoped for — from you. I've a clean record as men go. Kept fairly clear of women the last five years. It's harder in this climate. But if a man can't be master of himself, he's not worth a row of beans. Nothing could stop me now from trying my luck. But we're such real friends, Claire, that I did want to feel sure I had your good-will before I made a bid for hers.'

And she said, very low, letting her stifled emotion creep back into her voice, because he would not hear or heed: 'You have every ounce of my good-will, Dixon. I say it from the bottom of my heart.'

To her complete surprise he put out a hand, enclosing hers in a hard grip; and the knowledge pierced her like a dagger-thrust — that was the most she could hope to have from him, ever. If he married Chrystal, she would have to endure the sight of them together all her days.

She could not speak; neither, for a few minutes, could he. Then he said in a changed voice:

'I'll be up there this evening. They're taking dinner to Baba Maharishi, themselves and the Sinclairs. Desmond asked me at the polo if I'd like to join them. He may have an inkling. He's that rarity, a husband who has remained a lover.'

Abruptly he stood up. 'I think I'll go. I've rattled you, I'm afraid, more than you're fit for. Thank you, *thank* you, Claire. Take things easy —— A book —?'

She attempted no protest, for fear she might say too much. He wrung her hand again and went out. She sat there rigid till his footsteps faded away. Then, like a memory from another life, came the thought of Jasper. She had not even mentioned his coming. What matter? What did anything matter — now? When the pain becomes too bitter, something snaps in the heart.

Suddenly she bowed her head, covered her face with both hands, and cried — and cried.

Chapter IX

This unavailing gift at least I may bestow.

DRYDEN

IT WAS on that very morning following the Apharwāt adventure, that Sinclair found his chance for a talk with Chrystal, in whom he divined some emotional ferment at work. If a word from him, at this early stage, might help her, speak he must, for all his masculine reluctance to put a spoke in another man's wheel or to intrude on the privacy of a woman's heart.

She was over this morning for Lilāmani's lesson, and staying on to lunch. The lesson over, he had seen Tara go out with the child. Here was his chance to catch Chrystal alone.

At the open drawing-room door he paused. For she was sitting very still, gazing at the child's picture, and her position gave him a profile view of her face: the straight nose, the soft, resolute lips, the honey-coloured hair curled in her neck, growing low on her forehead. A lovely, serious face, so untouched by life's pains and penalties that it might well seem to Afzul Khan the face of an angel.

The child's picture — an ambitious attempt at a group of pines — had astonishing merits. Chrystal had been impressed with her advance in these two months, not taking sufficient credit for her own individual manner of teaching; but he did not believe that, just now, she saw a line of those trees and rocks.

While he hesitated, she looked up quickly, turned, and

saw him in the doorway. Encouraged by her smile, he came and stood beside her.

'Are you pleased with that?' he asked.

'Specially pleased.'

'How much of it is you?'

'Hardly a touch. I'm allowed to say what's wrong. I'm not allowed to put it right!'

He smiled. 'The little monkey has a mind and a will of her own.'

'She has a gift of her own. Every picture she makes must be hers, good or bad.'

'And "a stranger intermeddleth not with her joy,"' he quoted softly. 'She doesn't know her luck, having a true artist for drawing mistress. Have you ever considered' — he edged towards his aim — 'whether your true vocation is artist or woman? You have it in you to combine both, like Eve.'

'I wonder —?' she mused, without looking up. 'Lance is a man in a thousand. But I gather there was some rough going at the start.'

'No harm for the artist or the woman. Only one thing, Chrystal,' he added in a tone of quiet authority; 'if you do marry, it must be a man of your own race.'

She glanced quickly up at him.

'I didn't expect *you* to say that, Roy.'

'It's because I am — what I am, that I must say it. And because I care a great deal what comes to you.'

She gazed at him with illumined eyes.

'You care — a great deal?' The look, the question, told him that Claire Inglis had spoken with knowledge of his possible influence — an added responsibility.

'Is that so strange?' he asked, a hand on her shoulder.

'To me it seems a wonder of wonders. I'm so proud of your friendship, of helping your lovely Little Scrap to find herself. And I know you aren't just handing out sugar-plums.'

'Not I. You've a knack of making people care. You've made poor Sher Afzul care to distraction.'

His name was out now, take it how she would.

'Oh, I have. Did he tell you?'

'Yes. And you?'

Knowing so much he must know all: and she said, very low: 'Roy, I'm distracted. He's such a splendid man.'

His hand closed on her shoulder. 'That's the trouble. Chrystal, my dear, could you talk of it to me?'

And she said, with sudden vehemence: 'Yes, I could — to *you*; not to anyone else on earth. I do — love him. I can't bear the usual talk. But you understand.'

'Well, then, come up into the wood. Easier out there.'

Hatless, she went with him, and they walked among the quiet trees that had listened, unheeding, to a thousand human confidences. There he lured her into a partial account of that scene in the hut, of its indecisive issue.

'I told him,' she said, 'that he *must* give me time. He would not take "No" straightaway.'

'Poor devil. But soon or late, it must be "No." Doesn't something in you, deeper than this turmoil, confirm that "must"?'

She stood still in the path and looked up at him, beset by a queer sensation that he radiated light. Then, as if needing support, she leaned against a tall tree, very fair and young, in her creamy yellow frock patterned with shadows.

'Yes — it does,' she answered, in her soft, resolute voice. 'But it's hard to think clear when one can only feel — and feel. Oh, Roy! I can't *bear* to hurt him so. Like sticking a dagger into my own heart.'

'Don't I know it?' he said, in a tone that almost upset her control. 'But believe me, Chrystal, the fascination is partly physical, partly natural response to his genuine feeling for you. If you did not see him for several months, it would subside. I speak from experience.' He paused, checked by his own innate reserve. 'I myself went through the same kind of crisis not long before I married. I was swept off my feet in the same fashion. She was nothing like so fine as your Afzul. I only mention it to show that I know what you're up against. And remember this: marriage depends on more than being in love. It's a spiritual bond. Failing that, it has no deep roots; no aim beyond personal pleasure and the getting of children. Forgive me if I'm too frank ——'

'Oh, please be frank,' she beseeched him. 'I love Afzul partly because he's so fierce and real.'

He smiled. 'Well, *I* can be fierce and real too! My only aim is to help you through this dark tunnel — and out the other side. Bear in mind the other side. Have you been in love before?'

'N-no. I think not.'

'That makes it harder. But you have grit and a sense of values. You might be happy with Afzul just at first, if his world and yours would let you. But they won't. And it couldn't last. You are too much of your period, too little pliable for the inner changes that would be required of you. And a crashing failure, a break after marriage, would be worse for you both. There's more in it than being young together. There's growing old together. Would Afzul, even for you, consent to retire and live in England? Could you face the prospect of growing old among those wild hills and alien people, cut off from your own world, your friends, your art —?'

'Oh, don't — don't!' She covered her face; a shiver ran through her and he put an arm round her shoulders.

'Now I've been too fierce. But I do want you to see ahead and you have the inner eye that can.'

She uncovered her face and smiled at him with wet lashes. 'Yes; terribly, I can.'

'Have I helped you, then, to feel — in spite of your tormented heart — that it *must* be "No"?'

Colour stirred in her cheeks. 'I'm afraid — you have.'

'Don't be afraid. Give yourself time; and one day you'll be glad of it — when you have found your destined Englishman. Good luck to him!'

She looked amused. He had diverted her mind.

'There's no one, that I know of, coveting the honour.'

'Isn't there? Has it never struck you that Verney is only standing by because you're obviously looking elsewhere?'

'Dixon —? Never. Anyway, he's a bit too old.'

'A crumbling ruin! Well under forty.'

'But truly, he's Claire's friend.'

'He's not *your* friend. Consider that next time you're together. See if I'm quite off the mark.'

She sighed: 'Where's the use — now?'

'Well, it might help a little, in this cruel business of hurting Sher Afzul, to know you'd be hurting a good man of your own race if you let the Pathan have his way.'

She glanced at him. 'Clever of you, Roy.'

'It's not meant in that way. Consider it. Even Afzul must know he's asking for the moon. But only you can tell him so. Does Verney not attract you at all? I get an impression that he does.'

Her colour deepened.

'I think your impressions would mostly — be right. I do like him a lot. I could like him more.'

'He's a man you could make a life with. But don't keep Afzul Khan dangling on a thread —— Hullo, we're caught out.'

It was Lilāmani, running through the trees, like a gleam of light in her yellow frock.

'Chrystal! Prithvi — *there* you are. We've hunted everywhere.'

He held out his arms and swung her off her feet, enjoying her silver laughter; and together they three went back to the hut, Roy keeping a hand under Chrystal's elbow, mutely bidding her be of good courage.

For Chrystal, that brief talk was cardinal, a hinge on which her emotional life turned, though she did not recognise it till much else had come to pass. Roy's intuition had discerned her mood more clearly than she realised, but not all at once would she admit the full effect of his plain speaking persuasive personality, of the fact that, throughout, he had stood beside her, not over against her. Not even to him could she reveal how deeply the spirit of her race affirmed his insistence on that hard refusal. Not all at once could she damp down the flame lighted in her when Afzul had held her and kissed her as he had done yesterday. Was it only yesterday?

And those glimpses of his own world, designed to attract her, had instead too clearly shown her that in it her veritable self could neither live true life, nor love true love. At first there might be the thrill of adventure, having the courage of one's conviction. But Roy's appeal had made her forward-looking mind see too clearly the inevitable end. Not once had he spoken as an elder to a younger, which would have stiffened her all through. He had spoken as a fellow human being, who had passed through the same dark tunnel and come out on the other side. She was to bear in mind the other side — the other man.

Those words called up a vision of Dixon's face: its decisive lines and jutting nose, the glint in his grey eyes when he smiled. She had caught a lifelike sketch of him at that picnic: and he never guessed. It was Dixon — she knew it now — who had first attracted her, with his brains and his humour, his refreshing unlikeness to the average modern young man.

Looking backward, she recalled her first impression of him on that long-ago afternoon in Peshawar, when he came to see Claire, who was fussing over some fad of Jasper's. So Chrystal had been left to entertain the clever, abrupt Police Officer, who had earned her gratitude by entertaining her himself. Decidedly, it would have been Dixon, had not her swift interest in Sher Afzul been clinched by Station disapproval. Undeniably Roy's hint of the other's deeper feeling for her was not without effect: but Afzul — Afzul ——

He must not be kept dangling on a string. She would deal the blow by letter. She could not bear — for him or herself — the emotional stress of seeing him again.

At lunch she was absent-minded; Roy, in the kindest way, treating it as a joke, waking the child's delicious laughter.

She returned to an empty hut: Eve at the Residency, enjoying a long day of music with Lady Thorne; Lance down at polo, where Roy had gone to join him. Late in the afternoon both came back and announced an impromptu dinner picnic, down at Baba Maharishi's tomb, for the full moon; just themselves and 'the Roys.'

After a pause Lance added casually: 'As Verney was lounging round at the polo, I asked him in to make the half dozen. No complaints, I hope, my pretty maid?'

'Of course not,' she lightly dismissed a move that set her wondering if Lance, unaware, had been prompted by Roy. It was so unexpected that it jerked her a trifle. And it was too soon. She was not in the mood. It prompted a perverse feminine impulse to stiffen herself against any deliberate attempt to withdraw her from the magnetic attraction of Sher Afzul Khan.

But by the time their party was assembled, and they were riding down in pairs through a forest belt of noble trees, the perverse impulse had subsided. To be friendly and natural with Dixon, to accept what befell, was her only way of showing gratitude to Roy — a man she could admire and deeply love without any emotional stir inside, a true fellowship of the spirit. Nevertheless, she contrived to ride down with Lance; Dixon following with Tara; Eve and Roy leading, in great form.

Their dinner picnic was laid under a giant maple on the grassy slope overlooking Kashmir Valley; and beyond it the Great Ones kept watch and ward. The place derived its name from the tomb of a Moslem saint, lying solitary in a cathedral not made with hands — the heavens for roof, mountains for pillars, moon and stars for altar lights. The tomb itself, under a regal cloth, was cased in lattice work, sheltered by walls and a verandah of carved cedar wood.

Chrystal, leaving things to chance, found herself between Roy and Dixon, who talked mainly to the men. When conversation lapsed, he sat beside her in a silence that made her aware of him in a new and disturbing way.

Once, to break the spell, she turned and asked casually: 'Have you seen Claire these last few days? I'm a sinner. I've not been there since Monday, about her etchings. She was looking so revived.'

'I was with her this afternoon,' he said, an odd gleam in

his eye. 'She looks better because she's rested and peaceful. But it's only skin deep. Any serious worry would bowl her over.'

The directness of that made her wonder if he knew about Apharwāt? Claire ought not to hear of it indirectly. She would go there tomorrow without fail.

While they all smoked and drank coffee, poured from a giant thermos, clouds came wandering up the valley, threatening to obscure the moonrise that was the object of their journey.

'Oh, that faithless moon!' groaned Eve. 'So pampered by overworship in this worshipful country. She simply won't behave, for all my abject salaams when she was new.'

And while Roy spoke of the moonrise on Apharwāt, Dixon said in Chrystal's ear: 'Have you been inside the shrine? Would you care to come and have a look at it?'

'I'm not very keen on tombs,' she confessed, in spite of a sudden eagerness to do almost anything he asked of her.

'There's some fine cedar-wood carving in the verandah.'

'Is there? I'd like to see that.'

'Come along, then, before the light fails.'

They rose and moved away, the rest not heeding.

Outside the verandah they halted, and Dixon said suddenly, 'I forgot — it's holy ground. Shoes not allowed inside.'

'We can take them off,' she said. 'The grass is warm.'

When she had removed hers, he took them from her and set the two pairs side by side near the verandah opening. 'For all the world, she thought, as if they were put out to 'be cleaned!'

But he was looking so serious that she refrained from the foolish remark and went on into the shrine, examining with critical interest the details of the complete design.

She could feel him now standing near her left shoulder, almost touching it with his arm. Again his silence had that disturbing quality; and there shot through her the startled thought — 'Is it coming now?' The last thing she had dreamed of. One on the top of the other: life had no artistic sense. She could only pray that she might be mistaken; but her prayer, like most of its kind, was vain.

'Chrystal,' he said suddenly, 'my information may not interest you. But I want you to know — I love you. You're the first thing in life for me. It's not a sudden flare-up. It has been going on for months.'

'Oh, Dixon!' She clenched her small hands, and the pain in her voice made him say quickly:

'Don't worry. I'm simply telling you, because I can't be near you any longer and not tell you, though it's plain to see you only have eyes for that favoured Pathan.'

Because he didn't say 'that damned Pathan' she almost loved him.

'Is it so terribly plain to everyone?' she asked. 'Are they all talking?'

'Naturally. But who cares? You don't.'

'Not for myself. Only — for him. I know the sort of things they say. It makes me furious.'

'That I can understand,' he said. 'Don't let it push you to lengths you might regret afterwards.'

'It almost could ——'

She checked herself; and he said, in a hardened tone: 'What lengths *are* you prepared to go? Is he mad enough to hope you may marry him?'

'Yes.' The word was a mere breath.

'*That* I can understand,' he said again, with a sudden vehemence more moving than any lover's declaration. 'Could *you* dream of such a thing?'

It was a moment when nothing but the truth would serve.

'Yesterday, I did feel — as if I could. But oh ——'

She wrung her hands together; and the little despairing gesture went through him like a spear-thrust. Yet he did not touch her. She seemed suddenly miles removed. He must, none the less, know where she stood.

'Chrystal, if he asks you outright, refuse him, I beg of you — for your own sake, not for mine. You probably don't care a row of beans ——'

'Oh, I *do*. I hate hurting you.'

The words appeared to be wrung from her; and to him they were like dew on parched earth. She was no longer miles removed.

'You darling girl,' he said, very low; and his hand closed on her shoulder with a sharpness that at once startled and steadied her. It was more the gesture of a friend than the possessive grasp of a lover.

She would have edged away from an encircling arm; but the strong hand on her shoulder, like Roy's this morning, gave her a sense of utter confidence in him worth more than any thrill of passion. Here was a man she could trust with the whole of herself; rely on to the end of ends. Why did this dark stirring in her blood withhold her from telling him so?

Before she had command of herself, he was speaking again:

'I know I'm at a disadvantage; years too old. No film-star fascination about me. But my heart has never before been an offer. Take or leave the thing, it's your property. And — listen here, Chrystal. You're not the sort who could pull off a life-bond with a Pathan, fine specimen though he is.'

Her sigh admitted as much; and he went on: 'If I can feel that you're not indifferent to me, that you *could* give me something genuine, some day, when you've pulled through all this, I can stand by and wait. It's a harder job when you're going eight and thirty than when you're five and twenty; but, even on a grain of hope, I'd wait till all's blue.'

His quiet tone implied no lack of fervour, but a resolute avoidance of emotional appeal in her present state of heart. And — she could only turn her face to him in the waning light, an ache in her throat, the prick of tears behind her eyes.

At the look in his, she forced herself to speak — no false word of comfort, but again the truth.

'Dixon,' she said, 'I'm proud that you care. I'll treasure in my heart every word you've said tonight.'

Sharply he caught her hand in his.

'That's good enough for me. Don't worry — darling. We'll leave it till you're ready — if ever? Time to be getting back, now.'

He suddenly pulled her towards the verandah opening.

'What a precious lot of carving you've examined! Damn it all, where *are* those shoes?'

The explosive note in his voice, clashing oddly with his commonplace words, was the only sign he gave of all that was at work in him.

Some zealous caretaker had moved the infidel shoes; but he found them and thrust hers at her, not offering to put them on for her; giving her the relief of something practical to do.

As she watched him kneeling down, fastening his own, her heart melted in her with gratitude — with more than gratitude.

Chapter X

Whom does love concern beyond the lover and the beloved? Yet its impact deluges a thousand shores.

E. M. FORSTER

THAT night sleep deserted her. After Apharwāt, and all that came of it, she had slept the profound, renewing sleep of youth. But tonight there was more than emotional disturbance at work in her. There was discord; the pull of two opposing forces that seemed each to capture a separate part of her; a dual state of being unknown in her limited experience. And until she could be resolved into her single-minded self again, there was no sleep in her. Undressed, it seemed useless to lie in bed, staring at rafters, when the world outside was drenched with the moonlight.

Pulling a low chair to the open door she sat there till her troubled mind absorbed a measure of the night's serene and selfless calm.

With a detached fragment of it, she could marvel now at this imperious emotion exalted by poets and novelists, whose fervours she held had always tended to discount as probably intensified for effect. Tonight the potent thing at work in her veins was forcing her to admit that perhaps they wrote of it more truly than she had given them credit for; reminding her that her own secret adventuring self had always wanted to reach the out of reach, to defeat Fate, to prove love an invincible reality.

But which love — ? The emotional urge, the half-fearful fascination that had swept her towards Afzul? Or the subtler, deeper disturbance wrought in her by Dixon, without aggression, without demand?

Afzul's kiss and her own instinct had told her that he would be a fierce lover, perhaps a fiercer husband. He had said more than once, 'A man must be master in love'; and the real Chrystal would not have it. Something impermeable in her would remain unattached always: an inhuman touch that the Englishman might possibly understand; the Pathan never.

Dixon's 'information' and his manner of giving it had served him better than he would be likely to guess. If she wanted the hard core of love, she would find it in Dixon Verney. If he did not fascinate her, he had stirred in her tonight something precious and unaccustomed; a whispered promise of happiness more lasting and secure than she could possibly hope for as wife of Afzul Khan; a sense of utter reliance and trust that were bread and meat to her soul. He was an authentic, earthly man, with no pretence about him. He would respect her art, even if he lacked the sympathetic understanding which made that masculine Lance the destined mate for Eve. He would respect her tiresome spirit of independence — of the 'cat that walked alone in the wild woods, waving its wild tail.'

One must live out of the whole of one's self, or grow crooked. To the whole of herself Afzul would never appeal, for all his splendid manhood. Dixon would, by virtue of his race as well as his fine quality — if only he could, in time, arouse her as the other had done. The body — she now perceived — must be a fully consenting partner. That was the difficulty and the glory of the love that justified marriage.

And out there, cool and unconcerned — the moon entangled among pines, the quiet, undemanding night. Alone with this loveliness, it seemed almost a pity that one should be troubled by any other desire than the instinctive longing to be lifted up into it, to become one with it — the artist's way of salvation. But the woman in her argued that peace and serenity might be bought at too high a price: refusal of all human intimacy, all disturbing emotions; living flesh and blood chilled to the austerity of carven stone. Better the torment and the ecstasy and all the conflicting elements that were the essence of life. One must accept the whole of it in order to render even a small part of it with truth; that much she had grasped, even at what Lance called her 'tender years.' And theories were 'junk' unless one at least tried to act on them. So good-bye to vain dreams of a human life untormented by human distractions.

Now, before she could hope to sleep, she must choose — with her few grains of wisdom — between her love of Afzul, strong in its present appeal, and her incipient love of Dixon, that held a promise of deeper, more lasting happiness. Success in marriage — Roy had said — hung on even bigger things than being in love. 'A spiritual bond': the words struck home. That was the real need of her nature. And her decision must be immediate, in Afzul's case, though refusing him now would amount to ultimate acceptance of the older man, who had been standing by, giving her time.

Roy's quiet command, 'It *must* be "No,"' came to her in his very voice. Yet still Afzul walked to and fro in her heart — his lithe movements, his big laugh, the gleam in his tawny eyes. She could picture him walking to and fro tonight in his hotel room, counting on her answer, unable to credit the extinction of his hope. 'He must not be kept dangling by a thread': Roy was her Bible in this difficult affair. Would it were possible for any hand but her own to cut the thread! A letter it must be: written while conviction was clear. It might be clearer in the morning. One could not tell. So she would write it now: rewrite and post it tomorrow.

She took paper and pencil and sat there staring at the blank sheet. How did one deal a death-blow in terms that were kindly yet convincing? Sentence after sentence her brain approved, her heart dismissed. At last, in despair, she wrote down whatever came first.

My dear Afzul:

I think you must know what my answer is bound to be. [*'He can't and he won't know it,' her critical self spurned that cautious opening.*] *Taking counsel with my mind has not made my heart cool; but it has shown me that in a life's bond, like marriage, there is more than the heart to be reckoned with. There are claims we can't ignore to our people and our race. You did see that yesterday, though you tried not to see it too clearly. I believe we could be happy together for a time; but I know it could* only *be for a time. And how much worse for us both if I had to leave you after marriage! Better, far better, to face the impossibility now, and accept — 'No.'*

Honestly, I can give no other answer. It's not race pride or prejudice — you know that. It's because too many other big things are against us.

Please face this, Afzul — though I hate writing it — like the brave man you are. Don't throw up all that England has given you. Stay in the regiment. You are a fine officer. And afterwards, when this hurt is healed, marry some girl of your own clan who will be worthy of you, in ways that I could never be, and give you all that I never could, though I might break my heart in trying to do it.

This is the hardest letter I've ever had to write. But it's the truth; and that must come first always, even if it hurts.

Allah will bless you and send you comfort in time, because of your courage. I feel honoured that you have loved me. I will remember you always.

CHRYSTAL ADAIR

Please, please don't *try to see me again. It would be quite useless and it would hurt us both too much.*

As she wrote those last words, tears welled up and spilled over; but he would not know. Letting the half-sheet of paper fall into her lap, she lay back with a shivering sigh. The night's magical influence fell like dew on her aching sense of having dealt him a sword stroke, when she would fain have crept once more into his arms. Truth must come first, she had glibly written; but truth escaped one in every direction. One could only follow some inner guide — the greater Self according to Roy — and hope for a glimmer of light beyond the black tunnel.

Dixon —? It well might be.

The moon had sailed almost clear of imprisoning trees; below her a drift of cloud white as a swan's wing; jagged pine twigs and a tuft of needles etched on her radiance.

Bright and dark struck sharp on each other — that was life.

Comfort crept into her, from that heavenly reassurance of Beauty, strange source of the heart's uplifting: Beauty that is the splendour of Truth. Her limbs weary, her troubled confusion straightened out, she stole quietly to bed and to sleep, 'accepting everything beneath the sun.'

Chapter XI

For him the night of striving
Brings forth the strife of day;
His feet are unarriving
Upon the eternal way.

GERALD GOULD

To SHER AFZUL KHAN, on fire of a love, the brief pause imposed by that distracting and adorable girl was torment unalloyed. It would certainly be two days. It might be three: an eternity to his natural desire for swift fulfilment, even at the risk of shattering the thing he ardently craved. Richly equipped with his human heritage — the physical glory of man — he was only half alive, as yet, to the greater glory of mind and spirit.

And impatience was sharpened by the cruel uncertainty of the issue. Her response to his kiss had told him the chief thing he needed to know. Yet the very knowledge that she cared and could still resist him stung his Pathan pride to the quick. For him a kiss of that nature, given and returned, could not be other than a prelude to marriage. He himself would never have kissed her so but for the love he had seen in her eyes; and it distressed him that she, who had become his earthly divinity, should yield so far and yet remain doubtful of going farther. It was a matter of religion and race custom rather than any moral inhibition; marriage being, for the Moslem, a social obligation. The Pathan, whose love of women equals his love of money, would not hesitate to go with harlots or bazaar women, or even with Peshawari dancing boys who wear the rose above the ear, but he would never play at love-making; even were purdah lifted, with potential wives and mothers of the race. It is the West's casual attitude in this regard that bewilders men of the East and undermines their normal respect for white women.

Afzul had heard from an older cousin — once a soldier — how, before the war, these were reckoned inaccessible to any man of dark skin; a belief completely shattered when Indian troops returned from France, bringing tales of things seen and heard and done that had lowered the prestige of the whole white race. He himself, at school and at Sandhurst, had learnt to esteem their masculine code of character, had admired their girls shyly, from a distance, even in the friendly English atmosphere. Only this one had set his manhood on fire; had given proof that she loved him; and yet she would not ——

Pride and passion alike insisted that, in the end, she must, or he could hardly have endured those few days of torturing suspense. He would not go where he might meet her. He would not even play polo with Desmond and Sinclair, whose appeal to wisdom had not stayed his fated course. All day he climbed the surrounding hills with his gun, to weary himself; but no amount of 'leg breaking' could weary his iron frame, his tireless youth.

At night he was tormented with visions of her: swinging up her racket for a back-hander, the rhythm and beauty of her young limbs, too bare for all men to see; the gleam of her golden hair, the fragrance that came with her always, as if she were a flower. Now she would seem deliciously near him, close against his heart, as in the hut; now beyond reach, like strange thoughts and dreams that vanish on waking. Beneath her softness he was aware of an inner resistance that the male in him wanted to break down and the lover must needs respect, as he respected her uncomfortable honesty, though it jerked him often over trifles of no account. And he feared, more than a trifle, her critical spirit, fostered by this art that meant so much to her. He could not endure criticism in a woman to her man. As husband he must in all things be her master, her recognised superior.

In Peshawar he had felt nearer to her and her people. Changes unnoticed had been wrought by those few weeks among his own devil-may-care people; a race with no nerves, no complexities of thought or conduct, yet seldom failing in loyalty to their own unwritten code of life and death. After renewed contact with the simpler Moslem mentality, its clear outlook on men and things, he felt oppressed by these complications of so-called civilised life, and the fetish of 'good form' that had been drummed into him at Sandhurst; his Pathan self constantly tripping up the correct, officer self that he wore like a uniform and aspired to wear like a second skin. But no man could extinguish the spirit of race. Though shame might follow, instinct would prevail.

It was still strong on him, the pull of his uncompromising country, the pleasure of tramping or riding through it with Abdul Jān, Afridi of Afridis, tall and lithe, high nose and ruddy complexion; on his own shale or screed, a living fragment of earth; his rifle as much a part of him as the arm that wielded it.

Together, in pursuit of human quarry, they had tramped or ridden miles upon miles; passing from gully to gully, now among naked rocks, now through scrub or woodland, where black bear lurked in their dens and little musk deer slid by like ghosts and gay manāl pheasants flashed in the sunlight. Mile on mile of utter silence; but for the echoing clatter of hoofs, a stray rifle-shot, or broken rocks falling down and down — a remote, desolate sound. Or it might be a burst of flutes and drums, the wild chanting of some party on the march: goodly young men, supple and straight, keen-eyed as eagles, each one a trained warrior; rifles across their shoulders, knives in their girdles. Five times a day, being good Moslems, they would halt for prayer, master and man on an equal footing at prayer, at meals, and at war. One had need of prayer in that bleak, fierce country. It made this grassy hill station with its madness of many balls appear childish. No free action, as the Border understood freedom.

And his own stifled passion had been stirred by the night

of wild Khuttak dancing, at his sister's wedding; no relation to its dead-alive travesty in the mixed ballrooms of Anglo-India. In the Free Land all were male dancers, whirling or stamping, in perfect rhythm, to the squeal of flutes and mutter of drums that set the blood racing in a man's veins.

He need only shut his eyes to see and hear it all: the high centre pole with its cluster of lamps, throwing feelers into the darkness, where clansmen, in their scores, sat enspelled from eight at night till two in the morning. At the word, a hundred dancers in tunics and peaked turbans came dashing into view; circling, stamping, shoulder to shoulder; swords swung aloft, blades whistling and flashing, while the men twisted and leaped and thudded with their heels, now heavy as elephants, now light as gazelles. When the drums died down and fell to muttering, the hundred melted into darkness. And out of that darkness with a piercing yell sprang the prima donna of the evening: a magnificent boy of twenty, whirling like a dervish to the sound of drums and tabors; the players rushing in to join him, leaping and twirling at dizzying speed; clansmen crazed with excitement clapping and shouting themselves hoarse. No scene to excel it, East or West.

The women, debarred from any form of dancing, were not shut out from the fun. Behind screened windows they sat, seeing and hearing all. More than ever, after long absence, he approved those fine women of his race, their character and courage, the dignity and ordered freedom of their lives, that made many white women of the 'society' kind seem more like petted lapdogs than responsible mothers of men. And his very approval had stirred a whisper of doubt that was heresy to his heart — could he, should he, take to wife one whose thoughts were not as their thoughts, nor her way as their ways? Would he, so diversely mated, have peace in his home — the first need for a man? The few in his land who had chosen foreign wives declared that English girls gave more trouble than others, most of them returning to their own kind. And the thought of children with Western blood in their veins troubled him more than all.

But again, they would be her children; and his pride would be unbounded if he could so far conquer the prejudice of the white race in this loveliest of women. So he had hardened his heart against the desired betrothal with Selima; and had angered his mother, because he could not give the true reason for his seemingly unreasonable behaviour. It was parental friction that shortened his stay and sent him off to visit his friend, the heir apparent of Swat.

For all his brave words in the hut, he did not by any means feel sure if they would ever accept a *Feringhi* [1] bride. He had no real wish to leave his regiment and the good-fellowship of British officers: but if Anglo-India would cold-shoulder Chrystal as his wife, he still crazily hoped for a life with her in his own land. Others, to his knowledge, were living there with Pathan husbands — French, Australians, Americans, even a Scot from her own country.

But romantic dreams were discouraged out of hand by his hard-headed friend Abdul Jān, whose English training had gone little more than skin deep. He liked the good money and the sporting life. He was planning to marry a Pathan bride of his own clan, now being educated at the first Border school for girls, inspired by a brilliant and beautiful dancer who had married a Khan, and opened some years ago by a Kohat chieftain's son serving in the British Border Police. More than fifty pupils now, Abdul said; and the one-time dancing girl, a vigorous old lady, keen as ever on the magic word, education.

Abdul had gone off shooting, but returned on the third day of Afzul's probation — as he named it to himself. Here was a chance to try the effect of his bold proposal on a Pathan tempered by years of English education. To that end he was invited for lunch, to be followed by singles at tennis.

He came: and Afzul broached the ticklish subject while they slacked over coffee and cigarettes in his bedroom, to get away from the hotel crowd.

Abdul received his tale with a grunt of disfavour. And the Pathan expletive, '*Ishtāg farullah,*' [2] fired Afzul's temper.

[1] Foreign. [2] God forbid!

'*You* insult, to my face, that loveliest girl, knowing that insult to a woman means death, that in this cursed country my hands are tied.'

Abdul Jān, a cooler specimen, could smile at a lover's anger, but would permit no libel on himself.

'I do not insult any woman, Sher Afzul, Tiger of the Jungle. I call on God to forbid such madness, as much for her as for you. Can you suppose our good Colonel Sahib, a friend to this Indianising, would accept in his regiment an English girl calling herself Mrs. Afzul Khan? Would our other officers and ladies accept her, for her lovely eyes? You know the answer. They also would say "God forbid," rightly upholding their pride of race.'

At that clear statement of an impossible position, Afzul felt and looked crestfallen. He admired his Colonel. He knew all about pride of race. But passionate love was driving him blindly along a path marked 'dangerous'; a path he would normally have avoided and have warned others to avoid.

'You think the Colonel would not wish me to remain in the regiment with an English wife?' he asked, all fire gone from his tone.

'I would bet a hundred rupees on it,' the other answered. 'And I don't bet rashly, loving money even better than women. You yourself could not, in God's name, marry any but a Moslem.'

'That,' said Afzul, in a low tone, 'she might possibly become.'

'And would her people in India receive a white woman turned Moslem? Would your people accept her, *if* she would go there with you? I don't believe it. No, my friend, choose a wife of your own clan; educate her in the Kohat school, where many Pathan maidens are being fitted to become wives of such as we. I don't want to be left desolate in the regiment, though our white officers are friendly enough. Gopāl Singh is chucking it in the autumn. Have you heard?'

'No. What now?'

The Afridi grinned.

'A man cannot live for ever without his woman. And Gopāl loves his money, as we do. It's like pulling out a sound tooth when he must send so many rupees to his father-in-law, who is always making some fresh demand. Gopāl emptied his heart to me one night after you left. He will take service with Patiala, and soon be a captain because of his English training. Then he can live Indian style with his wife and family; get more money, perhaps. And that clever little Brahmin — no soldier — will shift into Transport or Pay Department with his Kinnaird College bride. At Christmas I will marry my Fatima ——' He sucked in his thick lips. '*That* is a girl. And there you have the tale of our bungalow — lacking only Sher Afzul Khan.'

Afzul shook his head. 'No more bungalow for me.'

The Afridi remained unconvinced.

'Be a *pukka* Pathan, Afzul. Put this fair girl out of your thoughts. Come shooting with me till our leave is up. Then you will be cured of your madness.'

For answer Afzul exploded in his native tongue.

Abdul, nothing dismayed, stood up and clapped him on the shoulder.

'All the thanks I get for offering a friend's advice. Come and work it off on the tennis courts. Have a grand slam at your enemy!'

For a couple of hours they played singles. Men of keen eye and quick hand, equally matched, they fought out each game point by point, Abdul coming off conqueror.

'That means I'll win you over yet!' he triumphed.

'You can start crowing on a dunghill when you do,' Afzul flashed back, good humour restored.

Hope rode higher in him as they returned to the hotel for sherry and savoury morsels, just in time to escape a violent downpour. Steel rods of rain smote the earth in rushes, as if some Titanic gardener were spraying it to clear off human parasites. Then it fell in sheets, as though the heavens were dissolved.

'Neatly missed,' said Abdul, and went off to play bridge.

Afzul discovered in the rack a letter he had noticed earlier. Letters rarely came his way. Chrystal's writing —— His heart turned over in him. Distracted between hope and fear, he carried it up to his room, sat down, and opened it.

At a glance he took in the first few lines. Then it was as if something blinded him. He sat there hardly breathing; empty of life, as if a bullet had been fired at close quarters into his heart.

Slowly he emerged from this strange state, and read the remainder in a fury of rage and pain. Abdul's advice — that he had spurned in his proud assurance — repeated by her. 'Marry some girl of your own clan,' when she knew — she knew ——

Bismillah! She could kiss him from her heart on Apharwāt, and two days later she could write *that.* What man could fathom the way of a woman?

Only two sentences near the end soothed him like the touch of her hand: 'I feel honoured that you have loved me. I will remember you always.' But what use — if the sword of division sundered them for ever?

It was a fact his mind refused to grasp. And the pitiless rain drummed and drummed in his ears, imprisoning him in this box of a hotel full of self-satisfied English people, who would turn their contemptuous back on Chrystal if she became his wife. This Indianising position was impossible. What they gave with one hand, they took away with the other. Live their lives — yes. Marry their girls — no. In a spasm of frustrate fury he could have gone down and murdered them all, without a qualm in his Pathan soul. He would fain, like Samson, have taken the verandah pillars and pulled the hotel down on the top of the whole crowd — innocent, irritating people, who had done him no harm. Then he would head straight for the Free Land: and good-bye to their milk-and-water civilisation.

Yet for all his inner fury, he remained sitting on the quilt of a civilised bed staring at half a sheet of paper, numbed by the sense of incredulity that dulls the edge of a grief too sharp to be realised except by degrees.

Only the fact that she had touched the fatal letter, that her voice seemed to speak from it, withheld him from tearing it to shreds. It was bitterness unspeakable to know that he had awakened passionate response in her — up to a point. Beyond that point he seemed powerless to move her; powerless to give up the attempt, though she begged him not to see her again.

Never again. It was as though a dagger-thrust stabbed out his eyes. What did she suppose he was made of? How should he not, in this small station, go wherever he might have a chance of seeing her? His desperate need of her blinded him to everything except the commanding urge to marry her, no matter what came of it.

Bitterly he recalled how, for love of her, he had crushed his secret doubts; how his pride had gloried in the knowledge that she loved him, the belief that she would not deny that kiss from her heart. And now — this: insulting his manhood, humbling him in the dust. Like the rest of her race, what she gave with one hand, she took away with the other.

One thing was certain — if he remained in his box of a bedroom much longer, he would explode. The rain had ceased. He would go up into the dripping forest along the ridge that looked out over Kashmir: anywhere away from these people. What matter — to her, or to himself — if he never came back at all?

Chapter XII

We are the lords of life, and life is warm;
But Nature says, 'My children most they seem
When least they know me: therefore I decree
That they shall suffer.

MEREDITH

CHRYSTAL had not, after all, gone to see Claire the very next day. After rewriting and posting Afzul's letter, she felt in no mood to go where she must talk of him. Better also, for Claire, to wait till she could speak of it all calmly, as she could not do yet.

Only with difficulty could she speak to Roy, when he came over next morning to suggest a ride that afternoon. It was to be a mild paper-chase affair, such as Lilāmani loved: he to start ahead, scattering torn paper in, or out of, his track; they to hunt him up hill and down dale. That would suit Chrystal far better than a difficult talk with Claire; and it might help to deaden the ache inside.

When Roy left, she walked a little way with him. He said nothing, leaving it to her; and at last she forced out the bald statement: 'I've written to Afzul. I've just posted it.'

'Good girl,' he said; but his eyes, that looked so deeply into one, were saying more than that.

'I don't feel good. I feel bad and cruel and horribly unhappy.'

'No wonder. It's a hateful job. But I honestly believe he'll thank you for it in the end, even if he never tells you so. A man often needs to do that. In matters of the heart, you women instinctively see deeper than we do. Nature looking after the race, perhaps.' He glanced at her sidelong.

'What of last night? D'you still think I'm wrong about Verney?'

'No. You're terribly right. He told me so.'

'Good Lord! I never dreamed it was imminent. And did he get the *coup de grâce* also?'

'Not definitely. He didn't ask. He simply told me he would stand by — your words. Perhaps he'd heard of Apharwāt.'

'You bet he'd heard.'

'When he spoke of Afzul, he didn't mention it.'

'Didn't he? That's the man for my money. For yours too, I hope — later on.'

'Yes,' she said, very low. 'I hope — later on.'

He gave her hand a friendly squeeze, and they talked of other things. She had sent Claire a note to announce her coming visitation; not till the afternoon, because of Lilāmani's lesson.

It was a morning of cloud and mist. She had just left Stream Cottage when the sight of a familiar figure set her tingling with annoyance. Peter, of all people, with his loose figure and his jauntiest air. Suddenly she remembered that she had promised to play tennis with him this very afternoon — and had forgotten all about it. She must wriggle off the hook somehow. Claire was not to be set aside for any Peter in creation.

He raised his cap, grinning all over his face.

'Luck to meet you. I was coming to tell you there's no hope of tennis. They are all death on golf; and I don't blame them. The most sporting course in Asia! Also there's a match on. Come and wander round with me, Chrystal, I'll show you how. It's high time you started learning the noble and ancient game.'

'So noble and so ancient that it bores me stiff,' she informed him, aware that she uttered sacrilege.

A flush darkened his face, but he let her down more easily than she deserved.

'You only say that sort of thing to rile me. Why *do* you like to rile me, Chrystal-girl?'

'I suppose it's my evil disposition,' she murmured meekly, riling him worse than ever.

'Look here, that's the limit.' He flung out both hands in a familiar and irritating gesture of wrath. 'Evil disposition! D'you want me to tell you for the *n*th time—?'

'No, I *don't*.' It was she who flung out a hand now, warding him off. 'And I can't stay here fooling any longer. I'm due for a drawing lesson. About this afternoon: just as well the tennis failed. I'm booked for tea with my one and only aunt. She isn't a bit well. I've had to put her off once. I can't do it again. We can have our tennis any day. Don't howl about it, Peter. Do be reasonable.'

'Reasonable?' He was furious. 'You're enough to drive a sane man dotty. You promised.'

'Don't pile it on. I only said I'd play. And now I say I'm sorry—I clean forgot——'

'Damn! Well, but look here'—his pet apostrophe—'if you must do Mrs. Inglis, let me call for you after tea and take you round the links, or a walk if you prefer?'

Prefer? His persistence and insensibility would wear down a rock. But she must get rid of him for the moment.

'All right,' she agreed briskly. 'You can call for me. The rest depends on Claire. I don't make *any* promise: remember that.'

Before he could answer, she turned up to the hut, waving at Lilāmani, who ran down to meet her.

'Oh, Chrystal, I been waiting and waiting. I thought you'd forgotten.'

'Never.'

She flung an arm round the child, and they went in together.

She was well on her way to the Lynch hut that afternoon, battling with a sudden downpour of rain, when the awkward thought cropped up—how about Dixon? Must Claire be told of his astonishing proposal? Since she had not accepted him, he might prefer nothing to be said. She decided to say nothing unless she was cornered.

She found Claire alone in the drawing-room, lying back among cushions; a changed woman from the Claire, elated over a new etching, whom she had seen only five days ago. In that moment of shock the girl knew how sincerely she loved her.

'Oh, Claire, are you ill again?'

'I'm afraid so. But very glad to see you after all these empty days.'

Her sad eyes, lingering on the girl's face, impelled Chrystal to kneel down by the sofa for her greeting kiss, and she found herself gathered into Claire's arms.

They kissed, and Claire still kept an arm round her.

'Things have happened in these few days,' she said, 'that may upset our plans and be tiresome for you. Bring that little chair to the sofa, and I'll tell my dismal tale.'

She said it lightly, but her eyes betrayed her; and Chrystal thought: 'Something has downed her. As if she hadn't enough already.'

Her own sorrowful tale seemed by comparison of small account. It could wait.

Claire was telling her how she had suddenly felt bad three days ago, without giving any reason for the calamity; how the State doctor called in by Grace had said much the same as Doctor Ewart, only more so. Gulmarg was too high for her. She ought to go Home at once and see a specialist, have proper heart treatment, and stay at Home for the present.

'Too much India; too many hot weathers — that's my commonplace complaint,' she said without a shade of self-pity, which made it sound the sadder.

'Wouldn't you love to go Home?' Chrystal urged by way of comfort.

'Yes — of course I would.' She didn't sound much like it. She hadn't a kick left in her. 'But, darling, how *can* I?'

'In this hot weather —? No. But afterwards?'

'I didn't mean weather. I meant Jasper.'

'Damn Jasper!' said Chrystal softly; and Claire tapped her with decision, but without severity.

'You're a bad child. But the immediate worry is that

Doctor Blake says I *must* go lower down as soon as I can travel. Srinagar's too muggy. He suggests Nathia Gully. It's near Murree, but not so high. And——' She closed her eyes, as if to hide what Chrystal ought not to see. 'Jasper has changed his dates. He's arriving the day after tomorrow.'

'Lord! What a blow!'

It was out before she could put on the brake; and this time Claire really tried to look stern.

'Chrystal, you *must* behave, or I can't talk things out with you as I want to do.'

She was promptly penitent. 'I will behave, as far as I'm able. But please, I can't pretend that I love my male cousin or whatever he likes to fancy himself. What's making him so previous?'

She didn't dare ask if he were being deserted by Priceless Pam; but Claire smiled, as if she guessed at some unspoken impertinence.

'The heat has knocked him up. He wants looking after. Much use I'll be in that line. Doctor Blake won't hear of my moving into Nedou's. I've got to lie up more or less, till I am fit for easy travel. What Jasper will say to all that, Heaven only knows. As for Home——' She drew in her lip to steady it.

Chrystal—her own dilemma half forgotten—leaned forward, speaking urgently, not as niece to aunt, but as woman to woman.

'Claire, please listen. I can speak plainer than a doctor; and somebody must speak up when things get to such a pass. I may seem a selfish beast, but my heart isn't exclusively occupied by Chrystal Adair. It loves you very much. It's going to help you through this dismal business if permitted.'

'You darling child.'

Claire's thin hand pushed off her soft linen hat and stroked her hair. A suspicion of tears in her eyes impelled Chrystal to speak her mind without reserve.

'I'm permitted? Very well. What I want you to do is this. Serve Jasper, on arrival, with the doctor's ultimatum. If you raise any question about it, you're done down. Of course he'll hate it. He'll think he can't possible manage without your tender care. I'm getting terribly bold! But it might be no harm for him to find out what all of us must — I suppose — that we can pull through a lot more than we think we can.'

At that Claire closed her eyes again, and a spasm of pain crossed her face.

'"Out of the mouths of babes and sucklings,"' she murmured. 'Such a wise child.'

'Perhaps learning to be. A horrid uncomfortable process.'

Before Claire could speak, Mrs. Lynch was in the room flourishing a bottle and a medicine glass. She wore a lovely green silk tea-gown and moved less briskly than usual. Radiating health and happiness, she seemed a cruel contrast to the sad and stricken Claire.

While she measured out the medicine, Chrystal thought: 'Here's a doctor woman, who says what she thinks. I'll rope her in.'

Aloud she said: 'Claire never told me she had collapsed, or I'd have come sooner. You won't *let* her go to that pandemonium hotel, will you, Mrs. Lynch?'

'I will *not*.' A twitch of her long mouth confirmed the words.

'And you'll back up the need for going Home?'

'You can count on my backing,' said Grace Lynch, 'for all that's necessary to her salvation, even for putting a wee bit stiffening into her body and nerves. I'm writing to Lady Leigh at Nathia Gully. It's Government headquarters, you know. They'll be simply delighted to welcome her; give her a quiet corner till she can find something suitable. I wish I could take her over there myself.'

And Chrystal, seeing her chance, said briskly: 'Well, I'll do my best. You can count on me for that, if I *am* a giddy young thing.'

'You —? Excellent.'

She could feel Claire being taken aback, and was glad to have got it out in the other woman's presence.

'My *dear* girl,' Claire protested; but Chrystal waved her

away. 'Don't worry. Mrs. Lynch and I are in command!' She turned to Grace. 'You have the pull, being a doctor. I can only be your *chela;* faithfully obey orders.'

'I take you on, then,' said Grace crisply. 'I'm quite good at giving orders when I'm on my own!' She held up a warning finger. 'Don't dare say anything that might worry her — my *chela!*'

She flashed her quick smile at the girl, laid a hand on Claire's forehead, and went out, carrying with pride and dignity her burden of a new life to be.

'She's the most vital person I know,' Claire murmured. 'There's life even in the touch of her hand.'

Quickly she put out her own hand as Chrystal sat down again.

'Darling, what *does* this mean? You're happy with Lance and Eve?'

'Oh, I am. They're an almost unbelievable pair; but such *pukka* bits of human nature, that they must be believed in!'

'Well, then, why —? you can't run away in the middle of the season.'

'I can, if I choose. And I do choose.'

Claire looked searchingly into her eyes. 'I wonder why you do choose?'

'Aren't you sufficient reason? We belong.'

'Yes, we do, in more ways than one.'

It was a comfort to hear the contented note in Claire's voice that had been sounding so half alive.

'But even for your sake,' this privileged Chrystal boldly added, 'I couldn't bring myself to stay behind and minister to a bereft Jasper.'

Claire smiled at that without a murmur of reproof. 'I wouldn't dream of asking you to. But I didn't think you'd want to leave Gulmarg — and your Pathan.'

The word was out; and Chrystal thought, 'Now I'm for it.'

Crushing her hands together, she asked: 'Have you been hearing tales that you ought to have heard from me? I mean — about Apharwāt?'

'Yes. I did hear of that — from Dixon.'

'Where did he hear it?'

'At the Club.'

'Oh, I *hate* them all!' Chrystal flashed fiercely. 'I can imagine all the nice *kind* things they said.'

'But, darling — can *you* imagine —?'

Chrystal heard the pain in her voice.

'No — I can't,' she said, forcing a surface hardness. 'I did think I could, because of — what happened up there. Oh, Claire, he loves me desperately. And I do love him.'

Useless to put on false armour. The pain was too fresh.

'But does he actually suppose —?'

'He did — knowing that I care.'

'Chrystal! Did Sir Roy not speak to you?'

'Yes. The very next day. They met us up there. He spoke to Afzul then. He's a wonderful man. I love him.'

'I thought so. I love his wife too. They're so refreshingly unlike anything out here.'

A long pause. Chrystal guessed what was coming.

'And — Dixon? Did he not say anything at the picnic?'

The directness of it so startled Chrystal that she could only gaze at Claire, wondering — wondering ——

For a few moments Claire steadfastly returned her look; then she lowered her lids. But Chrystal, in a flash, had seen the secret thing — the reason for her own instinctive reluctance to speak of that evening. She was naturally not supposed to see, or to say a word on so embarrassing a subject, but her own frustrate longing levelled all barriers of age and discretion, leaving only the pain of their human hearts.

Her fingers closed sharply on Claire's left hand.

'Oh, Claire — is it *that*?' she ventured softly.

Claire drew a slow breath and opened her eyes, gazing without a word at the fair face that Dixon loved.

It was Chrystal who spoke. 'Darling, what a hopeless tangle all round.'

'*Is* it hopeless for you?' Claire asked in a careful voice. 'If you can't seriously think of marrying a Pathan —?'

Chrystal had half forgotten all that, smitten by Claire's

tragedy, of which she could not speak. And now it was poor Afzul: one woe treading on another's heels.

'I did seriously want to, when he asked me up there.' She could not, would not, mention Afzul's kiss. 'But Roy spoke of it in the loveliest way. He *does* understand. He does admire Afzul. Then Dixon spoke of it, the very same evening.' She looked pathetic. 'So I've been hammered at. And of course a bit of me knew it wouldn't work — in the long run.'

'It couldn't: and it might be a very long run,' Claire reminded her. Again a pause, and then, 'Did Dixon only speak of that?' she persisted, 'pressing her breast against a thorn.'

For the first time in her life, Chrystal actively wished that she could tell a flat lie. But even that would not serve; since Claire, amazingly, seemed to know.

'He spoke of himself too,' Chrystal admitted, 'in the humblest way — a man like that.'

'Yes — a man like *that!*' Claire echoed, unable to keep the bitterness out of her tone. She could more easily bear pain for herself than for him. 'And you — refused him?'

'He didn't ask,' she said; 'he only wanted me to know he was there, if ever I could ——'

'And could you ever? He said you had an eye for character. Are you, with all your gifts, too young to understand his quality? He's no idealist, no fancy lover. He's real all through.'

'Oh, I know that. I've know it all the time.'

'And — nothing more?'

'I think there might be. There nearly was, at first. But he was your friend, and so much older. Then Afzul got in the way.'

'Is he definitely out of the way? Tell me, Chrystal. I think I have a right to know.'

'Of course you have.'

It was useless trying to soften steel-tipped facts; and Chrystal told all, as best she could. Of Dixon she could only say: 'He's not the kind of man to be content with a half giving. And he deserves all. Some day I hope —— But you see, just now, I'm almost hating India because it has meant so much to me. If I married Dixon, I would have to live here always — mostly Frontier.'

'Not for so long as if he were a younger man,' Claire steadfastly pleaded his cause. 'You'd get over that feeling. Or he might retire earlier. He would give up more for you, Chrystal, than most of these charming, aimless young men, who talk glibly about "adoring" a girl, and wouldn't put themselves out an inch, if I know them, for the adored. One needs liking as well as love, for marriage: and it often lasts longer. I think Dixon has a year's furlough nearly due. It might be easier for you in England to *feel* his quality, not only to see it.'

'Yes, it might,' Chrystal pensively admitted. 'But, dear, you mustn't distress yourself.'

'I do. I blame myself,' Claire said, with stifled vehemence. 'I ought to have spoken about Afzul at the start, when I saw you were attracted. But you're an independent creature; and you seemed so cool-headed, I never dreamed it could go as far as this.'

'Nor did I, honestly. If you had been obstructive, it wouldn't have put me off Afzul. It would only have made friction between us.'

'That's how I saw it. And I wanted your friendship so much. I felt the responsibility, but I was a good deal taken up with my own — difficulties.'

Her throat constricted so sharply that she could say no more; and Chrystal, cut to the heart, was on her knees again, Claire holding her close. It was she who broke down and cried, as she had not cried for years, chiefly for Claire, who was loving her, though she had stolen her one and only; dabbing her eyes, calling her 'my sweet,' as never before.

Resolutely, at last, she gulped down her foolish sobs and sat back on her chair, head lifted with a touch of self-scorn.

'Oh, these men! Why *do* they plague us like this?'

'We're necessary to them, darling, in a number of ways,' Claire gently reminded her. 'Some of them wish we weren't!' she added, slipping with relief from the personal to the general aspect of their dilemma. 'But even they can't escape the common human frailty of exalting one man or woman above all the rest. I once heard passionate love aptly called "an exciting and necessary kind of madness." It *is* exciting; and it is necessary. But it's not all cakes and ale.'

'It's *not.* It can hurt like hell,' Chrystal, the novice, put it in stronger terms than the woman whom it had hurt almost to death. 'When I think how it's tormenting my poor Afzul now. When I see what *some* wives have to suffer' — she looked very straight at Claire — 'I think Nature's inspired plan brings most of us more pain than pleasure. And — oh, damn! There's that wretched Peter coming to fetch me after tea, simply to badger me again; to walk round the walls of Jericho and blow his tin trumpet!'

Claire laughed at that, and it was a treat to hear her laugh. 'Poor Peter! So persistent. Be merciful to him.'

'I won't be merciful to a persistent Peter when I've had to hurt Afzul so cruelly. He's not constant. He's dense and pig-headed. Far more pleased with himself than with me. If he tries another futile plunge, I'll squash him flat. The merciful touch has been my bane. Here comes tea, and he'll be hauling me off soon after. But you won't be deserted any more, I promise — darling, darling Claire.'

On a swift impulse she leaned forward again; and their long kiss said all that ever could be said between them on their tragic tangle that might have sharply sundered them, had Claire been a different make of woman. Instead, it linked them closer, not merely as aunt and niece, but as women, caring for men, yet craving a respite from that 'exciting and necessary madness' — love, desired or undesired.

Chapter XIII

The wild perplexity of blood and thought —
How scared and snared in burning bonds of fate!

GERALD GOULD

Too soon Chrystal knew for certain that persistent Peter was going to ask for it once again. Well, this time he should have it — in words of one syllable, if they alone would serve.

The downpour had ceased and rolled on to higher peaks. Vast white clouds, mountain-high, gleamed with the effulgence of 'clear shining after rain.' But Peter decreed that the ground was too sodden for golf, though enthusiasts were already creeping out like snails. Chrystal hopefully suggested the Club, where she could choke him off with people or a game of darts; inevitably he persisted, true to type.

'Grand evening for a good old tramp,' he suggested; and she sighed.

'Lovely — if you'd only let me go alone.'

He looked reproachful.

'No sense in that,' he said; and he believed it. 'Besides, you're engaged to me for the afternoon. And — who knows?'

He eyed her so eloquently that she tingled, not with embarrassment, but with antagonism. The fact that she was suffering acutely, on account of Afzul and Claire, didn't make her feel pitiful. It hardened her to deal him the blow direct.

'The afternoon, indeed! I'll give you an hour. And we'll make it a walking match. Come on.'

He was frankly scornful. 'As if I couldn't beat you hands down.'

'Try, then!' she twitted him.

'Oh, drop it, Chrystal. Come up along the Circular Road. Bits of that forest make me think of Bonnie Scotland.'

Impossible to tell him that he could not have chosen a worse place for an appeal to her heart than that memory-haunted path.

With a perversity common to life, the forest had seldom looked more lovely: the trees, heavy with raindrops, changed by the sun into quivering, flashing jewels; all Kashmir below them bathed in amber and gold; wave on wave of hills empurpled with rain, half seen, half veiled in wandering mist. Resolutely Chrystal closed her mind against it. Resolutely she set the pace; and for all his boasting, she nearly walked Peter off his legs.

At last, suspecting her tactics, he lost patience, stood still in the empty path, and took hold of her arm.

'I say, Chrystal, stop it. I didn't come up here for you to make a fool of me.'

'It's you making a fool of *me*,' she retorted, freeing her arm, an ice-blue gleam in her eyes. 'Can't you give me credit for knowing my own mind, Peter? I've told you straight — how many times? — that I don't love you, so I can't and won't marry you. I wouldn't — even if you were the only thing between me and perdition. Is that plain enough for you?'

He seemed to take it in this time. His brick-red face turned a queer colour, and his blue eyes blazed.

'I'm only a Scot. So not good enough,' he said, with contained fury. 'You're a changed girl up here, Chrystal; and it is easy to see what's the cause of it. You'd marry me fast enough, no doubt, if I was a damned Pathan. Doing young Lochinvar. Carrying you off to Apharwāt — taking advantage ——'

'He's taken *no* advantage, then or any time,' she retorted. Her controlled Northern anger went deeper than his. At that moment she could almost have killed him. But being, on the surface, a civilised young woman, she could only add, in a deliberately hardened voice, 'I'd marry *him* sooner than you, any day.'

As she spoke, her quick ear caught a rustling sound among the trees above the path; the snap of a twig, as some animal moved through the undergrowth. In her wrought-up mood it faintly startled her; but her whole attention was claimed by an infuriated Peter.

Stricken in more than his vanity, he completely lost hold on himself. He came close to her, thrusting his face at her.

'Chrystal, that's a lie — a cruel lie.'

'I do *not* tell lies. It's the truth,' she insisted, the ring of it in her tone.

Desperate now, he again caught her by the arm.

'It's madness. It's impossible. Whatever comes to me, *swear* you won't marry that half-tamed devil.'

'I won't swear anything to anyone. It's my own affair.'

(And the thought flashed: 'If Afzul were here, I'd accept him, whatever came of it.')

But he was not there; and she could only reiterate her declaration of independence. 'I'll marry whom I choose. It's no concern of yours.'

Vainly she tried to release her arm. He clung to it, beside himself ——

And now there were sounds above the road that startled them both: a scrambling and a cracking of boughs as if that hidden animal were rushing down upon them.

'Heavens! What *is* it?' cried Chrystal, jerking backward.

Peter, startled also, lost hold of her, just as the flying figure of a man pounced on him with the spring of a panther. And Chrystal, in a tingle of terror and excitement, recognised Sher Afzul Khan.

Bareheaded, in the tennis flannels of civilisation, he sprang at the detested Grant, with a sputter of guttural Pushtu more like the growl of a leopard than human speech.

Peter, staggering backwards, had the strength of rage in his limbs. One blow he let out at the fierce dark face. Then Afzul had him in a vice, bearing him steadily to the ground. The back of his head struck earth with a dull thud, while Chrystal, a few yards away, stood petrified. Her body stopped. Her mind stopped, as if a lightning flash had struck it.

Suddenly she became aware of Afzul's terrible intent. His fingers were closing relentlessly on Peter's throat.

'We Pathans deal death,' he growled, 'for insult to a woman or a blow to a man. You called her liar. You struck at me. You won't get a chance to call me Pathan devil again, you son of a ——'

Peter's eyes were starting; his face distorted. In another moment a helpless man would be killed before her eyes; and Afzul — Afzul would hang for it.

Fear and horror stabbed her spirit broad awake. A moment she struggled with a nightmare inability to move or speak. Then she sprang forward, a hand on his right arm.

'Afzul, stop! It's murder.' And in a lower tone she added: 'He's *not worth* it.'

Startled and moved by her touch, awakened to the issue of his violent impulse, Afzul relaxed his grip, flinging Grant aside as if he were a rat.

'She's right,' he rubbed it in. 'Your life is *not* worth mine. In my own land you would die for this. Now, thanks to her concern for *me*, you can go to hell your own way. You don't lay hands on her again.'

Grant, choking and half stunned, struggled to his feet.

'You'll hear more about *this*, you murdering devil,' he panted, fingering his bruised throat, 'as sure as I've got a tongue in my head.'

Afzul, spurning him, moved towards Chrystal; and Grant lunged blindly, his head still throbbing.

'You don't lay hands on a white woman in *my* presence.'

Afzul's fingers closed gently on Chrystal's arm.

'*You* get out of this.' His voice was steel-hard, as she had never heard it. 'You owe it to her that you're able to do so. Say another word, I'll knock you senseless.'

Peter, not heeding, turned on Chrystal the strangest look; putting a hand to his head, as if he might collapse without further assistance. Only a desperate effort saved him from that final indignity.

'You'll hear more of *this*, you bloody scoundrel,' he repeated sullenly, in the unconscious accents of melodrama. Then he turned and stumbled away, disappearing round a bend in the road.

Chrystal, for the first time in her life, felt as if she were going to faint; but a vital sensation awakened her.

Afzul's eyes were looking into hers, as they looked on Apharwāt. His arms were round her, and she, overwhelmed by his touch, yielded once more to her own commanding emotion.

Forgetful that anyone, at any moment, might come upon them, they clung together across the gulf that divided them, in one desperate kiss that hurt her to the soul, because a sane, submerged fragment of her knew it must be the last, though three parts of her could hardly bear to let him go.

Now he was drawing her to a rocky ledge by the road side; holding her tenderly, yet resisting her attempt to free herself.

'My beautiful, my belovéd,' he murmured. 'No letters — nothing — can separate us now.'

Reluctance to pain him, and her own longing to echo his words, could not quell the inner compulsion aroused by Roy, confirmed by Dixon, by all that had gone to the writing of that difficult letter, which he calmly proposed to ignore.

'Afzul — Afzul ——' She half freed herself at last. 'I daren't say "Yes" to that. I've told you I can't. I've told you why. There are too many forces pulling us apart.'

He shook his head.

'No forces can prevail, if I have all of *you*.'

'But it's not all of me that is consenting to — to this. There's something in me every time that holds back from complete giving; and there would be, always. Too many big things are against us.'

'Big things?' he flared up again. 'Isn't *this* the biggest thing for both of us?'

She could not honestly deny it; and only the extreme of honesty would serve in her desperate hour.

'Yes, in one way it is,' she truthfully admitted, though it weakened her steadfast refusal. 'If —?'

'If—?' He pressed her, tightening his hold, summoning all the force of his male energy to beat down her strange resistance to the strongest force in nature.

'Oh, I told you — *if* we could live our own lives in a world of our own ——'

'And *I* told you,' he capped her, 'I would throw up all that England has given me for this one best gift.'

She clenched her hands in a desperate effort to withstand — not the argument for marriage — but the man.

'No — no. I couldn't let you. And I — truly I couldn't throw up everything, either.' Suddenly the tragedy of it all overwhelmed her afresh. 'Oh, Afzul ——' she began, but her voice gave way: and again she was in his arms, without power or will to resist the fervour of his kiss.

At last, in despair, she pulled herself together, laying both hands on him, pressing him from her.

'Dear, dear Afzul, this *must* be good-bye. Let me go, as you love me. And let me go alone.'

'Not alone. You might meet that speckled cad again.'

The reminder of a completely forgotten Peter awakened a new concern for Afzul.

'He said you would hear of this. Do you think he would dare to tell —?'

'I think not.' Afzul's eye glinted at the recollection of that man's throat under his fingers. 'If he tells part, people will want to know more. One man doesn't half strangle another, in your polite little world, for nothing. If he dares to speak, I could speak also. But I think he won't — chiefly because of you.' Again he flared up. '*You* would never marry him. I heard that.'

'Never. I don't really want to marry anyone, Afzul. I know that sounds unnatural to you.'

He gravely considered her youth and feminine charm. 'Yes; for woman or man it is unnatural. Marriage is an obligation to the family, to the race.'

'Yes; that is how it should be.' He had given her a point and she pressed it home. 'For that very reason, don't you see,' she urged, 'marriage between us would be wrong for the family and the race? We are both very much of our race and country. We should each find barriers inside that we could neither break down nor understand. So you must — you *must*, please, accept my letter as my real decision. I couldn't have written words that would hurt you so unless something inside me felt absolutely sure that this cruel wrench would be best, for both of us, in the end. Please let me go.'

With a stab of pain he recalled her 'Please take me home'; the elation in his heart, the sense of fate foreordained — so few days ago. From those heights he had tumbled down to this — the end of all things. For he recognized at last that her will could not be shaken either by his passion or by her own. And he stood there gazing down at the slender, resolute girl, within an arm's length of him, yet for ever out of reach, taking in the black finality of it all: pure East in his acceptance of the accomplished fact.

'Where are you going now?' he asked, in a suppressed voice. 'Won't you let me walk with you this last time? I won't say anything to trouble you. I only want to be near you a little longer. Not to be pushed away.'

'I don't want to push you away.'

She could barely command her voice. For she had heard the note of surrender in his; and it was as well that he did not know how much harder he was to resist in this gentler vein. He would do as he said, he would not trouble her; but her human heart would trouble her the more, although she had seen in his face the tiger unchained. His bold attack on Peter might possibly have shaken her resolve, had not Roy's influence already turned the scales.

She could not face the long walk to Stream Cottage. The Lynch hut was nearer: and suddenly, achingly, she wanted Claire. Only to Claire could she speak of all this. Not a soul, mixed up in Gulmarg affairs, must know. Impossible to go home till she could behave as if nothing more had happened than the dismissal of 'Peter's latest.'

'I'm going now to my aunt, Mrs. Inglis. Come.'

In silence they walked back along the familiar path, under

a sky transformed by early evening light into a sea of confluent splendour. And Chrystal, as before, must close her mind against it all for a different reason; must deliberately harden herself against the appeal of his silent presence by recalling that terrible scene, by telling herself that he must have hovered above her and Peter deliberately listening; a strain of crookedness in him more alienating than any savage impulse.

It would have surprised and puzzled her had she guessed that he himself was only concerned at having given her a fright and at the tiresome law that had prevented him from squeezing the life out of Grant. Once, tormented by the sense of her nearness, he gently slipped his fingers round the hand that hung at her side, holding it as if it were a flower, not speaking or venturing a glance at her half-averted face; stirred to the depths when she very lightly returned his pressure.

At sight of people in the distance, he released her hand; giving it back to her, as though she had graciously lent it to him for his comfort. She herself, by now, could scarcely believe that this was the same man who had half throttled Peter under her eyes.

Nearing the Lynch hut, they stood still; and it was Afzul who spoke.

'Chrystal, you lovely girl, I don't ever forget that it is to your courage I owe my life, for what it is worth.' And she had simply not thought of that. 'You are in my mind always as the girl who would not be afraid. Your light hand on my arm was stronger than all the fury in my veins. But for that, I would now be leaving Kashmir in a hurry, to escape the indignity of your law courts and — the rope.'

Deeply moved, she could only say: 'Afzul, I am thankful. At first I felt petrified.'

'You are thankful that I shall live? Yet you have no use for me. Strange ——'

'But you know, you *know*,' she said, with sudden fervour, 'that I would have use for you, if —?'

'Ifs and buts,' he broke in bitterly. 'Little words; yet

they can wreck our lives. I leave Gulmarg at once. You needn't fear to see me any more.'

'Not fear,' she corrected him, 'but pain.'

'Yes. I have given you enough — while only wishing to give you all that was best.'

And she, charged with feeling, could only say in a soft, urgent voice: 'You won't leave the regiment? That would give me pain.'

'I don't wish to leave it. But just now — I don't want English people. I want my own country. I can make no promises — even to you.'

She sighed. 'It's natural you should feel like that. For me — Pathans and their country will have a special place always in my thoughts, in my heart. I shall never forget.'

And his deep voice answered, '*Al Rahīm, al Rahmān* — in the name of Allah the compassionate, the merciful, may you be blessed for ever.'

Taking her hand, he kissed it once — and again.

Overcome, she laid her right hand on his bowed head, as if blessing him in return.

He straightened himself and looked at her. Neither could speak. She heard him draw a deep breath as he turned from her, and walked away out of her life, not once looking back.

Chapter XIV

One day does not kill another; grief's hour does not make less of love's.

CONSTANCE MALLESON

BLINDED with tears, she stumbled into the narrow verandah and stood still, wiping them away, taking deep breaths to steady herself. Then she walked, unannounced, into the small drawing-room.

She found Claire half sitting up, propped with cushions, and over by the mantelpiece stood Dixon — seen for the first time since their picnic talk — smiling at her without a shade of reminder in his eyes.

The sight of him, so close upon her parting with Afzul, gave her a stab of pain. It gave her also a keener sense of his quality — a safe feeling that, at this shaken moment, was balm to her heart.

'If I'm flagrantly interrupting,' she addressed Claire. 'I can easily go on home.'

'No, you don't,' said Dixon so sharply that Claire laughed and held out her hand.

'You certainly don't! Why so soon again?'

And Chrystal, who had longed for the relief of telling her all, letting her tears flow unchecked, did her best to keep up the light note.

'Not according to plan! It was because of — what happened.'

'Finishing off poor Peter?'

'Yes: done *finish*,' Chrystal said, with decision.

'Thought he looked fairly done in when I saw him,' was Dixon's comment; and she glanced round in faint alarm.

'*Have* you see him?'

'I passed him near Nedou's, looking — well, distinctly queer. As I came up, he swerved off behind the building. You must have downed him badly.'

'I had to. But it wasn't only me. I ——'

Her control suddenly gave way. She was on her knees by the sofa.

'Oh, Claire, there was a clash. Rather startling ——'

Dixon came quickly forward.

'Don't go upsetting her, for Heaven's sake. She's brighter this afternoon.'

Chrystal looked up through a mist of tears.

'*This* won't upset her. It's my funeral. I — I've seen Afzul again.'

Claire's arm went round her, but Dixon spoke.

'If I'm in the way, I'll clear out. I'd like to see you home, but I can turn up again in half an hour.'

Her lips quavered into a smile. 'It's my turn to say — no, you don't. It was a clash — Afzul and Peter. I couldn't bear people to know. But I can trust you not to say a word.'

'At your command, not a syllable. Try to forget I'm here.'

He moved away and sat down near the fern-filled open hearth, where she could not see him, but she could feel him. She heard the click of his cigarette-case, the hiss of a lighted match. It was no relief now to tell her strange tale, putting a constraint on herself, because of his presence. Yet she could say things to Claire that it might be well for him to know. Not that even Claire could be allowed to hear all. No word of Afzul's murderous intent, or of her part in checking him. She only told of Peter's excitable state, his angry words, and the sudden appearance of Afzul that resulted in a violent tussle between them; Peter getting the worst of it.

In her simple and direct phrasing, she presented, unawares, a moving picture of Afzul in his twofold aspect: the violence that sprang from rage at Peter's unparliamentary behaviour, and his own despair over her letter; the gentleness and courtesy of that other Afzul, who had escorted her to the hut and blessed her in the name of Allah.

Trying, as bidden, to forget the silent presence, she let fall allusions to Afzul, here and there, that hurt Dixon beyond measure. Before all was said, he went quietly out and strolled in the verandah till she should need his services.

Chrystal, hearing him go, laid her head on Claire's shoulder and let grief have its way with her.

And there was this kindest of women — whose talk with him she had cavalierly torpedoed — murmuring endearments and comforting her, for the second time that afternoon. What did they mean by it, these men, making a Niobe of her, Chrystal, who never cried or flopped her head on a convenient shoulder?

Her collapse was brief as it was complete; all tension relaxed, all bottled-up grief released, in that rush of healing tears. Now she sat up briskly, flourishing a handkerchief puff and pocket mirror because Dixon must not suspect.

'I'm a proper idiot today, and you're an angel not to tell me so.'

She spoke lightly; but Claire answered with her slow, wise smile: 'Tears were given for relief. You're no idiot, my plucky child; and I'm no angel. I'm only a tired and faulty human woman.'

'Utterly human and understanding. That's what makes you the angel you've been to me, even when I went my own way, unheeding. Not quite unheeding, ever. I've blessed you for the rope you gave — the rope that hasn't hanged me, after all!'

'Came rather near it,' Claire reminded her.

'Rather near. But Jasper needn't know.' His name recalled the impending crisis. 'Oh, how I'll hate leaving those Roys and Eve! Lilāmani will squeal.'

'Dear, I *wish* you'd stay.'

'I can't — I won't. And when I say that, I mean it, as poor Afzul's had to realise. There's always a snag in the best-laid plans. I think those Roys are soon going off somewhere, camping among these grand hills.'

'Are they? Lady Sinclair told me, a few days ago, that Sir Vincent wants very much to see her husband and talk over the book while he is at leisure. I think they now mean to go there first. Come back here, perhaps, in early September when the rains may be petering out. It's the best month up here.'

'That's a bright spot. We'd meet again. I could carry on the lessons. Can you give me an idea when you'll be fit for the transfer?'

'Doctor Barker hopes in a week or ten days.'

'Well, I'll be ready when you are. The bottom's knocked out of my universe. I'm only afraid of an upset for you when Jasper has to face the music.'

Claire set her lips. 'A good deal hangs on that.'

'You *will* serve him with an ultimatum? Promise.'

Claire looked away towards Dixon's empty chair; then she said slowly: 'In the dire circumstances, I think I can promise. I have to consider that the children need me. Neither they nor Jasper would benefit if I let India kill me outright.'

'A sound argument. Rub it in.' She stood up briskly. 'I must go now, you dear, or they'll get thinking I've eloped with Peter! Wretched Peter, choked off at last.' With a mental shiver she remembered how. Once more she flicked the powder puff over her face. 'Do I look fairly normal?'

'You look lovelier than you've any business to, if you don't mean business. Tantalising the poor man.'

'Oh, I don't want to tantalise him. What can I do to spoil the effect?'

'Nothing. I'm sure he'd rather be tantalised and have it unspoilt. Dixon,' she called softly, and her voice seemed to caress his name.

He promptly appeared on the threshold, very straight and alert, looking from one to the other.

'You've not been upsetting her?' he asked; and it was Claire who answered him.

'Certainly not. She came, very rightly, to report at headquarters. Now take her home.'

'She doesn't need taking, thanks,' Chrystal remarked to no one in particular.

'She's going to be taken, whether she needs it or not,'

Verney retorted, holding out a hand to Claire. 'As she cheated us today,' he said, 'I'll look in tomorrow.'

And Chrystal, stooping to kiss her, thought: 'After tomorrow — Jasper. Enough to kill her outright.'

But even her youth was already discovering that human beings are tougher within than without. Claire would survive standing up to Jasper, backed by Grace; but it would be a painful interlude.

And now she herself must cross the marg with another man beside her, who said little and loved her a great deal; sorrowing also, but not as one without hope. Strange how, once again, these two were struck sharply on each other; and today she felt more alive to the contrast, to the dislocating dual appeal: in Afzul, the fascination of exploring strange lands; in Dixon, the deeper sense of security and understanding. With him her mind and spirit felt at home; while her heart and senses were still perturbed by that other, not yet free from his potent spell. At present she craved a respite from the exciting and necessary madness, her own or another's: with Afzul more exciting, with Dixon more necessary. Just now the lack of excitement pulled strongly in his favour. Three urgent men in one afternoon would be the limit.

At first he talked chiefly of Claire.

'Something knocked her endways a few days ago,' he innocently remarked. 'Perhaps it's just as well she's had to see another doctor, or she might have slain herself, hanging on here because of you, refusing to go Home because of Inglis and his "fancy heart," as Eve aptly called it.'

'If ever there *was* a pampered husband——' she broke out; and he shot an amused glance at her.

'I don't seem to see you pampering yours!'

She smiled back at him, liking that casual reference to his heart's desire.

'If ever I weakly wanted to, I should remember Jasper — and refrain. Dare I tell you? I've been very bold. I've begged her to hand him an ultimatum about leaving this and going Home. Mrs. Lynch is backing me.'

'Good luck to your joint efforts. Claire tells me you'll go down with her.'

'Of course I will.'

'You don't mind leaving this place — now?'

'I mind letting down Eve, just when she'll be losing Lance. But she'll understand that my first job is — to see after Claire.'

'Quite. And she may need it. If I know Inglis, he'll stump her by just taking it for granted that she can't do anything so unwifely as to desert him because some rotten doctor has got the wind up over her case. That fellow gets every damned thing his own way by taking for granted all that ministers to his comfort, including Claire. It would give him a wholesome shock if she were to go off with another man. But can you picture Claire?'

Chrystal's gaze dwelt a moment on the profile of the unsuspecting other man.

'I almost wish I could; though I love her best as she is: a large, understanding person who will never let herself be downed by life, because she has a sense of values and a sense of humour.' Since he was speaking his mind today and encouraging her to do so, she ventured a question. 'Have you known Claire for long?'

'I knew her and liked her before they went Home,' he said. 'But our *pukka* friendship has only been running for the last six months. She's a man's woman in the best sense. A man can make a real friend of her and feel he's on sure ground: love her, in fact, without risk of falling in love.'

Chrystal pondered his frank statement and the effect of that unflattering certainty on poor Claire.

'I wonder,' she said, 'would you call that a merit or a lack?'

He regarded her for the first time with the unveiled look of a man in love.

'That's a shrewd question for sweet-and-twenty.'

'If it's indiscreet,' she said quickly, 'it needn't be answered.'

He looked amused. 'The whole of our talk is bordering on the indiscreet. But we can trust each other. So — what matter?'

She glowed at that. It was the keystone of their relation, that sense of comradeship, of deep trust: something founded on a rock; the liking that Claire said outlasted passionate love. But she remained silent; and he made an honest attempt to answer her question.

'I should call it — partly a merit and partly a lack. A merit of mind and character; a lack of — well, some feminine essence. Can't put it clearer. Vocabulary isn't my strong suit.'

Chrystal smiled. She wondered if he were generously trying not to say that Claire lacked charm. And he, merely trying to express himself, went on: 'You, for instance, have got a mind and you use it; so a man could be friends with you — but at his peril.'

'That's the curse,' she sighed. 'I wish I wasn't perilous. I do like a man's friendship so much.'

The right sort of love doesn't exclude friendship,' he pointed out, in a different voice. 'You could have both.'

And she heard herself saying, without emphasis: 'I'm grasping. I would like to have both.'

'You shall,' he said, 'when you're ready for both.'

The simple statement aroused in her a deeper warmth of feeling than he had ever yet evoked; but not now could she answer him as he deserved to be answered when she was ready, as he had said.

It seemed that he understood as much; and, by virtue of his thirty-seven years, he understood how to wait. For he added, after a brief pause: 'I hope you won't mind, but I told Claire I'd like to come along with you two when you leave, to be of any use I can on the journey. It's laying a lot on you.'

'It is,' she murmured. 'I'd be thankful. And Claire would feel she needn't worry.'

'She's had her dose of that, poor dear. I can't actually go down with you, in the queer circumstances: Inglis arriving with his favoured lady; Claire slipping off with me, taking you by way of chaperone — so they'd say!'

'They would! And it might look rather pointed. So — what?'

'I leave a few days earlier on my own. Join you at Srinagar, where she must have a night or two. Escort you to Nathia Gully; and stay there, if permitted, for the last week of my leave. So that's that.'

'All but Jasper.'

'The unknown quantity. He might even have the bright idea of going with her.'

'Priceless Pam and all?' Chrystal boldly asked, since they were being indiscreet.

'Don't ask me! I'm not his keeper.'

'Well, Pam or not, I should fade out.'

'So would I. Rough on Claire; but Inglis sticks in my throat. He justifies all the libels uttered about the I.C.S., a much-maligned body of men. Well, when he comes, it will be seen.'

In speaking, he stood still under a dense group of pines, not far from Stream Cottage. They smiled at one another, Chrystal feeling more stable and comforted than she could have believed an hour ago.

'Thank you,' he said in his direct way, 'for giving me the walk. You must be feeling fed up with demanding males.'

The fact that he could recognise that, and say it, raised him several cubits in her esteem. 'I was, rather. But from this one I haven't noticed any demands.'

His long mouth twitched. 'I've the common sense and common pride not to batter at a closed door. But before we part I'm going to make one demand.'

'Oh, what?'

His smile had a tinge of bitterness.

'Don't be alarmed. It's simply that I *must* know — is it really all over between you and Sher Afzul Khan? I didn't hear the end of your tale, you see. I thought it might be easier for you, with Claire alone.'

'It was easier. Very kind of you.'

'Not exactly. It was hurting me more than a bit.' He looked hard at her. 'I take it that your Pathan gave Grant a pretty rough handling.'

'I'm afraid he did.' She avoided his look. 'He caught

Peter being very aggressive. To him it seemed like insulting me. And with them it's death to insult a woman.'

He nodded. 'They deal it too. Fine fellows they are in many ways. I suppose he came as near it as he dared, in a not-Free Land.'

Chrystal, aware of his lurking suspicion, kept the door of her lips. 'He was very angry,' she admitted; no more.

'I don't blame him. Grant's not out of the top drawer. And for me, only one thing matters now. *Is* it all over?'

His eyes deeply were searching hers; and, like Claire, he had the right to know.

'What he wanted is over. I won't see him again. But in my heart — it's not yet all over.'

And he surprised her by saying, 'If it was, you'd not be the girl I'm willing to wait for till the heavens fall.'

He held out both hands to her, and she gave him both her own. He seemed to hesitate, looking down at them. Then, still more surprisingly, he asked, 'Did the other fellow kiss them?'

'Yes.' It was a mere breath.

And he said, with decision: 'Then I won't. I'll wait till I win the right to kiss *you*.'

She had never come so near to loving him.

Resolutely smiling, he released her hands. Then he too walked away, like Afzul, without looking back. In their utterly different fashion, they were real men, those two: and this afternoon, between them, they had lifted her opinion of their kind.

Chapter XV

The wrong is mixed. In tragic life, God wot,
No villain need be....
We are betrayed by what is false within.

MEREDITH

CLAIRE INGLIS lay awake that night into the small hours confronting an ultimatum far more drastic than anything imagined by the pair who were so concerned for her ill-health, so little aware of her true malady. A chill had settled on her heart since that moment of shock when she had heard Dixon's voice talking of Chrystal, sublimely unaware, revealing, to her of all people, his suppressed love for Chrystal: the love that she had crazily imagined he was hiding from herself, for reasons of his own. Of late months, it had become a habit of her life, this satisfying friendship, heightened by the suspicion of a stronger feeling. The belief that she had stirred his blood and won his admiration had given her a secret sense of warmth. In the glow her heart had opened like a late-flowering rose, only to suffer the fate of many autumn roses nipped by the first breath of winter. Though the moment of shock had passed, the inner chill persisted; as if one had sat too long over a fire at night, and found that it had quietly gone out.

Yet the stream of life still rushed on past the frozen point of grief; carrying yesterday, bringing tomorrow; anticlimax treading on the heels of climax; day relentlessly following day, whether dreaded or desired. And by some means one must carry on, because despair was the negation of life. Grief might benumb all urgencies, yet they remained, and must be dealt with to the best of one's power.

And there was irony in the thought that none would be more concerned than Dixon could he guess that his supposed love had tempted her, almost, to discard pretences and give the last half of her life to the service of reality — the service that was perfect freedom. And Chrystal, whom he craved, was squandering her pristine fervours on an impossible young Pathan. At thought of the girl, given so much more than she could cope with, jealousy stirred like a snake in her breast; but she loved Chrystal too well to let that form of poison defile her mind.

Nothing remained but to make a bid for the kind of freedom she least desired: to confront Jasper with an ultimatum such as even Chrystal would not dare to advocate. While she lay alone, after they left her, a slow conviction had taken possession of her that, if she went Home now, she could not — would not — come out again at all, simply to act as unpaid housekeeper to a man who bestowed all his reputed charm on others, giving her alone the benefit of his moods, his indigestion, and his nervous heart.

Her own sinful aberration — could he dream of it — might hurt his vanity and serve as a grievance. That it would not deeply affect him otherwise she had good reason to believe.

In any case, he would now never know. Her secret was her own affair; more tragic than sinful, in her modern view; but she chose to castigate herself with the old-fashioned word. Though technically she had never sinned against Jasper — as he had probably often done against her — she knew herself, in mind and spirit, no wife; knew that at times he found her cold, when he favoured her with a rare access of husbandly attention. Too often, while her body consented, her spirit remained detached, making an inner discord, since she did not easily disentangle one from the other.

For many years now she had let him go his own way; not making heavy weather — as he would say — over his marital aberrations. In return she cherished a privacy of the spirit, which had of late included her heart. With the first he had no concern; and little enough, it seemed, with the second. Whether his own heart had also strayed, she would not dream of asking him. She knew him quite capable of making love with his senses only, of having no deep feeling even for his Priceless Pam. Of him it was peculiarly true that self-satisfaction was nourished on self-deception; the two generating a form of selfishness that was less an affair of deliberate self-seeking than a blank inability to perceive or understand another's point of view. She would be up against that very disability if she could bring herself to say decidedly, before leaving Gulmarg, 'Never again.'

It would be, in many ways, easier to write from England: a concession to weakness — mainly physical — that she dismissed as 'shirking tactics.' And there were practical objections also. If she was not returning, all her books and other treasure must go with her, or she might never see them again.

A reasonable space between her two difficult announcements might be more merciful to him and less of a strain for her. Much would depend on his initial mood, on his manner of receiving the lesser shock of her transfer to Nathia Gully. How he would receive either shock she simply could not tell; so little real knowledge she had of him after all these years. If he had any feeling of sorts for Pam, any idea of a break-away on his own account, he might almost be grateful to her — afterwards, though he would never admit as much.

They were both nearing the age that tends either to bring achievement, or vague discontent, especially to the ill-mated; a craving for emotional change and excitement, a capacity to feel young again, if another could only see one so, as she had hoped that Dixon might do.

Instead, worn out in the service of husband and children, she was condemned to any change devoid of emotional adventure or renewal of youth. Acutely she realised, also, that a virtual breaking-off of one's marriage was no mere matter of snapping a single thread. It would involve a dragging up of roots and fibres. There were habits of thought and feeling that would go on automatically. One could never quite own oneself again.

And the way this major crisis had been sprung upon her put a severe tax not only on her nerves, but on a mind that detested jerks and friction of any sort; a mind that moved in large, simple sweeps and wanted life to follow the same gracious rhythm. Instead, it was thrusting on her the sharpest friction imaginable; a possible call to resist, unflinchingly, the very man to whom she had always given way, for no higher reason than her own willingness to pay almost any price for domestic peace. The awkwardness of their immediate position, the prospect of his own physical discomfort would probably blind him to any fanciful need of hers. The one thing he never could credit was the simple truth; living, as he did, in a maze of comfortable pretences. And he had no inkling of the wifely welcome awaiting him.

It had all been so sudden that time would not allow of preparing him for that which his soul detested — even more than cold mutton and limp salad — the facing of uncomfortable facts.

She had only just been able to catch him with a deferred wire: 'Booked rooms. Am ill again. Obliged to stay here.' The rest she must spring on him soon after his arrival. Useless to lay plans or to frame sentences in advance when there was no knowing how the other might shatter one's best-laid arguments. Better leave the moment to force its own issues. An ounce of spontaneity was often worth pounds of forethought.

In a country where so many wives spent years in England, their little world need not know of the break, which would ease matters for him. She had said not a word, even to Grace, beyond her intention to leave Gulmarg and go Home if possible in late September. Grace herself had been overjoyed by a surprise wire from John:

Coming week-end. J. L.

Puzzled at first, she had realised, in a flash, the motive behind that sudden move.

'I told him you were ill,' she said, 'and he promptly pictured me slaying myself on your account. The strong thumb isn't so effective through the post. Lovely of him, but he ought not. Such a racket of a journey, for a few days.'

'It's like him,' was all that Claire could say, envying Grace to the depths of her soul. That was how a man like Lynch expressed himself. In that moment, she dared not think of Jasper, except to feel shame at the fact that it would give her greater pleasure to see John again than to see her own husband.

And Grace insisted that she was not to trouble about being in John's room. It would be no hardship doubling up; and there was the small dressing-room.

Though she purposely said little on the subject, happiness emanated from her like a light. They talked chiefly of India, with the prospect in view of Claire's non-return; a fact she had barely grasped as yet. Now, with shame, she realised that complete banishment from this strangely compelling country would hurt her more than a permanent parting from Jasper. India leaves an indelible impression on those who remain long enough in her sun and shadow to be permeated by them, who have experienced the power of her spaciousness and peace to tranquillise the most turbulent spirit.

Claire would take back to England a deeper and more various mind than she had brought there with her wedding outfit; a fadeless memory of many Indias, all unknowable, yet dearly familiar and unforgettable. Up here, the healing influence of the mountains, their beauty and aloofness, had entered into her; till the shock of Jasper's coming and Dixon's disclosure had almost undone, in a few days, the good of these reviving weeks with Grace.

Now she lay alone in the dark, listening to the far-off music of waterfalls, sleep hanging heavy on her lids, yet refusing its balm to her troubled mind; till tomorrow had become today, and weariness obliterated even the advent of Jasper, even her own sentence of banishment from the land that had given her more than it had taken away.

It was early afternoon, and she was dozing uneasily among her cushions when a familiar step in the verandah set her heart beating thickly. And a moment later Jasper entered unannounced, very spruce and pleasant-looking in his pin-striped grey summer suit, bringing with him the faint pleasant smell of leather and scented soap, as if he were fresh from a bath that had washed off the dust of the road. So seen, he was almost good-looking; but there were querulous lines about his mouth, and even as he smiled at her she detected in his eyes a flicker of irritation over some trifle that would start their talk in the wrong key.

'No *salaam dō* needed for *this* Sahib,' he said, stooping to kiss her with just the right touch of effusion. It was the kind of possessive kiss from which she shrank instinctively; yet he barely returned the pressure of her fingers that closed on his hand.

'Nice sort of welcome for the jaded traveller,' he lightly reproached her. 'You sounded fairly fit a week ago. Hope it's just a passing flop.'

Taking her hesitation for assent, he proceeded to cheer her with his own characteristic form of welcome; a full-blown grievance over the inferior bedroom assigned to the Commissioner of Peshawar.

'Even if you *are* a bit of a crock,' he reproached her, 'you might have bestirred yourself to go over and see about it, instead of letting me in for a first-class row on arrival.'

'What's the matter with your room?' she asked dutifully, prepared for the worst.

'That's what you should have discovered. A wretched cubicle they've foisted on me. More like a loose box than a bedroom. Rotten cupboard accommodation. Gramophone next door, and an east window with light curtains. I'll be dragged awake at unearthly hours, when I'm needing all the sleep I can get, after weeks of insomnia from the heat. After all, I *am* a Commissioner, not a damned subaltern or a polo pony — as I told the bureau young woman, who had the impertinence to take it as a joke.'

'I'm really very sorry, dear,' she edged in a word at last.

'But they didn't get much notice. In ten days they can give you the room I originally booked. A Captain Dearmer and his wife are doubled up in it now.'

'Well, they might shift *him* for a Commissioner.'

'The Dearmers mightn't see the logic of that. She's not very well ——'

'Which doesn't affect *my* case,' was his characteristic comment. 'If you'd been moving in yourself, you'd have fussed around fast enough. But for me, it's no matter.'

'You *know* that's a lie,' she countered, with the stillness of controlled anger and clinched decision in her heart.

It was the first time she had been goaded into using the unbecoming word; and he stared in amazement. Raked by the searchlight of her wide-set, candid eyes, his very soul writhed away from her; but he brazened it out in his airy fashion.

'Queer language, Claire, to your husband! If my remark was a libel, accept apologies ——'

'You know it was a libel,' she answered, unappeased. 'You know my first concern is always to ensure your comfort. If I couldn't create a non-existent room, at least I'd have gone over there, ill as I am, to do what I could, even at the risk of fainting in public. But at present I'm not allowed to leave the sofa more than a few times a day. No question of going out or walking uphill. Grace is a doctor herself; and I've reason to be thankful for it.'

'Yes, yes, of course,' he said, without conviction, sinking into the softest chair available. There was no cushion, because Grace had piled them all behind Claire. With difficulty, unassisted, she dragged one out and handed it to him.

So used he was to accepting her ministrations, so little used to seeing her ill, that he took the cushion with a mechanical 'Thanks very much,' and pushed it between his shoulder blades. 'Lord, I'm tired and worried to death.'

A wave of sick depression flowed over her. He had the male knack of imposing his moods on any available female belonging.

'Nice awkward position your flop has landed me in. Not much fun languishing *solus* at one small table, Pam at another, propping a novel against her water-bottle. But having arrived together, if we sit together and go out together for tennis or what not —?'

'Much the same as at Peshawar,' she murmured as one who was not personally concerned with the matter.

'Oh, we're well known in Peshawar. You and old P. B. are there, and they accept our platonics by now. Up here it's another story. Nice for us, harmless philanderers, generating tittle-tattle, while you lie here, virtuously aloof, playing the invalid ——'

'I am *not* playing the invalid,' she took him up sharply. Her cold anger had been rising while he sat there self-engrossed, stone blind to her changed aspect, that had led her to expect unflattering comment. He seemed literally incapable, at present, of seeing anything except the wrong room and the awkward position for his Priceless Pam. By his insulting implication, he was bringing on himself, untimely soon, the announcement that she would normally have deferred for a day or two.

'I'm *not* playing the invalid,' she repeated, to his mutely astonished gaze. 'And it's not a passing flop. I didn't want to bother you on arrival with rather serious news. But your attitude is goading me into it. The facts are these. I had a nasty attack and collapse a few days ago. Grace called in Doctor Blake, who thoroughly examined me and said the same as Ewart, only more so. I need complete rest for some time and — freedom from worry.' She emphasised the last. 'As this place is too high, he has ordered me to Nathia Gully when I'm able to move. After that, about September' — she drew a difficult breath — 'I positively must go Home for special heart treatment, he says, if I'm to pull through at all.'

'Home? Heart treatment?' he echoed, slowly grasping all that those two words involved; above all, the expense — his first consideration in life, unless his personal comfort were involved. 'Easy for doctors to talk. Where's the money coming from, with school bills and cuts in pay and running that big house at Peshawar?'

'The money?' Again she treated him to the disconcerting candour of her eyes. 'You needn't worry about that. My few investments have depreciated badly, but I can sell out enough, at a loss, to cover immediate costs. Your expenses are heavy enough.'

And still he stared at her, moving his lips in the way he had when he was served with something unpalatable and had no prompt evasion at command.

'I don't understand you, Claire,' he complained at last, more truly than he knew. 'You've laid your plans to bolt, it seems, without reference to the person most concerned.'

'And you, it seems, can't open your mouth without insulting me,' she answered bitterly, stiffening herself to deal him the final blow. 'I have laid *no* plans — the whole thing has been sprung upon me since I wrote last. I *am* referring it to the person most concerned — though you don't give me that impression, except as regards expense. And I propose to relieve you of that.'

Seeing himself put in the wrong, he changed his tone of voice from the aggrieved to the persuasive — the attitude she had most reason to fear.

'My dear girl,' he said more gently, 'no one's insulting you. What a notion! In spite of doctors' orders to lie flat, you seem inclined to mount your high horse this morning. *Can* you see me left lamenting in Peshawar, without my model wife to oil the wheels and keep me company?'

She tried to smile at his pleasantry. 'I've never seen myself as a model wife.'

'Well, you always have been, so far. I'd be lost without you,' he generously admitted, patting her hand that lay limply beside her. 'Come now, Claire, ask yourself, is it fair, is it kind to desert me in this cavalier fashion, in my uncertain state of health? You know how I rely on you in every way. A few months of going slow at Nathia Gully might make another woman of you. Then I'll get back the model wife you've been without fail till this unpleasant turn of the wheel.'

It was the plea she had dreaded: a plea virtually unanswerable, had they both been otherwise. Only two things saved her from surrender: the insistence on his own uncertain health and the implicit ignoring of her more serious condition. Even so, in her weakened state, it would be fatally easier to give in.

'It *is* hard lines,' she admitted, gently withdrawing her hand. 'But it might be worse in the end for us both — not to mention the children — if I stayed out here now, and perhaps let you in — for funeral expenses.'

'Oh, my *dear* girl!' He edged away instinctively from serious issues. 'We needn't jump to such horrid conclusions. You're naturally feeling a bit nervous just now, so you exaggerate.'

'I'm not feeling nervous.' Her voice hardened again. 'And you can ask Doctor Blake if I exaggerate. He was quite explicit. Too much India. Too many hot weathers. A judgment on me, in fact, for overdoing model wifehood. The willing horse has dropped in the shafts. Horses do, you know, when they're pushed too hard. Something snaps inside.'

'And who's been pushing *you* too hard?' he queried, with the obtuseness of the man who has never doubted the justice and wisdom of his own acts.

'Life,' was her comprehensive answer.

'Oh, well — !' he sounded relieved. 'Lots of us could say that. But we can't all throw down our hands because of it.'

The harder note in his voice relieved her also.

'We've no right to throw down our hands at all,' she agreed, 'because the cards are against us. Unhappily, some of us are driven to it. That's my case, I'm afraid.'

'Oh, rot. You aren't that sort,' he flattered her, with the comfortable certainty that no mere wife could let down Jasper Inglis.

'No, I'm not that sort,' she temporised, still reluctant to shock, and possibly hurt, the man whom she had instinctively shielded from hurt or discomfort all her days. Never had the force of habit been so painfully brought home to her.

'It makes me hate all the more what I've got to say, Jasper. I had very little sleep last night, facing several unpleasant truths and arriving at very difficult decisions. You must please accept them *as decisions;* not as matter for argument.'

She drew in her lip. Uncomfortable sensations warned her that she could not, physically, stand much more of the strain he was putting on her through inability, or refusal, to perceive the extent of her plight. In the simplest, briefest terms she told him that she was under orders to leave Gulmarg; that, in late September, she and Chrystal would return to England.

After that, a pause and a deep breath — nerving herself for the worst.

'There,' she said, 'I shall remain. That is my difficult decision. When I leave India — it must be *for good:* partly on account of health, but chiefly because I find I can't honestly go on living with you any longer — as your wife.'

She spoke without looking at him; but in every nerve she was aware of his abnormal stillness; his inability to credit her with decisive action independent of himself and his demands.

She ceased speaking; and there fell an ominous pause. When at last he spoke, his voice had an edge to it.

'Have you taken leave of your senses, Claire? Or is all this a blind' (she knew it must come) 'for going off with another man? Verney's been after you, has he? I've been sceptical of the platonic touch.'

She listened to the last in a frozen fury that could find no relief in scathing retort. For a second or two — a pause between two hammer strokes — it seemed as if her heart stopped beating.

Then she heard herself saying, in a voice as frozen as her fury: 'You have a positive genius for misjudging others. Dixon Verney — my very dear friend' — she caught her breath — 'is in love with Chrystal.'

And he actually said: 'Hard luck! I wouldn't have thought it: the born bachelor.'

Skilfully he side-stepped away from her harsh indictment, and she was only aware of relief that he had taken her word for it.

Then, to her unspeakable dismay, he leaned forward, patted her shoulder, and took her by the arm.

'Look here, my dear. I'm not accepting any of this tall talk. You've got whimsies in your brain, because you're sick. I can see you are. You look a rag!'

'I feel it,' she said, with closed eyes. 'Do please have mercy on me and believe what I say. It's the truth. I've come — to the end — of my tether.'

'But — but what's wrong with *me*, in Heaven's name?' he asked, so blankly that she could almost have laughed, only laughter might dissolve in tears. 'I let you go your own way. I'm no *zubberdast* like Lynch.'

'Oh, it's not that — not that,' she murmured. How did one say such things? 'You are forcing me, Jasper, to a detestable necessity. But now, at last, it must be the truth between us. For years and years you have been slowly killing my love — the kind of love I had for you long ago. Don't ask me why. These things can't be explained. I — I can't love... the man you are. And you don't know how to love, as I understand the word. I only know there's a dead thing in my breast. And God Himself can't bring a dead love to life again.'

She was actually saying things that she could not have credited herself with saying to this man. And she heard him gasp. She had verily given him the shock of his life.

'I feel — I feel,' he said, 'as if I'm listening to a mad woman; not to the woman I've known and implicity relied on for seventeen years.'

She opened her eyes at that. 'Have you known me, Jasper, I wonder?'

'Begins to look as if I never have,' he answered in an inimical voice.

'Have you ever really tried to know me?'

'Oh, Lord! What next?' He spoke now with the impatience of a shallow nature oppressed by a demand to face tragic issues. 'I can't stand much more of this — on the top of that journey and all. You forget, *I*'ve got a groggy heart also.'

Again laughter threatened — mirthless laughter: but she must hold herself in till he was gone; and surely he must go soon.

'I'm very sorry,' she murmured; 'I didn't mean to spring it all on you now. You forced me to, by the things you said.'

'Oh, yes. *I*'m always the one to blame ——' His old tag was half a relief. 'Am I to understand that you definitely want to clear out? Drop me like a bad potato — children and all?'

'No — not the children.' She drew a shuddering breath.

'Hand them over to the bolting wife, eh?'

'No — no!' she said, clinging to consciousness, like a drowning man to a spar. He seemed determined to misunderstand. 'I don't mean that. I mean, of course, I would be with them as usual. They needn't know till they're older. I wouldn't take a penny from you for myself; and — if you should want to marry again, I would make things easy for you, without degrading my proper pride. In fact, I'll do any mortal thing I can — short of coming out here to live with you again. This must be — *the end*.'

'Good God!' he cried. No evasion now. He had grasped, at last, the ungraspable truth.

And, even as he spoke, a masculine voice was shouting in the verandah: John Lynch.

A different Jasper said, 'Damn the man, butting in.'

'After all, it's his own drawing-room,' Claire feebly murmured, her voice sounding very far away.

Two minutes later, Lynch entered his own drawing-room to find — no Grace; but Inglis staring as if he had seen a ghost; and his wife on the sofa, her head fallen back among the cushions, in a faint that looked like death.

Chapter XVI

Baffled, get up and begin again,
So the chase takes up one's life, that's all.

BROWNING

IT WAS not Death, who seldom arrives at the acceptable moment; and, for Claire, extinction might have been a mercy, hard on the heels of her first and last resolute attempt at self-assertion. She remained unconscious long enough to frighten Grace and Doctor Blake, but at length, half reluctantly, she returned to face life — a state of being so difficult, so full of complications, trivial and tragic, that one hardly dared to breathe.

And today she had done rather more than breathe. She had said things that could not be unsaid: had perhaps hurt Jasper more than she deemed possible. For seventeen years he had relied on her, had loved her in his fashion: and she had failed him utterly, just when he most needed comforting over that 'loose box' of a bedroom. Such, at least, would be his view of her desperate bid for freedom.

Her first coherent thought, on emerging from merciful darkness, had been, 'Oh, dear, what a pity!' Yet how instinctively one clung to life, for all its ironies, cruelties, and uncertainties. By now, she could almost feel grateful to Grace and Doctor Blake for dragging her back from the edge of beyond.

It was after dinner. She was lying on the sofa, while Grace and John sat together, in deep, undemonstrative content, near a crackling fire of wood and pine-cones, lit by Grace more for cheerfulness than for warmth. A late shower had left a chill in the air; and Claire, with a deeper chill at her heart, felt thankful to lie thus inert, to watch the little leaping flames and savour the scent of burning wood. Jasper, she was told, had faded away directly she came round, with tactful remarks about leaving her to rest and get over it.

Grace had allowed herself only a veiled allusion to him just before dinner.

'I hope all this means that you *did* manage to pull it off?'

And Claire had answered, 'Yes, I did — just manage ——'

Not a word of the more drastic pulling-off — the real cause of 'all this'; though later on Grace would have to know. She was the one person besides Chrystal who must be told, if only for practical reasons. None but Grace could she trust to collect her treasures and see them safely despatched to England. But all that must wait.

Now it was enough to lie there at peace while they fancied she was dozing; to take a disinterested pleasure in watching that satisfactory pair. There sat John, solidly content, having faced his rush journey of forty-eight hours — much of it through the fiery furnace — simply to assure himself that Grace was not being slain by her tiresome friend and to enjoy two or three days of her society. Grace herself was loving him for it, under a show of skin-deep disapproval; and she, Claire, was not being allowed by either of them to feel herself in the way. In a sense, they had her to thank for the treat they both so patently relished; and Claire, watching them, thought, not for the first time, that none could fully know John who had not seen him in his 'unbuttoned moods' with Grace. Temperamentally they were poles asunder; merged in heart, yet each maintaining personal independence of mind and character.

Lying there, outside the picture, deliberately holding her thoughts on them, she was still intermittently aware of Jasper, in the background, annoyed and aggrieved — if no more — at her unwifely behaviour. She had banished the actual man, but his ghost would trouble her for a long while yet. He had become a habit, mental as well as physical; and he was forcing her now to worry over his grievance, knowing how actively he hated discomfort in any form; until, with an odd jerk, she reminded herself that his bedroom was no longer her affair. Pam would now become the receptacle of grievances that would temper her diet of flattery. She would deal coolly and capably with the bedroom vexation; and Claire found herself perversely resenting the favoured one's intrusion when she ought to be feeling relieved. It was the kind of relief that brought little satisfaction; only a flat feeling that there was nothing to push against any more. It would take time for full realisation to penetrate her bruised mind and enable her to grasp the sense of personal freedom that would lighten and enlarge her life.

'Like the poor prisoner of Chillon,' she thought inconsequently, yet not inaptly, recalling the poignant line, 'Even I regained my freedom with a sigh.'

Wearily she stirred and turned on her cushions. Grace heard her at once, though John was talking, and sprang up.

There were steps and voices outside, Chrystal and Sir Roy. How dear of them, coming to enquire. And if Grace needed any extra inner sparkle, it was provided by the friendly greeting between John and Roy, her husband and friend.

Chrystal had been terrified at the news of that long fainting fit. Roy had offered to walk across with her and have a few words with Lynch, whose services to himself neither he nor Tara would ever forget.

It was a keen pleasure when Lynch, after greetings, proffered a cigar and suggested a stroll, 'not to smoke out the women'; though Sinclair, knowing his man, thought, 'There's a practical reason behind it, or he wouldn't be Lynch.'

And the practical reason came out forthwith.

'I ran up here,' he remarked, 'just to make sure that Grace wasn't taking any risks; too completely turning doctor over poor Claire.'

'"Some" run,' was Sinclair's comment on the achievement; and Lynch chuckled.

'Some breather also. Furnace at full blast down there. — But my point is this: Claire's badly crocked up. She'll be needing a good bit of attention.'

'Hasn't her husband come up?' asked Sinclair, and Lynch regarded him with that curious lift of his lids.

'You don't know Inglis, I believe?'

'I don't.'

'No loss. A broken reed, at best, for this sort of thing. Also, quite between ourselves, I suspect serious friction, from the look of them when I arrived, and the awkward way he drifted out of the picture directly she came round. I wonder — could your wife come along now and then, give Grace a chance to slack off? If I fuss at her direct, she stiffens. It's the nature of a woman who's got a nature!'

'You can count on Tara,' Sinclair assured him. 'She would gladly do anything to help Mrs. Inglis or ease Grace. We owe her a debt too; and we like Mrs. Inglis immensely. Count on us; and Chrystal will be here a good deal.'

'Yes. But young things like running round.'

'Not Chrystal — just now.'

'Why? What's up?'

They looked straight at each other; and Lynch read the thought behind Sinclair's eyes.

'Not Sher Afzul Khan? Seriously?'

'Yes; on both sides. I persuaded her against it; but it has hit them both hard.'

'Bad luck. You did them a good service, though they may not see it yet awhile. Hope it doesn't make a promising officer chuck the Army. It's going to be a serious crux in this affair of Indianising. — But we mustn't start on any such fertile theme. I'm grateful to you and Lady Sinclair.'

'My dear Lynch,' Sinclair took him up, 'it's a trifle to ask of us, seeing all that we owe to you.'

Lynch waved away his own trifle with a large hand; and Sinclair added: 'You may also be glad to know that we're planning to leave this with the two of them. Sir Vincent couldn't get here to see me, so they want us on a visit over there. I'm only awaiting Blake's verdict, so that we can travel together.'

'Good. Claire's a fine woman. She's had a hard time of it with that man. She ought to be in bed now.'

'And we ought to be getting back. I'm glad we came.'

'So am I. You've eased my mind considerably.'

Sinclair collected Chrystal, and they strolled home across the open marg under a sky of flashing stars; Chrystal saying little, Roy deep in his own thoughts.

She found his quiet presence singularly soothing; and tonight she needed soothing. Dixon was leaving tomorrow; and Gulmarg would feel emptier without him than it had any business to feel, for a young woman not yet in love with him. The passionate response evoked in her by Afzul was subsiding to a dull ache, which she was doing her best to ignore. Yet perversely she could not achieve a stroke of painting to distract her mind. And today's post had brought her an envelope containing a picture postcard of Apharwāt, with nine Indian words in Afzul's square handwriting:

Al Rahim, al Rahmān, yād bād rōz-i-girān. Read aloud, they had a musical rhythm. The recurrence of the long 'ā' gave a sonorous splendour to so many Eastern words; and beneath them he had written in English: 'Because of your command, I will not leave the Army. Afzul.'

Nothing of the rest could she understand; and she could not bring herself to ask Lance or Eve, who only knew of her written decision.

No word had been said by either beyond a casual remark from Lance: 'Afzul, my best polo-player, has melted into the landscape; and I met poor old Grant today looking as glum as if he were attending his own funeral. Whose scalp will you be hanging at your girdle next, you devastating damsel?'

'Oh, *don't* call me that,' she had pleaded, with such acute distaste that he had looked hard at her a moment, as if he would like to kiss her himself.

Instead, he had answered gravely: 'Humble apologies. It's the wrong epithet for you.'

If either had an inkling of Dixon's plight, they gave no sign. It would be a horrid wrench parting from them, her favourite human beings — the artist and the worker. The English side of India had given her nothing more memorable than those two and the fine thing they were making of marriage.

When the twin huts came in sight, she said suddenly, 'Roy, there's something I want to show you — alone.'

'What now?' he asked, looking round at her, coming out of his dream.

'It's a card I've got from Afzul. Part of it not in English. I *must* know what it means; and I can only ask you.'

'Right,' he said, slipping a hand under her elbow. 'Come on up. We can slip round the back into my little sanctum.'

It was a small, Spartan room: two chairs and the paper-strewn table where he worked. On it — one touch of Tara — a vase of tall blue Jacob's-ladder to delight his eye.

Silently she handed him the card, watching his face with a muffled stir at her heart. He frowned at first, then smiled and shook his head.

'Poor fellow. He's hard hit; but he shouldn't have sent you this.' Without looking up at her, he read:

> *In the name of Allah the Compassionate, the Merciful, remember the days that are gone.*

There fell a difficult silence. Tears ached in her throat, but she was determined not to break down.

'Those first words,' she said, very low, 'he spoke when he left me.' Then, perceiving her slip, she added quickly: 'I saw him again, Roy, afterwards. I can't tell you now; but I will — over there. When it hurts less.'

'Yes, over there,' he said. 'I'm glad we don't separate. I rather think it's a permanent attachment.'

The pleasure of that became so entangled with the pain that her control very nearly gave way.

He seemed to understand. It was his gift of gifts. Taking her left hand in his right he pressed it hard, and strangely said: 'It's worth remembering also the days that are to come. If you *have* hurt him badly, Chrystal, you've done him a good service. I'm glad he'll stick to the Army, not make it a cause of race hatred. We most of us manage to live down even the unforgettable.'

She could smile at him now. 'I knew you would somehow make it hurt less.'

'I've suffered unforgettable things. Most of us do,' he said simply. 'The Sword of suffering often brings Wisdom.'

And she left him with the threatened tears unshed, the strangest mingling of pain and exaltation in her heart.

A week later they left Gulmarg, the five of them. Lilāmani wept at parting from the hut and the stream and Eve and 'that Ian baby.' But tears were dried by the promise of meeting again, perhaps even a return in September. Chrystal's unshed tears took longer to subdue; and the heavens wept also, which did not ease the ache, though it did ease a little her regret at leaving those rain-soaked hills.

And social Gulmarg, enjoying a brilliant season, was only aware of ripples on the surface of waters deeply stirred; none dreaming that the course of six lives had been drastically changed in as many weeks; while the unconcerned, in their hundreds, went on dancing and racing and pursuing golf balls; flaying God's grass from the Meadow of Flowers.

Chapter XVII

We are the music makers,
We are the dreamers of dreams.
. . . . . .
For we are the movers and shakers
Of the world, for ever, it seems.

A. O'SHAUGHNESSY

TARA leaned back among the blue-and-yellow cushions of their covered *shikara* and smiled at Roy; her smile, these days, had a lovely brooding quality like a gleam of light on tranquil water. But the question that emerged was purely practical.

'A tiffin party for the five of us?'

'Five — yes, if you can call us a "tiffin party."' He tilted a look at her. He was sitting upright, hands clasped round a lifted knee. 'We don't sound like it: Edom, the Guru, Aruna, and ourselves. Some sort of picnic: a good vegetable curry and plenty of fruit — not forgetting coffee and cigars — would suit those three and us also.'

'"The order is obeyed."' She quoted Gulbaddan. 'And where shall it be, O *Swami*-Sahib?'

'How about the upper terrace of our Chasma Shahi for the last of it? Good-bye is a hard word when it comes to leaving this paradise and one of the finest men of any race that I've ever met. That shrine of remembrance will make it at once easier and harder.' He gazed at her — pondering. '*Will* it be a little hard for you leaving all this, in spite of the big things tugging at your heart?'

And now she could say, with truth: 'More than a little

hard. The beauty and wonder of your India will live in me always — the most magic spring and summer of my life.'

His fingers closed sharply on her hand.

'It will live in both of us always. When we get back to the familiar life and its duties, we won't merely repeat the past. We'll do all the old things in a new way.'

'And if I hadn't come out,' she mused, 'I wouldn't have understood about the new way hidden in your heart. It was as if something led me, something even bigger than my longing. And now ——'

'Yes, now ——' he echoed, his gaze so eloquent that she dropped her lids, as if she would veil the secret thing that was not yet known to any but themselves.

And the *shikara* sped smoothly on, poled by a stalwart Kashmiri and steered by his wife, with her short paddle at the stern; nosing its way through a lane cut in the dense reeds, where dark-red dragonflies flitted and a warbler was singing a small song to itself. On and out into clear water that shimmered like an opal, with every tint of the changeful sky. Drifts of mist, moonstone blue, veiled the rice-fields and backwaters. Plumes of smoke, bluer than the mist, rose from houses on the shore, where grazing ponies neighed to one another and a shepherd boy called to his scattered flock. The plop of a fish far out and the lapping of water against their boat sounded loud in the quiet.

Boats carrying market produce were stacked with melons and cucumbers, marigolds and lotus pods. From an alley-way of willows a barge sauntered out, piled high with love-lies-bleeding, pure crimson lake; its reflection staining the water as it went. Whole gardens of it glowed in dry patches between the dikes; not for its beauty, but for use in colouring food; and blazing beds of marigold for temple offerings. The lotus-fields towards Nishāt Bagh were all overblown; the cuplike seed pods already purpling; the leaves lifted on long stalks, their vivid undersides catching the light. In every detail of the picture there was a harmony of line and colour that satisfied more than the eye.

September was nearing an end. On the higher peaks fresh

snow had fallen. All the trees in the valley — poplars, willows, and chenars — were splashed with gold, as though a beam of sunlight had left its imprint on the leaves. For these two the year had swung round full circle: a year of deepest dark and highest light. They were in Srinagar for a farewell week after their fortnight of riding and camping in higher regions, not quite 'according to plan,' because of the coming child — a prospect so welcome to both that neither had felt irked by the restrictions it entailed. Roy himself — with a strange certainty of prevision — had foreknowledge of a second son, heir to neither title nor lands, but to a higher heritage of the spirit, godson of his Guru and of Lance, his rediscovered friend.

Between two expeditions, taken easily, they had spent a few days in their deserted hut, enjoying Gulmarg at its loveliest, almost empty of summer invaders. For custom and fashion curiously decreed a general return to Srinagar in the very month when Gulmarg became a paradise of rain-washed hills, blue distances, and translucent air. Only a few incurable golfers deferred the evil day.

Once again they climbed Apharwāt, foregoing the rough descent to the lakes. Once again they took their fill of Kashmir and her guardian summits; looking down into the misted valley through a rain of golden birches, across rocks aflame with scarlet leaves of saxifrage; every mighty peak from end to end sharply clear against the porcelain-blue of a September sky: a vision that summoned the spirit to a far journey. They had spent hours up there in a felicity more than mortal. They had laid plans for their journey down to Bombay with Chrystal and Claire. First Agra, for its glories and Dayālbagh; then Udaipur, where Chrystal would see the best of Rajput genius, and Bāpu would see the child with his daughter's name and promise of her loveliness. Then Bombay — and Home.

Meantime, they were enjoying a brief taste of houseboat life away from the crowd, moored to the lovely little Isle of Chenars; discovering in its tangled undergrowth, a pitiful scatter of marble pillars and fragments of a small pavilion:

one more lost Moghul dream. Ruins, ruins everywhere, under all this lavish natural beauty.

Eve was with them, and 'that Ian baby,' on their way down to join Lance. They would travel with Roy to Murree, where Lance would meet them. He had furlough due; they might be at Home next summer. At the Residency Grace was installed with her newly arrived son, awaiting Doctor Blake's leave to face the motor journey and rejoin her man after the longest separation since their marriage.

Aruna, staying with friends at the Mission hospital, came often to see them. Her brilliant pair, devoted yet constantly quarrelling, had returned to Peshawar, Sinclair having secured through Vincent a post for Surāj as a junior master at Islamia College, with Indian history and literature for his subject. Rajini, later on, would help Aruna with her *Mahāla Samiti*[1] and social-service work, the crying need of India. After much friction and flashes of jealousy, it had been decided that Aruna should have the wish of her heart — to adopt the two little daughters left by Surāj with an unwilling married sister at Udaipur.

'Between us,' mused Roy, 'Aruna and I have not done so badly for that promising pair, who might otherwise have broken their wings against the bars of their cages.'

'You've done wonders,' Tara declared. 'They're fascinating creatures.'

The houseboat was in sight now, though still far off. There they could not be to themselves because of Eve and Lilāmani; and Tara, with a glance at him, drew a blue envelope out of her embroidered bag.

'What is it now?' he asked, aware of something astir in her.

'It's a letter that came in today's *dāk* from Thea — about Vernon. He's been up there this month on leave. I hadn't heard for some time. So I hoped "it" had subsided. Suddenly, the other day, I remembered that I never answered his last about some special air exploit that he was rather proud of. Not wanting to seem unkind, I wrote — quite a

[1] Women's Institute.

short one, saying *Shahbash* and giving news of his Fairy. And oh — it *is* queer the way chance trifles turn a scale. Read it, yourself.'

His interest pricked by curiosity, he took the sheet of blue paper and read:

I want you to know this, Tara dearest, about Vernon; to know how grateful I am for the way you've handled my bewitched Babe. One sort of woman would have been bored, and snubbed him and hurt him. The other sort would have let him flirt with her, kept the whole thing on the physical level of making love. You, by letting him write — by the way *you wrote — lifted the whole thing. Hardly seeming aware of it, yet keeping in touch. He showed me one of your letters, besides the last, which brings me to the tale of the charmer that didn't! She's the pukka grass widow out of Kipling, with a taste for snaring the freshest and nicest boys available. Rather more than pretty, in a deceptively demure style; and Vernon has the Desmond weakness for that sort of thing.*

Of course I soon saw what was up; detesting her, but not daring to utter, lest I play into her hands. Naturally there came a day when he *saw what she was after, and no doubt the poor darling hated it and wanted it about equally.*

Well, that day she took him for a ride; flattered him and persuaded him to dine with her alone. Coming back here to change, he found a letter from you, after a long silence. You *know what was in it; and I know how it worked. He just sent a note round with some lame excuse. Then he came straight to me and told me everything, as simply as if he had been twelve years old. He said your letter had pulled him back like a jerk on the reins when a pony stumbles; and it pulled extra hard because he had felt rather sad that you didn't answer his last about doing well in that dash over the Border.*

The whole thing is off; and I'm now gently drawing his attention to a delicious girl here, just to play with. No marrying, I've told him, for at least three years. I wish my very bachelor Theo would look that way. Paul — the Ubique Gunner — has got himself engaged to something at Hyderabad. I haven't even seen a snap of it yet; and I'm faintly alarmed. You never know what sort of undesirable alien marriage may pitchfork into a harmless family.

But nonsense apart, thank you again, dearest of Taras, for your unbeknown good deed. I can't tell you how happy we've been together since you torpedoed the charmer.

I long to get you both back again. Your Roy is a lucky, lucky man, which I'm sure he doesn't need telling ——

Roy looked up from those words at Tara's profile, its mingling of delicacy and strength, the clear skin warmed by wind and sun and health renewed.

'Yes, a damned lucky man — who *doesn't* need telling,' he said gravely; and she turned to him with smiling eyes.

'You forget it's not all *my* doing. If you hadn't told me to let him write, I should have damped him down for the good of his young soul; and the charmer would have got him. When I tell Thea, she'll thank *you*.'

'"Each is both,"' he reminded her, glancing sidelong, as voices over the water drew their attention to the houseboat, where Eve and Lilāmani stood on deck calling, 'Coo-ee,' waving them a welcome home.

And another day of days dropped into the lake, like a pearl from a silver thread.

Chasma Shahi again: the same, yet subtly changed by the passing of spring and by the fact that it was no longer their shrine. Orchard boughs were heavy with fruit; trees flecked with amber and tawny gold. Only the roses still made a brave show in their second blooming.

On the stone *chabutra* of the upper terrace they sat at the low narrow table with cushions for seats, two women and three men — England, America, and India, all wearing Indian dress. 'Good augury,' the Guru had remarked, by way of benediction.

A green glass bowl full of roses was flanked by silver baskets piled with pears and apricots, grapes and walnuts, that Sri Samādhi cracked between his strong lean hands. Today he talked more than usual, knowing himself with those who cared for the things he had to say; and beneath his suave tones one felt the core of steel that gave his least request the air of a command; the stillness at the centre that drew others out.

Their picnic meal was almost over; Gulbaddan had served coffee and cigarettes. The two women had wandered down into the rose garden to find Tara's friend, old Rāmanand. Sri Samādhi, cracking walnuts for himself and Roy, was talking of a possible visit to England, recalling an earlier experience which had disappointed him on the whole. Expecting to find the civilised West more enlightened mentally than his own land, he had found instead a dismaying scepticism and indifference to things of the spirit, except among a select few. But now he understood there was a change in the air: a spirit of seeking, of hunger. Radhakrishnan had written of eager young audiences attending his lectures; clerks, teachers, salesmen, students — men and women who had more or less lost their religion — standing in crowds, after a hard day's work, on the chance of hearing a Hindu philosopher lecture on a deeply religious view of life.

'Because of this awakening interest,' he said, 'my friend would have me once more visit England and speak to these young audiences, who, I am assured, would listen — if only because listening has become the "fashion," he added with his touch of dry humour.

'Too much the fashion in God's own country,' Edom admitted. 'They want me to go back there for a talking tour, having discovered the man behind certain outspoken articles that have made some folks sit up. Well, suppose I did go, the highbrows would be falling over each other to sample that queer product — millionaire-into-Brahmo. All the elegant ladies, with long noses and jade earrings and empty lives, would gulp down my platitudes; go home with a fit of spiritual indigestion: and in a week — pouf!' He snapped his bony fingers. 'In at one ear, out at the other — that's the curse of the listening vogue. And we're passing on the habit to India, with the movies in full blast, and radio coming soon. To see a peasant audience at a talkie is a sight for laughter or tears, which way you take it. Huddled together, by the hour, not a laugh among them, gulping it all down: gangsters at gunplay, Chaplin chucking a custard pie in the other fellow's face, rape or rapture — all one to them.'

'So it may seem,' the Guru interposed. 'Yet they are worthy of better fare. Though few can read or write, they are no fools; their patience and content are born from no mere pig-trough philosophy. They often go hungry, but on the whole they are happy, because their faith is great and their needs are few.'

'You've hit the nail, Guru-*ji*. I've lived among them for close on a year, and I'll maintain against the world that the average Indian peasant is a happier man in himself than any Russian or American mechanic. Take him all round, he's sober, kindly, and content, living in his queer pantheon of gods and goddesses. And the man who "Montagues" that content will deserve the damnation he likely won't get.' He shot a quick look at Sinclair. 'I've had some good talk around all that, this summer, with a certain clever and charming woman, who came over to seek me out, hoping I'd return with her and enlighten my fellows. I told her she'd far better stay and learn from India, instead of tempting a free man back to a mechanised world. She may see my point yet.'

The gleam in his grey eye lit a thought in Sinclair's mind, 'Sits the wind in that corner?' And Edom, catching his glance, thrust out an expressive lower lip.

'I'd like to have you meet her, Sinclair. She's sprung from the best of our élite — the pick of us; the most generous and intelligent, open to all breezes of the spirit. They count for more than they guess. Just through being what they are, they may quicken a better understanding with your people, Sinclair: a will to believe the best; on both sides, instead of being in a damned hurry to impute the worst.'

'It's got to come,' Sinclair stated; and the Guru, watching both men, intently, had ceased to crack nuts. 'It's the one thing needful, not only for ourselves, to give the world clear proof that, whatever happens, the British Empire and America will stand shoulder to shoulder.'

Edom twinkled. 'We're ready for it, when you are —

the best of us. Take it from me that, as a whole, we sincerely admire the best of *you*. But admiration — as friend Balzac has it — is apt to be fatiguing for the human species. Too much looking up gives a crick in the neck. Most folk feel more comfortable looking down.'

'We Indians,' Sri Samādhi quietly remarked, 'have had too much experience of that little human weakness in our rulers. Better all round to try looking level for a change. That is the only aspect between friends.'

'Looking level, as *we* do.' There was a new warmth in Edom's tone. 'We three — India, England, and America' — his bony finger indicated each in turn, 'drawn together by something bigger than Chance. Prophetic? Who knows? It's for us to help make it so. Must the world be devastated by another hideous war just to teach us the simple necessity of hands across the sea? — But here I am, as usual, talking your heads off!'

He laughed and looked from one to the other, knowing himself forgiven. 'And I'm due for another leave-taking this afternoon. Young Dayālanand. Don't forget the Garden of the Lord, Sinclair. It's the seed of big things to come. The boy's going back there now.'

He rose, holding out a hand to each. 'We'll meet again. It is written. You've a great work before you, Sinclair, and you do honour to a great tradition. If your governing classes have glaring faults, they have greater virtues. Nothing in this age of dictators and proletariats can fill their place. I look forward with confidence to our next meeting.'

He saluted them Eastern fashion; and went his purposeful way, leaving the others to face a more difficult parting, though they also might confidently hope to meet again.

'You *will* come to England,' Sinclair urged, 'and give the new young a chance to hear your words of wisdom?'

Sri Samādhi gravely regarded the *chela* he had grown to love beyond all others.

'That will be seen. Whatever befalls, my spirit will never lose hold of yours, in this life or in any life to come. I make neither promise nor plan. When the right time arrives, I know it, and act accordingly. It may be when your great work is nearing its end. Then I would come and lecture to an audience of one — my *chela.*'

'That's when I shall need you,' Sinclair said with feeling, 'when the disabling wonder creeps in — what hope that one's work may achieve the purpose that has been its breath of life?'

'The Devil's whisper. You must not heed it. Artist or teacher can but give and give to the uttermost. He cannot force others to receive his gift, though he may persuade them. You have attained — very nearly — to inner fulfilment. You have proved, by practice, that, when the senses cease from troubling, the soul emerges astonished at its own strength. The "toothaches and pimples of daily life" are seen in true perspective. Such experience not only satisfies and enriches, it changes the man himself; and the light within you must come out, illumining your work, your relation to others. They will feel it, without knowing what they feel.'

'A few have already told me so,' Sinclair admitted to this man, as he would not have done to any other. 'It is strange.'

'Not so strange to one who knows the nature of the seed that bears such fruit.' He looked shrewdly at the younger man's face. 'Your age? Nearly forty?'

'Next June.'

'A good age for achievement. Not too young to look for recognition, nor too old for first-rate mental activity. But remember, the mind is ageless. Look always ahead, never backward. The Past cannot be changed. But every present action is shaping a future that can be changed. Choice and will are no illusions, though they may be conditioned by the cards dealt out to you. My friend Radhakrishnan has wisely said that, without a measure of free will, personal consciousness is a superfluous luxury.'

Sinclair smiled. 'That man has wit as well as wisdom.'

'Yes. And both are needed for ability to perceive Truth — the meaning and wonder of life, in great things and small — with a liberated mind. That is my gift to you, Roy — a liberated mind.'

That first use of his Christian name so moved Sinclair that speech was difficult; and Sri Samādhi, perceiving it, reverted to matter more impersonal.

'For your two countries the message is clear: fusion of spirit between an enlightened India and an England proffering the fellowship of the true leader, more concerned for influence than for power. At present too many small grievances and the cool disdain of the average white man make many aspiring Indians blind to vast benefits. Everywhere they see only the surface aspect of your people — aimless pursuit of pleasure and futile activity. No eyes for any world outside their own.'

Sinclair sighed and crushed out the stub of his cigarette. 'That's the perennial curse of the situation. But mercifully, there's always the little leaven at work.'

'Yes — and among ours too, with their many so-different failings. You will find the little leaven in Dayālbagh: proof that one man's initiative, lit by a spark of genius, can bring mighty things to pass. Every great movement has sprung from a dream in the mind of one man. So it will always be. For a dream is a living seed; and centuries of history bear witness that, in spite of all the wise men who prophesy failure — and are always right! — *the* dream, in the end, prevails.'

At that Sinclair raised his hand, a new light in his eyes! '*Guru-ji*, giver of many gifts, you have given me my watchword — perhaps my title — the Dream Prevails ——.'

For a few moments they looked at each other in silence. The two women were coming up the steps. It was the end. Yet between those two, even at parting, there could be no farewell.

Chapter XVIII

Joy and woe are woven fine,
A clothing for the soul divine;
Under every grief and pine,
Runs a joy with silken twine.
It is right it should be so;
Man was made for joy and woe.

BLAKE

ALONG a strip of level path, among tall pines and ilex, Claire Inglis walked alone. After three months of peaceful days and real sleep at night, she looked and felt a different woman. She could now enjoy two short walks every day; and the sparkle in this late September air had brought a faint colour to her cheeks. Chrystal, in these three months, had revealed the hidden gold of her nature as never yet. They were working together regularly at the etchings and paintings for their joint book, to which Roy was gladly giving the prestige of his name. Lady Leigh's interest and friendly spirit warmed her heart. She could and did tell herself that she had much to be grateful for. Yet, deep down, there still persisted a curious numb sensation. Two central facts gone at a stroke: the man and his needs, however tiresome, the friend and potential lover. At Home, with the children needing her, loving her, it would pass; but in this detached state — for all her increased love of Chrystal — the real Claire felt, at times, intolerably alone; more so than ever in these last few days.

For Dixon had lately written that Lynch had granted him ten days' special leave. With Chrystal's permission, he would spend it up at Nathia Gully; and Claire had seen a look in the girl's eyes, when she spoke of it, that had tightened her own heart to endure the sharpest pang of all.

He had now been up for five days. No sign so far of the expected crisis. They were all friendly together: Dixon tactful and charming almost to excess; Chrystal determined not to let her feel out of it, as, in cold fact, she knew herself to be.

This afternoon they had gone off somewhere, not riding; and Claire wondered stoically what that might bode? The obvious possibility made her feel more than ever alone: a sensation curiously intensified by a letter received from Jasper that morning. It was the first sign he had given since the day of her unwifely welcome. She had brought it out with her to re-read more calmly, while resting on the wayside seat round the corner, the present limit of her stroll.

Here the pines had been cut away, giving an unbroken view of mountains shading from blue to purple, wave on wave of hills, crowned with their diadem of snow. But beauty, impregnated with pain, could hurt as well as heal: always that aching under-sense of life's failure to meet its high demand on sense and spirit.

Today no call of beauty could mitigate the very mixed sensations aroused in her by the unexpected contents of Jasper's letter.

Dear Clair, he wrote,

I hope you have more or less recovered by now from the severe shock I gave you by turning up too soon. I was fool enough to fancy I should be welcome — but let that pass.

I have not written sooner because I had to find my own bearings in the extremely awkward situation you sprang upon me; letting me down as you did by your inconsiderate, not to say unnatural, behaviour. Please note that I have at least given you *time to pull up in health before serving you with my decision.*

In view of certain things you said, I have decided that separation doesn't meet the case. It's an unnatural condition, and ought to be abolished. Frankly I need a permanent woman in my life. So it's only fair that I should be placed in a position to marry, when formalities permit; and the honour you have refused will be welcome to another — I need name no names.

As you wish to keep the children — which would certainly be better for them — she and I are willing to accept the odium of being reckoned, in a technical sense, the guilty parties. It might be a bad mark against me for higher promotion. But that need not worry you; and I have no particular wish to stay on late in India, even if my health would permit. The point is that you can safely take up the case against me without any fear of my letting you *down by coming the penitent husband over you.*

I'm ignorant as to the proceedings when 'parties' are in different hemispheres, but a lawyer will put you wise. I'll send you a letter that can be shown in court, and you can tell the children what you like, when you like. I can trust you not to blacken my face unduly; and if Madge — a pukka *Inglis — would care to see me any time later on, I would be agreeable. All necessary money payment can be arranged through lawyers. So we needn't correspond again direct. You needn't even bother to make out a polite answer to this deplorable epistle. If you will kindly write on a postcard 'I agree,' with your initials, it will be the last favour required of you by your one-time husband.*

J. INGLIS

Clearly she had cut his vanity to the quick, if not his heart. That it might have been a salutary operation gave her generous nature no satisfaction at all. His letter, though unkind in tone, was at least straightforward. And there an end of her inglorious married life: a bond that lacked meaning and reality unless it linked the deeps together. If there were any deeps in Jasper, no plummet of hers had ever reached them. Without question she shared his view that separation was an unnatural state of life. Live together — or a clean break. That he actually offered her the clean break would have seemed too good to be true, had it set her free — for Dixon. At every turn the spirit of irony mocked her with its demoniac laughter.

Mechanically folding up her letter, she discovered that tears were trickling over her cheeks; not for the loss of a husband she could not love, but for loss of a love she had never possessed. Spurning herself, she rose and moved to the edge of the path, deliberately tore Jasper's letter into smallest fragments, and flung them, with a sweep of her arm, down into the valley. A light wind caught them. They frisked like yellowish butterflies; gave it up at last, and were gone.

As she turned away, feeling chilled and tired, voices came to her from across the gully — a deep dip in the path that swerved outward again and round the next shoulder of the hill. Through the trees she could see two figures: unmistakably Chrystal and Dixon. The girl's laughter sounded clear and sweet. They were coming her way: coming, perhaps, to tell her the one thing that she hardly knew how to bear.

Careless whether they saw her or not, she turned and walked quickly off in the other direction. That she must reach Windy Ridge well ahead of them, and steel herself to face whatever they might, or might not, have to tell.

The other two had paused to take in the full sweep of misty valley, autumn-splashed forest and shining peaks. Verney's quick eyes had caught sight of Claire by the rail; had seen that strange gesture, half tragic, half defiant; had seen the whole woman, in a flash, as with new eyes. Her lack of beauty or charm was offset by her finely proportioned figure, by an air of dignity and nobility that curiously smote him at a moment when his whole being was absorbed in the girl who stood quietly beside him — so near, yet still so distractingly out of reach.

It was not in him to realise how the alchemy of love had sensitised his perceptions, giving him a far clearer vision of people and things, quite other than the shrewd insight that had made him Lynch's right-hand man. He only knew that his thwarted love for Chrystal had become a consuming flame, such as he would scarcely have credited in himself or another a year ago. Until now there had always been something in him impervious that resisted the feminine lure, that refused full surrender to any commanding emotion. But this enchanting girl penetrated to depths unstirred before. She had fused his mind and heart into a singleness of assent such as he had never experienced; and he did not know how he could bid her good-bye, in less than a week, without dishonouring his Spartan resolve not to press her again till he got Home in February. One must give her time to win clear of all she had been through; time, perhaps, to miss him a little and be glad to see him again.

Stirred almost intolerably by her silent presence, he stole a glance at her profile — so fair, so still, with the far-off look in her eyes that came only when beauty was wafting her miles away. He wanted fiercely to pull her out of her dream and take her in his arms; take his own chance of response or rebuff. But the habit of years prevailed. He remained standing there, seemingly absorbed in the familiar view, scarcely seeing it, because his mind was completely astray.

And Chrystal, unaware of all that, was also thinking less of the mountains than of sensations revived in her by his coming; a deep content in having him there; a glow that had been lacking in Gulmarg, because her heart was still centred on another man. No word from Afzul since that moving postcard; and it was better so. Yet, unwisely, she had half hoped for — she knew not what. As hope died down, something else had died down too, reminding her how Roy had said that the attraction was partly physical, that if she did not see or hear of him for several months it would subside. That was the kind of thing one half resented and refused to believe; but Roy understood the human heart no less than the spirit. She had been reading his *Out of the Dust*; and more than ever she felt proud of winning his friendship, grateful to him for shifting her mind again towards Dixon. He was proving, not merely his love, but his worth, at every turn, by matter-of-fact doings and refrainings, not one of them lost on her quick perception.

Now, here he stood beside her, his silence making her feel more profoundly aware of him than any inadequate attempt at speech.

This much she knew: that, if they married, they could rely on each other to the utmost. Their house would be founded on a rock. She believed he would respect her personality and her art, if with less understanding than Lance — who really had music in him — could give to Eve.

At that moment, as if guessing her mood, he turned abruptly; and a tingle in her veins awoke the thought, '*Is* it coming, after all?'

But he only said in a matter-of-fact voice: 'That was Claire over there by the railings. Did you notice?'

'No,' she said, ashamed, 'I didn't. I was noticing the mountains.' She looked across at the empty path. 'Gone!'

'Yes, I think she saw us. Walked away faster than she ought to do. Queer.'

But for Chrystal it was tragic; which could not be said.

'Perhaps she wasn't feeling sociable. She seemed worried this morning. I think there was a letter from that tiresome Jasper. She won't ever be free of his naggings unless they have the sense to make it a clean cut.'

'Devoutly to be wished. But oh, Lord, the complications! Enough to scare one off matrimony, except that the gods first make us mad, to serve their own ends. Good thing, anyhow, to get her out of India. It was killing her. I'm glad you two go along with the Sinclairs.'

'Yes. It was Roy's inspiration. Lovely. They make me feel like five o'clock on a May morning, those two. We're to stay at their fine old place for a bit, and get on with our joint book. The sister, who has Claire's little Norman, is to bring him there; and they want me to carry on with the Fairy's lessons. Luck all round.'

'Excellent. For how long, I wonder?'

'I haven't a notion. My parents may emit a murmur, but I feel now as if I belong to Claire. Anyway, I'll keep you informed of our movements.'

'Thanks — yes.' There was an odd constraint in his voice. '*My* movements,' he added, 'won't be of any account till February the first. Four months hence.' He looked at her intently, pain and passion in his gaze. 'A hell of a time to wait. But you're worth every minute of it, if —?'

Her quickened sympathy and imagination saw in a flash those empty months — empty for her also. A wave of emotion surged through her; and she heard herself saying, in her softest voice, 'Is it terribly necessary to wait?'

'*You* ask that?' His face was transfigured.

'Of course *you* should be asking it!' she murmured, assuming a lightness that belied her heart.

'Don't tantalise me, Chrystal.' He sounded half angry. 'D'you mean — what your words imply?'

'Of course I mean it. I wouldn't tantalise *you*, Dixon.'

She gave him the full light of her eyes. And he, unpractised lover that he was, laid an arm round her shoulders, palpably hesitated a moment, then tightened his hold and kissed her — a quick, hard kiss, as if, even now, he could not let himself go.

For her, that good moment was shot through with a stab of pain. A sudden anguished memory of Afzul's kisses, the mingled fear and rapture of her surrender. Could he have so desired it, Afzul had his triumph at that moment. He had won from her the kind of kisses that she would fain have given only to the man who could command the whole of her: had, in a sense, stolen Dixon's birthright.

A dry sob shivered through her.

'You darling!' he breathed: and at last he took her in his arms. Yet he could not tell her now, could probably never tell her a hundredth part of his love. It was incommunicable, except in a hundred everyday acts of loyalty and tenderness, that she might or might not rate at their full value.

At the sound of footsteps he promptly released her.

'In the public path! Ought to be ashamed of myself.'

But there was a triumph of gladness in his voice that moved her almost as much as his kiss.

'Come on home.' He slipped a possessive hand through her arm. And suddenly a chill breeze from nowhere shivered her deep content.

They must go home — and tell Claire.

BOOK FOUR

THE RAINBOW BRIDGE

Chapter I

Strange, when it strikes to within, is the known;
Richer than newness revealed.

MEREDITH

SAINT MARTIN'S summer that year surpassed its reputation. The autumn sunshine had a mellower quality than the blaze of August, with its overblown borders, its hint of decay in the heart of abundance. November's dying glory held a whisper of promise; not, 'Take down, it is finished,' but, 'Take down, it is beginning.'

It was as if summer had actually returned to wave farewell, coupled with a greeting to the wanderers, who had come back to their own after many days. The September gales had swept through England while the trees could resist the assault on their leaves. Now stillness had fallen like a spell on wood and moor and garden. Becalmed clouds brooded above them with the bright rounded fullness of fine weather. No breeze shivered the brittle glory of the beechwood that had given the place its name. And in Sinclair's eyes, not all the greater glory of Himalchān could excel that one wood in its sunset splendour: the gracious symmetry of trunks and limbs, the noble contours and cascade of leaves, ranging from every tone of yellow to russet and red-gold. So he had seen them when he left home: so he had found them on arrival; as if, like the Sleeping Beauty, they had remained enspelled until he came again.

It was a full week now since their day of delight: a week to linger in the memory of all who shared in the joy of that long-delayed return. Aunt Jane — perpetrator of bromides —

had written of it as 'the return of the prodigal': an implication that would have prickled the earlier Roy.

It moved him now only to a flick of dry humour: 'Good old Die-Hard! Must dig a thumbnail into me, just to make me feel I really *am* home again!'

Her thumbnail dig had been Lady Roscoe's only share in this first week of very mixed sensations, realised only by Tara. Both were glad to have Chrystal and Claire still with them, also the small Norman, cheerfully annexed by Lilāmani as 'a new kind of brother,' one that had lived in India and could exchange cryptic remarks with her in Hindostani. Nell, who was shy of him, clung to Tara like a barnacle, lest she might vanish again, if allowed to go out of sight. As for Prince, Roy's golden retriever, after a few enquiring sniffs, he had gone half crazy with the abandoned joy of doghood, unhampered by any tiresome code of dignity or restraint. In his esteem, such senseless restrictions were confined to human beings and cats. Moonstone, Lilāmani's smoke-blue Persian, knew all about that. Deigning to recognise her absentee master with due detachment, she purringly insinuated herself against him with a casual air of affection.

Only one welcome was perforce delayed. Nevil could not be there to greet them. But they had dashed off in the new car to Hillside; and he would soon be home.

Today there had been a small lunch party for more greetings: Christine, Roy's only sister — a small finished creature like their mother — married now to a lesser light in the Foreign Office: Lord and Lady Avonleigh — Derek and Gabrielle — neighbouring landowners and close friends. Last, possibly best, there was Roy's favourite godfather, Cuthbert Broome, once a famous novelist; still, at eighty-six, more shrewdly observant and alert than most of his fellows five and twenty years younger. His 'thatch of tow,' now silver white, seemed thick as ever, and a quenchless spark of youth glinted in his sea-blue eyes. For Roy he was still 'Jeffers,' the man who had backed him and believed in him when his own father doubted; had set his feet on the ladder to literary fame, and had lived long enough to see his faith justified in full. Their love for each other was rooted in masculine reserve; but already Broome had discerned inner changes that even Roy's few intimates might never discover at all. He was staying for three nights, as they had much to talk of, and he liked a rest between two car journeys.

That they were all overjoyed at the wanderer's return was more or less taken for granted, since they were English, fearing sentiment as a man fears goloshes or a dicky; and their lively lunch ended in an adjournment to garden chairs under the twin beeches on the lawn, where the November sun, strong as May, conjured the leaves into flakes of amber light.

There they were all sitting now, with coffee and sweets and cigarettes, facing the fine old house: flat-fronted, creeper-covered, the French windows of the drawing-room curved outward and framed with the last feathery gold leaves of an ancient wistaria. The short wings at either end blazed with many shades of Virginia creeper, and the east wing ended in his mother's tower room; once her sanctuary, now his own, for work or meditation. The house itself — shrine of how many loyalties, griefs, and joys — stood, like others of its kind, as witness to 'the ancient beauty for which man was made and that men are always unmaking.'

Roy found himself responding to sights and scents of home as to a known voice not heard for years: a voice that recalled half-forgotten memories of another self in other lives. His return to it all gave him a profound sense of completion, in spite of a curious discord between his own inner changes and the eternal sameness of house and wood and estate; the surface sameness of the lives around him, sunk in the deeply rutted groove of English country ways. All the good folk who had known him since childhood had accepted his reappearance among them with a friendly 'Good-day, sir. Glad you be back again,' as if he had merely been up to Scotland for a week or so; though there were others who welcomed him with deep feeling for his father's sake and his own.

The fact that his long absence had not been connected with anxiety or uncertainty was mainly Tara's doing. Being Tara, she had not troubled to mention her notable service rendered in that line. But he had it now from Helen, rightly proud of the way in which she had carried her secret burden, letting none of them suppose otherwise than that he was detained abroad owing to important literary work. And he himself had not failed to let her know what he thought of her unobtrusive achievement: holding his corner of England for him, while he was doing larger work for England elsewhere.

Keyserling was right. Man's highest achievement was usually that which he performed alone outside the circle of marriage. Woman, the responsible altruistic partner, should be given as much working responsibility as possible. Tara loved it all: she should not lose the fruits of her achievement. For, although his body was back in England, the Indian book in hand would still absorb most of his time and energy. The link with his mother country was not broken. If England was here, India was here also, not only within himself. The house was full of his mother. And his fancy still saw the ghost of a small gracious figure, in opal-tinted *sari*, moving along the grass paths of the rose garden, snipping off dead blossoms and murmuring to live ones, as if they were personal friends.

Today it was Tara's mother — 'Helen' to them all — who strolled with Claire along the paths. Claire, in a soft-blue woollen dress, her thick short hair framing her face, looked years younger than Claire of Gulmarg, in whom some vital spring had seemed to be broken. She was still too thin for her large frame, but she moved with a natural dignity and poise that came from within. She was taller by half a head than the slender woman who walked beside her, with a trim figure and elastic step that suggested the early fifties rather than the late sixties. Her dull gold hair, very grey at the temples, had faded to fawn colour: a shade lighter than the dress she was wearing, with its touch of old lace and authentic emeralds. They looked like striking up a friendship, those two; and no better fate could befall Claire than to call Helen Despard friend.

He himself was sitting with Broome and Gabrielle, a woman of rare worth and something more than intelligence;

one to whom he could speak of India as a unity in diversity, only recognised by those who could probe beneath the surface confusion of many faces and many tongues. Christine and Robin had been obliged to leave early for some political function. Derek and Gay were remaining for tea. They would soon be turning up again. He and Tara would be running over there in the new car. Fifteen or twenty miles was quite a neighbourly distance in this mechanised era. Derek, friendly and humorous, partial to children, had joined Norman and Lilāmani, who were very busy quarrelling, without rancour, over 'my India' and 'your India'; Norman's India being Peshawar and Kohāt; Lilāmani's, Kashmir and the brief, exciting glimpse of Udaipur, which had startlingly renewed her lapsed intimations of 'used to be before.' She liked Norman because he wasn't 'too much a boy,' whatever that might imply; but she would not let him be assertive over India. It was her country far more than his, by reason of her Indian grandmother and a splendid 'big grandfather in King's clothes' with whom she had fallen in love at sight. Chrystal had been allowed to make a watercolour sketch of him — a fine rendering of the strongly marked features, the deep-set eyes, the silver beard; and Lilāmani had been promised a copy painted specially for her.

Chrystal, at the moment, was sitting apart with Tara, talking of the pair who strolled in the rose garden.

'Helen has caught on to Claire, just as I did,' Tara remarked, watching them. 'And if Helen catches on, you're done for!'

Chrystal laughed softly. 'Claire wouldn't see it so. She can still hardly believe that the inspired plan isn't a myth. And she deserves all the good that's going, after the hard knocks she had out there.'

The inspired plan amounted to a proposal by Lady Despard that she and Claire should live jointly in her Black and White House, so close by that the garden marched with a part of Roy's estate. It was too large for her alone, but she loved it too well to think of letting or selling; nor would she, in her wisdom, live always with Roy and Tara, let them plead never so. She would share it gladly with Claire and her children, would enjoy having young things with her again. And Claire — who had been visualising rooms or a cramped villa — was still a trifle dazed at the changed prospect, hardly able to take it in; unaware that Roy himself had originated the happy idea. They were now obviously discussing details that were forcing Claire to take it in, as Chrystal perceived from the light in her eyes, the faint flush in her cheeks. And her own heart glowed with gratitude to this pair who had so casually slipped into her life, so vitally altered it, in more than surface ways.

She herself was staying on with them, to complete the threefold book, a lasting reminder of beauty unseizable, of joy shot through with sharpest pain, that would always be linked in her mind with Kashmir. Her mother had received the news of her delayed coming with mild surprise, yet without protest. Chrystal, her father's favourite, had always been the difficult daughter; and her coming marriage increased her sense of detachment from the rather cramping atmosphere of her Scottish home.

'After all,' she had written, 'if Claire had not collapsed, I should still be in India; and there's a wonderful feeling of India in this utterly English country house.'

She would go home for Christmas; return to Claire in February for the coming of Dixon, would perhaps be married at Easter, and good-bye to the cherished independence on which she had set such store. Too early her woman-self had been wrecked on a man. Perhaps not altogether wrecked, in view of Dixon's quality, she mused, looking down at her new fire opal set in brilliants; a stone she could wear, without superstitious qualms, because she was October. Roy called it her fetter; but his words of congratulation on her news gave him the privilege to say what he pleased.

Greatly she liked the look of him sitting there under the beeches; no Rajput noble now, as at Chasma Shahi, but an English country gentleman in his grey-green tweed flecked with yellow. And that splendid old man with the young light in his eyes made a picture worthy to set beside Sir Lakshman

Singh, who had allowed her to attempt that portrait sketch. She was reproducing it, secretly, as her Christmas gift for Roy, who had saved her — she could admit it now — from a marriage that might have spelt tragedy for her, and for Afzul no less. A sudden vision of his unforgettable face and figure sprang to her mind: triumphant in possession, stoically accepting defeat, bending over her hand, blessing her and walking out of her life without looking back. Would it please him, or madden him, to know that, for all her hard refusal, he had given her sensations that no other — not even Dixon — could give her again.

A small sigh shivered through her. A wandering cloud blotted out the sun. Their brief illusion of summer was gone ——

They were all gathered in the drawing-room for tea: a lofty room of pale walls and moulded ceiling, little altered since Sir Nevil's day, except for some weeding-out of furniture and fewer water-colours on the walls; the tall French windows curtained in gold brocade, a log fire leaping and crackling, Prince and 'Mrs. Moon' on the hearthrug in friendly accord. Here was England — country-house England — at her homeliest and happiest. Not the mere week-end country house, nor the country house of tradition — autumn shooting, winter hunting, summer punctuated with local cricket matches and garden parties, as it had been, more or less, in Lady Roscoe's 'good old days.'

With the advent of Sir Nevil Sinclair and his Rajput bride, the individual had replaced the type. He had never conformed to the Sinclair tradition. Still less so did the son of his courageous marriage, a man whom the Time Spirit seemed to be using for its own mysterious ends.

So it appeared to Cuthbert Broome — one little given to random fancies — as they sat together that evening in great content over the blazing fire in the library, friendliest of rooms, still quick with the invisible influences of those who had stamped on it their twofold personality. For he had known it forty years ago, when Nevil Sinclair and his

Lilāmani had used it as a refuge from 'husband relations'— puzzled and prejudiced and not too friendly to the bride of an alien race.

There she still hung above the writing-table, Nevil's first portrait of her; an Eastern child-woman of seventeen, who had taken more than his heart into her hands; had changed a gifted dilettante into a man and a famous artist. And here sat he — who had outlived them both — with their son, in the meridian of life; recalling the many-sided boy he had been, appraising the finely balanced man he had become in these two bewildering years of absence from home duties and home ties. Even from early days Broome had discounted the surface impression of selfishness, because his mother spoilt him; had seen promise of great things, in the boy's genuine concern with problems entirely outside himself and the urgencies of youth. And tonight he clearly perceived how the true Roy had prevailed. This was a man with a call, though he would never so regard himself; one that might be dubbed egoist by those who failed to perceive how little thought of self, or of personal advantage, coloured his devotion to this work that fired his imagination and dominated his life.

Tonight, also, Roy himself was aware of a mental comradeship, a community of outlook that spanned the gulf of more than forty years between them. For the two could talk not only as friends but as fellow writers, who had both kept clear of the writing world; a world of coteries and jealousies and back-scratching, that had given to writers, as a whole, a worse name, in these regards, than they possibly deserved. Here was one of the few men to whom he could speak from his heart of India and the spirit behind his coming book. For if Broome knew little of that strange country, he possessed his full share of the disinterested interest of the artist; the spark of imagination that enables a man to appreciate things entirely outside his ken.

By virtue of that shared quality, Roy found himself drawn into a vivid account of his few illuminating days at Dayālbagh, his contact with the unique personality of the dreamer, the born leader and practical thinker, who had succeeded in linking the age-old wisdom of Yoga with the best elements of civilised life.

'No mere record,' he concluded, 'of college and hospitals and model industries can give you the remotest idea of the spiritual driving force that informs that mixed community of Moslems, Bengalis, Maharathas, and the rest, linked in one brotherhood of right living and right thinking. And the God in the machine is just an alert, ordinary-looking man, who began as a telegraph clerk, sceptical of spiritual things, yet driven to seek for some living truth in which he could believe. Fourteen years he spent in looking for his Master, an essential element in their spiritual life: saw him in a vivid dream and knew the actual man at sight — just as I knew my Guru when we met,' he concluded, with a very straight look at the shrewd old man, who was apt to dismiss that kind of talk as 'fancy bread.'

'None of your sceptical twinklings, Jeffers! I don't draw long bows for effect. And, *pace* Aunt Jane, I've *not* spent these two years in riotous living. I've been steeping myself in the world's oldest wisdom, under the guidance of a man head and shoulders above any I've known. Hope you meet him one of these days. Such men as he and the Sahib-ji are difficult to credit except at first hand; but, having known both, I can accept, if you can't, the staggering statement that, when the Sahib-ji's call came, every detail of his ideal Garden City existed clearly in his imagination. As he had seen, so he created the Garden of the Lord — believe it or not, as you please.'

The old man nodded, visibly impressed.

'As a mere writer, of course I know something of that. "Came the whisper, came the vision ——" But to conceive and visualise a whole city is more on the lines of orchestral composition — the ultimate mystery of artistic creation. An impressive achievement, in any case.'

'You'd be the more impressed if you could see the impossible stretch of country where that dream came true: a deserted river-bed, all stones and sand, where no green thing could flourish. No experts to help him. Nothing but experiment, patience, and faith. From a thousand trees, hopefully planted—one survived. It was noted; others of the same kind put in; heroic attempts made to fertilise those acres of lifeless dust. And what result?'

'Fairy tale?' queried Broome.

'No: stark truth. Nine thousand trees are flourishing there now, flowers and fruit and crops. It's just symbolic of the way they face their problems: the way all problems should be faced. No shrugging of shoulders and "Where's the use?" I'll see that my Nevil doesn't catch that modern trick.'

'And where does the Yoga business come in?' asked Broome. 'Frankly I jib at that word, Roy. A damned lot of cheap charlatanry mixed up with it over here.'

'And it's done a deadly lot of damage,' Roy agreed. 'It put me off originally. But I always had a sneaking idea that there was less wrong with Yoga than with the way people used it; the fraudulent stuff talked by esoteric humbugs, who have merely picked up smatterings of a deep truth.'

'That's the style.'

'Well, it's not *my* style; and it's not the Sahib-ji's either. The driving force in his city is a practical religion, without forms or dogma or priestly hocus-pocus. Twice a day they come together—over two thousand of them; no seats, no altar, only a centre platform for the Sahib-ji with his chair and peacock fan. The whole meeting, mostly silent, has a Quakerish air, profoundly impressive. There's chanting and general singing; and in the evening an impromptu talk from their leader. "The rest is silence": and the effect of that silence, impregnated with faith and aspiration, must be felt to be understood.'

'*That* I can believe.' Broome neither looked nor sounded sceptical. 'They've got conviction; the thing of all others that we lack in our overcivilised world. You can't hang living truths on loosened pegs: and all our pegs are loose, more or less. We need a few men like your Sahib-ji to hammer them in again.'

'In my own line,' said Roy, 'I hope I may be working to that end.'

'And am I to be allowed a squint at any of it?'

'Tomorrow it will be thrust on you, my Guru of the West! Tonight, I think we'd better follow the family move to bed. I heard Tara outside about fifteen minutes ago. Probably after offering something hot to the veteran. But she refrained.'

'That precious wife of yours is too good to be true.'

'There you go again—rampant sceptic. Talk of the younger generation! I've proved her true in little things and great. You'll prove her good in another five minutes! I'd lay my right hand you'll find something hot out there, waiting for you in a thermos.'

And so it proved.

Chapter II

. . . Our heart's home
Is with infinitude . . .
Effort and expectations and desire
And something ever more about to be.

WORDSWORTH

ROY'S habit of early waking, for dawn meditation, was less conformable to the life and climate of England, especially in winter, than to that of India. Yet he had no intention of renouncing a custom of proven value, not only to the spirit but to the whole of his day's employ: a fact recognised by Tara, who, more often than not, shared his morning hour.

To discard, for that brief while, thoughts and problems of personal life, to keep the sun in his mind's heaven — even if the actual sun were in eclipse — engendered a dawn mood that coloured the rest of the day; keeping his head cool, as if in solitude, while his hands carried on the normal work of life. It was the change of motive and mental attitude, of which he became increasingly aware, affecting not only himself but others, as Sri Samādhi had said. 'Be a lamp to yourself,' had been his parting word, 'and you will be a lamp to others also.'

Today, waking very early, Roy slipped quietly out, not waking Tara, and donned his Indian *choga*, worn only in his mother's tower room. When he reached it, a line of light under the door made him wonder — had he forgotten to turn it out? Could Hester be indulging in a fit of unearthly early zeal?

Entering softly, inhaling the faint fragrance of sandalwood, he had his answer.

There, on his mother's low-carved chair, sat a small figure — Lilāmani, in pushmina dressing-gown and fur slippers, a dark plait hanging between her shoulders, small hands clasped, gazing up at the lifelike portrait of Sir Lakshman that filled part of the wall by the window. With a start she turned and sprang up, facing him, no alarm in her eyes, though she knew she was trespassing.

'Prithvi Rāj,' she breathed, gazing at his Indian dress. 'How lovely!'

He took her lifted face between his hands and kissed it.

'I couldn't think why the light was on. What are *you* doing up here at this time of day?'

'Doing *puja* with Bāpu,' she said simply. 'I *do* love him. But best when he's all white, even the beard.'

'So do I,' her father agreed, perceiving that the fine-boned face of the picture lacked a certain mellow beauty, that only comes with age when the fire of the spirit burns clear within.

She looked up at him watchfully.

'D'you fearfully mind that I came?'

'Fearfully,' he answered, with so grave a look that her lips quivered into a smile.

'You don't — *truly* you don't. D'reckly I peep in here, it's almost India. Something wokened me too early, and I had too many thinks. I often have — Udaipur, Bāpu, and Aruna.'

'Always India?' he asked in a level tone.

'Yes — nearly.'

A catch in her breath said more than the words; and because he understood too well, he paid no heed. Sitting down in the low chair, he took her on his knee and felt her small shiver of content.

'Too cold up here,' he said, 'for playing truant so early in the morning!'

'But *I'm* not cold. I switched on the 'lectric.'

He glanced at the gleaming stove and laughed.

'A practical fairy!'

'Well, you see I thought if I went and got a cold through

coming here, you wouldn't let me come again. May I sometimes — now I'm eight? And because I'm Lilāmani, too?'

She looked up at his mother's portrait, the last and loveliest, painted when his father returned from France and realised that the War was going to cost him more than his left arm.

Quaintly she murmured, 'I *wish* that other Lilāmani could be here with us.'

His hand tightened on her thin little body.

'So do I,' was all he could bring himself to say; so, too, sharply the words pricked his heart — after thirteen years.

She noticed nothing, absorbed in the picture.

'Bāpu said — I am like her.'

'You are. I hope you'll be more and more like her when you grow up.' On impulse he added, pointing at the sandalwood chests under her portrait: 'Those are full of lovely things she used to wear, *saris* and shoes and bangles. I'll show you one day. Perhaps, if you're an extra good girl, I'll give you one of her *saris* for a Christmas party frock.'

She hunched up her shoulders and clasped her hands in ecstasy.

'Oh, you *are* a Prithvi! — Can't I see them now?'

'No. You must go back to bed. And I must stay here.'

'To say your prayers?' she asked gravely.

'Yes; and to work. But first I'll carry you back, to keep you warm.'

He lifted her up and she nestled to him, sharply recalling that dread evening in Srinagar when he almost believed he had lost her, and she had sprung out of the dusk into his arms. There had been another bad moment at Udaipur; so strangely and deeply she had been affected by the whole place and by that noble old man, who had rejoiced to hold her in his arms. More than once Roy had thanked his stars that he had insisted on that promise — 'never again'; or they might have lost her indeed.

As he stooped to tuck her up, she clung to him with her sudden fierce intensity.

'Oh, you are — you *are* a Prithvi Rāj. I won't forget about those *saris*.'

Nor would he. It was as if the other Lilāmani had prompted him, so suddenly the impulse had arrived.

Back in her shrine, he stood a long while before her picture looking and looking, as he used to do, till the inner stillness deepened and a sense of her presence invaded him, as it had done on the night of his hard decision to leave the near call for the far, in the firm belief that the inextinguishable lamp of her spirit was leading him on to some high achievement, some invisible end——

As the stir in his veins subsided, he said, under his breath, 'Motherling, are you satisfied now?'

There could be no answer: but his spirit knew, while his heart echoed the wish of his own child that the 'other Lilāmani could be here.'

Turning away from her — from the five Rāma-Sita panels, each revealing a new aspect of her beauty — he sat down on the low window-seat and flung open the curved casement to this mild November morning. In a sky darkly clear, the stars were turning pale. The moon, nearly full, hung low above the beechwood, silvering its rounded contours; and the garden far below was drowned in mist. Taller trees rose out of it, as he had seen — how often — the world's greatest mountains rising from an ocean of mist, shouldering the stars that flashed out there with a brilliance hardly known in this temperate England.

It would never quite subside, his intermittent longing for stark snow peaks and high, inexpressible skies. His spirit was at home among those shining peaks, those leagues of ice and snow, where the stars were not merely stars, but 'bright shoots of everlastingness,' and the sparkling air seemed to come from some other planet. But, if India held his spirit, England held his heart, his allegiance to the land of his father's people.

And here, in his mother's shrine, as the child had said, it was almost India. Here he could achieve a measure of detachment, surrender himself to that which was working through him; in faith that his dream of a harmonised England and India must, in the end, prevail. His Guru had spoken.

Here was the imperishable essence of her who had seen her own brave marriage to England as a symbol of some ultimate union between the countries mingled in the personality of her son. There hung her gold phulkari, near the table with her casket. Her row of brass *lotahs* still gleamed on the mantelpiece beneath the strip of vellum, with those words in gilt lettering that he had learnt by heart, because of the music they made in his mind, long before he could grasp their meaning: 'There is no likeness of Him whose name is Great Glory. Deathless they become who, in heart and mind, know him as heart-dwelling.'

He knew now, as he had only half known it two years ago. That pearl beyond price was India's gift to him. He saw many things clearly now that had been hidden from him when he first dreamed of the book-to-be. The sun in his mind's heaven revealed vistas that opened on to infinity, lighting up innermost recesses of thought and high purpose. Emotions might pass; illumined moments fade; but work remained, enduring and austere, the cornerstone of an artist's integrity.

Through the influence of his Guru, he had arrived at seeing life and its problems with a measure of the detachment that is the hidden strength of Indian character, a mental quality deeper than mere fatalism. 'Accepting everything beneath the sun' — that was the essence of Hinduism, the essence of wisdom, East or West. Life would infallibly bring its meed of uncertain pleasures and unexpected sorrows, but there remained the ancient truth that 'the will, powerless over circumstance, is free to determine the habits of the soul.'

Here was sanctuary: here he could work in peace, relying on Tara — high priestess of the shrine — to shield him from untimely intrusions. During the last two days, thoughts long dammed up had begun to flow again like mountain streams in spring. Astonishing, he still found it, the power and wonder of creative renewal. Past experiences glowed in him like a chain of fires on a range of distant hills: and here, in the quiet English dawn, he felt new power stirring within him, such as a tree may feel at the time of rising sap and uncurling leaves. Yet his mind remained calm as a mountain lake, a mirror for stars and moon and all the company of heaven.

By now the actual heavens quivered with beams of the unrisen sun. Light was invading the stronghold of shadows; trees down below more clearly seen. Stars had vanished; only the white fire of Jupiter, planet of the morning, gleamed among lacelike twigs of birches patterned on a tremulous sky.

Deliberately he yielded his mind to the influence of the hour that is neither night nor day, as a swimmer yields his body to unfathomed seas, with a strange sensation of security in helplessness.

I am thy Dawn, from darkness to release——

The familiar *mantra* carried him leagues away to the eternal snows of the spirit...

Yet half of him was aware of the door-handle softly turned, of Tara bringing the low chair and sitting close beside him in her long blue cloak. His hand found hers; and together they watched the mingling of softest blues and greys and pearl-white clouds faintly touched into life. One long drift threw up a mottled corona like a feathery aurora borealis that changed from moon-colour to sun-colour as the east brightened. And suddenly, among dark tree-tops, the sun's rim winked a fiery eye.

Two birds flashed past the window, black against the brightness, down into the garden, seeking worms.

Another day in their new life had begun.

THE END